LOGOS AND LAW IN THE LETTER OF JAMES

SUPPLEMENTS TO
NOVUM TESTAMENTUM

VOLUME C

LOGOS AND LAW
IN THE LETTER OF JAMES

The Law of Nature, the Law of Moses,
and the Law of Freedom

BY

MATT A. JACKSON-McCABE

BRILL
LEIDEN · BOSTON · KÖLN
2001

This book is printed on acid-free paper.

Library of Congress Cataloging-in-Publication Data

Jackson-McCabe, Matt A.
  Logos and law in the letter of James : the law of nature, the law of Moses, and the law of freedom / by Matt A. Jackson-McCabe.
    p.   cm. — (Supplements to Novum Testamentum, ISSN 0167-9732 ; v. 100)
  Revision of the author's thesis—University of Chicago, 1998.
  Includes bibliographical references (p.) and index.
  ISBN 9004119949 (cloth : alk. paper)
  1. Law (Theology)—Biblical teaching. 2. Bible. N.T. James—Criticism, interpretation, etc. I. Title. II. Series.

BS2785.6.L34 J33 2000
227'.9106—dc21   00-050733
                                                                    CIP

Die Deutsche Bibliothek – CIP-Einheitsaufnahme

Jackson-McCabe, Matt A.:
Logos and law in the letter of James : the law of nature, the law of
Moses, and the law of freedom / by Matt A. Jackson-McCabe.. – Leiden ;
Boston; Köln : Brill, 2000
  (Supplements to Novum testamentum ; Vol. 100)
  Zugl. : Chicago, Univ., Diss., 1998
  ISBN 90–04–11994–9

ISSN   0167-9732
ISBN   90 04 11994 9

PRINTED IN THE NETHERLANDS

For A. J. and Jeremy

CONTENTS

ABBREVIATIONS

AB	Anchor Bible
ABD	*Anchor Bible Dictionary*
AJP	*American Journal of Philology*
ANF	*The Ante-Nicene Fathers*
ANRW	*Aufstieg und Niedergang der römischen Welt*
APOT	R. H. Charles (ed.), *Apocrypha and Pseudepigrapha of the Old Testament*
ATR	*Anglican Theological Review*
BA	*Biblical Archaeologist*
BAGD	W. Bauer, W. F. Arndt, F. W. Gingrich, and F. W. Danker, *Greek-English Lexicon of the New Testament*
BDF	F. Blass, A. Debrunner and R. W. Funk, *A Greek Grammar of the New Testament*
BHT	Beiträge zur historischen Theologie
Bib	*Biblica*
BJS	Brown Judaic Studies
BWANT	Beiträge zur Wissenschaft vom Alten und Neuen Testament
BZNW	Beihefte zur *ZNW*
CBQ	*Catholic Biblical Quarterly*
CNT	Commentaire du Nouveau Testament
CSCO	Corpus scriptorum christianorum orientalium
Ebib	Etudes bibliques
FB	Forschung zur Bibel
GCS	Die Griechischen christlichen Schriftsteller
HNT	Handbuch zum Neuen Testament
HR	*History of Religions*
HTKNT	Herders theologischer Kommentar zum Neuen Testament
HTR	*Harvard Theological Review*
HUCA	*Hebrew Union College Annual*
HUT	Hermeneutische Untersuchungen zur Theologie
IBC	Interpretation: A Bible Commentary for Teaching and Preaching
ICC	International Critical Commentary
JBL	*Journal of Biblical Literature*

JJS	*Journal of Jewish Studies*
JR	*Journal of Religion*
JSJ	*Journal for the Study of Judaism*
JSNTSup	Journal for the Study of the New Testament, Supplement Series
KEKNT	Kritisch-Exegetischer Kommentar über das Neue Testament
LCL	Loeb Classical Library
LSJ	Liddell-Scott-Jones, *Greek-English Lexicon*
MGWJ	*Monatsschrift für Geschichte und Wissenschaft des Judentums*
MNTC	Moffatt New Testament Commentary
MPG	J. P. Migne (ed.), *Patrologiae cursus completus. Series Graeca*
NHMS	Nag Hammadi and Manichaean Studies
NICNT	The New International Commentary on the New Testament
NIGTC	The New International Greek Testament Commentary
NovT	*Novum Testamentum*
NovTSup	Novum Testamentum, Supplements
NRSV	New Revised Standard Version
NTD	Das Neue Testament Deutsch
NTS	*New Testament Studies*
ÖTKNT	Ökumenischer Taschenbuchkommentar zum Neuen Testament
OTP	J. H. Charlesworth (ed.), *The Old Testament Pseudepigrapha*
PVTG	Pseudepigrapha Veteris Testamenti graece
RAC	*Reallexikon für Antike und Christentum*
RB	*Revue biblique*
RevScRel	*Revue des sciences religieuses*
RGVV	Religionsgeschichtliche Versuche und Vorarbeiten
RivistB	*Rivista biblica*
SB	Sources bibliques
SBLSP	*Society of Biblical Literature Seminar Papers*
SBS	Stuttgarter Bibelstudien
SO	*Symbolae osloenses*
ST	*Studia Theologica*
SVF	H. von Arnim (ed.), *Stoicorum veterum Fragmenta*
SVTP	Studia in Veteris Testamenti pseudepigrapha
TDNT	G. Kittel and G. Friedrich (eds.), *Theological Dictionary of the New Testament*
TSK	*Theologische Studien und Kritiken*
TU	Texte und Untersuchungen
TZ	*Theologische Zeitschrift*

WBC   Word Biblical Commentary
WTJ   *Westminster Theological Journal*
WUNT   Wissenschaftliche Untersuchungen zum Neuen Testmament
ZKT   *Zeitschrift für katholische Theologie*
ZNW   *Zeitschrift für die neutestamentliche Wissenschaft*

Concerning References to the Ancient Sources

Where possible, abbreviations for ancient literature given in the Society of Biblical Literature Handbook have been followed. For other ancient works, the abbreviations list of *TDNT* has been used as a guide, though some have been slightly modified. References to *SVF* are to volume and entry number unless explicitly identified otherwise.

ACKNOWLEDGMENTS

This study is a revised version of a dissertation submitted to the Department of New Testament and Early Christian Literature at the University of Chicago in December, 1998. Its publication gives me an opportunity to express, once again, my gratitude to my teachers. Hans Dieter Betz, Adela Yarbro Collins, Arthur J. Droge, John J. Collins, and the late Arthur W. H. Adkins have provided not only invaluable guidance and encouragement, but models of excellence in scholarship that I can only hope to have approximated in these pages.

I would also like to thank David Moessner and the Editorial Board of Supplements to *Novum Testamentum* for publishing this study. I am especially grateful for the very insightful criticisms and suggestions of their anonymous reviewers. I have followed them wherever possible, and the result is a substantially improved manuscript. Many thanks are also due to Zeba Crook, who proofread the entire manuscript and, with the help of Nicholas Jesson and Kelly Quinn, compiled the indices. Their help was made possible by a generous grant from the Niagara University Research Council, for which I am most grateful. It goes without saying, of course, that all remaining problems are my own responsibility.

Finally, and always, I would like to thank A. J. for her patience and constant encouragement, and Jeremy for giving his daddy perspective on the whole project. The dedication of this study to them is a small symbol of their important role in its completion.

INTRODUCTION

The Letter of James ranks among the most enigmatic works of early Christian literature. One searches critical scholarship in vain for any consensus on fundamental questions regarding its place in emerging Christianity. Roughly equal numbers of scholars argue that it represents an authentic work of James, the brother of Jesus, as argue that it is pseudonymous;[1] that it was written in Palestine, as that it was written from the diaspora; that it is to be included among the earliest works of the New Testament, as that it is among the latest. Some, moreover, have argued that the Letter of James has no place in early Christianity; that it was originally a Jewish work only subsequently "christianized" by the insertion of references to Jesus Christ, who is in fact explicitly mentioned only twice (Jas 1:1; 2:1).

As there is no certain attestation of James prior to the third century,[2] the historian is dependent above all on evidence internal to the work itself for locating it within early Judaism or Christianity. The evidence, however, is frustratingly scanty. The address of the letter to "the twelve tribes who are in the diaspora" has suggested to some that it was composed in Jerusalem, and thus no later than the mid-60's CE. However, the possibility that a pseudonymous author has assumed the guise of James of Jerusalem, and the fact that Jas 1:1 must in any case be understood as a highly symbolic address,[3] renders this supposition most uncertain. Other elements of the letter which have often been taken as indications of its provenance, such as the author's good Greek diction or the reference to the early and late rains in Jas 5:7, must be considered equally tenuous.[4]

---

[1] Over the history of the discussion, one also finds, though less frequently, suggestions that the author is James the son of Zebedee, or some otherwise unknown James.

[2] For references see M. Dibelius, *James: A Commentary on the Epistle of James* (11th ed., rev. H. Greeven; Hermeneia; Philadelphia: Fortress, 1988) 51–52. All references to Dibelius's commentary in the present work cite this edition, unless otherwise noted.

Throughout this study, I will refer to the letter and its author as "James." The latter is done only for the sake of convenience and is not intended to convey my advocacy of any particular theory of authorship.

[3] See M. A. Jackson-McCabe, "A Letter to the Twelve Tribes in the Diaspora: Wisdom and 'Apocalyptic' Eschatology in the Letter of James," *SBLSP* 35 (1996) 510–15.

[4] For a recent survey of the various views regarding James's provenance see P. H. Davids, "The Epistle of James in Modern Discussion," *ANRW* 2.25.5 (1988) 3622–25.

Somewhat more promising are indications of the rhetorical situation envisioned in the letter. Of particular importance in this regard is James's relation to Paul. This issue, however, is quite controversial in its own right. Interpreters argue variously that James's critique of the notion of "faith without works" is a polemic against Paul himself; that it is a correction of a "misunderstood" (by James) or "misused" (by others) pauline idea; or that it has no connection to particularly pauline ideas at all. Resolution of this controversial problem depends largely on one's reconstruction of James's view of "faith" and "works," and its relation to his interest in law (cf. 1:25; 2:8–12; 4:11–12).

Ultimately, then, one who wishes to locate the Letter of James within ancient Judaism or Christianity has little more to work with than his or her reconstruction of its religious thought. Of course, the first and most basic requirement of any attempt to define James's place within (or without) emerging Christianity on this basis is some broad reconstruction of the origins and development of early Christian thought more generally. Most often in the history of scholarship, such reconstructions have been imagined on an essentialist paradigm. Luther's well-known assessment of the Letter of James and its place in early Christianity is quite instructive in this respect. James, according to Luther, "is flatly against St. Paul and all the rest of Scripture in ascribing justification to works." Moreover, though its "purpose is to teach Christians,"

> in all this long teaching it does not once mention the Passion, the resurrection, or the Spirit of Christ. He names Christ several times; however he teaches nothing about him, but only speaks of general faith in God . . . All the genuine sacred books agree in this, that all of them preach and inculcate [*treiben*] Christ . . . But this James does nothing more than drive to the law and to its works.[5]

In short, the Letter of James "has nothing of the nature of the gospel about it."[6] Luther ultimately concluded, therefore, that James "is not the work of any apostle."[7] Indeed, it is reported that on at least one occasion Luther anticipated the later critical theories of the non-Christian authorship of the letter by suggesting "that some Jew wrote it who probably heard about Christian people but never encountered any."

---

[5] E. T. Bachman, ed., *Luther's Works* (Philadelphia: Muhlenberg, 1967) 35. 396.
[6] *Ibid.*, 35. 362.
[7] *Ibid.*, 35. 396.

Since he heard that Christians place great weight on faith in Christ, he thought, "Wait a moment! I'll oppose them and urge works alone." This he did. He wrote not a word about the suffering and resurrection of Christ, although this is what all the apostles preached about.[8]

As emerges quite clearly from these remarks, Luther's evaluation of James and its place in early Christianity was determined in large measure by two related assumptions: first, there was some essential message, or "gospel," that was common to "all the apostles"; and second, this essential message underlies "all the genuine sacred books." This model for imagining Christian origins is at least as old as competing Christian claims of originary orthodoxy over against divergent, decadent heresy. As a hermeneutical approach to the New Testament canon, one sees a critical step in this direction already in Irenaeus's view that the "Son of God," through Matthew, Mark, Luke and John, "has given us the Gospel under four aspects."[9] Indeed, the assumption that a single such essence—often, as with Irenaeus and Luther, spoken of in terms of "the Gospel"—underlies each of the various writings of the New Testament is reflected in the very formulation and arrangement of the canon itself.[10]

Such an essentialist approach to early Christianity is, at least for the historian, quite problematic.[11] Simply put, the historian has "neither a theoretical basis nor an empirical warrant" for assuming the persistence of any given trait, over time, which might be taken to constitute the "essence" of Christianity.[12] And while historical criticism, as Harry Gamble has rightly observed, "has traditionally disregarded the canon as irrelevant for the interpretation of individual documents,"[13] the influence of this long-standing paradigm on the modern critical study of Christian origins and the New Testament

---

[8] This suggestion was reportedly made in the Summer or Fall of 1542; see *Luther's Works* 54. 424.

[9] *A. H.* 3.11.8. This approach to the gospels is correlated with the later use of the titles "Gospel according to" by H. Y. Gamble (*The New Testament Canon: Its Making and Meaning* [Guides to Biblical Scholarship, NT Series; Philadelphia: Fortress, 1985] 35; cf. 76).

[10] See Gamble, *New Testament Canon*, 73–82.

[11] The appropriateness of this model for the theologian is another matter, but one that need not be addressed for the purposes of the present study.

[12] On the problem of using an essentialist (monothetic) paradigm for the classification of historical phenomena, see the very important essay of J. Z. Smith, "Fences and Neighbors: Some Contours of Early Judaism," *Imagining Religion: From Babylon to Jonestown* (Chicago and London: University of Chicago Press, 1982) 1–18. The phrase "neither a theoretical basis nor an empirical warrant" is taken from p. 4.

[13] *The New Testament Canon*, 80.

should not be underestimated. In fact, though perhaps not as overtly
so, such an approach continues to inform critical scholarship on the
Letter of James.

This is nowhere more evident than in the interpretation of "the
implanted *logos*" (ὁ ἔμφυτος λόγος) which, according to the author
of James, "is able to save your souls." "That the gospel, if obeyed,
is able to save a person's self [cf. ψυχή]," writes one interpreter of
Jas 1:21, "is certainly a truism of the N[ew] T[estament]."[14] This
assumption regarding the centrality of "the gospel" in early Christian
or, in this commentator's terms, "New Testament" soteriology manifests itself no less definitively, if more subtly, in the comparisons
which various interpreters have formulated to illuminate the meaning of James's "implanted *logos*."[15] Arnold Meyer and M.-E. Boismard,
who argued for the non-Christian origin of James as a whole (so
Meyer) or at least of Jas 1:17–21 (so Boismard), adduced passages,
respectively, from Cicero's *De Legibus* and the *Apostolic Constitutions* in
support of the thesis that the association of "implanted *logos*" with a
perfect law in James results from a dependence on the Stoic equation of human reason with natural law. With the rejection of these
scholars' more general views regarding the non-Christian origin of
James or of this passage, however, has come a (usually tacit) rejection of their interpretation of its *logos*. Regardless of their views regarding the philosophical origin of this expression, those scholars who *do*
identify James as a Christian work have generally ignored the relevant passages from Cicero or the *Apostolic Constitutions*, and emphasized, rather, the similarities between the language used in connection
with the *logos* in James and the treatment of "the Gospel" elsewhere
in the New Testament. Thus, for example, Martin Dibelius, who
reasoned from James's description of the "implanted *logos*" as that
"which is able to save your souls" that, regardless of the expression's
philosophical provenance, James's *logos* must be interpreted as "the
'saving' word—*hence, the gospel*."[16] If James is a Christian work, it is
evidently reasoned, then the *logos* which, according to its author, "saves"
must be that which is the unique possession of Christians, the essence
of Christianity; in a word, "the Gospel." Such reasoning finds par-

---

[14] P. H. Davids, *The Epistle of James: A Commentary on the Greek Text* (NIGTC;
Grand Rapids: Eerdman's, 1982) 95.
[15] For what follows, see the detailed discussion below in Chapter One.
[16] Dibelius, *James*, 113 (emphasis mine).

ticularly vivid expression in Martin Klein's recent interpretation of the λόγος ἀληθείας of Jas 1:18. "Mit Bezug auf Gott," Klein writes,

> sind es vor allem zwei 'Worte', die so bezeichnet werden können: die Tora und die christliche Verkündigung. *Da es sich nun beim Jakobusbrief um ein christliches Schreiben handelt, wird auch mit dem 'Wort der Wahrheit' in irgendeiner Form die christlische Verkündigung gemeint sein.*[17]

One suspects that the "riddle of James," which has become almost proverbial since the publication of Meyer's *Das Rätsel des Jacobusbriefes*, results as much from the inadequacy of the interpretive paradigms brought to the work as from the ambiguities in the text itself; that it is a consequence, particularly, of treating the category "Christian" as though it connoted some essential and static *sine qua non*. Whatever the case, it is the guiding assumption of this study that neither the simple classification of the Letter of James as "Christian" nor its presence in the New Testament canon provide a sufficient basis on which to formulate conclusions regarding its understanding of what constitutes the "word of truth" or the means for "salvation." In fact, while I do classify James as a Christian work, I will argue that it is precisely comparison with Cicero's *De Legibus*, the *Apostolic Constitutions*, and other works whose authors draw on the Stoic theory of natural law, which best illuminates its correlation of ὁ ἔμφυτος λόγος with a law that is both "perfect" and "of freedom." The fabric of James's soteriological thought has been woven from Jewish, Christian *and* Greek philosophical discourse. The demonstration of this claim, the elucidation of its significance for understanding the religious thought of the Letter of James more broadly, and its implications for the historian's attempt to locate this work within the early Christian movement, will be taken up in the pages which follow.

---

[17] Martin Klein, *"Ein vollkommenes Werk": Vollkommenheit, Gesetz und Gericht als theologische Themen des Jakobusbriefes* (BWANT 139; Stuttgart, etc.: Kohlhammer, 1995) 131, emphasis mine. Klein considers the usual description of this "proclamation" as "the gospel" to be problematic inasmuch as the latter term most often refers specifically to Jesus's death and resurrection, which are scarcely mentioned in James (*ibid.*). Note at the same time, however, his comparison of James's "law of freedom"—precisely inasmuch as it is "identical" with the λόγος ἀληθείας—with Pauline concepts: "Es [sc. the 'law of freedom'] umgreift also auch die Funktionen, die bei Paulus das Evangelium von Jesus Christus und die Gabe des heiligen Geistes innehaben" (*ibid.*, 144).

CHAPTER ONE

IMPLANTED *LOGOS* IN THE INTERPRETATION
OF JAMES

Among the earliest extant interpretations of "the implanted *logos*" (ὁ ἔμφυτος λόγος) described in the Letter of James as that "which is able to save your souls" (Jas 1:21) is that of an anonymous Greek exegete whose explanation is preserved, with some minor variations, in the Greek commentaries attributed to Oecumenius and Theophylactus.[1] The implanted *logos*, according to this interpreter, is human reason: it is that which makes us "rational" (λογικοί). It is associated, moreover, particularly with the general human ability to distinguish "the better and the worse" (τοῦ βελτίονος καὶ τοῦ χείρονος).[2] A quite similar interpretation, though one at least not obviously dependent upon that of Oecumenius and Theophylactus, is found in the commentary of the 12th century Syriac exegete Dionysius bar Salibi. He too explained this phrase with reference to the human ability, "implanted" in our nature by God, to make ethical distinctions: *in natura enim inseruit Deus, ut amet bona et odio habeat mala*.[3] In addition, Dionysius identified the implanted *logos* itself as "natural law" (*legem naturalem*); the "perfect law of freedom" of Jas 1:25 is thus

---

[1] It is difficult to date this interpretation in any precise way. The Oecumenius in question was bishop of Thessaly in the 10th century, and Theophylactus was an 11th century exegete; but M. Dibelius, at least, expresses doubts regarding these attributions, and dates the commentaries (or at least their contents) to "the Ancient Church," i.e., prior to the Middle Ages (*James*, 262). The accuracy of these attributions, in any case, matters little for our purposes. It is most doubtful that the interpretation of Jas 1:21 which concerns us here was the original contribution of either one, as both seem to have been above all collectors of prior comments. For the sake of convenience I will refer to the compilers of these commentaries simply as Oecumenius and Theophylactus.

[2] Oecumenius: MPG 119. 468; Theophylactus: MPG 125. 1145.

[3] I. Sedlacek, *Dionysius bar Salibi in Apocalypsim, Actus et Epistulas Catholicas* (CSCO, Scriptores Syri 2/101; Rome: de Luigi, 1910) 91; throughout this study I depend on Sedlacek's Latin translation of Dionysius's Syriac. That the *natura* in question is in fact human nature is clear from the prior paraphrase of 1:21, *excipite verbum insitum naturae nostrae* (*ibid.*, 91f), as well as from his comment on 1:25, quoted immediately below.

a "law which God from the beginning placed in human nature"
(*legem quam Deus ab initio posuit naturae humanae*).[4]

While it has generally been agreed by critical scholars that the author
of James does equate the implanted *logos* with the "perfect law of
freedom," and though it has often been noted that his association
of law and freedom finds precedents particularly in the Stoic sources,
the interpretation of James's *logos* in light of Stoic concepts of human
reason and natural law as found in these ancient commentaries has
found few advocates.[5] It has long been noted that the term ἔμφυτος
does not always carry its usual connotation of "innate" or "inborn";[6]
and the vast majority of James's interpreters have argued that the
context in which the term is used in this work militates against reading it in this sense.[7] This, in turn, is thought to preclude any substantive Stoic influence on James's use of the phrase ἔμφυτος λόγος.
Thus, when mentioned at all, the interpretation of James's *logos*
offered in these ancient commentaries is viewed as little more than
an odd relic of past interpretation, and one that merits no serious
consideration.[8] Martin Dibelius, whose interpretation of this passage

---

[4] *Ibid.*

[5] On the use of the term "natural law" in connection with Stoicism, see the
opening remarks of Chapter Two. On the relation of these early commentaries to
the Stoic understanding of human reason and natural law, see Chapter Three,
under the heading "Early Interpretation of James 1:21."

[6] Note the analogous discussion of the possibilities for translating this term by
those attempting to reconstruct Chrysippus's doctrine of implanted preconceptions
(ἔμφυτοι προλήψεις), on which see below, Chapter Two. The term ἔμφυτος, despite
the presence of a cross reference for it, is not discussed in *TDNT*, which omits the
promised entry on the term φύω; see *TDNT* 2. 537. The most extensive discussion
of the term seems to be that of H. Heisen, *Novae hypotheses interpretandae epistolae Jacobi*
(Bremen: 1739), which is cited by Hort, Ropes and Adamson. This work remains
unavailable to me.

[7] A notable exception is F. J. A. Hort, *The Epistle of St. James: The Greek Text with
Introduction, Commentary as far as Chapter IV, Verse 7, and Additional Notes* (London:
MacMillan, 1909) 37–38. Hort argued that the author of James would not have used
the term ἔμφυτος, the proper meaning of which is "inborn" or "congenital," to
describe the "outward message of the Gospel": "[h]e could never have used in that
sense a word which everyone who knew Greek would of necessity understand in
the opposite sense." A similar interpretation, though one argued more broadly from
the context of James 1, is offered by A. T. Cadoux, *The Thought of St. James* (London:
Clarke & Co., 1944) 19–24. Neither author, however, emphasizes Stoic usage in
particular. Those who argue for the Jewish authorship of James have argued along
similar lines; see on this below.

[8] So J. E. Huther, *Kritisch exegetisches Handbuch über den Brief des Jakobus* (KEKNT;
3d ed.; Göttingen: Vandenhoeck & Ruprecht, 1870) 84; cf. the later edition of the
Meyer commentary by W. Beyschlag, *Der Brief des Jacobus* (KEKNT; 6th ed.;
Göttingen: Vandenhoeck & Ruprecht, 1897) 83. See more recently the summary

remained essentially unchanged from the publication of the first edition of his commentary in 1921 to the final edition revised by Heinrich Greeven in 1964, formulates this position with admirable concision:

> if ἔμφυτος were to mean "innate, natural" here . . . then in accordance with Stoic concepts one would have to think of that portion of the cosmic Reason which is innate in every human being.[9] In fact, Oec, Theoph and Dionysius bar Salibi have interpreted it in just this way. Yet it would hardly be said of reason that it is able to save souls— an expression which here quite clearly must be understood eschatologically. In addition, the transition . . . to the theme "hearing and doing" [in Jas 1:22–25] precludes a reference to reason and demands a reference to the word, indeed, the "saving" word—hence, the gospel.[10]

That is to say, while the Stoics would scarcely say that human reason can be "heard and done"[11] or "save souls,"[12] such expressions are used of "the Gospel" in the early Christian literature. James's

---

dismissal by F. Mußner: "JUSTIN . . . spricht von dem 'dem gesamten Menschengeschlecht eingepflanzten Logoskeim'; in der altkirchlichen Auslegung von Jak 1,21 wurde teilweise mit diesem Gedanken operiert, so von ÖKUMENIUS, THEOPHYLACT und DIONYSIUS. *Doch daran denkt Jak sicher nicht*" (*Der Jakobusbrief* [3d ed.; HTKNT 13/1; Freiburg, etc.: Herder, 1975] 102 n. 2, italics mine). Cf. L. T. Johnson, *The Letter of James: A New Translation with Introduction and Commentary* (AB 37a; New York, NY: Doubleday, 1995) 202: "Rather oddly, Oecumenius and Theophylact take it to mean the ability to discern between that which is better and that which is worse."

[9] Dibelius refers at this point to A. Bonhöffer, *Epiktet und das Neue Testament* (RGVV 10; Gießen: Töpelmann, 1911) 97, on which see immediately below.

[10] Dibeius, *James*, 113; cf. the first edition of this commentary, *Der Brief des Jakobus* (KEKNT; 7th ed.; Göttingen: Vandenhoeck & Ruprecht, 1921) 107–8. Cf. the similar formulations of the problem by J. B. Adamson, *The Epistle of James* (NICNT; Grand Rapids, MI: Eerdmans, 1976; repr. 1984) 98–99; Davids, *Epistle of James*, 95; R. P. Martin, *James* (WBC 48; Waco, TX: Word, 1988) 49; and most recently M. Tsuji, *Glaube zwischen Vollkommenheit und Verweltlichung. Eine Untersuchung zur literarischen Gestalt und zur inhaltlichen Kohärenz des Jakobusbriefes* (WUNT 2.93; Tübingen: Mohr [Siebeck], 1997) 108 n. 58.

[11] Cf. Adamson, *Epistle of James*, 98; Davids, *Epistle of James*, 95; Martin, *James*, 49; see also S. Laws, *A Commentary on the Epistle of James* (Black's; London: Black, 1980) 82.

[12] Cf. J. H. Ropes, *A Critical and Exegetical Commentary on the Epistle of St. James* (ICC; Edinburgh: T & T Clark, 1991 [= 1916]) 172; also Laws, *Epistle of James*, 82; C. H. Felder, "Wisdom, Law and Social Concern in the Epistle of James" (Ph.D. diss., Columbia University, 1982) 74; F. Manns, "Une tradition liturgique juive sousjacente à Jacques 1,21b," *RevScRel* 62 (1988) 85; Davids, *Epistle of James*, 95. The description of ἔμφυτος λόγος as that which "saves souls" receives particular emphasis in this context by Klein, who argues, in addition, that reading Jas 1:21 along the lines of Justin's adaptation of the Stoic *logos* would make sense only "in eine Missionspredigt, aber nicht in die Gemeindeunterweisungen" (*Ein vollkommenes Werk*, 135). Justin and the author of James, however, make quite different use of this Stoic idea; cf. the discussion of Justin in Chapter Three with that of James in Chapters Four and Five, and especially in the Conclusion.

command to "receive" the implanted *logos* is even more frequently emphasized in this connection: such a command, it is argued, excludes understanding this *logos* as something "innate"; and this is taken to preclude interpreting it along Stoic lines.[13] Moreover, it has often been pointed out that the expression δέχομαι τὸν λόγον (cf. Jas 1:21, δέξασθε τὸν ἔμφυτον λόγον) is found in a number of Christian works, typically with reference to "the Gospel."[14] Finally, the reference in Jas 1:18 to the fact that God "gave birth to us by means of a *logos* of truth (λόγῳ ἀληθείας)" has itself been an important—and indeed, for some, decisive—consideration in the interpretation of Jas 1:21:[15] not only is the phrase λόγος ἀληθείας used in other Christian works with explicit reference to "the Gospel" (cf. Col 1:5, Eph 1:13 and 2 Tim 2:15), but the verse as a whole recalls the common Christian notion of "re-birth" or "new creation."[16] In short, as Adolf Bonhöffer

---

[13] So Huther, *Kritisch exegetisches Handbuch*, 84; Adamson, *Epistle of James*, 98f, and esp. *idem, James: The Man and his Message* (Grand Rapids, MI: Eerdmans, 1989) 397; Davids, *Epistle of James*, 95; Martin, *James*, 49. Cf. further J. B. Mayor, *The Epistle of St. James: The Greek Text with Introduction, Notes, Comments and Further Studies in the Epistle of St. James* (3d ed.; London: MacMillan, 1913; repr. Classical Commentary Library; Grand Rapids, MI: Zondervan, 1954) 68; Ropes, *St. James*, 172; J. Chaine, *L'Epître de Saint Jacques* (2d ed.; EBib; Paris: Gabalda, 1927) 29f; J. Moffatt, *The General Epistles: James, Peter and Judas* (MNTC; London: Hodder and Stoughton, 1928) 25; J. Marty, *L'Epître de Jacques. Etude critique* (Paris: Alcan, 1935) 53; Johnson, *Letter of James*, 202; P. Perkins, *First and Second Peter, James, and Jude* (IBC; Louisville: John Knox, 1995) 104.

[14] Dibelius, *James*, 114; H. Windisch, *Die katholischen Briefe* (3d ed.; HNT 15; Tübingen: Mohr [Siebeck], 1951) 11; Laws, *Epistle of James*, 82; F. Vouga, *L'Epître de Saint Jacques* (CNT, d.s. 13a; Geneva: Labor et Fides, 1984) 63; Johnson, *Letter of James*, 202.

[15] See, e.g., Huther, *Kritisch exegetisches Handbuch*, 84; B. Weiss, *Die katholischen Briefe. Textkritische Untersuchungen und Textherstellung* (Leipzig: Hinrich's'sche Verlag, 1892) 96; Beyschlag, *Der Brief des Jacobus*, 83; M. Meinertz and W. Vrede, *Die katholischen Briefe* (4th ed; Die Heilige Schrift des Neuen Testamentes 9; Bonn: Hanstein, 1932) 24–25; Chaine, *L'Epître de Jacques*, 30; Mußner, *Der Jakobusbrief*, 102; J. Cantinat, *Les Epîtres de Saint Jacques et de Saint Jude* (SB; Paris: Gabalda, 1973) 104; Adamson, *Epistle of James*, 99 and n. 10; Johnson, *Letter of James*, 202. Dibelius rejected this particular line of argument: given his literary assessment of James, he felt that "one cannot rely upon such evidence from other sayings" (*James*, 113, n. 30). He in any event interpreted both the λόγος ἀληθείας and the ἔμφυτος λόγος with reference to "the gospel."

[16] It is to be noted, though, that the interpretation of Jas 1:18 remains controversial. A variety of authors doubt whether it refers to a *new* creation at all; see F. Spitta (*Der Brief des Jakobus* [Göttingen: Vandenhoeck & Ruprecht, 1896) 45–47; Hort, *The Epistle of St. James*, 31–35; G. H. Rendall, *The Epistle of James and Judaic Christianity* (Cambridge: At the University Press, 1927) 63–65; C.-M. Edsman, "Schöpferwille und Geburt Jac I 18. Eine Studie zur altchristlichen Kosmologie," *ZNW* 38 (1939) 11–44 (though cf. *idem*, "Schöpfung und Wiedergeburt: Nochmals Jac 1:18," *Spiritus et Veritas* [Eutin: Ozolin, 1953] 43–55); L. E. Elliott-Binns, "James I.18: Creation or Redemption?" *NTS* 3 (1957) 148–61; O. J. F. Seitz, "James and

put it in his *Epiktet und das Neue Testament*, though the appearance of the term ἔμφυτος in Jas 1:21 might remind one of the Stoic sources, it is used in James "in einem ganz ungriechischen und in einem entgegengesetzten Sinn als bei den Stoikern." For "[w]ährend er hier [sc. for the Stoics] gerade die natürliche, allgemein menschliche geistige Ausstattung bedeutet, versteht Jakobus ... eine bestimmte, historisch in Jesus aufgetretene Lehre, die übernatürliche, geoffenbarte Wahrheit des Evangeliums!"[17]

JEWISH COMPOSITION AND STOIC *LOGOS*

There have been two notable exceptions to this general rule of disallowing substantive Stoic influence on James's concept of *logos*. Arnold Meyer, in 1930, and M. E. Boismard, in 1957, each argued that James's reference to ὁ ἔμφυτος λόγος is to be understood in light of the equation of human reason and natural law made by ancient Greek philosophers. It is interesting, and likely indicative of the status of the early commentaries in critical scholarship on James, that neither author cites Oecumenius, Theophylactus, or Dionysius bar Salibi in this context. In fact, there are no indications that Boismard was at all influenced by the earlier work of Meyer. It is all the more striking, then, that in both cases, this interpretation of James's *logos* is accompanied by doubts regarding the classification of James—or at least of a hypothesized source behind Jas 1:17–21—as a Christian work.[18]

---

the Law," *Studia Evangelica II* (ed. F. L. Cross; TU 87; Berlin: Akademie Verlag, 1964) 486; H. Frankemölle, *Der Brief des Jakobus* (2 vols.; ÖTKNT 17; Gütersloh: Gütersloher; Würzburg: Echter Verlag, 1994) 1. 297–305; Tsuji, *Glaube*, 68–69.

[17] *Epiktet und das Neue Testament*, 97. Bonhöffer referred particularly to the Stoic doctrine of implanted preconceptions (ἔμφυτοι προλήψεις) in this connection. Interestingly, when discussing in another context the controversial problem of Chrysippus's understanding of this doctrine, Bonhöffer argued that the term ἔμφυτος could only mean "inborn." See *idem, Epictet und die Stoa: Untersuchungen zur stoischen Philosophie* (Stuttgart: Enke 1890; repr. Stuttgart-Bad Cannstatt: Friedrich Frommann Verlag [Günther Holzboog], 1968) 192f, and further Chapter Two, under the heading "The Implanted Preconceptions and Human Reason."

[18] Spitta also argued that James's *logos* was innate in connection with his argument for the non-Christian origin of James. He did not, however, emphasize Stoic influence in this connection. See *Der Brief des Jakobus*, 49–52. Different again is L. Massebieau, "L'Epître de Jacques: est-elle l'oeuvre d'un Chrétien?" *RHR* 32 (1895) 249–83. While arguing that James was not originally a Christian composition, Massebieau nonetheless interpreted the "implanting" of *logos* in James as part of a "new creation."

In line with his broader thesis that a Jewish *Grundschrift* underlies our present Letter of James, Meyer argued that the "law of freedom" mentioned in Jas 1:25 and 2:12 is none other than "das ATliche Gesetz."[19] Pointing out that James's association of law and "freedom," as well as its description as "perfect" and "royal," could be understood apart from any peculiarly Christian ideas simply in terms of a merger of Jewish and Greek philosophical thought,[20] Meyer argued that the equation of the "law of freedom" with implanted *logos* in James 1 is also to be understood in this light. Greek philosophers, and particularly the Stoics, he observed, had long since identified true law with ὀρθὸς λόγος, "right reason." Cicero, in fact, had defined law as *ratio summa insita in natura*, and "therefore λόγος ἔμφυτος."[21] Citing *4 Maccabees* and the writings of Philo, he pointed out that it was not uncommon for Jewish authors of this period to view the Torah in light of the Stoic theory of law. Such authors, he argued, imagined that it was the Jewish people in particular who had been entrusted with natural law.[22] In a context such as this, then, a philo-

---

[19] A. Meyer, *Das Rätsel des Jacobusbriefes* (BZNW 10; Gießen: Töpelmann, 1930) 156; cf. 149–50. Meyer apparently follows Dibelius's analysis of Jas 2:8–12, which is the key passage for identifying James's law. According to Dibelius, James understands the love command not as "the chief commandment," but as "one commandment alongside others" (*Der Brief des Jakobus* [1921] 133; *James*, 142); cf. *Rätsel*, 149–50. Dibelius himself, however, had argued that James's use of the phrase "law *of freedom*" was "a clear indication that in his ritual and moral injunctions the author does not have the Mosaic Law in mind at all" (*James*, 18; *Der Brief des Jakobus* [1921] 16), but rather "the gospel" conceived as a new Christian law (*James*, 119; *Der Brief des Jakobus* [1921] 112–13). Meyer (*Rätsel*, 151f n. 7), though, rightly pointed out the tension between Dibelius's view that the love command in James is "one command alongside others" rather than "the chief commandment," and his subsequent remark that James's law "is a Christian law, and consequently it is not obeyed by being ever so careful in tiny matters, but rather by fulfilling the great commandment of love"; cf. Dibelius, *James*, 142 with 144 (= *Der Brief des Jakobus* [1921] 133 and 135). The problem of the relationship of the "law of freedom" to the Torah on the one hand, and to the love command on the other, is treated in detail in Chapter Four.

[20] *Rätsel*, 150–55.

[21] *Ibid.*, 156, with reference to Cicero, *De Leg.* 1.18. Meyer also refers in this connection to Justin's use of the term ἔμφυτος to describe the "seed" of reason (λόγος) which is implanted in all human beings, but does not make the significance of the passage for the interpretation of James explicit (*Rätsel*, 156 n. 7).

[22] Cf. Meyer, *Rätsel*, 158: "Gott hat in diesen Menschen [sc. Israel] eine andere vollkommene Natur erzeugt, daß sie recht leben und handeln können—würde Philo sagen." It is, however, most doubtful that Philo thought the Jewish people were of a different "nature" than others; for Philo, rather, Israel's distinction resides primarily in the sages of its history, and in the fact that Moses—the epitome of the

sophical term like ἔμφυτος λόγος would have taken on the more specialized sense of the Jewish national law.[23] Jas 1:18, therefore, where it is said that God "gave birth to us by means of a *logos* of truth," is to be interpreted metaphorically with reference to the fact that God, by giving Israel this law, bestowed upon them a "unique distinction before all his other creatures": "All other creatures are children of God through the creation; Israel is the first fruits through the law."[24]

A little more than a quarter of a century later, and apparently independently of Meyer, an analogous line of interpretation was advanced by M.-E. Boismard.[25] Arguing that the oft-noted similarities between 1 Peter and the Letter of James are to be explained in terms of their common dependence on an ancient baptismal liturgy,[26]

---

sage—left his people a written expression of natural law. See further on Philo's understanding of natural law below, Chapter Three.

[23] *Ibid.*, 157.

[24] See *Rätsel* 157–59: "Es handelt sich also auch I.18 um eine Zeugung durch das Gesetz; das ist ein bildlicher Ausdrück dafür, daß Gott den zwölf Stämmen durch das Gesetz einen einzigartigen Vorzug vor all seinen andern Geschöpfen geschenkt hat . . . Alle anderen Geschöpfe sind Kinder Gottes durch die Schöpfung, Israel ist Erstling durch das Gesetz."

[25] M.-E. Boismard, "Une liturgie baptismale dans la Prima Petri: II.—Son Influence sur l'Epître de Jacques," *RB* 64 (1957) 161–83. Boismard does not cite Meyer's study, and in fact seems entirely unaware of the relevant passage from Cicero's *De Legibus*.

[26] The "liturgie" upon which these—and several other NT works—are understood by Boismard to depend is not so much a written text as "un certain schème commun" which was "sujet à de nombreuses variations. . . . On ne peut donc parler d'une liturgie baptismale chrétienne primitive, mais d'un certain nombre de formes parallèles de cette liturgie, qui auront influencé *I Petr.*, *Jac.* Paul ou Jean" ("Une liturgie," 180). Boismard's account of the relationship between 1 Peter and James is in fact quite complex. He argues, for example, that 1 Pet 1:6–9 (and Rom 5:3–5) depends "more or less directly" on Jas 1:12—which is to say, upon the source which is supposed to underlie this verse—while Jas 1:2–4, on the other hand, depends on 1 Pet 1:6–7 (and Rom 5:3–5); see "Une liturgie," 162–67. This source analysis is in any case less than persuasive. Boismard's literary understanding of James as a collection of disparate and merely artificially linked materials, while not uncommon, is highly questionable. Regardless, his interest in establishing literary links between James and 1 Peter often leads him to overlook the argumentative structure of particular units of the former; cf., e.g., his treatment of Jas 1:19–20 ("Une liturgie," 170) with the analysis of these verses presented below in Chapter Four. The several similarities between James and 1 Peter are indeed intriguing, but they admit of a number of possible explanations, none of which, at least thus far, has been persuasively argued to the exclusion of the others. At any rate, it is more the relation of the thought of these two works than their literary relationship that is of concern in the present study. See further on the former issue below, Chapter Four, under the heading "Implanted *Logos* in light of the Torah and Judgment."

Boismard identified "the primitive 'core'" of that portion of it supposedly found in Jas 1:17–21 and 1 Pet 1:22–2:2 as a divine birth
"par l'effet de la Parole de Dieu."[27] Nonetheless, Boismard felt that
an "essential theological difference which separates 1 Peter from
James" was evident in these works' divergent conceptions of this
"word."[28] While that of 1 Peter is quite clearly "la prédication
évangélique," in James it is the law—indeed, the Mosaic law rather
than a new Christian one.[29] Noting "the philosophical tone of the
entire fragment" of Jas 1:17–21,[30] Boismard, like Meyer, argued that
the association of the law of Moses with the implanted *logos* reflects
"the themes of Jewish propaganda" which, in dependence on Stoic
thought, "emphasized the links between Mosaic law and the law of
human reason."

> [T]hese were not two different laws, but one and the same law expressed
> in two successive forms, in the form of natural law first, the λόγος ἔμφυ-
> τος, then in the form of Mosaic law, the λόγος γραπτός.[31]

In support of this view, Boismard cited a passage from the *Apostolic
Constitutions* where such a distinction between an ἔμφυτος and a γραπτὸς
νόμος is in fact evident:[32]

> O Almighty God, eternal one,
> > Master of the whole universe,
> > Creator and President of everything,

---

[27] *Ibid.*, 168.

[28] *Ibid.*, 172.

[29] *Ibid.*, 170–71. Boismard's identification of the law of freedom as the Mosaic
law is based primarily on his understanding of Jas 2:8–11. He does not, however,
present a detailed analysis of this passage, but apparently depends on the exposition of F. Spitta; note the repeated references to the former in *ibid.*, 171. Note that
Boismard suggests that Jas 2:1–13 also depends to some degree on the primitive
baptismal ritual; curiously, though, the question of the "law of freedom" [cf. 1:25
and 2:12!] is not explicitly raised in this connection; see *ibid.*, 175–77.

[30] Citing Jas 1:17, where the author refers to the unchangeableness of God; cf.
Boismard's reference to the similar idea found in the *Apostolic Constitutions*, on which
see below and esp. note 33.

[31] Boismard, "Une liturgie," 172: "ce n'étaient pas deux lois différentes, mais une
seule et même loi exprimée sous deux formes successives, sous forme de loi naturelle
d'abord, le λόγος ἔμφυτος, puis sous forme de Loi mosaïque, le λόγος γραπτός."

[32] Note that the ἔμφυτος νόμος of the *Apostolic Constitutions*, though specifically as
found in *AC* 8.12 (which Boismard does not mention), had already been correlated
with Oecumenius's interpretation of Jas 1:21 by Huther (*Kritisch exegetisches Handbuch*,
84), and echoed in a later edition of the Meyer commentary by Beyschlag (*Der Brief
des Jacobus*, 83). Both commentators, however, mentioned this passage only to dis-
miss it summarily as irrelevant for the interpretation of James.

the one who showed forth man as a (micro-)cosm of
the cosmos through Christ,
and who gave an implanted and written law (νόμον . . .
ἔμφυτον καὶ γραπτὸν) to him,
so that he might live lawfully as a rational being
(ὡς λογικόν) . . .[33]

Quite unlike 1 Peter, therefore, where "it is a question of a rebirth
by the Word of God contained in the apostolic kerygma," in Jas
1:18 "it is not a question of rebirth" at all. Much like Meyer, rather,
Boismard argued that for James (or at least James's source)[34]

it is the Jewish people who have been born once and for all when
God gave them the law, that law which was itself only the written
expression of the law inscribed in the very nature of the human being.
That way, the Jewish people were indeed the "first fruits of the creatures" of God.[35]

Perhaps influenced by his acceptance of Goodenough's theory regarding the non-Christian Jewish origin of the prayers from the *Apostolic
Constitutions*, Boismard concluded that though James itself is a Jewish
Christian work, the source which underlies Jas 1:17–21 is likely "a
pre-Christian form of the baptismal liturgy."[36]

---

[33] *AC* 8.9.8. I cite the translation of D. R. Darnell, "Hellenistic Synagogal Prayers,"
OTP 2.689 (Prayer 11), who however underlines the words "through Christ" as a
later Christian insertion; cf. Boismard's French translation in "Une liturgie," 172
n. 1. Boismard also cites in this connection *AC* 8.15.7ff, where God is described as
"the one who does not admit change; the one who by nature is unchangeable"
(trans. Darnell; cf. Jas 1:17), as well as 7.26.3, where it is said that God "implanté
(κατεφύτευσας) la loi dans nos âmes." Curiously, however, he does not refer to the
long prayer at 8.12.6–27, which gives the fullest account of this law and its relation to the law of Moses. See further on these prayers below, Chapter Three.
[34] See immediately below, with note 36.
[35] "Une liturgie," 172: "Dans *Jac.*, il n'est pas question de renaissance; c'est le
peuple juif qui a été enfanté une fois pour toutes lorsque Dieu lui a donné la Loi,
cette Loi qui n'était elle-même que l'expression écrite de la loi inscrite dans la
nature même de l'homme. Par là, le peuple juif était bien les «prémices des créa-
tures» de Dieu (I,18)." Note that on this interpretation, the λόγος ἀληθείας must be
taken with reference to the written law given to the Jewish people in particular (the
νόμος γραπτός) rather than to the ἔμφυτος λόγος which is given to all humanity.
[36] *Ibid.*, 172 and n. 1. There seems to be a certain equivocation on the question
of the source, however, as he later describes it as "juive ou fortement judaïsante"
("Une liturgie," 175). Cf. his appraisal of James itself: "c'est un écrit judéo-chré-
tien, émané d'un auteur, ou d'un milieu de pensée, pour qui la Loi mosaïque restait
la seule norme devant régler les activités morales de l'homme" (*ibid.*, 171).

CHRISTIAN COMPOSITION AND *LOGOS* AS GOSPEL

The analyses of James's "implanted *logos*" offered by Meyer and
Boismard have had little discernible impact on subsequent scholarship. The vast majority of James's interpreters have rejected these
scholars' respective theses regarding the non-Christian origin of the
letter as a whole or of this passage in particular. And this affirmation
of the Christian origin of James has resulted in a wholesale rejection of their interpretation of its *logos*. To be sure, the earlier arguments regarding the "un-Stoic" language used in connection with
James's *logos* are repeatedly cited. However, what Boismard and
Meyer had, in effect, suggested, was a more sophisticated model for
apprehending the meaning of *logos* in James: a model that allows for
traditions of diverse origins to be simultaneously at work in the text;
a model that allows for the possibility of a creative fusion of Jewish
and Greek philosophical traditions. One finds little or nothing in the
way of attempts to reckon with this model by subsequent scholars
who posit a Christian origin for James. The possibility that an analogous fusion might be at work if James is a Christian composition
has simply not been considered. Consequently, the relevant passages
from Cicero and the *Apostolic Constitutions* adduced by Meyer and
Boismard—much like the interpretations offered in the ancient commentaries—are rarely even mentioned by subsequent interpreters, let
alone seriously examined as potentially relevant for clarifying James's
concept of *logos*.[37]

---

[37] Works published subsequent to the appearance of these studies that neglect to
mention the relevant passages from Cicero's *De Legibus* and (in the case of those
published after Boismard's study) the *Apostolic Constitutions* in connection with the
interpretation of Jas 1:21 include M. Meinertz and W. Vrede, *Die katholischen Briefe*,
25; Cadoux, *The Thought of St. James*, 19–24; F. Hauck, *Die Briefe des Jakobus, Petrus,
Judas und Johannes* (6th ed.; NTD 10; Göttingen: Vandenhoeck & Ruprecht, 1953)
12; E. C. Blackman, *The Epistle of James: Introduction and Commentary* (Torch Bible
Commentaries; London: SCM, 1957) 62–64; L. Simon, *Une ethique de la Sagesse:
Commentaire de l'Epître de Jacques* (Geneva: Labor et Fides, 1961) 96–100; J. Schneider,
Die Brief des Jakobus, Petrus, Judas und Johannes: Die katholischen Briefe (9th ed.; NTD
10; Göttingen: Vandenhoeck & Ruprecht, 1961) 12; B. Reicke, *The Epistles of James,
Peter, and Jude: Introduction, Translation and Notes* (AB 37; Garden City, NY: Doubleday,
1964) 19–25; Dibelius, *James*, 112–14; E. M. Sidebottom, *James, Jude and 2 Peter*
(Century Bible, New Edition; Greenwood, SC: Attic, 1967) 34–35; W. Schrage,
"Der Jakobusbrief," in H. Balz and W. Schrage, *Die "Katholischen" Briefe: Die Briefe
des Jakobus, Petrus, Johannes und Judas* (11th ed.; NTD 10; Göttingen: Vandenhoeck
& Ruprecht, 1973) 21–22; Mußner, *Der Jakobusbrief*, 98–103; Adamson, *Epistle of
James*, 81–82, 98–100; idem, *James: The Man and his Message*, 397–99, 411–15; Laws,

The Thesis of a Superficial Stoic Influence

At most, one finds in such studies the suggestion that the use of the phrase ἔμφυτος λόγος in James represents an entirely superficial employment of philosophical language to couch a patently Christian notion. Dibelius, for example, wondered aloud "whether this usage employed by Ja[me]s is not somewhat influenced by philosophical concepts

---

Epistle of James, 81–85; Davids, *Epistle of James*, 95; Felder, "Wisdom, Law and Social Concern," 72–74; W. Popkes, *Adressaten, Situation und Form des Jakobusbriefes* (SBS 125/126; Stuttgart: Verlag Katholisches Bibelwerk, 1986) 136–56, esp. 146–51; Martin, *James*, 49; Frankemölle, *Der Brief des Jakobus*, 1.329–35; Perkins, *First and Second Peter, James, and Jude*, 103–5; Johnson, *The Letter of James*, 202.; Tsuji, *Glaube*, 108–15.

There are some minor exceptions. Whereas in the first edition of R. Leconte's brief commentary on James, published before the appearance of Boismard's essay, the ἔμφυτος λόγος was interpreted with reference to Jas 1:18 as "la Parole de Salut qui a procuré la régénération du fidèle," in the second edition, citing Boismard and several passages from the *Apostolic Constitutions*, he comments "or pour le judaïsme hellénistique, la Loi contenue dans l'Ecriture passait pour être inscrite dans la nature même de l'homme." The implications of this revision for Leconte's understanding of James's *logos* are not altogether clear, however, as he continues to interpret Jas 1:18 with reference to a "new birth." Cf. *Les Epîtres Catholiques de Saint Jacques, Saint Jude et Saint Pierre* (Paris: Les Editions du Cerf, 1953) 30 and note d, with *Les Epîtres Catholiques* (2d ed., 1961) 34–35 and note f.

J. Cantinat's *Les Epîtres de Saint Jacques et de Saint Jude* similarly interacts explicitly with Boismard's interpretation of James's *logos*. Oddly, however, the *Apostolic Constitutions* (and Cicero's *De Legibus*) receive no mention; see *Les Epîtres*, 95–97 and 102–106. Cf. in this respect R. Fabris, *Legge della Libertà in Giacomo* (Supplementi all RivistB 8; Brescia: Paideia, 1977), on which see below.

R. B. Ward cited Meyer's thesis (though not, explicitly, *De Leg.* 1.18) in connection with Dibelius's suggestion that James's phrase ἔμφυτος λόγος may have been influenced by Stoic language, but rejects the idea. While citing Justin's similar phrase as the "closest apparent parallel," and noting in addition *AC.* 8.12.8, as well as passages from Procopius of Gaza and Methodius (on the latter of which see below, Chapter Three), Ward dismisses their explanatory utility for James. In fact, Ward ultimately concludes that "no satisfactory linguistic parallels are available" which clarify the meaning of James's ἔμφυτος λόγος. See "The Communal Concern of the Epistle of James" (Ph.D. diss., Harvard University, 1966] 127–34, as well as the "Summary" at the beginning of his study.

Cicero, *De Leg.* 1.18, is mentioned in connection with Jas 1:21 by Windisch (*Die katholischen Briefe*, 11), as well as by Vouga (*L'Epître de Saint Jacques*, 63) and Klein (*Ein vollkommenes Werk*, 135 n. 90). Klein also refers in this connection to *AC* 7.33.3, where the author speaks of ἔμφυτος γνῶσις, but not to those passages from this work which treat the ἔμφυτος νόμος (*ibid.*, n. 91). Klein in any case considers Deuteronomy 30, not the Stoic sources, to be the model behind James's notion of an ἔμφυτος λόγος, even while conceding that the latter does reflect—albeit entirely superficially— Stoic terminology (*ibid.*, 136–37). None of these authors in any case discusses the passages in question at length, as each rejects the idea that substantive Stoic influence underlies Jas 1:21; see further on this below.

regarding 'seminal reason' (λόγος σπερματικός)";[38] but the question was for him in any case of no real consequence for the interpretation of the letter. Given his literary assessment of James as a "treasury" of earlier traditions linked only superficially to one another,[39] not only did he conclude that it, in any event, *"has no 'theology'*," but he posited in addition that, in the case of such paraenetic collections, *"it is not always possible to deduce from adopted concepts the intellectual environment of the author who appropriates them."*[40] Indeed, for Dibelius the possible Stoic provenance of this term was not even particularly significant for the interpretation of the phrase in its *immediate* context: "[e]ven if 'the implanted word' (ἔμφυτος λόγος) in 1:21 should actually prove to be an echo of Stoic terminology," he wrote, "the expression as Ja[me]s used it had obviously already been given a new meaning by the Christians."[41] Citing several Christian texts which use the term ἔμφυτος with no connotations of something "innate," Dibelius suggested that James, as with his command to "receive" this word, was "probably following an existing Christian usage"; and this, already, had re-defined the (possibly) Stoic expression in a manner wholly at odds with its original meaning.[42] In short, even if the phrase ἔμφυτος λόγος is to be considered one which has "a technical usage in the 'world'," it is at most one "whose actual meaning is either not understood or only half-understood by Ja[me]s."[43]

Interpreted along these lines, the question of the origins of this expression is purely academic. Thus, strikingly, the possible Stoic derivation of the phrase ἔμφυτος λόγος is not even mentioned by

---

Finally, the ἔμφυτος νόμος of the *Apostolic Constitutions* is also mentioned in connection with Jas 1:21 by M. Ludwig (*Wort als Gesetz: Eine Untersuchung zum Verständnis von "Wort" und "Gesetz" in israelitisch-frühjüdischen und neutestamentlichen Schriften. Gleichzeitig ein Beitrag zur Theologie des Jakobusbriefes* [Europäische Hochschulschriften 23/502; Frankfurt am Main, etc.: Peter Lang, 1994] 164). The issue of Stoic influence, however, is not raised in this connection. See further on Ludwig below.

[38] Dibelius, *James*, 114 (= *Der Brief des Jakobus* [1921] 108), referring to C. Clemen, *Primitive Christianity and its Non-Jewish Sources* (Edinburgh: Clark, 1912) 54—despite, apparently, Bonhöffer's rejection of Clemen's suggestion in *Epiket und das Neue Testament*. Cf. Dibelius's reference to the relevant passage from Bonhöffer in *James*, 113 n. 29 (= *Der Brief des Jakobus* [1921] 107 n. 2).

[39] See Dibelius, *James*, 1–11. The view is summed up well on p. 3 (with emphasis removed): "we may designate the 'Letter' of James as paraenesis. By paraenesis we mean a text which strings together admonitions of general ethical content."

[40] *Ibid.*, 21 (= *Der Brief des Jakobus* [1921] 19).

[41] *Ibid.* For the things which, in Dibelius's view, make this "obvious," see above.

[42] *Ibid.*, 113 (= *Der Brief des Jakobus* [1921] 108), citing *Barn.* 1:2; 9:9 and Ign., *Eph.* 17:2.

[43] *Ibid.*, 35 (= *Der Brief des Jakobus* [1921] 34).

Dibelius when he then proceeds to argue that the phrase "law of freedom"—which the author equates with ὁ ἔμφυτος λόγος—must be understood in light of Stoic concepts.[44]

The notion that James (or his "tradition") has taken a Stoic phrase, drained it of its philosophical significance, and filled it with an entirely new meaning has been advocated in various forms by a handful of scholars.[45] Given this approach, it is not surprising that, even among these authors, the passages cited by Meyer and Boismard are relegated to footnotes and parentheses, if mentioned at all.[46] Referring *inter alia* to Cicero's *summa ratio insita in natura*, Justin's ἔμφυτον σπέρμα τοῦ λόγου, and the ἔμφυτος γνῶσις of the *Apostolic Constitutions*, but emphasizing that the author of James describes his ἔμφυτος λόγος as that which "saves souls," Klein, for example, puts it this way: "So mag man zwar *in der Wortwahl* stoisch-philosophischen Einfluß konstatieren, *in der Sache* ist die Vorstellung vom λόγος σπερματικός für das Verständnis der Stelle [Jas 1:21] aber wenig hilfreich."[47] That is to say, given the divergences between the language used in connection with the ἔμφυτος λόγος in the Letter of James and that found in the Stoic sources, one is dealing at most with a superficial connection existing sheerly at the terminological level. Any further comparison between James and those works that *are* substantively influenced by Stoicism, therefore, would not prove illuminating. Regardless of the provenance of the phrase, James's *use* of it is in any event "ganz ungriechisch und unstoisch."[48] Thus even when inclined to see Stoic influence in James's concept of a "law of freedom," such scholars, like Dibelius before them, do not correlate this with James's equation of the "law of freedom" with ἔμφυτος λόγος.[49]

---

[44] See Dibelius's excursus on "The Perfect Law of Freedom" in *James*, 116–20.

[45] Windisch, *Die katholischen Briefe*, 11; Laws, *Epistle of James*, 83–84; Vouga, *L'Epître de Saint Jacques*, 63; Felder, "Wisdom, Law and Social Concern," 73–74; Frankemölle, *Der Brief des Jakobus*, 1. 329; Tsuji, *Glaube*, 108 n. 58; cf. Marty, *L'Epître de Jacques*, 53; Cantinat, *Les Epîtres*, 96 and 104–5. See further the comment of R. Fabris mentioned below in note 84.

[46] Note that neither Cicero nor the *Apostolic Constitutions* is even mentioned in this connection by Dibelius-Greeven, Laws, Frankemölle or Tsuji.

[47] Klein, *Ein vollkommenes Werk*, 135; emphasis mine. Klein, in fact, identifies Deuteronomy 30 as the "Schlüssel" for interpreting Jas 1:21, suggesting that the author of James simply couches a deuteronomistic notion in philosophical language; see *Ein vollkommenes Werk*, 136–37.

[48] So Frankemölle, *Der Brief des Jakobus*, 1. 329; cf. Bonhöffer, *Epictet und das Neuen Testament*, 97.

[49] So, particularly strikingly, Klein, *Ein vollkommenes Werk*, 152: "So dürfte die Rede vom λόγος ἔμφυτος letzlich ihren Ursprung in der deuteronomistischen Theologie

The Rejection of Stoic Influence

More often one finds interpreters dispensing with the Stoic evidence altogether. In this case, James's notion of a "saving" ἔμφυτος λόγος is explained by comparison with the use of planting imagery in early Christian missionary contexts, as for example in 1 Cor 3:6–8 (cf. φυτεύω)[50] and, above all, in the synoptic parable of the sower (Mark 4:3–20 pars.; cf. σπείρω).[51] Along these lines, one also finds comparisons with 1 Peter's description of "the word (ῥῆμα) which was announced to you as the gospel" as an imperishable "seed" (σπορά), or with the use of seed imagery in 1 John.[52] In a manner reminiscent of Boismard, in fact, some have argued that a common tradition underlies Jas 1:18, 21 and 1 Pet 1:22-2:2—a tradition associated, perhaps, with baptism.[53] Here, though, the tradition is considered to be a Christian one, and Boismard's detection of a difference between 1 Peter and James has generally been disregarded.[54] Indeed, Mußner considers the supposed baptismal *Sitz im Leben* of Jas 1:18, 21 itself to be decisive for the interpretation of both the λόγος ἀληθείας and ὁ ἔμφυτος λόγος as "d[ie] uraposolischen Paradosis," that is, as "the Gospel."[55]

---

des Alten Testaments haben, während die Spur des νόμος ἐλευθερίας eher zu griechischem Denken, besonders zu dem der Stoa führt"; cf. *ibid.*, 136–37. Cf. also Vouga, *L'Epître de Saint Jacques*, 65–66.

[50] It should be pointed out in this connection that the term ἔμφυτος derives not from ἐμφυτεύω, but from ἐμφύω; see, e.g., Ropes, *St. James*, 172. Of course, this does not of itself preclude comparison of Jas 1:21 with 1 Cor 3:6–8.

[51] Beyschlag, *Der Brief des Jacobus*, 83; Mayor, *Epistle of St. James*, 68–69; Meinertz and Vrede, *Die katholischen Briefe*, 25; Hauck, *Die Briefe*, 12; Reicke, *The Epistles of James, Peter, and Jude*, 21; Mußner, *Der Jakobusbriefe*, 102 and n. 2; Adamson, *Epistle of James*, 81; Davids, *Epistle of James*, 95; Martin, *James*, 49; cf. Cantinat, *Les Epîtres*, 105. See also F. Manns, "Une tradition liturgique," 87–89, who locates the roots of this terminology, as well as the "seed" imagery of 1 John and 1 Peter, in Jewish liturgical usage; cf. in this respect Fabris, *Legge*, on whom see below.

[52] 1 Pet 1:22–25 (cf. 1 Pet 1:23: λόγου ζῶντος θεοῦ καὶ μένοντος); 1 John 3:9. See Beyschlag, *Der Brief des Jacobus*, 83; Moffatt, *The General Epistles*, 24; Manns, "Une tradition liturgique," 89; cf. Hauck, *Die Briefe*, 11; also Cantinat, *Les Epîtres*, 105.

[53] See esp. Popkes, *Adressaten*, 136–56; Mußner, *Der Jakobusbrief*, 95–97 and 101–3; Schrage, "Der Jakobusbrief," 21; Adamson, *James: The Man and His Message*, 397; Hoppe, *Der theologische Hintergrund des Jakobusbriefes* (2d ed.; FB 28; Würzburg: Echter, 1985) 94. See also Fabris, *Legge*, on which see immediately below. Others are more reticent regarding the baptismal connection; see in this respect Davids, *Epistle of James*, 93; also Laws, *Epistle of James*, 18–20.

[54] Boismard's study is often overlooked altogether. Note, however, the works of Cantinat and Leconte discussed above in note 37, and the study of Fabris discussed immediately below.

[55] Mußner, *Der Jakobusbrief*, 95f, 102. Note that neither the *Apostolic Constitutions* nor Cicero's *De Legibus* is mentioned in this connection. Cf. Schrage, "Der Jakobusbrief," 21.

It is this line of interpretation which is advanced in Rinaldo Fabris's *Legge della Libertà in Giacomo*. Fabris's intensive study of the issue presents by far the most direct and sustained challenge to the interpretation of Meyer and Boismard to date. With an eye both to these scholars and to those, like Dibelius, who find Stoic influence behind James's association of law and freedom, Fabris formulates the problem in terms of a choice between interpreting James in light of an "ambiente biblico, giudaico" or an "ambiente greco-ellenistico,"[56] and finds decisively in favor of the former. He concedes, of course, that one does see analogies in the Greek, and particularly Stoic, sources both for James's equation of law with ἔμφυτος λόγος and for the various epithets given to the law in James.[57] The crux of his argument, though, is that the *context* in which such phrases are used in James is "tipicamente biblico e giudaico," and that one must therefore look exclusively to Jewish literature for the ultimate source and meaning of such expressions.[58]

The phrase ἔμφυτος λόγος is of particular interest to Fabris since it dominates the immediate context in which the "perfect law which is of freedom" is first mentioned, that is, Jas 1:19–27.[59] Indeed, he considers the interpretation of this phrase to be the decisive factor in determining the significance of the expression "law of freedom" for James.[60] Fabris observes that the former phrase was read in line with Stoic concepts already in the commentaries of Oecumenius and Theophylactus. Against such an interpretation, however, he argues that only limited analogies to James's phrase are found in the Greek literature; there are no expressions precisely parallel to it.[61] While

---

[56] See *Legge*, 13, 31 and *passim*. Note that throughout Fabris's study, the expression "biblico," which is used in opposition to "greco," "ellenistico" and "stoico," includes not only the Jewish scriptures, but the New Testament as well; see, e.g., his treatment of the phrase λόγος ἀληθείας, on which see immediately below. This peculiar dichotomy effectively excludes the possibility of hellenistic influence on any works later included within the Christian canon.

[57] *Ibid.*, 33–48.

[58] See esp. his ch. 3, "Il contesto della «legge di libertà»: il suo carattere biblico e guidaico" (*Legge*, 53–81), noting particularly the concluding comments on p. 81.

[59] *Ibid.*, 55–59.

[60] *Ibid.*, 113: "Infatti il λόγος, che ha il potere di salvare le anime 1,21 . . . è la «legge perfetta» . . . Perciò la comprensione di questa formula di *Iac.* 1,21 è decisiva per chiarire il significato della «legge della libertà»." Cf. *ibid.*, 27: "Si deve notare che questa esspressione di Giacomo 1,21 è decisiva per tutti gli autori, assieme all'altra λόγος ἀληθείας, di *Iac.* 1,18, per determinare la natura e il significato della «legge della libertà»."

[61] See *Legge*, 43: "Però nella letteratura e nei documenti greci non si trova la

very strictly speaking accurate, this claim is nonetheless quite misleading inasmuch as Fabris curiously neglects to mention, here or
elsewhere in his lengthy monograph, Cicero's definition of law in
terms of *ratio insita*, the ἔμφυτος νόμος of the *Apostolic Constitutions*, or
the ἔμφυτον σπέμρα λόγου of Justin—and this despite his interaction
with both Meyer and Boismard.[62] Indeed, the similar phrases to
which he refers in this connection are, apparently, only the Stoic
expressions ἐνδιάθετος λόγος and ὀρθὸς λόγος.[63]

As mentioned above, Fabris argues in any case that it is the context in which the phrase is used in James which is decisive: the treatment of the ἔμφυτος λόγος in James is "biblico e giudaico," not Greek
or Stoic.[64] The usual observations and arguments are made in this
connection: the ascription of "saving" power to this *logos* is particularly reminiscent of early Christian literature;[65] the theme of "hearing and doing" is typical of Jewish and Christian works;[66] the ἔμφυτος
λόγος is to be identified with the λόγος ἀληθείας of 1:18, which is
itself understood not only to refer "decisamente ad un contesto bib-
lico-giudaico,"[67] but to be a clear reference to "the gospel";[68] Jas
1:18 and 1:21, which are "perfectly parallel" to 1 Peter 1:22ff, reflect
ancient baptismal paraenesis.[69] Therefore, Fabris concludes, one must
attempt in the first place to locate precedents for the phrase ἔμφυτος λόγος in the biblical literature;[70] and this precedent, he argues, is
found in Jeremiah's expectation that God would place his law within
the human heart in the eschatological era.[71] More specifically, Fabris

---

formula λόγος ἔμφυτος, come in *Iac.* 1,21, dove essa rivela un caraterre stereotipo e
fisso"; see further 43f and 46.

[62] See *Legge*, 42–44; cf. 26f, as well as his extensive interaction with Boismard's
interpretation of Jas 1:21 on pp. 142–46.

[63] See Fabris, *Legge*, 43.

[64] *Ibid.*, 59.

[65] *Ibid.*, 62, 148.

[66] *Ibid.*, 63–64.

[67] *Ibid.*, 62, citing Jewish works such LXX Ps 118:43 and *T.Gad* 3:1, as well as
Col 1:5; Eph 1:13 and 2 Tim 2:15.

[68] See the discussion of Jas 1:18 in *Legge*, 134–42, esp. 138–40.

[69] *Ibid.*, 191; cf. 59–62 and his anticipation of this line of argument already on
58–59.

[70] *Ibid.*, 113: "Dato il carattere biblico e giudaico del contesto nel quale essa [sc.
the formulaic expression ἔμφυτος λόγος] è inserita, è indispensabile esaminare in
quale misura questo concetto della «parola impiantata» trova un riscontro in quel-
l'ambiente."

[71] *Ibid.*, 116, 130, 148–49; see further 113–21. This passage from Jeremiah had
already been adduced in this connection by a number of other authors; for a list
see *Legge*, 24 n. 46, and note in addition Cantinat, *Les Epîtres*, 105.

argues that James's ἔμφυτος λόγος is the law of love as the internalized "messianic law"; the equivalent, in essence, of what Paul conceives in terms of the holy spirit.[72]

LUDWIG'S *WORT ALS GESETZ*

Martina Ludwig's recent *Wort als Gesetz* represents another sustained attempt to interpret the Letter of James as a Christian work, and its *logos* without recourse to Greek philosophical sources. At the same time, this study differs significantly from those discussed above in that its fundamental aim is in fact to overturn the usual "gospel" interpretation of James's *logos*. It is Ludwig's contention that James's equation of law and *logos* is rooted in a Jewish "nomistic word theology" which first surfaces in works of the deuteronomistic school. Primarily on the basis of this thesis, Ludwig argues that James's *logos* is not "the Gospel," but the Torah.[73]

If there is promise in Ludwig's ability to conceive of James as a Christian work without immediately concluding that "the Gospel" must be its central soteriological category,[74] the form which her argument takes, unfortunately, is less than persuasive.[75] Among the chief problems is the apparent formulation of the question in terms of a strict dichotomy between "Jewish" and "Hellenistic" precedents for James's concept of *logos*. Given the overall aim of Ludwig's study, her use of these categories as mutually exclusive is less explicit than with Fabris. For example, her emphasis on the Jewish precedents for James's use of expressions like δέχομαι τὸν . . . λόγον,[76] "hearing

---

[72] See *Legge*, 133–81. Cf. with respect to this latter comparison Klein, *Ein vollkommenes Werk*, 158–59; further J. A. Kirk, "The Meaning of Wisdom in James: Examination of a Hypothesis," *NTS* 16 (1969–70) 24–38.

[73] See, e.g., the summary of the argument as found in *Wort als Gesetz*, 169: "Bestimmte Formulierungen aus Jak 1,12–25 sind . . . zufriedenstellend aus jüdisch-nomistischer Tradition zu erklären. Danach scheint es mir erwiesen, daß der Jak in 1.18.21–23 mit λόγος nicht das Evangelium, die christliche Lehre o.ä. bezeichnet, sondern das jüdische Gesetz." Interpretation of Jas 2:8–11 is presented as being of secondary importance: it is discussed along with other relevant passages found outside of James 1 only in order to provide "ein vollständigeres Bild der jüdisch geprägten Theologie des Jak" (*ibid.,*. 171; cf. 171–75).

[74] See in this connection also Tsuji, *Glaube*, 108–115, who relies in large measure on Ludwig.

[75] See my review in *JBL* 115 (1996) 372–75. I have drawn freely on portions of this review for what follows.

[76] *Wort als Gesetz*, 159–61.

and doing,"[77] and λόγος ἀληθείας[78] is not meant to refute Stoic influence on James's concept of *logos*, but to show that such usages can be understood apart from comparison with Christian treatments of "the Gospel." A similar aim underlies the compilation of Jewish texts that use agrarian imagery to speak of the internalization of the law in order to explain James's description of the *logos* as ἔμφυτος.[79] In short, Ludwig rejects the possibility of Greek philosophical influence on James's concept of *logos*, but the rejection is tacit—a function, apparently, of her thesis that James relies on a *Jewish* tradition of equating law and *logos*.

Ludwig's treatment of Philo's analogous equation of law and *logos* is especially suggestive in this respect. Philo's extensive reliance upon Greek philosophy, according to Ludwig, renders any similarity between his language and the "Jewish Word-terminology" "only accidental."[80] In fact, analysis of Philo's writings suggests that "the taking up of the nomistic Jewish Word theology is apparently not to be expected in authors heavily influenced by Hellenism."[81] Conversely, it would seem, one ought not expect James—which according to Ludwig *is* influenced by this Jewish tradition—to exhibit significant hellenistic influence. And in fact, the possibility that James's understanding of these terms has also been influenced by Greek philosophical thought is entirely overlooked in Ludwig's study. The interpretation of James's ἔμφυτος λόγος offered by Meyer, Boismard and in the early commentaries of Oecumenius, Theophylactus and Dionysius is passed over in silence,[82] as are the often discussed Stoic precedents for the work's repeated association of law and freedom.

THE PROBLEM AND THE THESIS

Whether by rejecting Stoic influence outright or by positing an entirely superficial adoption of Stoic terminology to convey a patently Christian

---

[77] *Ibid.*, 164–67.

[78] *Ibid.*, 151–57.

[79] *Wort als Gesetz*, 162–64. Cf. Ward, "Communal Concern," 130–33; Klein, *Ein vollkommenes Werk*, 136–37; Tsuji, *Glaube*, 109.

[80] *Ibid.*, 86.

[81] *Ibid.*, 194.

[82] Note that Ludwig does refer to the *Apostolic Constitutions* when discussing the expression ἔμφυτος λόγος; but she gives no indication that its phrase ἔμφυτος νόμος may be in any way indebted to Stoic thought. It is cited, rather, primarily because it "sounds like a clarification of Jas 1:21" (*ibid.*, 164).

meaning, those interpreters who view James as a Christian composition have uniformly rejected the proposition that its notion of a
"saving *logos*" might be illuminated by comparison with texts informed
by Greek philosophical tradition. The relevant passages cited by
Meyer and Boismard, like the commentaries of Oecumenius, Theophylactus and Dionysius bar Salibi, are scarcely deemed worthy
of mention, let alone substantive discussion. When cited, the passages are quickly dismissed as irrelevant to the interpretation of James.
The striking coincidence of terminology in this rather diverse series
of works has not led to their collection and systematic study.

Such a hasty dismissal of evidence, coupled with the fact that the
two authors who *do* detect substantive Stoic influence do so while
doubting the Christian origin of, at least, this portion of James, suggests that this state of affairs is symptomatic of a wider set of assumptions regarding the centrality of "the Gospel" in early Christian—or,
perhaps more to the point, "New Testament"—soteriology. If it is
taken to be a "truism of the New Testament" that the gospel saves;
if it is understood that the "*logos* of truth" in a Christian work must
naturally refer to "the Christian message"; then it is scarcely surprising that the philosophical notion of a *logos* innate in the human
animal would be seen as relevant to James only if it was originally
a non-Christian work.[83]

In any event, scholarship's consistent failure to reckon with the
possibility that James's correlation of law and *logos*—even if it is a
Christian composition—might represent a creative fusion of traditions of diverse origins is problematic. Despite the formulation of the
problem in the works of Fabris and Ludwig, it does not immediately follow from James's use of typically Jewish or Christian expressions in association with ἔμφυτος λόγος that the latter phrase itself was
coined entirely apart from Greek philosophical influence. As Dibelius
and others have recognized, it is quite possible that an expression
of philosophical provenance is simply used in James alongside expressions of Jewish or Christian origin.[84] At the same time, against Dibelius

---

[83] See the further discussion of this problem in the Introduction.

[84] Note, in fact, the apparent concession in Fabris, *Legge*, 81. Having concluded
regarding the context in which James's "law of freedom" occurs that "non solo il
complesso delle nozioni, ma anche il loro rapporto si spiega esclusivamente alla
luce della tradizione biblica e giudaica," Fabris goes on to write that the presence
of "[a]lcune somiglianze esterne di vocabolario con l'ambiente greco" does not alter
the fact that the "carattere biblico e guidaico" of James excludes "l'ambiente greco
e stoico come matrice delle nozioni di Giacomo." Rather, "al massimo possono

and others, it does not immediately follow from the fact that James speaks of ἔμφυτος λόγος in a manner uncharacteristic of Stoic discussions of human reason that the original meaning of the phrase is entirely irrelevant to James. Such facile conclusions bespeak a much too simplistic approach to the very complex problem of the merger of Jewish, Christian and Greek tradition in the early Christian literature. A number of ancient Jewish and Christian works sought to incorporate Stoic concepts into religious traditions with which they were not originally associated, and this inevitably resulted in the adaptation and modification of the philosophical ideas. If the treatment of ἔμφυτος λόγος in the Letter of James is not typical of Stoicism, neither is its Christian author a typical Stoic.

The question, however, remains. Is the expression ἔμφυτος λόγος in fact of Greek philosophical provenance? And if so, to what extent are its original connotations significant for understanding the religious thought of the Letter of James?

In what follows, I will show that the phrase ἔμφυτος λόγος was in fact coined in philosophical circles, in connection with the Stoic theory that human reason comprises a divinely given "natural" law. More specifically, the theoretical background of the phrase lies in the Stoic correlation of the inchoate *logos* with which humans are born with "implanted preconceptions" (ἔμφυτοι προλήψεις), that is, with the human animal's innate disposition to form concepts like "good" and "bad" (Chapter Two).

We shall see, further, that as the Stoic theory of law was adapted by various Jewish and Christian authors, it was, naturally, variously modified to accommodate aspects of these authors' thought which were alien to Stoicism. Most common is the identification of some body of instruction—the Torah or the teaching of Jesus—as a verbal expression of this innate natural law (Chapter Three). It is my contention that the Letter of James, with its correlation of implanted *logos* with the "perfect" law, a "law of freedom," presents another example of the Christian adaptation of this philosophical conception of law. Those aspects of James's treatment of ἔμφυτος λόγος which diverge from the discussion of human reason in the Stoic sources

---

suffragare l'ipotesi di *una assunzione materiale da parte di Giacomo della terminologia greca, però con un significato nuovo e diverso nel contesto attuale della lettera*" (emphasis mine). Fabris does not refer specifically to ὁ ἔμφυτος λόγος in this connection, but cf. 33–48, esp. 42–44.

result from the fact that James has incorporated the Stoic concept into a set of religious and historical convictions which derive from Jewish and Christian tradition rather than Stoic philosophy. In James it is assumed that the Torah represents a written expression of the implanted *logos* that all human beings possess by nature; and it is expected that the god who authored this law will execute an eschatological judgment in accord with it at the *parousia* of Jesus Christ (Chapter Four). Accordingly, *logos* and its opposite, human desire, are presented as the two "ways" upon which one can travel toward this judgment: the latter is characterized by "deception," manifests itself in "sin," and leads to eschatological "death," while the former is characterized by "truth," manifests itself in "good works" (ἔργα), and "saves souls" from death (Chapter Five). The soteriology of the Letter of James, in short, has been woven from strands of tradition that derive from Jewish, Christian *and* Greek philosophical discourse. The implications of this analysis for attempts to locate the Letter of James within early Christianity, and particularly in relation to Paul, will be discussed at the close of the study.

CHAPTER TWO

LAW AS IMPLANTED *LOGOS*:
CICERO AND THE STOICS ON NATURAL LAW

It will have been observed from the preceding chapter that a rather remarkable coincidence of terminology exists between Dionysius bar Salibi's commentary on the Letter of James, Cicero's *De Legibus*, and the *Apostolic Constitutions*. In each work the term "implanted" (ἔμφυτος, *insita*) is used, in the course of a discussion of natural law, to describe either that law itself or the "reason" (λόγος, *ratio*) with which it is identified. Further instances of this terminology can be adduced; for example, the "implanted natural law" (ἔμφυτος φυσικὸς νόμος) treated by Methodius, or "the seed of the *logos* implanted in every race of humans" (τὸ ἔμφυτον παντὶ γένει ἀνθρώπων σπέρμα τοῦ λόγου) that Justin correlates with the "natural law" manifested by and in Jesus Christ. Finally, one might also cite that text which Dionysius bar Salibi was interpreting, and which is the central concern of this study: the Letter of James itself correlates "implanted *logos*" with a law that is both "perfect" and "of freedom."

It is the purpose of this chapter to show that the recurrence of this terminology is not, in fact, mere coincidence. The similar language found in these otherwise widely disparate works is to be explained in terms of their common dependence on the Stoic theory of law. In order to demonstrate this point, it will be necessary to delve somewhat deeply into this important, but surprisingly neglected, aspect of Stoic philosophy.[1] Before turning to an examination of the evidence, though, a couple of introductory remarks are in order.

---

[1] P. A. Vander Waerdt describes the "detailed consideration" of the problem presented in his recent dissertation as "never previously attempted"; see "The Stoic Theory of Natural Law" (Ph.D. diss., Princeton University, 1989) 5. Cf. the earlier studies of H. Koester, "ΝΟΜΟΣ ΦΥΣΕΩΣ: The Concept of Natural Law in Greek Thought," *Religions in Antiquity: Essays in Memory of Erwin Randall Goodenough* (ed. J. Neusner; Leiden: Brill, 1970) 521–41; G. Watson, "The Natural Law and Stoicism," *Problems in Stoicism* (ed. A. A. Long; London: Athlone Press, 1971), 216–38; R. Horsley, "The Law of Nature in Philo and Cicero," *HTR* 71 (1978) 35–59; G. Striker, "Origins of the Concept of Natural Law," *Proceedings of the Boston Area Colloquium in Ancient Philosophy* 2 (ed. J. J. Cleary; New York: University Press of

Law was a subject to which the Stoic philosophers devoted a significant amount of attention. Treatises on the subject are associated with the most important names in the early movement: Zeno, Cleanthes and Chrysippus all wrote works entitled *On Law* or *On Laws*, as did Sphaerus and Diogenes of Babylon.[2] Unfortunately these works are entirely lost to us, with the exception of a couple of important fragments from Chrysippus's *On Law*. In fact, Cicero's *De Legibus* is by far the most extensive treatment of natural law that has been preserved from antiquity. The use of this treatise for reconstructing the early Stoic theory, however, is complicated by the fact that Cicero's primary source may have been Antiochus of Ascalon, a philosopher who had left the skeptical Academy to form his own breakaway "Old Academy," and whose thought represented a blend of Stoic and Platonic elements.[3] Accordingly, while it is clear by all accounts that the theory of law presented by Cicero is essentially the Stoic theory,[4] a number of authors have variously identified this or that detail of Cicero's account as departures from Stoicism. This question will in fact impinge on our discussion precisely at its most

---

America, 1987) 79–94. On Cicero's *De Legibus* in particular L. P. Kenter, *M. Tullius Cicero, De Legibus: A commentary on book I.* (Amsterdam: Adolf M. Hakkert, 1972); S. Benardete, "Cicero's *De Legibus* I: Its Plan and Intention," *AJP* 108 (1987) 295–309. Note also those studies published since the appearance of Vander Waerdt's dissertation: G. Striker, "Following Nature: A Study in Stoic Ethics," *Oxford Studies in Ancient Philosophy* 9 (1991) 1–73, esp. 35–50; P. Mitsis, "Natural Law and Natural Right in Post-Aristotelian Philosophy. The Stoics and their Critics," *ANRW* 2.36.7 (1994) 4812–50; J. G. DeFilippo and P. T. Mitsis, "Socrates and Stoic Natural Law," *The Socratic Movement* (ed. P. A. Vander Waerdt; Ithaca: Cornell University Press, 1994) 252–71. See also Vander Waerdt's own more recent studies: "Philosophical Influence on Roman Jurisprudence? The Case of Stoicism and Natural Law," *ANRW* 2.36.7 (1994) 4851–4900; "Zeno's *Republic* and the Origins of Natural Law," *The Socratic Movement*, 272–308.

[2] See the index in *SVF* 4, p. 100, under νόμος.

[3] The most recent and sustained argument for this position is that of P. A. Vander Waerdt, "The Stoic Theory of Natural Law"; see also *idem*, "Philosophical Influence on Roman Jurisprudence." For a sketch of the earlier discussion of the question see L. P. Kenter, *De Legibus*, 9–10. A good introduction to Antiochus of Ascalon is found in J. Dillon, *The Middle Platonists: 80 B.C. to A.D. 220* (Ithaca: Cornell University Press, 1977) 52–106.

[4] This point will become clear over the course of this chapter, and is at any rate not disputed in the secondary literature. Vander Waerdt's approach is properly cautious: "Cicero's account provides a check against which to evaluate the evidence that does survive from the early Stoa, but not a starting point for our enquiry" ("The Stoic Theory of Natural Law," 30). Nonetheless, he finds significant continuity from Zeno to Cicero (*ibid.*, 28)—and this despite his strenuous argument that Cicero's source was Antiochus of Ascalon.

critical juncture: the analysis of Cicero's treatment of the Stoic doctrine of "implanted preconceptions" (ἔμφυτοι προλήψεις) as it pertains
to his theory of natural law. Ultimately, resolution of the issue will
have little bearing on our present concern, which is simply to identify the theoretical basis for Cicero's definition of law in terms of
"implanted reason." For our purposes, it matters little whether this
basis is properly Stoic or Antiochan. Nonetheless, for the sake of
clarity, and because the Stoic theory is of interest in its own right,
the question will merit some attention. It will in any case be argued
that this aspect of Cicero's theory is essentially consistent with that
of Chrysippus.

A word too, finally, should be said regarding the use of the term
"natural law" in connection with Stoicism. While the significant steps
the Stoics took in the direction of a theory of natural law must be
counted among their most enduring and influential legacies, the precise nature of their contribution has been a matter of some debate.
It has often been noted that the terms "law of nature" or "natural
law" do not occur in the extant Stoic sources prior to Cicero and
Philo,[5] and at least one scholar has concluded that in Stoicism "the
real concern of the truly wise man was the positive correlation of
reason and nature (λόγος and φύσις), whereas the relation of law
and nature was still seen as an irreconcilable antithesis."[6] This conclusion, however, is the result of a rather misleading emphasis on
the actual terms "law of nature" or "natural law"—a restriction
which is problematic from the start given our extremely fragmen-
tary knowledge of the writings of the early Stoics.[7] As we shall see,

---

[5] Koester, e.g., takes this observation as his starting point in "ΝΟΜΟΣ ΦΥΣΕΩΣ";
see further on this the following note. See also Vander Waerdt, "The Stoic Theory
of Natural Law," 9–10 and 81–86.

[6] Koester, "ΝΟΜΟΣ ΦΥΣΕΩΣ," 527. Koester argues that the dissolution of the
Greek antithesis between νόμος and φύσις is achieved only when Greek ideas are
wedded to a Jewish emphasis on the law of Moses. In Philo's writings, he argues,
"[t]he new antithesis has now become that of the 'law of nature' and the numerous laws of men." Something resembling this latter antithesis, however, is already
evident in Zeno's *Republic*, on which see below. Moreover, such a thesis fails to
account for Cicero's use of similar terminology, as was pointed out by R. Horsley
in "The Law of Nature in Philo and Cicero," 35–59.

[7] It is indeed noteworthy that such terms are not in evidence for the earliest
Stoics. On the other hand, the absence of this term in the extant fragments of
Zeno—fragments which do *not*, it is to be noted, include even a single scrap of his
On Law—scarcely warrants Koester's assurance that it is "quite certain that Zeno
never used this term [sc. natural law]"; see "ΝΟΜΟΣ ΦΥΣΕΩΣ," 529. Cf. in this
respect Cicero, *De Nat. Deor.* 1.36, who speaks explicitly of Zeno's view of the *naturalis*

it is clear that the Stoics did, at least, define law in terms of a *logos* that was "positively correlated" with nature. And in fact, Chrysippus himself had spoken of law as φύσει . . . καὶ μὴ θέσει.[8]

For these reasons it seems to me that the terms "natural law" and "law of nature" are a fair designation of the law with which the Stoics were concerned whether or not they themselves ever used phrases like νόμος φύσεως or νόμος φυσικός, and I will not, therefore, avoid them. That being said, however, it should be emphasized that the Stoic "law," unlike the natural laws of most later thinkers, is not to be understood as an inviolable set of precepts that admit of codification. Not only is there no record of any attempt at a written formulation of this law in the early sources, but the theoretical principles that provide the basis for Stoic ethics in general, and the Stoic theory of law in particular, make such an attempt highly improbable from the start.[9]

Law as *Logos*

Fundamental to the Stoic theory of law was the identification of law and *logos*. Given the state of the evidence, it is possible to trace this formal identification with certainty only as far as Chrysippus; it is, however, rather difficult to believe that it was not already central to Zeno's notion of law as well.[10] Plutarch reports that in his *Republic*, Zeno had envisioned a state in which all human beings were fellow-

---

lex. While it is of course possible that Cicero himself has read this phrase into Zeno (or his source for Zeno's thought), the state of our sources prohibits such sweeping assessments as Koester offers here.

[8] Diog. Laert. 7.128. This distinction is echoed by Arius Didymus, who characterizes ὁ λόγος as φύσει νόμος (*SVF* 2.528). To this extent, Vander Waerdt's claim that "the early scholarchs avoid the term *nomos phuseos* because it is a singularly inappropriate term to describe their theory" would seem to go beyond the evidence; that such a term is "a singularly inappropriate" description of the Stoic theory is in any case questionable as, indeed, the title of Vander Waerdt's dissertation itself suggests. See "The Stoic Theory of Natural Law," 10.

[9] This is argued at length in Vander Waerdt, "The Stoic Theory of Natural Law"; see esp. pp. 89–99. See further B. Inwood, "Commentary on Striker," *Proceedings of the Boston Area Colloquium in Ancient Philosophy* 2, 95–101. For a different view see Mitsis, "Natural Law and Natural Right in Post-Aristotelian Philosophy," 4812–50.

[10] So also M. E. Reesor, *The Political Theory of the Old and Middle Stoa* (New York: J. J. Augustin, 1951) 9–10; Vander Waerdt, "The Stoic Theory of Natural Law," 38 and 123–134. Cf. also the comment of Cicero (*De Nat. Deor.* 1.36) that "Zeno believed the natural law to be divine, and that its function is to command what is right and to forbid the opposite," with the most commonly attested Stoic definition of law, on which see immediately below.

citizens, and in which the different local systems of justice (ἰδίοις δικαίοις) were replaced by the "universal law" (κοινὸς νόμος).[11] Plutarch does not describe this universal law further; but where the "world city" is discussed in later literature, its "law" or "constitution" is regularly identified as *logos*.[12] In fact, the identification of the universal law with *logos* is apparently assumed already by Cleanthes, who equates neglect of the former with ignorance of the latter in his *Hymn to Zeus*:

> For you [Zeus] have so welded into one all things good and bad that they all share in a single everlasting reason (λόγον). It is shunned and neglected by the bad among mortal men, the wretched, who ever yearn for the possession of goods yet neither see nor hear god's universal law (θεοῦ κοινὸν νόμον) by obeying which they could lead a good life in partnership with intelligence.[13]

In any event, the identification was made explicit at least by Chrysippus, as is clear from Diogenes Laertius's report that he had characterized the universal law (ὁ νόμος ὁ κοινός) as "right reason which pervades all things" (ὁ ὀρθὸς λόγος, διὰ πάντων ἐρχόμενος).[14]

Firmly in place in our later sources for Stoic philosophy, this identification of law and *logos* is in fact fundamental to a well-attested Stoic definition of law.[15] According to Stobaeus, the Stoics

---

[11] Plutarch, *Alex. Fort. Virt.* 329A–B (= *SVF* 1.262). Plutarch's report that Zeno said *all* people were citizens should be read in light of Diog. Laert. 7.32–33, where it is reported that Zeno held that only the virtuous were to be considered citizens of the universal politeia, while the non-virtuous were "aliens" and "enemies." It is most reasonable to conclude that Zeno held that all human beings have the *potential* to be citizens owing to their possession of *logos*, though only those who perfect their reason, and so live in accord with the cosmic law, actually are such. Cf. in this respect Philo's limitation of the term "world citizen" to the ἔμψυχοι νόμοι, on which see below, Chapter Three.

[12] See, e.g., Cicero *De Leg.* 1.23. Cf. the remark of Arius Didymus that gods and humans "are members of a community because of their participation in reason, which is natural law" (φύσει νόμος); for text and translation see A. A. Long and D. N. Sedley, *The Hellenistic Philosophers*, (2 vols.; Cambridge: Cambridge University Press, 1987) §67L (= *SVF* 2.528). Cf. in addition the use of such terminology by Philo and in the *Apostolic Constitutions*, on which see below, Chapter Three. See further the works of Reesor and Vander Waerdt cited above in note 10.

A tantalizing fragment from Heraclitus seems to suggest that he may have been an important precursor to the Stoics in this respect; for text, translation and commentary see G. S. Kirk, *Heraclitus: The Cosmic Fragments Edited with an Introduction and Commentary* (Cambridge: Cambridge University Press, 1954) 48–56; see more generally A. A. Long, "Heraclitus and Stoicism," *Philosophia* 5/6 (1975–76) 133–56.

[13] The translation is that of Long and Sedley, *The Hellenistic Philosophers*, 1.326f.

[14] Diog. Laert. 7.88; all translations of Diogenes Laertius are taken from LCL unless otherwise noted.

[15] M. Schofield writes that "the proposition that law is simply right reason

say that the law is good, being right reason commanding, on one hand, that which ought to be done, and forbidding, on the other, that which ought not be done.[16]

This definition is echoed elsewhere by Stobaeus, and is found with minor variations in the works of a number of other authors, including Cicero, Philo, Alexander of Aphrodisias, and Clement of Alexandria.[17] The fact that this definition is so widespread and never attributed to any particular philosopher suggests that it was rather standard Stoic fare. All of its elements, moreover, are at least present in the writings of Chrysippus, who not only, as we have seen, identified law as "right reason" (ὀρθὸς λόγος), but also wrote the following in the opening of his *On Law*:

> Law is king of all things human and divine. Law must preside over what is honourable and base, as ruler and as guide, and thus be the standard of right and wrong, *prescribing to animals whose nature is political what they should do, and prohibiting them from what they should not do* (καὶ τῶν φύσει πολιτικῶν ζῴων προστακτικὸν μὲν ὧν ποιητέον, ἀπαγορευτικὸν δὲ ὧν οὐ ποιητέον).[18]

Natural Law as Cosmic Logos

The Stoics closely associated the *logos* which is law with God. Cicero, for example, reports that "Zeno believed the natural law to be divine."[19] This association at times took the form of out-and-out identification. According to Cicero, Chrysippus "identifies Jupiter with the mighty law, everlasting and eternal, which is our guide of life and instructress in duty."[20] Again, Diogenes Laertius reports Chry-

---

employed in prescribing what should be done and forbidding what should not be done is a securely Stoic and indeed Chrysippean thesis"; see *The Stoic idea of the City* (Cambridge: Cambridge University Press, 1991) 68–69. Note further the attribution of a quite similar definition to Zeno by Cicero in *De Nat. Deor.* 1.36: "Zeno's view is that the law of nature is divine, and that its function is to command what is right and to forbid the opposite" (*Zeno autem . . . naturalem legem divinam esse censet, eamque vim obtinere recta imperantem prohibentemque contraria*). All translations of Cicero's works, unless otherwise noted, are taken from LCL.

[16] *SVF* 3.613: τόν τε νόμον σπουδαῖον εἶναί φασι, λόγον ὀρθὸν ὄντα προστακτικὸν μὲν ὧν ποιητέον, ἀπαγορευτικὸν δὲ ὧν οὐ ποιητέον.

[17] See *SVF* 3.614; Cicero, *De Leg.* 1.18–19; 1.42 2.8; 2.10; cf. *De Rep.* 33; Philo, *Jos.* 29; *Praem. Poen.* 55; *Migr. Abr.* 130; see further *SVF* 2.1003; 3.332.

[18] *SVF* 3.314; the translation is that of Long and Sedley, *The Hellenistic Philosophers*, 1.432 (§67R), with my emphasis.

[19] *De Nat. Deor.* 1.36.

[20] *De Nat. Deor.* 1.40: *Idemque* [sc. Chrysippus; cf. 1.39] *etiam legis perpetuae et aeter-*

sippus's view that "the law common to all things, that is to say, the right reason which pervades all things . . . is identical with this Zeus, lord and ruler of all that is."[21] On the other hand, the Stoics were apparently equally comfortable using language that indicated that God and the law were not, strictly speaking, identical.[22] Thus God is strictly identical with neither "universal reason" (κοινὸς λόγος) nor law in Cleanthes's *Hymn to Zeus*.[23] A passage from Plutarch might evidence a similar distinction on the part of Chrysippus, who also, according to Cicero, could identify the two.[24] Brad Inwood, in fact, has made the plausible suggestion that the Stoic (or at least Chrysippus's) "universal law" should be interpreted specifically as the will (βούλησις)—that is, the rational impulse (ὁρμή)—of Zeus, on the basis of the Stoic psychology of action.[25] The fluidity of the Stoic usage in this respect is perhaps to be understood in light of their similarly fluid use of the term "god."[26]

The association of law with the reason of God is also found in Cicero's *De Legibus*. In 2.8ff, Cicero attributes to the "wisest men" (*sapientissimorum*) the view that "the ultimate and primal Law is the mind of God, whose reason directs all things either by compulsion or restraint."[27] This law, he explains, is "coeval" (*aequalis*) with God,

---

nae vim, quae quasi dux vitae et magistra officiorum sit, Iovem dicit esse; cited according to LCL. Cf. Diog. Laert. 7.134 where τὸν θεόν is identified with τὸν λόγον; and note further the introduction to Chrysippus's *On Law*, where it is said that "Law is king of all things human and divine" (*SVF* 3.314).

[21] Diog. Laert. 7.88: ὁ νόμος ὁ κοινός, ὅσπερ ἐστὶν ὁ ὀρθὸς λόγος, διὰ πάντων ἐρχόμενος, ὁ αὐτὸς ὢν τῷ Διὶ, καθηγεμόνι τούτῳ τῆς τῶν ὄντων διοικήσεως ὄντι.

[22] Against Horsley, "Law of Nature," 42, who finds the tendency of Philo and Cicero to distinguish God from law as the "most significant" of all the indications of Platonic influence on the Stoic ideas of these authors.

[23] See *SVF* 1.537 (= Stobaeus, *Ecl.* 1.25.3–27.4), noting esp. the following clauses: Ζεῦ φύσές ἀρχηγέ, νόμου μέτα πάντα κυβερνῶν . . . κατευθύνεις κοινὸν λόγον, ὃς διὰ πάντων φοιτᾷ.

[24] Plutarch, *St. Rep.* 1050D; the extent to which the phrase τὸν τοῦ Διὸς λόγον . . . καὶ νόμον καὶ δίκην καὶ πρόνοιαν represents Chrysippus's own words, however, is not immediately clear.

[25] Brad Inwood, *Ethics and Human Action in Early Stoicism* (Oxford: Clarendon Press, 1985) 107f and 160. See further on this immediately below. Cf. in this respect Philo *Opif.* 3.

[26] See, for example, the Epicurean critique of Stoic theology reported by Cicero in *De Nat. Deor.* 1.36–41; see further Long and Sedley, *The Hellenistic Philosophers*, 1.323–33.

[27] *De Leg.* 2.8. I diverge from the translation of the LCL only in reading *principem . . . et ultimam* as descriptive of *legem illam* rather than the *mentem dei*; cf. in this respect 2.10, cited below, where the law, in a similar context, is described as *vera et princeps*.

"for the divine mind cannot exist without reason, and divine reason cannot but have this power to establish right and wrong."[28] Thus, before human beings ever began to codify laws, this "eternal law" (*legem sempiternam*) was in effect:

> For reason did exist, derived from the nature of the universe, urging men to right conduct and diverting them from wrong-doing, and this reason did not first become Law when it was written down,[29] but when it first came into existence; and it came into existence simultaneously with the divine mind.[30]

Cicero then offers a version of the standard Stoic definition of law which identifies the "right reason" in question more closely: "Wherefore the true and primal law, applied to command and prohibition, is the right reason of supreme Jupiter."[31]

These passages from *De Legibus* 2 occur in the context of a recap of the main points of *De Legibus* 1, which itself provides the theoretical basis for the *De Legibus* as a whole.[32] It is therefore not surprising that the association of the law with the divine *ratio* emerges clearly in book one as well, especially in connection with Cicero's argument that the common possession of reason (and therefore right reason) by the gods and humanity entails the common possession of law as well—a series of inferences that leads ultimately to the familiar Stoic thesis of the citizenship of gods and human beings in the cosmic *civitas*.[33]

Natural Law as Human Reason

Just as *logos*, according to the Stoics, is both a divine, cosmic force and a particular characteristic of the human animal, so too could the law comprised by this *logos* be conceived as both permeating the cosmos and internal to the human individual. While explicit testimony is lacking in the extant early fragments, the Stoic espousal of

---

[28] *Ibid.*, 2.10.

[29] Note that Cicero's own attempt to write up a law based on this "natural law" seems rather at odds with the early Stoic theory; see on this point above. In this respect, though, his project is not unlike later Jewish and Christian attempts to find verbal expressions of this law in their own traditions of instruction; see further on this Chapters Three and Four.

[30] *De Leg.* 2.10.

[31] *Ibid.*

[32] See the comments of Cicero in *De Leg.* 2.8, and those of Quintus in 2.9.

[33] *De Leg.* 1.23.

this latter view is nonetheless certain, at least from the time of Chrysippus. Suggestive in the first place is the fact that where the undoubtedly early Stoic concept of the human animal as citizen of the World City appears in later sources, it is consistently emphasized that the human's status as citizen owes to his or her share of the *logos* which constitutes the law of the Cosmopolis.[34] The most decisive evidence, however, comes from the sphere of the Stoic psychology of action. We have seen the specification of the law's function as "commanding that which is to be done and forbidding that which is not to be done" appears repeatedly in the Stoic sources. It is attributed to Zeno, quoted from Chrysippus's *On Law*, and is part of the standard Stoic definition of law found in a diverse body of ancient literature. It is therefore of great interest that Chrysippus understood these functions to be intimately bound up with the workings of the human *logos* as well.

All animal action, according to the Stoics, originates ultimately with "impulse" (ὁρμή).[35] Each impulse is itself prompted by a particular type of "presentation" (φαντασία), namely a "hormetic presentation," which "indicates to the animal the presence of something of interest to it, something which will contribute to its health, wellbeing, pleasure, the fulfillment of its individual nature, etc."[36] In the case of the mature human animal, the *logos* functions to provide a propositional content to the hormetic (and other) presentations that he or she experiences, and rational human action is caused by the impulse which results from assent to the proposition accompanying a given hormetic presentation.[37] Inwood makes the quite plausible

---

[34] See above, note 12.

[35] For the summary of the Stoic doctrine of impulse which follows I rely on Inwood's very illuminating study, *Ethics and Human Action in Early Stoicism*; see esp. pp. 47–53 on impulse as the cause of action. See further Long and Sedley, *The Hellenistic Philosophers*, 1.346–54, who offer translations of some of the basic evidence along with comments.

[36] Inwood, *Ethics and Human Action*, 56. As Cherniss points out (*Plutarch: Moralia* [LCL. Cambridge, MA: Harvard University Press, 1976; repr. 1993], 451–52 note c), the term ὁρμή, as is so common in Stoic schemes of classification, seems to have been used both in a more general way (i.e., to designate that movement of the soul which is generative of action) and with a more specific referent (i.e., as one species of the former, namely that directed toward something desired). The latter is to be contrasted with another species of the more general ὁρμή, namely the ἀφορμή, which is directed away from something rejected. See further the detailed discussion of the Stoic terminology in Inwood, *Ethics and Human Action*, 224–42.

[37] Cf. Diog. Laert. 7.86, where the *logos* is said to supervene "as the craftsman

conjecture that the Stoics would have held that an imperatival clause accompanies the hormetic presentation in addition to the propositional clause that accompanies all presentations.[38] For example, if a thirsty woman experiences the presentation of a glass of ice water on a hot day, her drinking that water will depend not only upon her assent to the proposition "it is appropriate for me to drink this ice water," but her obedience to the imperative "drink the ice water!" that her *logos* would issue subsequent to her assent to the aforementioned proposition. In short, rational human action is the result of one's obedience to the imperatival commands issued by one's own *logos* in response to hormetic presentations. Thus Chrysippus defined a human animal's impulse (ὁρμή)—impulse, that is, in the stricter sense[39]—as λόγος προστακτικὸς αὐτῷ τοῦ ποιεῖν, and ἀφορμή as λόγος ἀπαγορευτικός.[40]

This description of the human *logos* as προστακτικός[41] and ἀπαγορευτικός is rather striking in light of the widely attested Stoic definition of νόμος as λόγος ὀρθὸς προστακτικὸς μὲν ὧν ποιητέον, ἀπαγορευτικὸς δὲ ὧν οὐ ποιητέον. It is highly significant, therefore, that the definitions of human ὁρμή and ἀφορμή given above were in fact taken by Plutarch from Chrysippus's treatise *On Law*, a work which had used the terms

---

of impulse," as "a more perfect leadership" in action. (The translation of the latter phrase [τελειοτέραν προστασίαν] is taken from LCL; for τεχνίτης γὰρ οὗτος [λόγος] ἐπιγίνεται τῆς ὁρμῆς, however, I have cited the more literal translation of Long and Sedley, *The Hellenstic Philosophers*, 1.346 [§57A].) Assent is thus a necessary part of human action, and is in fact the locus of human ethical responsibility according to the Stoics; see further on this Inwood, *Ethics and Human Action*, 66–91.

[38] Inwood, *Ethics and Human Action*, 60–66.

[39] See above, note 36.

[40] Plutarch, *St. Rep.* 1037F. Inwood, *Ethics and Human Action*, 61, in writing that "Chrysippus seems to have defined an impulse as man's reason commanding him to act" has apparently read Chrysippus's τοῦ ἀνθρώπου as dependent upon ὁ λόγος rather than ἡ ὁρμή. While grammatically this is possible, the genitive is more likely dependent upon ἡ ὁρμή for two reasons. First, by Inwood's own account (*ibid.*, 107–8), it is not only *human* reason that commands; cf. in this respect *De Leg* 2.10: "... the divine mind cannot exist without reason, and divine reason cannot but have this power to establish right and wrong" (*neque ... esse mens divina sine ratione potest, nec ratio divina non hanc vim in rectis pravisque sanciendis habet*). More importantly, this definition must in any case be understood as concerning specifically ἡ ὁρμὴ τοῦ ἀνθρώπου since the impulse of non-rational animals is not governed by reason.

[41] Note that where LCL has προστατικός, SVF reads προστακτικός. I have found no indication that this confusion is based on textual variants; see further the edition of M. Pohlenz (*Plutarchi Moralia* (Lipsiae: Teubner, 1925) vol. 6, pt. 2, p. 12) which agrees with SVF with no indication of textual variants. The use of προστατικός in LCL is perhaps an oversight: προστατικός, from the verb προστῆναι, means "of or for a prostates [i.e. a leader]"; προστακτικός, meaning "of or for commanding," comes from προστάσσω, a term whose forms are used repeatedly by Plutarch in this passage.

προστακτικόν and ἀπαγορευτικόν to describe the functions of law in its opening lines.[42] Inwood quite reasonably concludes that this treatise

> must have been a work setting out in detail the relation of man to the will of Zeus ... In doing this he [sc. Chrysippus] seems to have developed a theory of the similarity of the mind of man and of god, and of the consequent need of a man to assimilate his will to that of god.[43] A man's correct actions (*katorthômata*) are the result of his impulses, obedience to commands to himself which are at the same time the commands of the Law of Nature, the will of Zeus.[44]

The fact that Chrysippus concerned himself with the topic of "impulse" in his treatise *On Law*, and that he moreover used the same terms to describe the functioning of human reason and natural law in this work, make it quite difficult to escape the conclusion that the identification of law with the *logos* of the sage was an important element of his theory of law.[45]

Several explicit statements of the identification of the law of nature with human reason are in fact found in Cicero's *De Legibus*, alongside its identification with the reason of God. In 2.8 Cicero writes that

> that Law which the gods have given to the human race has been justly praised; for it is the reason and mind of the sage applied to command and prohibition.[46]

This definition is obviously reminiscent of what we have found to have been a common Stoic definition of law. As in 2.10, it is altered only by a more precise identification of the *ratio* in question; this time, however, Cicero specifies that it is particularly the reason of the sage. The parallel between 2.8 and 2.10 is made explicit in 2.11. The text is corrupt but the sense is clear in any case:

> Therefore, just as that divine mind is the supreme Law, so, when [reason] is perfected in man, [that also is Law; and this perfected reason exists] in the mind of the wise man.[47]

---

[42] Plutarch, *St. Rep.* 1037F; cf. *SVF* 3.314.

[43] Inwood cites in this connection Cicero, *De Nat. Deor.* 2.58.

[44] Inwood, *Ethics and Human Action*, 108.

[45] Note also that Plutarch's critique of Chrysippus's *On Law* in *St. Rep.* 1038A seems to assume that Chrysippus had made this identification.

[46] *De Leg* 2.8; I have altered the translation of LCL only in rendering *ratio mensque sapientis* as "the reason and mind of the sage" rather than "of a *wise lawgiver*."

[47] *De Leg.* 2.11; I cite the LCL translation, which follows the conjectural emendation of Vahlen.

The identification of law with the *ratio* of the sage, as was the case with its equation with the *ratio* of God, is also clear from Book One. It emerges most clearly in *De Leg.* 1.18–19, where Cicero attributes to "the most learned men" (*doctissimis viris*) the view that

> Law is highest reason implanted in nature (*summa ratio insita in natura*) which commands what ought to be done and forbids the opposite. This reason, when strengthened and perfected in the human mind, is law. And so they believe that Law is intelligence, whose natural function it is to command right conduct and forbid wrongdoing . . . [Law] is the mind and reason of the sage . . .[48]

It is clear from the subsequent reference to the *mens ratioque prudentis* and the preceding mention of the *hominis mens* that Cicero's primary concern here is human reason. On the other hand, the general equation of law with "intelligence" (*prudentiam*) which naturally commands and prohibits might be spoken with reference to God or humanity,[49] and at least one author has in fact interpreted the initial definition of law as *summa ratio insita in natura* with reference to the divine reason which pervades the cosmos.[50] As this is precisely the definition which is of central concern to the present study, it requires closer examination. Which *ratio* in particular does Cicero have in mind here? Is a Greek λόγος ἔμφυτος, as Meyer suggested, in fact to be seen behind Cicero's Latin *ratio insita*? Is there any particular significance to the use of the term "implanted" in this connection?

The Development of Human Reason

I begin with the observation that the Stoic identification of natural law with human reason implies a developmental aspect to their theory of law. According to the Stoics, the human animal is born with only a potential *logos*, and cannot be properly described as "rational" until around the age of seven, at which time the *logos* becomes

---

[48] *De Leg.* 1.18–19: *lex est ratio summa insita in natura, quae iubet ea, quae facienda sunt, prohibetque contraria. eadem ratio cum est in hominis mente confirmata et confecta, lex est. itaque arbitrantur prudentiam esse legem, cuius ea vis sit, ut recte facere iubeat, vetet delinquere . . . ea est enim naturae vis, ea mens ratioque prudentis . . .* I have slighlty altered the LCL translation. Cf. also *De Leg.* 1.23.

[49] Cf. *De Leg.* 2.10: "For the divine mind cannot exist without reason, and divine reason cannot but have the power to establish right and wrong."

[50] Kenter, *De Legibus*, 81f.

"completed from the preconceptions" (ἐκ τῶν προλήψεων συμπληροῦσθαι).[51] This maturation at around seven years of age is to be sharply distinguished from the ultimate perfection of the *logos* attained only by the sage. Unlike the former, which occurs quite naturally and independently of any intentionality in every human individual, the latter occurs only through great intellectual effort, and is in fact rarely, if ever, achieved.[52] This initial maturation will be discussed more fully below. At present I wish only to emphasize that, inasmuch as it is the perfected reason (ὀρθὸς λόγος) which is identified by the Stoics as natural law, there is necessarily a developmental aspect in the theory.

While explicit evidence for early Stoic discussion of this natural consequence of their identification of natural law with human reason is lacking in the extant fragments, such a developmental aspect is in fact quite explicit in Cicero's *De Legibus*. The thought behind the corrupt passage from 2.10, where Cicero apparently identifies the law as reason "when it is perfected in the human being" (*cum in homine est perfecta*), and which thus exists particularly in "the mind of the sage" (*in mente sapientis*), is spelled out more clearly in 1.18. He begins by stating, as his initial definition of law, an obvious variant of the common Stoic definition discussed above: *lex est ratio summa insita in natura, quae iubet ea, quae facienda sunt, prohibetque contraria*. He then proceeds to clarify: "this reason, *when strengthened and completed in the human mind*, is law."[53] This statement obviously assumes a time when the *ratio* was less than "strengthened" and "completed," and this is precisely what one would expect given the Stoic account of the development of the human reason.

The particular developmental process which informs Cicero's *De Legibus* is stated more fully in 1.26–27. Having secured the premise of the providential governance of the universe (1.21) and the kinship of humans with God (1.22–25), Cicero rehearses a litany of the gifts that divine Nature has bestowed upon humans as a result of this family tie. Included among these are not only the senses, which serve as one's "attendants and messengers," but also the disclosure

---

[51] *SVF* 2.83; on the Stoic doctrine of preconception, see below.

[52] See Long and Sedley, *The Hellenistic Philosophers*, 1.381 (§61N).

[53] *De Leg.* 1.18: *eadem ratio cum est in hominis mente confirmata et confecta, lex est.* As was the case in the citation of this passage above, I have altered the translation of LCL; the emphasis in the translation, too, has been added.

of "vague conceptions of the most important things" (*rerum plurimarum obscuras . . . intelligentias*) which provide, "as it were, the foundations of knowledge" (*quasi fundamenta quaedam scientiae*).[54] Cicero continues, describing the further development of these "obscure conceptions" into the *ratio* itself:

> But, whereas God has begotten and equipped the human being, desiring it to be the chief of all created things, it should now be evident, without going into all the details, that nature herself—by herself—(*ipsam per se naturam*) goes a step farther; for, with no guide to point the way, she starts with those things whose character she has learned through the rudimentary and inchoate conceptions, and herself—by herself—strengthens and perfects the faculty of reason (*ex prima et inchoata intelligentia genera cognovit, confirmat ipsa per se rationem et perficit*).[55]

As Kenter has recognized, *De Leg.* 1.26–27 is to be understood in light of the Stoic view, mentioned above, that the human *logos* matures to the point where it can be described as properly "rational" as the result of a natural process involving preconceptions (προλήψεις).[56] According to Cicero, then, the mature human *ratio*—and ultimately, ideally, the "right reason" that is natural law—develops directly out these "obscure conceptions." Moreover, it is clear from Cicero's depiction of these "foundations of knowledge" as a divine endowment of the same order as the senses and the human form that he understands them to be innate in the human animal.[57] In fact, the Stoics did speak of a certain category of preconception which they described as ἔμφυτος, and it is undoubtedly this class of preconception that Cicero here has in mind. Thus for Cicero the potential *ratio* with which humans are born is intimately associated with the "implanted preconceptions" (ἔμφυτοι προλήψεις): human reason in the proper sense of the term develops naturally and directly out of them.[58] The fact that this developmental scheme is assumed in the initial

---

[54] *De Leg* 1.26; translation mine. The LCL translation of *intelligentias* as "meanings" fails to bring out the connection with the Stoic doctrine of conception and preconception; on this use of *intelligentia* in Cicero, see Marin O. Lisçu, *Étude sur la Langue de la Philosophie Morale chez Cicéron* (Paris: Société d'Édition «Les Belles Lettres», 1930) 114 and 126. On the textual problem here see Kenter, *De Legibus*, 111–112; the intention is sufficiently clear for our purposes in any case.

[55] *De Leg* 1.27; the translation is based on the LCL.

[56] Kenter, *De Legibus*, 111–12.

[57] *Ibid.*

[58] See further on this point below.

account of natural law, where law is defined as *ratio insita* (cf. λόγος ἔμφυτος), requires closer attention.

There is, however, an important preliminary issue which must first be sorted out. The Stoic doctrine of "implanted preconceptions" has been the subject of no small debate, and it has been suggested by more than one author that Cicero's belief that these are present in human individuals from birth represents a platonizing interpretation of the Stoic position.[59] It will be necessary to bring some clarity to the Stoic theory, and thus to Cicero's relation to it, before proceeding further. These questions are of obvious importance for the more general issue of the primary source for the *De Legibus* and its relation to the early Stoics. More importantly for our present purposes, this analysis will greatly illuminate the recurring use of the term "implanted" to describe the human *logos* or the natural law it comprises in the ancient literature.

THE STOIC DOCTRINE OF IMPLANTED PRECONCEPTIONS

The debate surrounding the Stoic doctrine of "implanted preconceptions" (ἔμφυτοι προλήψεις) concerns, specifically, the early Stoic understanding of their origin.[60] Both Chrysippus and Epictetus used the term ἔμφυτος to describe human preconceptions of basic ethical categories such as good and bad. It is clear by all accounts that Epictetus, in a manner reminiscent of Cicero, used this term to convey that these preconceptions are in some sense "inborn" in the human animal. There has been wide disagreement, however, regarding Chrysippus's use of the term and its relation to that of Epictetus. In what follows, therefore, it will be necessary to reconstruct Chrysippus's doctrine as far as possible without reference to the evidence of Epictetus.

---

[59] E.g., Kenter, *De Legibus*, 112.

[60] The most extensive discussions are those of A. Bonhöffer, *Epictet und die Stoa: Untersuchungen zur stoischen Philosophie* (Stuttgart: Enke 1890; repr., Stuttgart-Bad Cannstatt: Friedrich Frommann Verlag [Günther Holzboog], 1968) 187–222; F. H. Sandbach, "Ennoia and Prolêpsis in the Stoic Theory of Knowledge," *Classical Quarterly* 24 (1930) 44–51; reprinted with supplementary notes in *Problems in Stoicism*, 22–37; and M. Pohlenz, *Grundfragen der stoischen Philosophie* (Abhandlungen der Gesellschaft der Wissenschaften zu Göttingen 3/26; Göttingen: Vandenhoeck & Ruprecht, 1940; reprinted in *Stoicism*, [ed. Leonardo Tarán; Greek & Roman Philosophy 38; New York & London: Garland, 1987]) 82–103.

The Problem

The basic contours of the Stoic doctrine of conception and preconception are reported by Aetius:

> When man is born, he has the commanding part of his soul like a sheet of paper serviceable for writing upon. On this he inscribes each one of his concepts (τῶν ἐννοιῶν). The first method of inscription is through the senses (διὰ τῶν αἰσθήσεων). For perceiving something, e.g. white, they have a memory (μνήμην) of it when it has departed. And when many memories of a similar kind have arisen, then we say we have experience (ἐμπειρίαν). Experience is the mass of similar presentations (φαντασιῶν).

He continues:

> Of conceptions, some come about naturally in the aforesaid ways and undesignedly, but others through our instruction and attention. The latter are called "conceptions" only, the former are also called "preconceptions" (τῶν δὲ ἐννοιῶν αἱ μὲν φυσικῶς γίνονται κατὰ τοὺς εἰρημένους τρόπους καὶ ἀνεπιτεχνήτως, αἱ δὲ ἤδη δι᾽ ἡμετέρας διδασκαλίας καὶ ἐπιμελείας· αὗται μὲν οὖν ἔννοιαι καλοῦνται μόνον, ἐκεῖναι δὲ καὶ προλήψεις). Reason (ὁ λόγος), for which we are called rational (λογικοί), is said to be completed from our preconceptions (ἐκ τῶν προλήψεων συμπληροῦσθαι) over the first seven years of life.[61]

Preconception (πρόληψις) is thus a type of conception (ἔννοια). The term ἔννοια is used both in this more general sense, as the genus of which preconception is a species, as well as in a more restricted sense to denote a particular species of conception which contrasts with the preconception.[62] According to Aetius, the distinction between preconceptions and conceptions in this strict sense is one of origin: προλήψεις arise "naturally" whereas ἔννοιαι in the strict sense refer to those concepts which result from conscious intellectual effort.[63] Thus preconception can fairly be described as one's initial conception of something, which is as such rather ill-defined and in need of further refinement.[64] Both the natural origin of preconceptions

---

[61] SVF 2.83; the translation is that of Sandbach, "Ennoia," 25f.

[62] Pohlenz (Grundfragen, 84) speaks of "Ennoia im engeren Sinne" and as "Oberbegriff."

[63] Bonhöffer's limitation of the preconceptions to the "ethischen und ästhetischen Begriffe," (e.g. Epictet und die Stoa, 191, 193) and the concept of God (Epictet und die Stoa, 218–22), as well as his identification of them with the κοιναὶ ἔννοιαι have been well refuted by Sandbach; see "Ennoia," 26f and 23–25; also Pohlenz, Grundfragen, 84–85. Both result from his confusion of προλήψεις in general with the ἔμφυτοι προλήψεις. See further on this below.

[64] Cf. Sandbach, "Ennoia," 25: "This, then, is one distinguishing mark of the

and the rather general character of their content are apparently reflected in Chrysippus's definition of πρόληψις as ἔννοια φυσικὴ τῶν καθόλου.[65]

It is the precise meaning of this "natural" acquisition of the preconceptions that has been at the center of the scholarly debate regarding the Stoic doctrine of πρόληψις. At least one sense is clear enough from Aetius's own report: preconceptions result from the "natural" tendency of the commanding faculty to organize sensual experience, even before an individual has become properly rational.[66] It has long been noted, however, that while Aetius speaks of the "aforesaid ways" (plural) in which preconceptions can arise, he indicates only one such way, namely, by means of sensual experience.[67] It is therefore generally agreed that behind Aetius's account lies some source that had described more fully the "natural" and "undesigned" acquisition of preconceptions, and that something approximating such a source is preserved by Diogenes Laertius:[68]

> Of things conceived (τῶν νοουμένων), some have been conceived by direct experience (κατὰ περίπτωσιν), some by resemblance, some by analogy, some by transposition, some by composition, some by contrariety ... and some things are conceived by inference, like propositions and space; and something just and good (δίκαιόν τι καὶ ἀγαθόν) is conceived naturally (φυσικῶς); and by privation, for instance a man without hands.[69]

---

preconception; it is an undeveloped conception, as opposed to the thought-out definition"; further Pohlenz, *Grundfragen*, 83–84. The technical term for this refinement seems to have been διάρθρωσις; the evidence for this term comes primarily from Epictetus, but cf. Diog. Laert. 7.199. See further Bonhöffer, *Epictet und die Stoa*, 188–90.

[65] Diog. Laert. 7.54, citing from the first book of Chrysippus's Περὶ Λόγου. On the translation of this rather difficult phrase, see Sandbach, "Ennoia," 25 and 35 n. 12, who translates it as a "natural conception of the general characteristics of a thing." It has been variously understood but seems to suggest the rather general (which is to say, neither precisely nor adequately defined) nature of the information such a conception bears; so Sandbach, "Ennoia," 25; Pohlenz, *Grundfragen*, 84; Bonhöffer, *Epictet und die Stoa*, 203–4.

[66] Indeed the human *logos*, which is itself present at the time of an individual's birth only in a potential form, is "completed" by means of their accumulation.

[67] This, in fact, is introduced as πρῶτος τῆς ἀναγραφῆς τρόπος, upon which no "second" or "third" follows. This lacuna was apparently first detected by Zeller; see Bonhöffer, *Epictet und die Stoa*, 195.

[68] Upon this matter all the major expositors of this Stoic doctrine are agreed; cf. Bonhöffer, *Epictet und die Stoa*, 195; Sandbach, "Ennoia," 26; Pohlenz, *Grundfragen*, 82f.

[69] Diog. Laert. 7.52–53. The translation cited is a slightly altered version of Sandbach's translation; cf. "Ennoia," 26.

The "direct experience" which heads the list in this passage corresponds to the conceptions acquired "by the senses" in Aetius's account, with the rest of it apparently comprising his unspecified "aforesaid ways."[70] Most of the items on this list represent "some simple and unconscious mental operation from the data given by the senses" similar to that described already by Aetius in his illustration of the "natural" acquisition of preconceptions.[71]

Significantly, however, the only conceptions singled out by Diogenes Laertius as acquired "naturally" here are those of "something just and good." Assuming that something like this account lies behind the report of Aetius, therefore, we have a problem. Are we to understand that the concepts of "something just and good" are the only preconceptions (i.e., φυσικαὶ ἔννοιαι) on this list, or that they have a "natural" origin in a still more specialized sense than the other types of preconception? It must be pointed out at once that if Aetius has, in fact, relied on an account such as that found in Diog. Laert. 7.52–53, he provides clear and strong evidence for the latter interpretation: not only does Aetius characterize the acquisition of conceptions "by means of the senses" (διὰ τῶν αἰσθήσεων; cf. Diogenes Laertius's κατὰ περίπτωσιν)[72] as occurring φυσικῶς, but he explicitly classifies such conceptions as προλήψεις.

This much was clear to Bonhöffer. However, guided by his theses (i) that preconceptions concerned only conceptions in the spheres of ethics and theology and (ii) that all preconceptions were inborn, Bonhöffer nonetheless held that only the concepts of "something good" and "something just" from Diogenes Laertius's list were to be considered preconceptions. He argued that Aetius used φυσικῶς in a less technical sense when referring to the other conceptions to denote simply the "unsophisticated manner" in which a concept such as "white" was formed.[73] In fact Aetius, he contended, epexegetically appended the term ἀνεπιτεχνήτως to make this meaning clear.[74] Bonhöffer could not, however, dispense with Aetius's explicit class-

---

[70] So Bonhöffer, *Epictet und die Stoa*, 195; Sandbach, "Ennoia," 26; Pohlenz, 82f. See further Diog. Laert. 7.53 for the association of περίπτωσις with τὰ αἰσθητά.

[71] Sandbach, "Ennoia," 26; similarly Bonhöffer, *Epictet und die Stoa*, 195f.

[72] See above, note 70.

[73] Bonhöffer, *Epictet und die Stoa*, 194–96; cf. however *ibid.*, 192, where Bonhöffer regards precisely this interpretation of the term "natural" in the context of the general Stoic doctrine of φυσικαὶ ἔννοιαι as "unleugbar etwas Gekünsteltes."

[74] Bonhöffer, *Epictet und die Stoa*, 195.

ification of such conceptions as προλήψεις so easily. Calling this "den zweiten wunden Punkt der Stelle," he writes:

> I confess that I can only dispose of this obstacle by the assumption either that the author, with the division of the ἔννοιαι into *kunstlose* and *kunstmässige*, has thoughtlessly considered only the φυσικαὶ ἔννοιαι under the former so that, as in Epictetus 2.11, the division is therefore an *incomplete* one,[75] or that he has *mistakenly* extended the term πρόληψις to such concepts to which it, at least in the stricter sense, is not suitable.[76]

Such mistrust of the fundamental evidence for the Stoic doctrine of πρόληψις which Aetius's account provides was rightly questioned by Sandbach.[77] He showed that Bonhöffer's limitation of the preconceptions to concepts in the areas of ethics and theology was in any case misguided.[78] He pointed out further that if one assumes that some, at least, of the preconceptions were held to originate from empirical experience rather than being inborn in humans—an assumption warranted even apart from the evidence of Aetius[79]—the reports of Aetius and Diogenes Laertius are actually quite complementary:

> The two passages together give a perfectly consistent account of a preconception as the first conception of a thing, arrived at without special mental attention, and derived either directly or by some simple unconscious mental operation from the data given by the senses.[80]

Such mental operations as are described by Diogenes Laertius are simple enough, as Bonhöffer himself recognized, to warrant their characterization as "naturally" arising. The conceptions of "something

---

[75] See further Bonhöffer, *Epictet und die Stoa*, 194 on this supposition of an incomplete classification. Bonhöffer's belief that there was a "third category" of conception results from his mistaken limitation of the term πρόληψις to the ἔμφυτοι προλήψεις. In effect, this third category comprises all προλήψεις which are not at the same time ἔμφυτοι προλήψεις.

[76] Bonhöffer, *Epictet und die Stoa*, 196: "Ich gestehe, dass ich diesen Anstoss nur zu beseitigen weiss durch die Annahme, entweder dass der Verfasser, bei der Einteilung der ἔννοιαι in kunstlose und kunstmässige, nachlässigerweise unter den ersten nur die φυσικαὶ ἔννοιαι ins Auge gefasst hat, so dass also, wie bei Epictet II, 11, die Einteilung eine *unvollständige* wäre, oder dass er die Bezeichung πρόληψις *irrtümlich* auf solche Begriffe ausgedehnt hat, auf welche sie, wenigstens im engeren Sinne, nicht passt" (emphasis his).

[77] Sandbach, "Ennoia," 26.

[78] Sandbach, "Ennoia," 26f and 23–25. See further Pohlenz, *Grundfragen*, 84–85.

[79] See on this Epictetus, *Diss.* 4.8.6–10, where the πρόληψις of a carpenter is mentioned. It is difficult even in the case of Epictetus, who clearly believes in "innate" conceptions of ethical notions, that such a concept was held to be innate.

[80] Sandbach, "Ennoia," 26.

just and good" must thus be understood to arise "naturally" in a more specialized sense than is the case with the other preconceptions.[81]

What, then, is the nature of this more "natural" origin? Sandbach was well aware that Chrysippus himself, in a manner which recalls this passage from Diogenes Laertius, had spoken of ἔμφυτοι προλήψεις of "good" and "bad."[82] He rightly rejected, however, Bonhöffer's assertion that ἔμφυτος could mean nothing other than inborn, citing several examples to the contrary.[83] In fact, Sandbach argued, to interpret ἔμφυτος as "inborn" is "contrary to all the other evidence, and in particular inconsistent with the image of the soul at birth as a sheet of paper ready to be inscribed with conceptions."[84] He cited in addition the following passage from Cicero, which reports that the Stoics understood the concept of the Good to be arrived at by means of "analogy":

> Now notions of things are produced in the mind when something has become known either by experience or combination of ideas or analogy or logical inference. The fourth and last method in this list is the one that has given us the conception of the Good. The mind ascends by inference from the things in accordance with nature till finally it arrives at the notion of the Good.[85]

In fact, he argued, the especially "natural" origin of the concept of "something good" is itself clarified by this report. While all preconceptions are by definition "naturally" acquired, the origin of our concept of the Good results, in the words of the Stoic spokesman Cato, from the fact that "the mind ascends by inference from the things in accordance with nature till finally it arrives at the notion of Good."[86] That is to say, Sandbach argues, "we recognise the good through the force of its own nature."[87] Bonhöffer's contention that this pas-

---

[81] *Ibid.*, 28f.

[82] Plutarch, *St. Rep.* 1041E.

[83] Sandbach, "Ennoia," 28; so also Pohlenz, *Grundfragen*, 88–89. Cf. Bonhöffer, *Epictet und die Stoa*, 192f.

[84] Sandbach, "Ennoia," 28, apparently referring to Aetius, *Plac* 4.11, who describes the ἡγεμόνικον in this way.

[85] Cicero, *De Fin.* 3.33; cf. Sandbach, "Ennoia," 28–29.

[86] Cicero, *De Fin.* 3.33: *ab iis rebus quae sunt secundum naturam ascendit animus collatione rationis, tum ad notionem boni pervenit.*

[87] Sandbach, "Ennoia," 29. In the appendix to the reprint of this article, Sandbach revises this position, stating that the "nature" concerned with the term φυσικῶς "must be that of the man who forms the concept, not that of the concept itself" ("Ennoia," 33). However, he gives no indication of how, if at all, he understands this revision to effect his overall thesis of the origin of the ethical preconceptions in empirical experience. See further below.

sage referred to a conception of *the* Good—which is to say an ἔννοια in the strict sense as opposed to a more hazy πρόληψις of *something good*—is for Sandbach "unconvincing in itself," and in any case "impossible" in light of a passage from Seneca where a similar account is presented in the context of a discussion of the *initial* occurrence of the concept of the Good.[88] Finally, Sandbach also downplays the evidence from Diogenes Laertius by characterizing the entire sentence "something just and good is conceived naturally" as being, in any case, "a kind of postscript to the original list" added only because "the good, though conceived 'by analogy', was not covered by any of the examples given" elsewhere in Diogenes Laertius's source.[89]

For Sandbach, then, there can be no question of innate preconceptions in early Stoicism.[90] In the end, however, he found it "difficult," despite his own arguments to the contrary, "to feel confident that Chrysippus did not mean 'inborn' when he wrote the word [sc. ἔμφυτοι]." He thus settled upon the rather unsatisfying conclusion that Chrysippus's use of this term was "only a temporary aberration."[91] Ultimately, therefore, Sandbach merely replaced Bonhöffer's mistrust of the evidence of Aetius with similar misgivings regarding evidence from Chrysippus himself. Moreover, while Sandbach is undoubtedly correct in pointing out that at least *some* preconceptions are acquired only through sensual experience, his argument that the concept of the Good is also ultimately derived from sensual experience fails to convince. It is not altogether clear that Bonhöffer's detection of a subtle difference between Diog. Laert. 7.53 and *De Fin.* 3.33, whereby the latter passage concerns a well defined ἔννοια rather than a πρόληψις, is "impossible" in light of the evidence of Seneca, as Sandbach maintains. Indeed, Sandbach relegated to his endnotes

---

[88] Sandbach ("Ennoia," 29) refers to Seneca, *Ep.* 120, the topic of which is "how we *first* acquire the knowledge of that which is good and that which is honorable" (*quomodo ad nos prima boni honestique notitia pervenit*); the translation is cited according the LCL, with emphasis added. All translations of Seneca, unless otherwise indicated, are taken from LCL. Cf. Bonhöffer's treatment of this passage in *Epictet und die Stoa*, 215–16.

[89] Sandbach, "Ennoia," 29.

[90] Sandbach ("Ennoia," 29f) seems to attribute their presence in Epictetus to the "syncretism of the first century," at which time "Platonism gave to Stoicism a belief in inborn conceptions."

[91] Sandbach, "Ennoia," 28. J. M. Rist, in contrast, has no compunction about reading Chrysippus as intending "ingrained" rather than "inborn" ("The Criterion of Truth," *Stoic Philosophy* [Cambridge: Cambridge University Press, 1969, repr. 1990] 134).

mention of Seneca's additional assertion that while knowledge of the
Good is arrived at by means of analogy, Nature herself "has given
us the seeds of knowledge."[92] In addition, Sandbach's contention that
the notion of innate preconceptions contradicts Aetius's characterization of the commanding faculty at birth as a "sheet of papyrus
serviceable for writing upon" is an overly hasty and rather superficial
dismissal of Bonhöffer's position. Bonhöffer, in fact, had suggested
that the "implanted preconceptions," like the *logos* itself, are present
at birth only in "spermatic"—which is to say, potential—form, and
Sandbach nowhere answers this particular argument.[93]

   The possibility therefore remains open that certain preconceptions,
namely those of the ethical sphere, are in some sense inborn in individual humans. But is this in fact the case? And if so, how did the
Stoics explain their existence?

   It is Max Pohlenz who introduces the key evidence for the solution to this problem. Having rejected, with Sandbach, Bonhöffer's
contention that Chrysippus's use of the term ἔμφυτος was in itself
decisive, Pohlenz nonetheless cited a previously neglected passage
from Plutarch in which Chrysippus is criticized for his supposed contradiction of the "common conceptions":[94]

> and this [offense against common conceptions on the part of Chrysippus
> occurs] too in matters concerning good things and evil and objects of
> choice and avoidance and things congenial and repugnant (οἰκείων τε
> καὶ ἀλλοτρίων), the clarity of which ought to be more manifest than
> that of things hot and cold and white and black, since the mental
> images of these are incidental to the sense-perceptions entering from
> without (ἐκείνων μὲν γὰρ ἔξωθέν εἰσιν αἱ φαντασίαι ταῖς αἰσθήσεσιν
> ἐπεισόδιοι) whereas the former are generated intrinsically from the prin-
> ciples within us (ταῦτα δ᾿ ἐκ τῶν ἀρχῶν τῶν ἐν ἡμῖν σύμφυτον ἔχει τήν
> γένεσιν).[95]

---

[92] Seneca, *Ep.* 120.4, which continues: "some say that we merely happened upon
this knowledge; but it is unbelievable that a vision of virtue could have presented
itself to anyone by mere chance" (*Quidam aiunt nos in notitiam incidisse, quod est incredibile,
virtutis alicui speciem casu occucurrisse*); translated according to LCL. For Sandbach's interpretation of the "seeds of knowledge," see "Ennoia," 36 n. 23, and further below.

[93] Bonhöffer, *Epictet und die Stoa*, 194f.

[94] Pohlenz, *Grundfragen*, 89. It is not necessary to enter into the vexed question
of κοιναὶ ἔννοιαι here since they are not simply identical with ἔμφυτοι προλήψεις,
as Bonhöffer had believed, nor with the προλήψεις in general. See on this point
Sandbach, "Ennoia," 23–25, who is followed by Pohlenz (*Grundfragen*, 85 n. 1). See
further R. B. Todd, "The Stoic Common Notions: A Re-examination and Reinterpretation," *SO* 48 (1973) 47–75.

[95] Plutarch, *Comm. Not.* 1070C; all translations of Plutarch's works are taken from
LCL unless otherwise indicated.

Here the ethically oriented concepts are said to arise directly ἐκ τῶν ἀρχῶν of the human individual, and are on this basis explicitly distinguished from those originating "externally" by means of the senses.[96] The use of the term σύμφυτος to describe the "internal" origin of ethical notions such as good and bad, etc., is, moreover, strikingly reminiscent of Chrysippus's reference to the ἔμφυτοι προλήψεις of good and bad.[97]

The theoretical basis for the claim of the "internal" origin of human ethical categories, Pohlenz argued, is the Stoic doctrine of οἰκείωσις.[98] The Stoics had argued that the first sensation that any given animal experiences is one of self-awareness:

> . . . as soon as an animal is born it perceives itself . . . the first thing that animals perceive is their own parts . . . both that they have them and for what purpose they have them . . .[99]

Moreover,

> An animal's first impulse (τὴν πρώτην ὁρμήν), say the Stoics, is to self-preservation, because nature at the outset endears it to itself (οἰκειούσης αὐτῷ τῆς φύσεως ἀπ' ἀρχῆς), as Chrysippus affirms in the first book of his work *On Ends*: his words are, "The dearest thing (πρῶτον οἰκεῖον) to every animal is its own constitution (σύστασιν) and its consciousness thereof"; for it was not likely that nature should estrange the living thing from itself or that she should leave the creature she has made without either estrangement from or affection for its own constitution

---

[96] Cf. further *Comm. Not.* 1058F: ἀφ' ὧν [sc. τῶν αἰσθήσεων] σχεδὸν αἱ πλεῖσται γεγόνασιν ἔννοιαι; i.e. most, and thus *not all*, conceptions arise from sensual experience. Note that this statement is placed upon the lips of the "comrade" who approaches the skeptic Diadumenus after having been "confused" by the Stoics (*Comm. Not.* 1059A).

[97] So also Pohlenz, *Grundfragen*, 93.

[98] Pohlenz, *Grundfragen*, 89–93. S. G. Pembroke remarks that the term οἰκείωσις has "a persistent reputation for being impossible to translate" ("Oikeiôsis," *Problems in Stoicism*, 114); I shall simply use the Greek term. On οἰκείωσις generally see in addition to the work of Pembroke just mentioned R. Philippson, "Das erste Naturgemässe," *Philologus* 87 (1931–32) 445–66; Pohlenz, *Grundfragen*, 1–81; C. O. Brink, "Οἰκείωσις and Οἰκειότης: Theophrastus and Zeno on Nature in Moral Theory," *Phronesis* 1 (1955–56) 123–45; B. Inwood, "Comments on Professor Görgemann's Paper: The Two Forms of *Oikeiôsis* in Arius and the Stoa," in *On Stoic and Peripatetic Ethics: The Work of Arius Didymus* (ed. W. W. Fortenbaugh; New Brunswick, NJ: Transaction Books, 1983) 190–201; idem, *Ethics and Human Action*, esp. 182–201; and most recently T. Engberg-Pedersen, *The Stoic Theory of Oikeiosis: Moral Development and Social Interaction in Early Stoic Philosophy* (Studies in Hellenistic Civilization 2; Denmark: Aarhus University Press, 1990).

[99] Cited from Long and Sedley, *The Hellenistic Philosophers*, 1.347 (§57C).

(οὔτε γὰρ ἀλλοτριῶσαι εἰκὸς ἦν αὐτὸ [αὐτῷ] τὸ ζῷον, οὔτε ποιήσασαν αὐτό, μήτ' ἀλλοτριῶσαι μήτ' οἰκειῶσαι). We are forced then to conclude that nature in constituting the animal made it near and dear to itself (οἰκειῶσαι πρὸς ἑαυτό); for so it comes to repel all that is injurious (τὰ βλάπτοντα) and give free access to all that is serviceable or akin to it (τὰ οἰκεῖα).[100]

In a nutshell, the Stoics argued that the primary drive of all animals (including humans) is that toward the preservation of self. Providential Nature, moreover, endows all animals both with an awareness of their own "constitution" (σύστασις), and with a natural tendency to evaluate their experience subjectively, distinguishing those things which are helpful (τὰ οἰκεῖα) from those which are harmful (τὰ βλάπτοντα; τὰ ἀλλότρια) to that constitution.[101] Thus, Pohlenz argued, our ethical concepts form a special category of preconception inasmuch as they alone ultimately originate from something inborn in the human animal rather than from empirical experience.

Curiously, however, Pohlenz did not offer an explicit response to Sandbach's contrary account of their origin.[102] Consequently, when Sandbach added a supplementary note to the 1971 reprint of his "Ennoia and Prolêpsis in the Stoic Theory of Knowledge," he offered only one significant revision to his prior account: he conceded that his explanation of the "natural" origin of the concepts of "something just" and "something good" was "inadequate and unsatisfactory," and stated that the "nature" in question "must be that of the man who forms the concept, not that of the concept itself."[103] However, Sandbach gave no indication that his general thesis regarding the origin of these conceptions was any less secure as a result of Pohlenz's study. In fact, he remained rather cool to the latter's thesis:

---

[100] Diog. Laert. 7.85.

[101] Cf. Pohlenz, *Grundfragen*, p. 90: "Die Oikeiosis bewirkt also, daß das Lebewesen die Außendinge nicht nur objektiv wahrnimmt, sondern zu seinem eigenen Ich in Beziehung setzt und subjektiv als nützlich oder schädlich wertet. Den Wertmaßstab liefert unsre eigene Natur und das, was ihr gemäß ist und sie fördert."

[102] Pohlenz only interacts specifically with Sandbach to endorse the latter's rejection of both Bonhöffer's limitation of the preconceptions to matters of ethics and theology, and his identification of them with the "common conceptions." See *Grundfragen*, 85 and n. 1.

[103] Sandbach, "Ennoia," 33. Note, however, that he gives no indication that this revision is indebted to the work of Pohlenz.

I see no reason why this account [from Pohlenz] should not have been welcomed by a Stoic, but also no evidence of its connexion with ἔμφυτοι προλήψεις. In any case Pohlenz makes no claim that it is relevant to the way in which the concept of 'just' is formed.[104]

Indeed, such a renowned scholar of Stoicism as J. M. Rist could continue after the publication of Pohlenz's work to cite Sandbach's "masterly article" as a successful refutation of the notion that the early Stoa espoused beliefs in "innate" preconceptions similar to those found in Epictetus. "There is no other 'evidence' in the Old Stoic writers for a theory of any kind of 'inborn' belief," he writes; "their philosophy needs no such beliefs and should not be saddled with them."[105] In what follows, therefore, I shall re-examine the evidence cited by Sandbach from Cicero and Seneca with a view, specifically, to the respective theses of Sandbach and Pohlenz. Is Sandbach's assertion that there is "no evidence" to connect the "implanted preconceptions" to οἰκείωσις a fair assessment? Does his own reconstruction account for the evidence in a more satisfactory manner?

Cicero and Seneca on the Concept of the Good

The importance of οἰκείωσις to Stoic philosophy in general is clear from the complaint of Plutarch that "in every book of physics, yes and of morals too," Chrysippus repeatedly writes "ad nauseam that from the moment of birth we have a natural congeniality to ourselves, to our members, and to our own offspring" (ὡς οἰκειούμεθα πρὸς αὑτοὺς εὐθὺς γενόμενοι καὶ τὰ μέρη καὶ τὰ ἔκγονα τὰ ἑαυτῶν).[106] This doctrine, in fact, provided the starting point for all of Stoic ethics, as is clear from a variety of sources.[107]

One such source is the summary of Stoic ethics in the third book of Cicero's *De Finibus* whence, it will be recalled, comes the account of the origin of the concept of the Good that is so central to Sandbach's

---

[104] "Ennoia," 34.
[105] J. M. Rist, "The Criterion of Truth," 134 with notes 3–4.
[106] Plutarch, *St. Rep.* 1038B.
[107] See on this, in addition to the works mentioned above in note 98, A. A. Long, "The Logical Basis of Stoic Ethics," *Proceedings of the Aristotelian Society* 71 (1970/71) 85–104; Long and Sedley, *The Hellenistic Philosophers*, 1.350–54. Inwood (*Ethics and Human Action*, 194) comments that "Chrysippus wanted to make good his point about orientation [i.e., οἰκείωσις] because his entire system of ethics would be founded on it."

refutation of the idea of "inborn" ethical preconceptions in early Stoicism. It is with this passage, therefore, that I shall begin.[108]

It will be recalled that Sandbach argued that Bonhöffer's thesis of the inborn origin of the concept of "good" stood in clear contradiction to the position of Cicero's Stoic spokesman Cato, who attributed its origin to a process of analogy. Sandbach rejected Bonhöffer's contention that, since Cicero's Cato focused upon *the* Good where Diogenes Laertius spoke only of *something* good, the former was concerned specifically with the origin of a fully developed ἔννοια rather than a προλήψις.[109] Despite its dismissal by Sandbach, however, Bonhöffer's observation, as we shall see, is quite to the point. Cicero's Cato, in his remarks regarding "analogy" in *De Finibus* 3, is concerned with our acquisition of the concept of the Good in the strict Stoic sense of the term. The ultimate origin of the human ability to conceptualize the distinction between "good" and "bad" is another matter altogether.

It is important first of all to bear in mind the broader philosophical context in which the summary of *De Finibus* 3 was written, namely, in that of a sharp disagreement regarding the question of the nature of the Goal, or Highest Good.[110] Cato, as Cicero's Stoic representative, argues that the Highest Good consists of virtue alone. He rejects, therefore, the Platonic and Peripatetic view that "bodily advantages" such as health, strength, etc., contribute anything toward the Goal,[111] and for this reason rejects, too, the classification of such things as "goods" at all. Thus, for example, his treatment of health: "We deem health to be deserving of a certain value but we do not place it among the goods."[112] The Highest Good, which is to say virtue or *honestum*, is in fact the sole good.[113] In effect, the Stoic Cato makes a technical distinction between *bonum*, or the Good in the strict Stoic sense as virtue alone, and *aestimabile*, or "the valuable,"

---

[108] Cf. Pohlenz's treatment of this passage in *Grundfragen*, 86–92, and esp. 90–92; see also Engberg-Pedersen's analysis in chapters 3 and 4 of his *The Stoic Theory of Oikeiosis*.

[109] See above, pp. 48–49.

[110] See esp. *De Fin.* 3.22–31, 41–48, and the critique of the Stoic position in *De Finibus* 4; see further 5.15–23, which greatly illuminates the dispute. Cicero's *De Finibus* as a whole intends to present, with subsequent critiques, the positions of the Epicureans, Stoics, and Antiochus of Ascalon on this question.

[111] *De Fin.* 3.41–48.

[112] *De Fin.* 3.44: *Nam qui valitudinem aestimatione aliqua dignam iudicamus neque eam tamen in bonis ponimus*; I have slightly altered the LCL translation.

[113] See e.g. *De Fin.* 3.21, where Cicero's Cato speaks of *honestum, quod solum in bonis ducitur.*

under which fall those bodily advantages classified as "good" by the Platonists, Peripatetics, and more generally in common parlance.[114] This distinction is scrupulously observed throughout Cato's summary, and will in fact provide one of the chief points of Cicero's subsequent critique.[115]

Secondly, we must understand *De Fin.* 3.33, the specific passage to which Sandbach referred, in the context of the larger account of the development of the notion of the Good presented in *De Finibus* 3. Significantly, the concept of the Valuable, as the *prima divisio*, is said to occur to the human individual before that of the Good.[116] It represents a conceptualization of the distinction that is made naturally by all animals according to the doctrine of οἰκείωσις: the distinction between those things that are "deserving of choice" because in accord with nature, and their opposites, which are thus called the Non-valuable (*inaestimabile*).[117] The formation of the concept of the Valuable is thus the inevitable result of the combination of, first, the innate tendency of all animals to distinguish those things which are beneficial to their constitutions from those that are harmful, and second, the particularly human possession of *logos*, the natural tendency of which is to organize experience into concepts. In the development that results ultimately in the formation of the concept of the Good, therefore, the formation of the concept of the Valuable is second only to the practical recognition of that which is valuable, an ability which is innate in all animals.[118]

In contrast, Cato reports that the recognition of "that which can *truly* be said to be good" (*quod vere bonum possit dici*) is a subsequent development.[119]

---

[114] One senses nonetheless a certain tension in this distinction owing to the fact that the Good, as a concept, is a derivative of the Valuable. Thus while the Good is on one hand "supremely valuable" (*plurimi aestimandum*), it is nonetheless different from the Valuable (which is itself neither good nor evil) in *kind* rather than *degree*; see *De Fin.* 3.34. See further Pohlenz's references to analogous Stoic evidence in *Grundfragen*, 94.

[115] See, e.g., *De Fin.* 4.56–61. Cicero here takes the characteristically Antiochan view, apparently originally espoused by Carneades (see *De Fin.* 3.41), that the Stoics differ on this issue from the Peripatetics and Platonists only in terminology, not in substance; cf. *De Fin.* 4.3–5 and 21–23.

[116] *De Fin.* 3.20.

[117] *Ibid.*

[118] See *De Fin.* 3.16 and 3.20.

[119] *De Fin.* 3.20; emphasis mine. On the concept of the Good as a later development relative to that of the Valuable, see further 3.21–22.

Man's first attraction is towards the things in accordance with nature
(*ea quae sunt secundum naturam*); but as soon as he has understanding
(*intelligentiam*), or rather becomes capable of "conception" (*notionem*)—in
Stoic phraseology ἔννοια—and has discerned the order and so to speak
harmony that governs conduct, he thereupon esteems this harmony
far more highly than all the things for which he originally felt an
affection, and by exercise of intelligence and reason infers the conclusion (*cognitione et ratione collegit*) that herein resides the Chief Good
of man, the thing that is praiseworthy and desirable for its own sake
(*summum illud hominis per se laudandum et expetendum bonum*) . . .[120]

Cato speaks in this instance of the first recognition of the Highest
Good (*summum bonum*); there is however, as we have seen, only one
bonum in his system, and that is the virtue which comprises the Goal.
Honestum, he continues, is "that Good which is the End to which all
else is a means" and which "alone is counted among the goods."[121]

It is striking that Cicero's Cato associates the later development
of the concept of the Good with the ability to form ἔννοιαι. That
this term is used in its strict sense is clear from the following considerations. The formation of the concept of the Valuable, according
to Cato's scheme, had already occurred several stages prior to the
formation of that of the Good; thus the stipulation that the Good
can be arrived at only with the ability to form ἔννοιαι would make
little sense if he simply meant the general tendency of the rational
animal to form (pre-)conceptions from experience. More importantly,
the ability to form preconceptions occurs quite early in human development, and in any case well before one is capable of the type of
rational inquiry requisite, according to Cato, for recognition of the
Good.[122] Cicero's Cato associates the ability to form ἔννοιαι with the
possession of *intelligentia*, which, as is clear from the context, is characterized by a capacity for rational examination and inquiry (*cognitione
et ratione*). The formation of concepts by this intellectual means is, as
we have seen, the mark of ἔννοιαι in the strict sense, not προλήψεις.

We are now in a position to evaluate properly the notice concerning the origin of the concept of the Good in *De Fin.* 3.33 to
which Sandbach referred in his refutation of Bonhöffer. The characterization of the *notitia boni* as having arisen "from the things in

---

[120] *De Fin.* 3.21.
[121] *De Fin.* 3.21: *id bonum quo omnia referenda sunt . . . quod solum in bonis ducitur*; I
have slightly altered the LCL translation.
[122] *SVF* 2.83.

accordance with nature" by means of "analogy" (*collatione rationis*) is to be interpreted in light of the fuller exposition found in 3.20–21 which has just been examined. The "analogy" made from "the things in accordance with nature" to which he here refers, as is clear from 3.20–21, is not a simple mental process like those which occur automatically and result in the formation of preconceptions in the pre-rational stages of early childhood. On the contrary, it requires a properly rational mind and the ability to form ἔννοιαι in the strict sense of the term. Moreover, the "conception" that Cicero's Cato has in mind, as Bonhöffer had already recognized, is not of the hazy and ill-defined variety that characterizes preconception, but is in fact a conception of that which is good in the Stoic sense, as opposed to that which is merely "valuable." Cato's concern here, that is, is the manner in which one arrives at the concept of that which *the Stoic* considers the Good; and this notion, he reports, is attained by means of a rational analogy from those things which the individual had long since considered "valuable." In order to understand the ultimate origin of the concept of the Good, therefore, one must inquire after the origin of the concept of the Valuable. And this, it is clear, results from the inborn disposition, characteristic of all animals by virtue of οἰκείωσις, to distinguish between that which is beneficial for oneself and that which is not.

An examination of Seneca *Ep.* 120.4ff, the other passage to which Sandbach referred in arguing against the thesis of the innate origin of the concept "good," yields quite similar results.[123] The question addressed in this letter is "how we first acquire a conception of *bonum* and *honestum*."[124] Seneca, like Cicero's Cato, uses the term *bonum* in its strictly Stoic sense, identifying it on one hand with *honestum*, and distinguishing it, on the other, from *utile* ("advantageous," "useful"), which, like Cato's *aestimabile*, describes the advantages pertaining to the body.[125] Thus Seneca's chief concern is how one first arrives at a conception of *the* Good, which is to say *virtus* or *honestum*, not the ultimate origin of the human tendency to make ethical distinctions.[126]

---

[123] Cf. Pohlenz's treatment of Seneca, *Ep.* 120 in *Grundfragen*, 86–88, 92.

[124] *Ep.* 120.3: *quomodo ad nos prima boni honestique notitia pervenerit.* Note that LCL renders *notitia* as "knowledge," thus obscuring the connection with the Stoic doctrine of conception. Cf., however, Cicero's use of this term, on which see Lisçu, *Étude sur la Langue*, 114.

[125] *Ep.* 120.1–3.

[126] The bulk of the letter is in fact concerned with the further stimulus toward

Seneca proceeds to describe how one arrives at a notion of the (Stoic) Good in a manner that is once again reminiscent of *De Finibus* 3:

> our school of philosophy hold that *honestum* and *bonum* have been comprehended by means of analogy (*per analogia*) . . . Now what this "analogy" is, I shall explain. We understood what bodily health was: and from this basis we deduced the existence of a certain mental health also. We knew, too, bodily strength, and from this basis we inferred the existence of mental sturdiness.[127]

As in *De Fin.* 3.21 and 33, the notion of the Good is arrived at by analogy from those things that benefit the body, which is to say, by analogy from the concept of the *utile*.[128] Seneca does not pursue the question of the origin of this latter concept further. He does, however, make reference to "seeds" of the knowledge of the Good which have been given to the human animal directly from Nature herself:

> Nature could not teach us this [sc. the *boni honestique notitia*] directly; she has given us the seeds of knowledge, but not knowledge itself (*semina nobis scientiae dedit, scientiam non dedit*). Some say that we merely happened upon this knowledge; but it is unbelievable that a vision of virtue could have presented itself to anyone by mere chance.[129]

A similar reference is found in *Ep.* 108, where once again Nature is depicted as the giver of these "seeds" to all of humanity:

> It is easy to rouse a listener so that he will crave righteousness; for Nature has given the foundations and the seed of virtue (*fundamenta semenque virtutum*) to us all.[130]

Sandbach interpreted these "seeds" as a reference to "the facts observed" from which, apparently, the analogy to the Good is made.[131] In *Ep.* 121, however, Seneca discusses a type of knowledge given by Nature in a more direct way, and which stands in clear contrast to knowledge gained from empirical experience: "The teachings of expe-

---

the formation of this conception which comes from the observance of the deeds of great individuals; but the fact that one should find oneself in admiration of such deeds presupposes, as Pohlenz recognized (*Grundfragen*, 86–88), a prior evaluative disposition to distinguish good from bad.

[127] *Ep.* 120.4, 5; I have altered the LCL translation only in retaining the Latin terms *honestum* and *bonum*.

[128] Cf. the partial list of things considered "useful" at *Ep.* 120.2–3, which includes wealth, possessions, status, and physical strength.

[129] *Ep.* 120.4.

[130] Seneca, *Ep.* 108.8

[131] Sandbach, "Ennoia," 36 n. 23.

rience are slow and irregular; but whatever Nature communicates belongs equally to everyone, and comes immediately."[132] It is clear from the wider context of *Ep.* 121, moreover, that the knowledge given directly by Nature rather than won from empirical experience is rooted in an animal's natural desire for well-being. It results, in other words, from οἰκείωσις. Indeed, Nature is said to have "communicated *nothing* [to animals] *except* the duty of taking care of themselves and the skill to do so."[133] The "seeds" of the knowledge of the Good, therefore, result ultimately from the human animal's innate tendency to recognize that which is beneficial for itself.

οἰκείωσις *and the Implanted Preconceptions*

Given this analysis of the accounts of the origin of the concept of the Good by Cicero and Seneca, Sandbach's claim that there is "no evidence" to link the ἔμφυτοι προλήψεις to οἰκείωσις is scarcely an accurate assessment. His own account, in any case, fails to convince. It is in fact precisely οἰκείωσις which both Cicero and Seneca locate at the beginning of the development which, by way of analogy from the antecedent concept of the Valuable, results finally in our concept of the (truly) Good. Our ethical concepts, therefore, are not entirely the products of empirical experience, as Pohlenz well recognized:

> Empirical experience is indispensable [for the formation of the concepts of "beneficial" and "good"], but the primary cause lies in the nature of the λογικὸν ζῷον, in which the predisposition for the formation of the ethical concepts is contained.[134]

Such an origin gives the ethically oriented preconceptions a unique standing among other preconceptions. It is thus quite understandable that Diogenes Laertius has singled out the concept of "something

---

[132] Seneca, *Ep.* 121.20: *Et tardum est et varium, quod usus docet; quicquid natura tradit, et aequale omnibus est et statim.*

[133] *Ibid.*; cf. *Ep.* 121.23: *Haec [natura] nihil magis quam tutelam sui et eius peritiam tradidit*; the emphasis in the translation is mine. Note also that Seneca characterizes the initial stage of this natural self-understanding in terms reminiscent of preconceptions: one's constitution is initially understood *crasse . . . et summatim et obscure.* Cf. in this respect *De Finibus* 5, on which see below.

[134] Pohlenz, *Grundfragen*, 92: "Die Empirie ist dabei unentbehrlich, aber die primäre Ursache liegt in der Natur des λογικὸν ζῷον, in der die Anlage zur Bildung der sittlichen Begriffe enthalten ist."

good," even among the other preconceptions, as being "naturally" acquired. And thus, too, does Plutarch distinguish concepts such as "white" and "warm" from those of ethical categories like "good" and "bad," or οἰκεῖος and ἀλλότριος—this latter pair being technical terms in the doctrine of οικείωσις[135]—on the basis of the latter's σύμφυτος γένεσις.[136] Given the centrality of οἰκείωσις to the philosophy of Chrysippus in general, it is undoubtedly in this context that his characterization of the preconceptions of good and bad in particular as ἔμφυτοι προλήψεις is to be understood.

The link between the "implanted preconceptions" and οἰκείωσις is confirmed by a further examination of the "seeds" of knowledge or virtue to which Seneca refers, and which, as we have seen, are understood to have been given to human beings from Nature by means of οἰκείωσις.[137] This imagery of "seeds," as well as the analogous image of "sparks," of knowledge or virtue is also found repeatedly in Cicero's works. In one such passage, the "seeds" or "sparks" of knowledge and virtue are said to be "innate" (innata) in the human animal:

> Now if at our birth nature had granted us the ability to discern her,[138] as she truly is, with insight and knowledge, and under her excellent guidance to complete the course of life, there would certainly have been no occasion for anyone to need methodical instruction [i.e., philosophy]: as it is, she gives to us tiny sparks (parvulos igniculos), which we, being quickly corrupted by bad morals and opinions, extinguish, so that the light of nature never appears. For inborn in our constitutions are the seeds of virtue, which, if they were permitted to grow, would lead us by nature itself to happiness of life (Sunt enim ingeniis nostris semina innata virtutum, quae si adolescere liceret, ipsa nos ad beatam vitam[139] natura perduceret); as things are, however, as soon as we come into the light of day . . . we at once find ourselves in a world of iniquity amid a medley of wrong beliefs . . . we become infected with deceptions so varied that truth gives place to unreality and the voice of nature to fixed prepossessions.[140]

---

[135] Cf. Diog. Laert. 7.85.

[136] Plutarch, Comm. Not. 1070C.

[137] For a general discussion of the use of "seed" terminology, see Pohlenz, Grundfragen, 95–99.

[138] On the intimate relationship between οἰκείωσις, virtue, and the knowledge of "nature," see esp. De Fin. 4.25 and 5.41. While these passages come from Antiochan rather than Stoic sources, the assumed agreement between the Stoics and Antiochus on the crucial point in the former passage is to be noted.

[139] The beata vita is another expression for the "Goal," or "highest good"; see, e.g., De Fin. 5.12.

[140] TD 3.2f; I have altered the LCL translation only to bring out more clearly the imagery of the "seeds" and "sparks."

In another passage it becomes clear that these "seeds" are themselves nothing other than the implanted preconceptions:

> . . . the highest and noblest part of man's nature she [sc. divine Nature] neglected. It is true she bestowed an intellect capable of receiving every virtue, and implanted in it at birth and without instruction embryonic notions of the loftiest ideas (*ingenuitque sine doctrina notitias parvas rerum maximarum*), laying the foundation of its education, and introducing among its endowments the elementary constituents, so to speak, of virtue (*tamquam elementa virtutis*). But virtue itself she initiated—and nothing more (*sed virtutem ipsam inchoavit; nihil amplius*).[141]

The *elementa virtutis* are here quite clearly identified as the "little concepts" (*notitias parvas*) that Nature has "implanted" (*ingenuit*) in the human mind, and these "rudiments of virtue" are referred to elsewhere in this work as the "seeds" and "sparks" of virtue.[142] While Antiochan rather than properly Stoic in orientation, this passage nonetheless has significant points of contact with our Stoic sources. The idea that Nature only gives the individual the beginnings of the knowledge of virtue is by now familiar from Seneca, as well as from *TD* 3.2.[143] Moreover, as the passage continues, the Antiochan Piso emphasizes that the development of these "rudiments" into full fledged *virtus* and *honesta* ought to be the number one priority in life.[144] This sentiment, as we shall soon see, recalls in a striking manner Epictetus's conviction that the refinement and proper application of the ἔμφυτοι ἔννοιαι is the central task of the philosophical education, and likely reflects Chrysippus's own emphasis.

Sandbach also objected that Pohlenz had made no attempt to show the relevance of οἰκείωσις for the formation of the notion of "something just," which is singled out by Diogenes Laertius alongside that of "something good" as "naturally" arising. The details of the Stoic treatment of the origin of justice are notoriously difficult to reconstruct, and a discussion of the problems would lead us much too far from our present concern.[145] What is clear in any case is

---

[141] *De Fin.* 5.59. The LCL rendering of the final clause as "but of virtue itself she merely gave the germ and no more" correctly recognizes the connection of this passage with the "seed" terminology that appears elsewhere in *De Finibus* 5. I have nonetheless given a more literal rendering here, while otherwise following LCL.

[142] *De Fin.* 5.18, 43.

[143] Cf. also *De Leg.* 1.30 and 33, on which see further below.

[144] *De Fin.* 5.60.

[145] See on this question esp. Engberg-Pedersen, *The Stoic Theory of Oikeiosis*, 122–26; Inwood, "Comments on Professor Görgemanns' Paper," 190–99; Pembroke, "Oikeiôsis," 121–32.

that the Stoics did in fact locate the origins of justice in οἰκείωσις: "the followers of Zeno," Porphyry says quite explicitly, "make οἰκείωσις the beginning of justice."[146] Though the details are rather obscure, it is most probable that the Stoics placed the natural affection of parents for their offspring—an affection which was said to be providentially guaranteed by οἰκείωσις—at the center of their account of justice.[147] It is not insignificant, therefore, that Cicero describes this parental affection, too, as being "implanted" by Nature.[148]

Finally, it is to be pointed out against Sandbach that given the doctrine of οἰκείωσις, there is no contradiction between the Stoic theory of "innate preconceptions" and their characterization of the commanding faculty at birth as a *tabula rasa*. The human individual is born not with ethical conceptions *per se*, but rather, given its status as a "rational animal," with an innate predisposition to form these concepts.[149] Indeed, the practical ability to recognize that which is, generally speaking, "good" and "bad" for oneself, according to the Stoics, is not limited to the rational animal, but characteristic of all animals regardless of their ability to abstract from experience formal concepts of "good" and "bad." Nature gives to the rational animal the "seeds of knowledge," but not knowledge itself.

Epictetus on Implanted Concepts

Sandbach criticized Bonhöffer for taking Epictetus as his starting point for reconstructing the early Stoic doctrine of preconception. He argued that one ought rather examine first the evidence for the early Stoa and then read Epictetus to determine the extent of the

---

[146] Porphyry, *Abst.* 3.19 (= *SVF* 1.197): τὴν δὲ οἰκείωσιν ἀρχὴν τίθενται δικαιοσύνης οἱ ἀπὸ Ζήνωνος; on the question of the precise referent of "the followers of Zeno," see the comments of Pembroke, "Oikeiôsis," 122.

[147] It is scarcely accidental that Chrysippus's espousal of the natural origins of parents' affection for their offspring emerges from a fragment from the first book of his *On Justice* preserved in Plutarch, *St. Rep.* 1038B; see further *De Nat. Deor.* 2.128–29; *De Fin.* 3.62.

[148] *De Off.* 1.12: *natura . . . ingeneratque in primis praecipuum quendam amorem in eos, qui procreati sunt.* Cicero speaks here of the human animal in particular, whose affection for its offspring, however, differs only in degree from that of other animal species; cf. *De Off.* 1.11. See further *De Fin.* 5.66.

[149] Cf. Pohlenz, *Grundfragen*, 92: "Bei der Geburt sind die Begriffe freilich noch nicht vorhanden. Die Seele gleicht der tabula rasa, und es gibt in ihr keine Begriffe, weder fertige noch unfertige. Angeboren ist aber dem Lebewesen nach seiner seelischen Struktur durch die Oikeiosis die Tendenz und die Fähigkeit, zu den Dingen wie zu sich selbst wertend Stellung zu nehmen."

agreement.[150] From a methodological point of view, Sandbach's critique is a sound one; I have therefore had little recourse to the evidence of Epictetus in the preceding account of the Stoic doctrine of implanted preconceptions. Turning now to Epictetus, however, what emerges is an account that is in fact quite consistent with that of the early Stoa.

Epictetus says the following:

> we come into being (ἥκομεν) without any innate concept (φύσει ἔννοιαν)[151] of a right-angled triangle, or of a half-tone musical interval, but by a certain systematic method of instruction (ἔκ τινος τεχνικῆς παραλήφεως) we are taught the meaning of each of these things... But, on the other hand, who has come into being (ἐλήλυθεν) without an innate concept (ἔμφυτον ἔννοιαν) of what is good and evil, honourable and base, appropriate and inappropriate, and happiness, and of what is proper and falls to our lot, and what we ought to do and what we ought not to do?[152]

The contrast between concepts achieved by intellectual labor and those achieved "naturally" is familiar from Aetius as the distinction between concepts in the strict sense (ἔννοιαι) and preconceptions (προλήψεις), respectively; and that Epictetus considers these "natural concepts" to be preconceptions is in fact clear from the context.[153]

As Sandbach has pointed out, Epictetus elsewhere uses the term πρόληψις with reference to several conceptions which, by any account, must be understood, at least in the context of Stoicism, to derive from empirical experience.[154] In one lecture, for example, he discusses preconceptions of musicians, carpenters and other artisans, as well as of philosophers, to make a point that one needs to question and refine one's preconceptions in order to arrive at a more adequate understanding of their subject matter.[155] In the passage cited

---

[150] Sandbach, "Ennoia," 22–23.

[151] The LCL's translation of the phrase φύσει ἔννοιαν as "innate concept" anticipates the subsequent (and synonymous) ἔμφυτον ἔννοιαν. Cf. Justin *App* 6.3, who describes the name "God" as an ἔμφυτος τῇ φύσει τῶν ἀνθρώπων δόξα. (On the idea of an innate belief in God, see below.)

[152] *Diss.* 2.11.2f. The LCL captures the sense of the rather elliptical ἥκομεν and ἐλήλυθεν by translating them as "come into being"; cf. "come into the world" for τὸ ἥκειν in the translation of *Diss.* 2.11.6. Cf. in this respect Cicero, *De Leg.* 1.59: the introspective person will realize that (s)he "came into life" (*in vitam venerit*) well-equipped by nature. All translations of Epictetus are taken from LCL unless otherwise noted.

[153] *Diss.* 2.11.4, 10, 11.

[154] Sandbach, "Ennoia," 27.

[155] *Diss.* 4.8.6–10. Cf. the discussion of the πρόληψις of the Cynic's πρᾶγμα at

at the beginning of this section, though, Epictetus uses the phrase
φύσει ἔννοια synonymously with ἔμφυτος ἔννοια, which in the context clearly implies an innate concept, as even Sandbach recognized:
"it must be admitted that when we come to examine Epictetus he
can hardly be interpreted otherwise than as believing in 'inborn' preconceptions."[156] Once again, these "implanted preconceptions" concern ethical concepts in particular: while we do not "come with"
the concepts of music theory and geometry, we do come already
having preconceptions concerning ethical categories. He proceeds to
explain, in similar terms, the fact that everyone, educated or not,
makes ethical evaluations: "The reason for this is that we come as
if already taught by nature certain things in this area."[157] The attribution of such knowledge to nature's own instruction recalls Seneca's
discussion of the "seeds of knowledge" gained by means of οἰκείωσις,
and the similar passages from Cicero discussed above. And while
there is no explicit evidence that Epictetus understood the ἔμφυτοι
ἔννοιαι to result from οἰκείωσις (which does not receive extensive
treatment in his extant lectures in any case),[158] the connection is
nonetheless quite likely: not only are they present from birth, but
they comprise ethical concepts in particular.[159]

While all humans are thus born with ethical preconceptions,
Epictetus stresses that these, as such, are not sufficient to ensure the
correct assessment of one's experiences in terms of "good" and "bad."

> There lies the whole question, and there opinion (οἴησις) comes in.
> For men start with these principles upon which they are agreed, but
> then, because they make unsuitable application (ἐφαρμογῆς) of them,
> get into disputes.[160]

Diss. 3.22. The idea that such preconceptions require refinement clearly reflects the
technical Stoic distinction between πρόληψις and ἔννοια. This emphasis on the
importance of developing the former into the latter is in fact quite characteristic of
Epictetus, particularly in the ethical sphere. See on this immediately below.

[156] Sandbach, "Ennoia," 29.

[157] *Diss.* 2.11.6: τούτου δ' αἴτιον τὸ ἥκειν ἤδη τινὰ ὑπὸ τῆς φύσεως κατὰ τὸν τόπον
ὥσπερ δεδιδαγμένους; translation mine.

[158] That οἰκείωσις was nonetheless important for Epictetus is clear, for example,
from *Diss.* 1.19.11–15, where it is understood to be fundamental to all human
behavior.

[159] Cf. Sandbach, "Ennoia," 24f. Indeed, note esp. that when Epictetus asserts
in *Diss.* 1.22.1 that προλήψεις κοιναὶ πᾶσιν ἀνθρώποις εἰσίν, the particular preconceptions he has in mind are those of τὸ ἀγαθόν and τὸ δικαιόν—precisely those singled out as being acquired φυσικῶς in Diog. Laert. 7.53.

[160] *Diss.* 2.11.8; cf. 1.22.1–8. For the corrupting influence of opinion on this
process, cf. Cicero, *TD* 3.2, quoted above.

Epictetus, therefore, places this all important problem of "application" at the center of his notion of the true education:

> What then, does it mean, to be getting an education? It means learning how to apply (ἐφαρμόζειν) the natural preconceptions (φυσικὰς προλήψεις) to particular cases, each to the other in conformity with nature, and, further, to make the distinction, that some things are under our control while others are not under our control.[161]

While all preconceptions are acquired "naturally," so that the term φυσικάς in the phrase φυσικὰς προλήψεις in this passage could be used pleonastically rather than with reference to those preconceptions which are "natural" in a more specialized sense, it is clear from both the *Dissertations* in general and from this passage in particular that Epictetus's foremost concern, at least, are those preconceptions which are especially "natural," that is, the implanted preconceptions.[162] Thus the remainder of this particular lecture centers on this question: "Where, then, shall we place τὸ ἀγαθόν? To what sort of things shall we apply it (ἐφαρμόσομεν)?"[163] Indeed, the importance of mastering philosophy's subtle theoretical principles pales in comparison with that of learning to correctly "apply" our ethical preconceptions to particular experiences:[164] for while the improper application of them is the source of all evils,[165] proper application makes one "perfect."[166]

It will be recalled that preconceptions are themselves, by definition, rather vague and ill-defined conceptions. Prerequisite for proper application, therefore, is refinement and systematization (διάρθρωσις).[167] The first step in such a process is the confession of one's ignorance in the matter: only such an admission will lead to knowledge and

---

[161] *Diss.* 1.22.9–10; cf. 1.2.6. That which is under the control of the human is assent (συγκατάθεσις) to impressions (φαντασίαι); see above, note 37. Epictetus refers to this most often as "use of impressions" (χρῆσις φαντασίων) or something similar; see e.g. *Diss.* 1.1.7; 1.12.34; 2.19.32; and Frag. 4.

[162] So also Pohlenz, *Grundfragen*, 85: Epictetus "ist im wesentlichen nur an ihnen [*sc.* preconceptions of the ethical sphere] interessiert." Note also the use of the phrase φύσει ἔννοια to denote specifically the ἔμφυτοι ἔννοιαι in 2.11.2; and see further, in addition, n. 159 above.

[163] *Diss.* 1.22.11.

[164] See *Diss.* 2.17, and cf. esp. 2.17.1–3 with 2.17.29–40.

[165] *Diss.* 4.1.42: τοῦτο γάρ ἐστι τὸ αἴτιον τοῖς ἀνθρώποις πάντων τῶν κακῶν, τὸ τὰς προλήψεις τὰς κοινὰς μὴ δύνασθαι ἐφαρμόζειν τοῖς ἐπὶ μέρους.

[166] *Diss.* 2.11.10.

[167] See on this process esp. the whole of *Diss.* 2.17, which is entitled: πῶς ἐφαρμοστέον τὰς προλήψεις τοῖς ἐπὶ μέρους; see further the discussion of Bonhöffer, *Epictet*, 189–92.

progress, "for it is impossible to get a man to begin to learn that which he thinks he knows."[168] Having thus repudiated "opinion" (οἴησις), one can begin honest enquiry into the preconceptions with the goal of establishing a standard (κανών) which is higher than mere "opinion" for their practical application.[169] Indeed, the establishment of this "standard" is itself the very generative problem and continuing task of philosophy: καὶ τὸ φιλοσοφεῖν τοῦτό ἐστιν, ἐπισκέπτεσθαι καὶ βεβαιοῦν τοὺς κανόνας.[170]

While Epictetus's classification of the different types of conception is consistent with that of the early Stoics, the centrality of the ἔμφυτοι ἔννοιαι to the achievement of moral progress in his ethical system goes beyond anything explicitly attested in the scant extant evidence for the latter. However, given the Stoic understanding of rational human action as caused by the impulse resulting from assent to the propositional content of a given hormetic presentation, it would seem that an accurate conception of "the good" would be absolutely crucial for virtuous action for them as well. So, for example, a man's acceptance of some public office will depend upon his assent to the proposition "it is good for me to accept this office." Such assent will obviously presuppose some conception of what is "good" and what is not, on the basis of which the man will either give or withhold his assent to the proposition. If his conception of the good is incorrect, his assent to such a proposition may well—though not necessarily— issue in an impulse toward improper action;[171] conversely, the only way to ensure virtuous action would seem to be the possession of an accurate conception of the Good. That Chrysippus did, in fact, place a similar emphasis on the development of the ἔμφυτοι προλήψεις is suggested by Diogenes Laertius's grouping of several series of Chrysippus's treatises as works concerning τὴν διάρθρωσιν τῶν ἠθικῶν ἐννοιῶν.[172] Further evidence for the centrality of the ἔμφυτοι προλήψεις

---

[168] *Diss.* 2.17.1; cf. 2.17.39f and 2.22.17ff.

[169] *Diss.* 2.11.17f; a good example of this process is found in *Diss.* 1.22.11–16, where the question concerns the application of the term "good" to those things that are not under our control. Cf. also *Diss.* 1.28.28, where Epictetus refers more generally to the preconceptions as the "standards" people use for judging good and evil.

[170] *Diss.* 2.11.24; cf. 2.11.13–14.

[171] According to the Stoics, one can act "appropriately" in spite of his or her mistaken understanding of the Good; thus the Stoic distinction between "appropriate" and "right" action, on which see Long and Sedley, *The Hellenistic Philosophers*, 1.359–68.

[172] Diog. Laert. 7.199f; cf. the comments of Pohlenz, *Grundfragen*, 84 n. 1. Note also Plutarch's citation of Chrysippus's view that "physical speculation (τῆς φυσικῆς θεωρίας) is to be undertaken for no other purpose than for the discrimination of good and evil" (*St. Rep.* 1035D); cf. with this Epictetus, *Diss.* 1.22.11, cited above.

to the early Stoic understanding of moral development might also be seen in their role in the moral philosophy of Antiochus of Ascalon which, as has already been pointed out, is quite similar to that found in Epictetus. It is thus most likely that in this respect too, Epictetus's discussion of the ethical preconceptions simply reflects earlier Stoic teaching.[173]

Excursus: Belief in the Gods as ἔμφυτος

For the sake of completeness, and because the question will impinge to some degree on our discussion of Justin Martyr in the following chapter, the description of a supposed universal human belief in a god or gods as ἔμφυτος or its Latin equivalents in several ancient philosophical works also warrants some attention. Dio Chrysostom, in the oration entitled "The Olympic Discourse, or On the First Conception of God," describes the origin of the human belief in the divine as follows:

> Of man's belief in the deity (τῆς ... περὶ τὸ θεῖον δόξης) and his assumption that there is a god we were maintaining that the fountain-head, as we may say, or source, was that idea which is innate in all mankind (τὴν ἔμφυτον ἅπασιν ἀνθρώποις ἐπίνοιαν) and comes into being as the result of the actual facts and the truth ... being, one may almost say, a common and general endowment of rational beings (σχεδόν τι κοινὴν καὶ δημοσίαν τοῦ λογικοῦ γένους).[174]

Similarly, Justin Martyr characterizes the concept of "god" as "a belief implanted in the nature of human beings" (ἔμφυτος τῇ φύσει τῶν ἀνθρώπων δόξα).[175] That this position was characteristic of at least some Stoics seems clear from a quite similar assertion made by Balbus, the Stoic spokesman of Cicero's *De Natura Deorum*: "For innate in everyone, and as it were engraved upon the soul, is a belief in the existence of the gods."[176] Thus Seneca, too, writes:

---

[173] Note further that Epictetus's (and Antiochus's!) general emphasis on the proper refinement of our ethical notions is quite compatible with Inwood's reconstruction of Chrysippus's teaching on "excessive impulse," esp. as this relates to an individual's ethical conceptions; see *Ethics and Human Action*, 155–65, esp. 162–65.

[174] Dio Chrysostom, 12.39; cf. 12.27. Translations of Dio are taken from LCL unless otherwise noted.

[175] *App.* 6.3.

[176] *De Nat. Deor.* 2.12: *omnibus enim innatum est et in animo quasi insculptum esse deos*; translation mine. Cf. the Epicurean position as described at *De Nat. Deor.* 1.44: "For the belief in the gods has not been established by authority, custom or law, but rests on the unanimous and abiding consensus of mankind; their existence is therefore

> ... we infer that the gods exist, for this reason, among others—that there is implanted (*insita*) in everyone an idea concerning deity (*de dis opinio*), and there is no people so far beyond the reach of laws and customs that it does not believe at least in gods of some sort.[177]

Seneca characterizes the Stoic position regarding the *insita opinio* of the divine as one argument among others for the truth of the existence of the gods. The problem of the existence of the gods was the first division of Stoic theology,[178] and that there were indeed a variety of arguments made in this connection is clear from the second book of Cicero's *De Natura Deorum*. Cicero's reference to this particular argument in *De Nat. Deor.* 2.12 occurs at the conclusion of the first series of arguments presented by Balbo, and refers back, apparently, to the *consensus omnium* argument discussed in 2.5:

> Nothing but the presence in our minds of a firmly grasped concept of the deity could account for the stability and permanence of our belief (*opinio*) in him, a belief which is only strengthened by the passage of the ages and grows more deeply rooted with each successive generation of mankind ... The years obliterate the inventions of the imagination, but confirm the judgments of nature.

When, however, Cicero rehearses Cleanthes's explanation of this consensus in 2.13–15, there is no hint of a conviction regarding any innate belief in the existence of the gods found among its four causes.[179] In fact, this argument is mentioned neither in the context of Cicero's rehearsal of the arguments of Zeno, Cleanthes or Chrysippus,[180] nor is it, for that matter, ascribed to any other particular philosopher. Indeed, it is not discussed further by Balbus, and goes without mention in the Academic critique of Stoic theology presented in book three.[181] It would thus seem that this argument had

---

a necessary inference, since we possess an implanted—or better, an innate—notion of them (*quoniam insitas eorum vel potius innata cognitiones habemus*)"; I have slightly altered the LCL translation. Cf. *De Fin.* 4.4 for a similar juxtaposition of the terms *insita* and *innata*.

[177] *Ep.* 117.6.

[178] For the divisions of Stoic theology, see *De Nat. Deor.* 2.3.

[179] Cleanthes is said to have argued from divination, the beneficence of the universe, the awe inspired by the display of nature's power as instanced, e.g., in storms, earthquakes, etc., and above all the orderliness of the heavens.

[180] For the particular arguments of Zeno see *De Nat. Deor.* 2.20ff; on Cleanthes, 2.13–15; on Chrysippus, 2.16–19.

[181] Cotta's critique of the *consensus omnium* argument is limited to the following comment: "Then is anybody content that questions of such moment should be decided by the belief (*opinione*) of the foolish? and particularly yourselves, who say

at best a marginal place in the source of Cicero's *De Natura Deorum*, and this might suggest that it was in fact a later development in Stoic theology.[182] Assuming, however, that it was a viable Stoic position at least by the time of Cicero, we might fairly inquire as to its philosophical basis: in what sense, given the constraints of Stoicism, might this belief be described as ἔμφυτος?

In *De Leg.* 1.24, Cicero writes that humans alone have a *notitia dei* and attributes this fact to the unique kinship (*agnatio*) that humans have with the gods. This kinship resides in the human possession of the rational soul which, unlike the "fragile and perishable" elements of the human animal derived from the mortal sphere, was "implanted by God."[183] The human possession of *ratio* is for Cicero crucial for the formation of the *notitia dei*, but not simply because it is requisite for concept formation in general. The possession of the *ratio*, according to Cicero, *necessarily* entails recognition of its ultimate source, and thus a belief in the existence of the gods:[184] "Thus it is clear that man recognizes God because, in a way, he remembers and recognizes the source from which he sprang."[185] The reference to memory in this latter explanation, however, has a curiously Platonic ring to it, and it is possible, as Kenter has suggested, that Cicero has here merged "Platonic elements with the doctrine of the Stoa."[186]

Seemingly more congenial to Stoicism, on the other hand, is the account provided by Dio Chrysostom. Dio, as we have seen, argued that the ultimate source of the concept of God was an ἔμφυτος ἅπασιν ἀνθρώποις ἐπίνοια which, unlike the conceptions of God that come from poets and lawgivers, arises "naturally without a mortal teacher

---

that all the foolish are mad?" (*De Nat. Deor.* 3.11) The argument had already been dealt with from a somewhat different angle in the context of Cotta's critique of Epicurus; cf. *De Nat. Deor.* 1.62–64.

[182] Bonhöffer, *Epictet und die Stoa*, 219, is reluctant to attribute such an argument to Zeno and Cleanthes, but assumes its presence at least in the theology of Chrysippus.

[183] *De Leg.* 1.24: *animum esse ingeneratum a deo*. That Cicero has in mind here specifically the *rational* soul is clear from the fact that the Stoics held the human to be unique among other mortal animals owing to its possession of reason, not soul, which latter, on the contrary, characterizes all animals by definition; see on this Long and Sedley, *The Hellenistic Philosophers*, 313–23; further Inwood, *Ethics and Human Action*, 21–26. Cf. in this connection *De Leg.* 1.23 with Cicero's reference to the "divine" element in humans at *De Leg.* 1.59.

[184] So Pohlenz, commenting on this passage: "Auch die Gotteserkenntnis wurzelt also in der Struktur unsrer Physis" (*Grundfragen*, 100).

[185] *De Leg.* 1.25.

[186] Kenter, *De Legibus*, 105.

and mystagogue, without deception."[187] More precisely, the belief in the divine arises as a result of two factors:[188] "because of the kinship (ξυγγένεια) which [God] has to them [sc. humanity] and the many evidences of the truth."[189] The latter "evidences" are those provided by natural phenomena: the orderliness of the astral movements, the abundance of benefits received from nature, etc.[190] The former reference to the "kinship" between human beings and the gods, on the other hand, recalls the account of Cicero discussed above. It has been suggested, in fact, that Cicero and Dio here draw upon a common source, perhaps Posidonius, for their understanding of an innate concept of God.[191] Dio's explanation of the significance of this "kinship" for our concept of god, however, is rather different from that of Cicero:

> ... the feelings of the human race towards their first and immortal parent, whom we who have a share in the heritage of Hellas call πατρῷον Δία, develop step by step along with those which men have toward their mortal and human parents. For in truth the goodwill and desire to serve which the offspring feel toward their parents is ... present in them, untaught, as a gift of nature and as a result of acts of kindness received (ἀπὸ τῆς φύσεως καὶ τῆς εὐεργεσίας ἀδίδακτος ὑπάρχει), since that which has been begotten straightaway from birth loves and cherishes in return (τοῦ γεννηθέντος εὐθὺς ἀντιφιλοῦντος καὶ ἀντιθεραπεύοντος), so far as it may, that which begat and nourishes and loves it ...[192]

---

[187] Dio Chrysostom 12.27: γινομένη κατὰ φύσιν ἄνευ θνητοῦ διδασκάλου καὶ μυσταγωγοῦ χωρὶς ἀπάτης. I have altered the (protestantizing) translation of LCL, which reads "without the aid of human teacher and free from the deceit of any expounding priest," and read καὶ μυσταγωγοῦ with ἄνευ θνητοῦ διδασκάλου rather than with χωρὶς ἀπάτης.

[188] So also Pohlenz, *Grundfragen*, 102.

[189] Dio Chrysostom 12.27; my translation. Note the textual problem here. διά is to be preferred to ἐδήλου since the subsequent explanation of the ξυγγένεια and the μαρτύρια depict them as sources rather than consequences of the δόξα θεοῦ; see further below. Note also that the immediate juxtaposition of two finite verbs without a coordinating conjunction seems rather odd. Pohlenz (*Grundfragen*, 102) follows this same reading, though there is no indication that he is aware of a textual problem here.

[190] Dio Chrysostom 12. 28–34. The fingerprints of Cleanthes are perhaps to be detected here.

[191] See the references given by Cohoon, *Dio Chrysostom* (LCL; Cambridge: Harvard University Press, 1977) 5.30f n. 2. Pohlenz assumes the dependence of Dio upon Posidonius, characterizing this position as generally recognized (*Grundfragen*, 101, with references in n. 2).

[192] Dio Chrysostom 12.42.

The key element of this discussion is the parallel experiences one has vis-à-vis one's mortal and one's divine parent. A child's good-will toward its mortal parents is "natural"; it is an "untaught" response to the love (s)he experiences from his or her parent. This latter love of a parent for its offspring, on the other hand, is itself, according to Chrysippus, providentially guaranteed by οἰκείωσις, as was pointed out in connection with our discussion of the "natural" origin of the concept of "something just."[193] While Dio, to be sure, cites the parents' kindness toward their child as a crucial factor here, his language suggests that the whole *reciprocal* relationship is in effect guaranteed by nature.[194] One might compare in this respect the asser-tion of Cicero's Stoic Balbo that the newborn child "untaught and by nature's guidance" seeks its mother's breast.[195] Thus too could we understand Philo's claim that one's "desire for [kin and country] may be said to be born and grow with each of us and is a part of our nature as much as or even more than the parts which unite to make the whole."[196]

Whatever the case, our initial belief in God, the "first and immor-tal parent," arises ultimately as a result of this same dynamic accord-ing to Dio.[197] Indeed, the "first breast" that feeds the child is that of "the earth, its real mother": it is the air which "after breathing into it and quickening it, at once awakens it by a nourishment more liquid than milk and enables it to emit a cry."[198] Humans, according

---

[193] Plutarch, *St. Rep.* 1038B; see above pp. 61f.

[194] Cf. the proofs adduced by the Stoics from Nature for the natural social ten-dency of humans in, e.g., *De Nat. Deor.* 2.128–29 and *De Fin.* 3.63. Cf. further the apparently common Stoic discussion of non-human animals which seem "naturally" to cooperate, esp. the sea pen discussed in *De Nat. Deor.* 2.123–124 and Philo, *De Animal.* 60 and 93. Cf. with this position Aristotle's view, cited by Inwood ("Comments," 198) that "the thing produced is *oikeion* to its source ... but to the product the source is nothing, or less important" (such "products" including human children). This passage from Dio Chrysostom may in fact fill a crucial gap in the evidence for the Stoic doctrine of social οἰκείωσις (felt, for example, by Pembroke ["Oikeiosis," 124f]) by emphasizing precisely the newborn child's love for its parents.

[195] *De Nat. Deor.* 2.128.

[196] *Abr.* 63: ὧν [συγγενῶν καὶ πατρίδος] ὁ πόθος ἑκάστῳ τρόπον τινὰ συγγεγένηται καὶ συνηύξηται καὶ μᾶλλον ἢ οὐχ ἧττον τῶν ἡνωμένων μερῶν συμπέφυκε; translated according to LCL. Cf. *De Fin.* 5.65, where Cicero traces one's affection for, among others, one's family and fellow citizens, to "the fact that children are loved by their parents."

[197] Note esp. the description of God as προπάτωρ in 12.29 and πατρῷον Δία in 12.42.

[198] Dio Chrysostom 12.30–31.

to Dio, are thus unable to feel anything other than wonder and love for the deity.[199] In fact, Dio can speak rather loosely of a similar recognition and honor toward God even on the part of plants and non-rational animals which, unlike humans, are of course incapable of formulating ἔννοιαι at all.[200]

The scant nature of our evidence surrounding the Stoic position on the origin of the human belief in the gods prohibits the drawing of any decisive conclusions. It is noteworthy, however, that what evidence there is leads us back once again to the doctrine of οἰκείωσις. Thus the description of the human belief in the deity, by at least some later Stoics, as ἔμφυτος would seem to provide still further confirmation of Pohlenz's general contention that the implanted preconceptions must be understood in light of the Stoic doctrine of οἰκείωσις.

Conclusions

The Stoics distinguished two types of concepts. Concepts (ἔννοιαι) in the strict sense of the term are the result of conscious intellectual effort and begin to be formed only when one has achieved an initial state of rational maturity. Preconceptions (προλήψεις) occur "naturally," that is, from simple mental processes which do not require conscious intellectual labor, and begin to form, apparently, almost immediately. While empirical experience is necessary for the formation of all concepts according to the Stoics, fundamental ethical concepts such as "good" and "bad" form a special class of preconception, called implanted preconceptions (ἔμφυτοι προλήψεις). These derive ultimately from the tendency, innate in all animals, to subjectively evaluate experience in terms of that which is beneficial for oneself and that which is harmful. Humans are not born with ethical conceptions *per se*; nonetheless, as rational animals in whom concepts naturally begin to form almost immediately, they are predisposed to the formation of these conceptions *regardless of the nature of their experiences*.[201] The imagery of "sparks" and especially "seeds" of knowledge or virtue is often used to describe this potential and inevitable

---

[199] Dio Chrysostom 12.32.
[200] Dio Chrysostom 12.35. An actual ἔμφυτος δόξα or ἐπίνοια of God, of course, is nevertheless the peculiar endowment of the *rational* animal; see 12.27 and 12.39.
[201] The same cannot be said, for example, of the concepts of "white" and "black"; thus the distinction reported by Plutarch at *Comm. Not.* 1070C.

ethical knowledge with which humans are naturally endowed. In what was perhaps a later development in Stoic theology, a posited universal human belief in the deity was also explained with reference to this dynamic, and itself described as ἔμφυτος.

Our interest in the role of the implanted preconceptions in Cicero's theory of natural law has led us into a rather long digression, but the matter is one of great import for our present study. This Stoic doctrine is an important piece in the puzzle of the recurring use of the term "implanted" to describe either human reason or the natural law it comprises in a range of ancient literature. In order to clarify this point, let us now return to Cicero's definition of law in terms of "implanted reason."

NATURAL LAW AS "IMPLANTED REASON"

Implanted Preconceptions, Human Reason, and Natural Law

It is Cicero's view that divine Nature endows individual human beings with certain "obscure concepts" in order to provide them with the "foundations of knowledge." While it is sometimes supposed that this view represents a platonizing interpretation of the Stoic doctrine of preconception, we have found that this is not a necessary conclusion. The Stoics themselves argued that a certain class of preconception was different from all other concepts in that they arise not simply from empirical experience, but, ultimately, from the inborn self-awareness and self-love guaranteed by οἰκείωσις. There is thus no reason to suppose that Cicero deviates from Stoic theory in locating the divine endowment of these preconceptions at the beginning of the development of human reason, and ultimately too, therefore, of "right reason" or natural law.[202]

In fact, this position is best understood in light of Chrysippus's own view of human reason. We have seen that human reason, for the Stoics, is the product of development. Existing only in a potential form in newborn humans, it reaches an initial state of maturity only around the age of seven, when it is "completed out of the preconceptions" (ἐκ τῶν προλήψεων συμπληροῦσθαι).[203] This latter statement

---

[202] As I will suggest below, platonic influence on Cicero's understanding of the ἔμφυτοι προλήψεις themselves is in fact likely; nonetheless, their role in the theory of natural law as presented by him is intelligible quite apart from such influence.

[203] *SVF* 2.83.

must be viewed in light of Chrysippus's understanding of *logos* as an "assemblage" of concepts and preconceptions.[204] Humans are not properly "rational"—which is to say, one's *logos* is not a *logos* in the proper sense of the term—until a sufficient complement of preconceptions has been formed to allow for the higher thought processes which result in concepts in the strict sense of the term.[205] It is only at this point that one begins to apprehend one's rational nature and, thus, that one can begin to form a concept of the (Stoic) Good.[206] Nature takes the human animal this far; henceforth it is the responsibility of the individual to cultivate his or her *logos* into the "right reason" of the sage, which is natural law. Prior to this initial maturation one has only a potential *logos*: an assemblage, it is to be inferred, of preconceptions alone.

As Kenter recognizes, it is this Stoic theory that underlies the description of the maturation of human reason in *De Leg.* 1.26–27.[207] The maturation of the *ratio* is here described as a natural process— it is effected by "Nature herself"—and the explanation of the completion of the *ratio* as arising from "obscure" and "insufficient" concepts rather obviously recalls Aetius's report that the *logos* is "completed out of the preconceptions." In fact, Cicero's description of these "obscure concepts" as "the foundations of knowledge" is quite reminiscent of his description, elsewhere, of the implanted preconceptions as the "seeds" or "sparks" of knowledge or virtue.[208]

According to Cicero, then, the first stage in the developmental process which results in mature human reason is the divine endowment of "implanted preconceptions." Unfortunately, there is no explicit evidence among the early Stoic fragments for this association of the potential reason with which humans are born and the ἔμφυτοι προλήψεις. On the other hand, given Chrysippus's definition of *logos*

---

[204] *SVF* 2.841: ἐννοιῶν τέ τινων καὶ προλήψεων ἄθροισμα. See further Inwood, *Ethics and Human Action*, 72–74; "assemblage" is his translation.

[205] It is not altogether clear, however, how the Stoics envisioned the ability to exercise higher orders of thought to result from the formation of a certain number of preconceptions in the human mind.

[206] See Pohlenz, *Grundfragen*, 92: "Erst wenn der Logos sich vollendet hat, kann daraus der klare Begriff werden, daß das wahrhaft Gute das ist, was unsrer Natur als λογικὸν ζῷον entspricht." See further on this the discussion of *De Finibus* 3 above.

[207] Kenter, *De Legibus*, 118, with further parallels.

[208] Cf. *De Fin.* 5.59, comparing esp. the *rerum plurimarum obscuras nec satis . . . intelligentias* of *De Leg.* 1.26 with the *notitias parvas rerum maximarum* treated there, and described elsewhere in *De Finibus* as the "seeds" or "sparks" virtue (e.g., 5.18). Cf. further the "sparks" of virtue discussed in *De Leg.* 1.33.

as an "assemblage" of concepts and preconceptions, it seems a rather small step to describe the "spermatic" *logos* with which humans are born as an assemblage, as it were, of "implanted preconceptions." Thus just as virtue is a disposition of the *ratio*, so too could the implanted preconceptions themselves be described as the "seeds" or "sparks" of virtue. In fact, as we shall see in the following chapter, the *Apostolic Constitutions*, under clear influence of the Stoic theory of law, understands the natural law given to the human animal at its creation to be comprised by the "seeds of divine knowledge"—knowledge which it refers to elsewhere as "implanted knowledge" (ἔμφυτος γνῶσις).

Similarly, there is no explicit evidence in our scanty sources for the early Stoics that this theory of the development of the human *logos* was discussed in connection with natural law. It is however rather difficult to believe that Chrysippus, at least, had not understood and reckoned with this rather obvious implication of his identification of that law which is φύσει καὶ μὴ θέσει with the *logos* of the sage. As will become clear in the subsequent chapter, the incorporation of the Stoic doctrine of implanted preconceptions into a theory of natural law was, in any case, certainly not Cicero's own innovation. A number of ancient works, none of which can plausibly be linked directly to Cicero's *De Legibus*, share this theoretical approach to natural law. What is more, it is precisely here that one finds the recurring terminology that is the central concern of this chapter: the description of natural law or, as in *De Leg.* 18, the *logos* which comprises it, as "implanted."

Natural Law as ratio insita

Cicero's statement in *De Leg.* 1.27 that Nature "strengthens" (*confirmat*) and "completes" (*perficit*) the *ratio* echoes *De Leg.* 1.18, where law is defined as "reason, when it is strengthened and completed in the human mind" (*ratio cum est in hominis mente confirmata et confecta*).[209] As we have seen, however, the natural maturation referred to in 1.27 results, according to Stoic theory, in a *ratio* that is "complete" only insofar as it has become capable of rationality in the proper sense of the term. It is not yet the "right reason," characteristic of the sage alone, that is natural law. In fact, Cicero explicitly and repeatedly states that law is the *mens* and *ratio* of the sage in particular, including

---

[209] *De Leg.* 1.18; translation mine.

once immediately following this definition of law as *ratio . . . confirmata et confecta*.[210] Similarly, Cicero specifies on several occasions that law is not simply reason (*ratio*), but *right* reason (*recta ratio*) in particular.[211] Finally, law is associated with both virtue and the highest good:

> [I]t is undoubtedly true that to live in accordance with nature is the highest good. That signifies the enjoyment of a life of due measure based upon virtue, or following nature and living according to her law, so to speak; in other words, to spare no effort, so far as in us lies, to accomplish what nature demands; among these demands being her wish that we live by virtue as our law.[212]

Certainly wisdom, virtue, and attainment of the highest good do not accompany the natural maturation of the *ratio*! Thus while *De Leg.* 1.26–27 concerns the initial stage of maturation which occurs naturally in the development of human reason, 1.18–19 deals with the final perfection of human reason in the mind of the sage.[213]

Whatever the case, the developmental aspect of the Stoic theory of natural law is clearly in view when Cicero writes, in 1.18, that "the same reason, when it is strengthened and completed in the human mind, is law." This identification obviously assumes a time when reason was less than "strong" and "complete." What is more, the use of the demonstrative pronoun *eadem* ("the same") here specifies that the reason in question is that of the previous sentence: the *ratio* which becomes law when "completed in the human mind," that is, is the *ratio summa insita in natura*. Does this, then, imply that the phrase "implanted reason" refers particularly to the potential, *spermatic* reason with which Nature endows the human animal?

At least one author has interpreted the phrase otherwise. Kenter, in his commentary on *De Legibus* I, explains it, rather, with reference to the cosmic *logos* which pervades universal nature.[214] This

---

[210] *De Leg.* 1.19; cf. 2.8 and 2.11.

[211] *De Leg.* 1.23; 1.33; 1.42; cf. *De Rep.* 3.33, and further *De Leg.* 2.10.

[212] *De Leg.* 1.56; cf. further 1.18, where law is identified with *prudentia*; and 1.60, where *prudentia* is described, in the context of a discussion of the happiness which accompanies the highest good, as a *virtus* of the mind's eye in "selecting the good and rejecting the opposite."

[213] Against Vander Waerdt, *The Stoic Theory of Natural Law*, who argues that Cicero, depending upon Antiochus of Ascalon, has consciously altered the Stoic theory so as to identify natural law with the reason of the average human adult. This argument is most dubious in light of several indications to the contrary mentioned in this paragraph.

[214] So Kenter, *De Legibus*, 81f.

interpretation suggests itself primarily in light of *De Leg.* 2.8–11, where Cicero presents a summary of the theoretical position he had outlined in book one. Here, Cicero emphasizes the identification of natural law with the *ratio* or *mens* of both God and the human sage, and Quintus remarks that Cicero has "touched on this subject several times before."[215] Given the fundamental importance of this dual identification to Cicero's general theory of law, one might expect that he would include references to both the *ratio divina* and the *ratio hominis* in his initial account of the law in 1.18–19. If so, reference to the former could be found only in the phrase *summa ratio insita in natura*. The phrase *insita in natura* would in this case be comparable to Chrysippus's characterization of ὁ νόμος ὁ κοινός as ὁ ὀρθὸς λόγος, διὰ πάντων ἐρχόμενος.[216] The use of the demonstrative pronoun *eadem* in the following sentence might thus serve to emphasize the gods' and the human animals' common possession of "this same reason"— a point argued in detail in *De Leg.* 1.21ff.

This line of interpretation, however, is most doubtful. It is to be observed in the first place that the term *natura* appears often in the *De Legibus*, and by no means always with reference to universal nature. In at least one other passage, in fact, it is clear from the context that the term is used specifically with reference to human nature, despite the absence of the limiting genitive *hominis*.[217] The immediate context of *De Leg.* 1.17–19, too, indicates quite clearly that the *natura* in question is to be interpreted specifically with reference to human nature. *De Leg.* 1.18–19 as a whole is introduced as an inquiry into the "origins of justice" (*iuris principia*), and the account of law

---

[215] *De Leg.* 2.8–11.

[216] Diog. Laert. 7.88; cf. *Hymn to Zeus* (*SVF* 1.537, p. 122, lines 8ff), where Cleanthes speaks of the κοινὸν λόγον, ὃς διὰ πάντων φοιτᾷ.

[217] See *De Leg.* 1.27: "But, whereas God has begotten and equipped man . . . it should now be evident that nature, alone and unaided, goes a step farther; for, with no guide to point the way, she starts with those things whose character she has learned through the rudimentary beginnings of intelligence, and, alone and unaided, strengthens and perfects the faculty of reason." Note esp. that Cicero passes to this contrast between God and *natura* after having just used the two interchangeably; see 1.26–27. Cf. further the use of "nature" in 1.33—a passage which is, however, apparently corrupt; see on this Kenter *De Legibus*, 132–33. Cicero's fluid use of the term "nature" is not at all peculiar in this respect; see Long, "The Logical Basis of Stoic Ethics," on the wide use of the term φύσις by the Stoics generally, and further the discussion of Philo's use of the term in E. R. Goodenough, *By Light, Light: The Mystic Gospel of Hellenistic Judaism* (New Haven: Yale University Press, 1935) 49–54. See also in this connection Engberg-Pedersen's provocative argument for the importance of human, as opposed to divine, nature in Stoic philosophy more generally in *The Stoic Theory of Oikeiosis*.

which it includes is itself offered with this aim in mind.[218] It is important to note, therefore, that Cicero has asserted, just prior to this account, that the "nature of justice . . . must be sought for in *human nature*."[219] The importance of human nature in particular for Cicero's overall point, in fact, becomes quite clear at the conclusion of his initial account of law at 1.18–19:

> Now if this [preceding account of law] is correct, as I think it to be in general, then the origin of Justice is to be found in Law, for Law is a *natural force; it is the mind and reason of the sage*, the standard by which Justice and Injustice are measured.[220]

Justice, that is, is "natural" inasmuch as it derives from law; and the law, in turn, is natural to the extent that it is identical to the reason *of the sage*. Indeed, it is to be noted that—excluding, of course, the possibility of the definition in question—1.18–19 contains not a single reference to the identification of the law with the divine *ratio*. Nor does Cicero's argument at this point depend upon this identification. Cicero, in fact, does not attempt to secure his interlocutors' concession that the cosmic *ratio* will be relevant to their discussion at all until 1.21.

As far as I have noted, in fact, Cicero elsewhere uses the term *insita* only with reference to the nature or *animus* of the human being.[221] In fact, the term appears in Cicero's works in conjunction with themes and ideas associated particularly with the ἔμφυτοι προλήψεις: it is used as a description of virtue,[222] in connection with οἰκείωσις,[223] and even in direct connection with the Stoic doctrine

---

[218] *De Leg.* 1.18.

[219] *De Leg.* 1.17: *natura enim iuris explicanda nobis est eaque ab hominis repentenda natura;* I have altered the translation of LCL only in adding emphasis, and in rendering *hominis natura* as "human nature" rather than the more gender-specific "nature of man."

[220] *De Leg.* 1.19: *quod si ita recte dicitur, ut mihi quidem plerumque videri solet, a lege ducendum est iuris exordium; ea est enim naturae vis, ea mens ratioque prudentis, ea iuris atque iniuriae regula.* I have altered the translation of LCL only in the addition of the emphasis and in rendering *prudentis* as "of the sage" rather than "of the intelligent man." Regarding the latter, it seems to me rather clear in the context of the *De Legibus* that it is the Stoic identification of the law with the reason of the sage that Cicero has in mind here; cf. Kenter, *De Legibus*, 83.

[221] Cf. *T.D.* 1.57; 4.26–27; *De Off.* 3.32; *De Nat. Deor.* 1.17; *De Fin.* 1.31; 4.4; *Pro Sexto Roscio Amerino* 53; *Topica* 31; *Against Verres* 2.48, 139, 177; *Pro Murena* 30; *Brutus* 213; *Against Piso* 15; *Pro Cluentio* 4.

[222] *Pro Murena* 30.

[223] Cf. *Pro Sexto Roscio Amerino* 53, where a father's love for his child is described as *insitam*, with the Stoic doctrine of social οἰκείωσις. One might also mention in this connection Cicero's description of his love for Rome as such in *Verr.* 2.139,

of conception.[224] While there is thus good precedent for Cicero's use of the term *insita* in connection with human nature, and even in connection with the ἔμφυτοι προλήψεις, its use in connection with divine nature would be quite peculiar.[225] Indeed, when, in another work, Cicero wishes to convey the notion of the omnipresence of the *vera lex*, he chooses a phrase more directly reminiscent of Chrysippus's: *diffusa in omnes*.[226]

If, then, the *natura* into which reason has been "implanted" according to *De Leg.* 1.18 is thus human nature,[227] the phrase *ratio insita* would seem to be used with particular reference to the initial endowment of reason in its potential, less-than-complete state. In fact, Cicero's use of the term *insita* in this connection, recalling as it does the Greek ἔμφυτος, is quite striking given the foundational role played by the ἔμφυτοι προλήψεις in his theory of law. The perfected human reason which is identified with natural law is, in its initial form, comprised of "implanted preconceptions." Cicero's usage, it would seem, simply applies the technical description of the inchoate preconceptions

---

with which one can compare *De Fin.* 5.65–66. See further the report in *De Fin.* 1.31 that some Epicureans had expanded upon Epicurus's doctrine of the Goal, which was rooted in the belief that humans from birth naturally seek pleasure and avoid pain, by arguing that this judgment rests not only with the senses, but is *naturalem et insitam in animis nostris*; such a position is perhaps to be understood as the adaptation of Stoic ideas for the support of Epicurean ethics.

[224] *TD* 1.57; *Top.* 31. Note also the description of all human beings' notions (*cognitiones*) of the gods as *insitas . . . vel potius innatas* in *De Nat. Deor.* 1.44, which admittedly, however, is given in an account of Epicurean theology; cf. though the use of the identical phrase by Cicero in *De Fin.* 4.4 in connection with a report of a Platonic/Peripatetic view concerning the universal desire for knowledge on the part of human beings.

[225] Kenter cites several passages to demonstrate the synonymity of *insita* and *innata*, all of which refer to the nature or *animus* of the human being; he does not, however, comment upon the possible significance of this fact for the interpretation of the account of law at *De Leg.* 1.18. See Kenter, *De Legibus*, 82.

[226] *Rep.* 3.33; cf. Chrysippus's διὰ πάντων ἐρχόμενος (Diog. Laert. 7.88) and Cleanthes's διὰ πάντων φοιτᾷ (*SVF* 1.537; p. 122, lines 8ff). It is noteworthy that even in this passage the cosmic *ratio* manifests itself in human beings in their experience of their *own* nature. Thus when Cicero describes this *lex* further as *naturae congruens*, it becomes clear that the *natura* that he has in mind at the very least includes the *natura hominis*; for "[w]hoever does not submit to it [sc. the "true law"] is fleeing from himself and denying his human nature, and for this very reason will suffer the worst penalties, even if he escapes what is commonly considered punishment"; the translation is an adaptation of that of LCL.

[227] Cf. in this respect Dionysius bar Salibi's paraphrase and explanation of the ἔμφυτος λόγος of Jas 1:21: Excipite verbum insitum naturae nostrae; *h.e. legem naturalem innuit. In natura enim inseruit Deus, ut amet bona et odio habeat mala* (Sedlacek, *Dionusius Bar Salibi*, 91–92); see further on this Chapter Three. Cf. in addition Justin's reference to the ἔμφυτος τῇ φύσει τῶν ἀνθρώπων δόξα of God.

as "implanted" directly to the "spermatic" reason which the latter comprise.[228]

In fact, the number of other ancient works which exhibit similar terminology in analogous contexts confirms this interpretation. These works will be considered in detail in the following chapters, but the most striking instances can at least be mentioned here. In the *Apostolic Constitutions*, too, God's initial gift of a natural law to the human animal is equated with an endowment of "the seeds of divine knowledge," also called "implanted knowledge" (ἔμφυτος γνῶσις), while the law itself is described as an ἔμφυτος νόμος. Similarly, the incomplete *logos* possessed by all humans is described by Justin as the ἔμφυτον τοῦ λόγου σπέρμα (cf. σπορά), while the teaching of Christ, who brings this *logos* to perfection, is "right reason" or natural law. It is precisely this theoretical understanding of law, in fact, that Dionysius bar Salibi brings to his explanation of the ἔμφυτος λόγος of the Letter of James: it is interpreted with reference to the ability to make ethical distinctions,[229] "implanted" in human nature by God, and identified further with "natural law."

In sum, Cicero's definition of law as *ratio summa insita in natura* is to be understood in light of the Stoic correlation of the potential reason given to humans by nature with an initial endowment of ἔμφυτοι προλήψεις. Moreover, given the analogous descriptions of either human reason or the natural law it comprises as "implanted" in a variety of ancient works, it is clear that the phrase *ratio insita* was not Cicero's own idiosyncratic coinage. This latter point is all

---

[228] Cf. further in this connection *De Leg.* 1:24: "For when the nature of man is examined, the theory is usually advanced . . . [that] a time came which was suitable for sowing the seed of the human race (*serendi generis hominis*). And when this seed was scattered and sown over the earth (*quod sparsum in terras atque satum*), it was granted the divine gift of the soul. . . . the soul was implanted (*esse ingeneratum*) in us by God." I have altered the LCL translation only by rendering *ingeneratum* so as to make the continuation of the "sowing" metaphor more explicit. See further on this passage above, n. 183.

While one might object that the use of the term *summa* to describe this *ratio* is problematic for this interpretation, it is perhaps more significant that the term most often used in the common Stoic definition presented here to describe perfected reason—namely *recta ratio* (cf. ὀρθὸς λόγος); cf. *De Leg.* 1.23; 1.33; 1.42; 2.10; *De Rep.* 3.33—is avoided. *Summa*, unlike *recta*, might be taken simply with reference to the divine nature of the *ratio* rather than specifying its "right" or "perfect" state. The former point is in fact made elsewhere in the *De Legibus*; see 1.23, with which compare 1.59. Cf. further Justin, *App.* 3.3: μέρους τοῦ σπερματικοῦ θείου λόγου, on which see below, Chapter Three.

[229] Cf. on this point, too, the commentaries of Oecumenius and Theophylactus.

the more significant for our purposes given Cicero's heavy dependence upon some Greek source or sources for the theory of law
espoused in his *De Legibus*. It is safe to conclude, that is, that Cicero's
source had defined natural law in terms of λόγος ἔμφυτος. The author
of this source is impossible to identify with any certainty, and the
question is, fortunately, not crucial for the present study. The problem is nonetheless of interest in its own right, and merits at least
brief consideration.

RATIO INSITA AS λόγος ἔμφυτος:
THE GREEK SOURCE OF THE *DE LEGIBUS*

In general it is fair to say that Cicero was not a particularly original philosopher. By his own admission, his philosophical writings
were intended primarily to bring Greek ideas to the Roman world.
His *De Legibus*, at least with respect to the theory of law presented
in its first book, is no exception.[230] Cicero is in fact quite explicit
about his use of sources in this treatise, particularly with respect to
his treatment of the central issue of the natural origins of law and
justice.[231] His dependence in this matter is so great that the Epicurean
Atticus, the primary interlocutor of the *De Legibus*, quips sarcastically:

> And, of course, you have lost your independence in discussion, or else
> you are the kind of man not to follow your own judgment in a debate,
> but meekly to accept the authority of others![232]

Cicero assures Atticus that such facile acceptance of prior intellectual authority is not his usual procedure, but is in this case prompted
by the profound importance of his subject matter and his desire for
a secure theoretical foundation for his work.[233]

It cannot be doubted that the source for the theory of natural
law used in book one of the *De Legibus*, like those of Cicero's other

---

[230] On the intention of Cicero's philosophical writings, see *De Fin.* 1.1–12; *De Nat. Deor.* 1.1–14; *TD* 1.1–8; *Acad. Pr.* 5f. Cicero's attempt to use the Stoic theory of law as a foundation for a concrete body of legislation in the *De Legibus*, how-ever, is almost certainly original, at least in its Roman context; see on this imme-diately below. Note, though, the similar Jewish and Christian moves discussed in the following chapters.
[231] *De Leg.* 1.18; 1.36.
[232] *De Leg.* 1.36.
[233] *De Leg.* 1.37.

philosophical works, was Greek. This is clear first of all from his comments regarding the lack of prior Roman concern for questions of legal theory as opposed to those regarding legal minutiae.[234] A further indication lies in the etymology of the Greek term νόμος given in 1.19, to which Cicero adds his own Latin etymology of *lex*.

On the other hand, there has been some question as to which Greek author, precisely, provided Cicero's main source.[235] Several scholars have argued that Cicero's source was not a proper Stoic, but rather Antiochus of Ascalon, a personal acquaintance of Cicero and founder of the breakaway "Old Academy" whose philosophy is treated by Cicero in both the *De Finibus* and the *Academica*.[236] This philosopher is best known for his belief in the essential agreement of the Platonists, Peripatetics and the Stoics; his philosophy, accordingly, presented something of a synthesis of the thought of these three schools. In fact, Cicero interacts explicitly with Antiochus in *De Leg.* 1.54, when Atticus recognizes that Cicero's view on the dispute concerning the Good agrees substantially with that of Antiochus.[237] Whether agreement in this matter implies a dependence on Antiochus throughout the *De Legibus*, however, is far from clear. Other indications of Antiochan influence cited in support of this idea are suggestive, but not decisive.[238] Certainly, one can at least say that the use of Antiochus would have been consistent with Cicero's hope to win approval for his theory of law from the "Old Academy," the Peripatetics *and* the Stoics—among whom he, like Antiochus, finds essential agreement.[239]

Even if Antiochus was Cicero's primary source, however, it is by no means clear that one should thereby reckon with a radical alteration of the Stoic theory of law in the *De Legibus*. Cicero himself elsewhere writes of Antiochus of Ascalon that "had he made very

---

[234] *De Leg.* 1.14. See further Vander Waerdt, "Philosophical Influence on Roman Jurisprudence," 4867–70.

[235] For a sketch of the positions, see Kenter, *De Legibus*, 9–10.

[236] So most recently Horsley, "The Law of Nature"; Vander Waerdt, "The Stoic Theory of Natural Law."

[237] *De Leg.* 1.54; note however Cicero's hesitation: *cui* [sc. Antiochus] *tamen ego adsentiar in omnibus necne mox videro*.

[238] Especially those cited by Horsley, "The Law of Nature in Philo and Cicero," 42–50; see further the discussion immediately below.

[239] *De Leg.* 1.37–39. The view regarding the essential agreement of these schools on the question of the *summum bonum*, however, apparently goes back to Carneades, and is to this extent consistent with Cicero's skeptical leanings; see *De Fin.* 3.41. For Antiochus's dependence upon Carneades in this matter see *De Fin.* 5.16.

few modifications," he would have been "a perfectly genuine Stoic."[240]
On the face of it, then, the question would thus seem in any case
to be at most one of "modifications" of the Stoic theory.[241] The substantive question, that is, is this: even if Antiochus was the primary
source for this work, in what way, if any, does his theory of law
represent a departure from the Stoic theory?

In its basic outlines, at least, the theory of natural law presented
in the *De Legibus* is unquestionably Stoic. As we have seen, its central points have clear precedents in our sources for the early Stoics.
Cicero takes the Stoic identification of law with human reason as
the point of departure for his theory, and in fact repeatedly offers
variants of a common Stoic definition of law as "right reason applied
to commanding and prohibiting."[242] The *ratio* in question, for Cicero
as for the Stoics, is both the cosmic *ratio* of God and human reason. The notion that gods and humans are members of a common
state in virtue of their similar possession of reason is also clearly
Stoic in origin.[243] So too, the developmental aspect of Cicero's theory of law draws upon the Stoic account of human reason and its
development; and it is rather difficult to imagine that Chrysippus
had altogether overlooked the implications of the latter for his
identification of natural law with the *logos* of the sage.

In fact, even if one should grant the supposed indications of
Antiochan influence found by Horsely and Vander Waerdt, these
represent only minor modifications of the Stoic theory—albeit, in
the case of Vander Waerdt, a slight modification with far-reaching
implications. For Vander Waerdt the most consequential change
effected by Antiochus was the ascription of "appropriate actions"
(καθήκοντα) rather than "right actions" (κατορθώματα) to natural law:
"a simple technical modification, though one motivated by fundamental revisions in Stoic psychology."[244] Horsley, on the other hand,
finds two significant divergences from Stoicism in Cicero's account.[245]

---

[240] *Acad. Pr.* 132.
[241] Thus Dillon (*The Middle Platonists*, 80–81), who finds it "very likely that the
discussion of Natural Law in Cicero *De Legibus* I is basically Antiochan," nonetheless points out that "none of this is original to Antiochus."
[242] *De Leg.* 1.18, 33, 42; 2.8, 10.
[243] *De Leg.* 1.23; cf. *De Fin.* 4.7.
[244] Vander Waerdt, "Philosophical Influence," 4873. Vander Waerdt's position is
problematic in any case, as Cicero's law is explicitly identified with the reason of
the sage in particular; see above n. 213, and the discussion to which it is appended.
[245] Horsley, "The Law of Nature in Philo and Cicero," 40–42. A third point

The first is Cicero's predilection for phrases like "divine mind" or "mind of God." While perhaps suggestive of platonic influence, this does not, in and of itself, represent a significant alteration of the Stoic theory.[246] Horsley's second point, and that which he finds to be the "most significant" indication of non-Stoic influence, is the fact that Cicero "clearly distinguish[es] God from the law," whereas "Stoic doctrine had identified God with law as well as with reason."[247] As was pointed out earlier in this chapter, however, strict identification does not appear to have been the early Stoics' only valid option for describing the relationship between God and law or *logos*.[248] On the other hand, the consistency with which this distinction is maintained in the *De Legibus*, along with Cicero's predilection for describing God as "lawgiver," might suggest platonic influence—especially given that both tendencies are also characteristic of the more obviously platonizing Philo.[249] Be that as it may, one cannot in any case fairly speak of a substantive departure from the original Stoic theory.

Potentially more consequential for the present study are indications of platonic influence in connection with Cicero's understanding of the implanted preconceptions.[250] While, as we have seen, it is not the case that Cicero's notion that these are present from birth owes to platonic influence, such influence might nevertheless be seen in both his references to memory in this connection and his apparent view that humans have implanted preconceptions which extend beyond the sphere of ethics and belief in the deity. The Stoics, we have seen, included among the ἔμφυτοι προλήψεις only those concepts whose origin lies in οἰκείωσις: above all one's ethical concepts, though apparently for some (later?) Stoics, at least, also a belief in God. Cicero, on the other hand, speaks of the "obscure notions of many things" (*rerum plurimarum obscuras intelligentias*) which Divine Nature gives to the human animal.[251] This statement would seem to suggest

---

made by Horsley concerning the frequent use of the term θεσμός applies not to Cicero, but to Philo, who, Horsley argues, also depends upon Antiochus. On Philo's theory of law and its relation to that of Cicero, see Chapter Three.

[246] In fact Horsley himself recognizes that there is some evidence for a similar use of the term νοῦς among the early Stoics; see "The Law of Nature in Philo and Cicero," 41 n. 15.

[247] *Ibid.*, 42.

[248] See above, under the heading "Natural Law as Cosmic Logos."

[249] Horsley, "The Law of Nature in Philo and Cicero," 42.

[250] See Kenter, *De Legibus*,112; further Pohlenz, *Grundfragen*, 97–99.

[251] Cicero, *De Leg.* 1.26.

preconceptions from a wide range of topics beyond those discussed in this connection by the Stoics, and Cicero in fact speaks elsewhere in *De Legibus* 1 of "shadowy concepts, as it were, of *everything*" which the individual human "from the start has formed in soul and mind."[252] That platonic influence is in fact at work here is suggested by an interesting passage in the *Tusculan Disputations*, where Cicero discusses the platonic theory of *anamnesis* using Stoic sounding terminology:

> in no other way was it possible for us to possess from childhood such a number of important ideas, implanted and as it were impressed on our souls and called ἔννοιαι (*insitas et quasi consignatas in animis notiones, quas* ἔννοιαι *vocant*), unless the soul, before it entered the body, had been active in acquiring knowledge.[253]

This passage is somewhat reminiscent of *De Leg.* 1.25, where Cicero explains why it is that all human societies evidence some belief in a deity: "Thus it is clear that man recognizes God because, in a way, he *remembers* and recognizes the source from which he sprang." Interestingly, a synthesis of the Stoic "concepts" and the Platonic "ideas" was also apparently effected by Antiochus of Ascalon.[254] This may provide further evidence for Cicero's dependence upon Antiochus for his presentation of natural law, though the presence of similar ideas in Cicero's other works has led at least one scholar to conclude that Cicero has effected this merger himself.[255]

Whatever the case, the importance of this innovation for Cicero's general theory of law is negligible. Cicero's primary interest in the implanted preconceptions, both in 1.26 and in 1.59, is in any case ethical. Thus, referring back to 1.26–27, Cicero writes that

> those inchoate concepts (*inchoatae intelligentiae*) to which I have referred, which are imprinted in our souls (*in animis inprimuntur*), are imprinted

---

[252] *De Leg* 1.59: *principio rerum omnium quasi adumbratas intellegentias animo ac mente conceperit*. The translation and emphasis are mine. It is perhaps possible to interpret *principio* in 1.59 more loosely and, therefore, to take the reference more generally to the "natural" formation of preconceptions which occurs even before an individual is properly rational, and thus to all preconceptions rather than the ἔμφυτοι προλήψεις in particular. Note, however, the preceding reference to "how nobly equipped by Nature (s)he [sc. the human individual] entered life," which recalls rather strongly the passage concerning the divine endowment of the *obscuras intelligentias* in 1.26; cf. Kenter, *De Legibus*, 235.

[253] *TD* 1.57; I have deviated from the LCL only in rendering *insitas* as "implanted" rather than "innate."

[254] Dillon, *The Middle Platonists*, 91–96.

[255] So Pohlenz, *Grundfragen*, 99.

in all souls alike . . . In fact, there is no human being of any race who, if he finds a guide, cannot attain to virtue.[256]

So too, in 1.59: after speaking of "shadowy concepts, as it were, of everything" which form "from the start" in the human mind, Cicero goes on to explain how the development of these concepts leads ultimately to a conception of the *summum bonum*.[257]

In sum, given the several indications of platonic influence in the first book of his *De Legibus*, it is quite possible that Cicero depends upon Antiochus of Ascalon for his theory of law. However, it is by no means clear that his general theory differs substantially from that of the Stoics. The instances of platonic influence perhaps add some distinctive color to the Stoic theory, but they do not alter it in any substantial way. The theoretical foundation that allowed for Cicero's definition of law as "implanted reason" is wholly Stoic in origin.

The question of Cicero's source in any case matters little for our present purposes. By the first century BCE at the latest, law had been defined in terms of λόγος ἔμφυτος in connection with the Stoic theory of natural law. This is suggested not only by Cicero's explicit attribution of this definition to prior (Greek) authority,[258] but, as we shall see in the following chapters, by the similar language found in the *Apostolic Constitutions*, in works of Justin Martyr and Methodius, in early commentaries on the Letter of James and, in fact, in the Letter of James itself.

---

[256] *De Leg.* 1.30, I have slightly altered the LCL translation.
[257] *De Leg* 1.59–60.
[258] I.e., to "the most learned men"; see *De Leg.* 1.18.

CHAPTER THREE

THE LAW OF MOSES, THE TEACHING OF JESUS,
AND NATURAL LAW

Among the enduring effects of Alexander the Great's incursions into
the East was a vast and multi-faceted interplay of Greek and Jewish
culture.[1] Despite the rhetoric generated in response to the Hellenistic
reform of Jerusalem and, especially, Antiochus Epiphanes's subsequent attempt to suppress traditional Jewish piety altogether, the Jews
of this age were not faced with a choice between "Judaism" and
"Hellenism." Hellenization was simply a fact.[2] What confronted the
Jews of the Hellenistic and Early Roman periods was rather the
challenge of producing a synthesis of Greek and Jewish ways that
would yet preserve a distinctively Jewish identity amid the international
Hellenistic culture.[3] The literary and other remains of the Jews of
the Hellenistic age reveal a wide range of responses to this challenge.

One strategy, the impact of which would continue to be felt in
subsequent centuries, particularly as Christian theology developed,
involved the Jewish appropriation of Greek philosophical tradition.[4]
A number of Jewish intellectuals found the rigor and insights of
Greek philosophical discourse compelling. Rejection of their own religious heritage in favor of one or another school of philosophy, however, was scarcely the only option. On the contrary, what one finds
in the extant literature are various attempts to bring the two traditions

---

[1] See esp. V. Tcherikover, *Hellenistic Civilization and the Jews* (trans. S. Applebaum;
Philadelphia: Jewish Publication Society of America, 1959; reprinted with a preface by J. J. Collins, Peabody, MA: Hendrickson, 1999); M. Hengel, *Judaism and
Hellenism: Studies in their Encounter in Palestine during the Early Hellenistic Period* (2 vols. in
one; Philadelphia: Fortress, 1981).

[2] See S. J. D. Cohen, *From the Maccabees to the Mishnah* (Library of Early Christianity;
Philadelphia: Westminster, 1989) 34–45; also M. Hengel in collaboration with
C. Markschies, *The "Hellenization" of Judaea in the First Century after Christ* (trans. J. Bowden;
Philadelphia: Trinity Press International, 1989).

[3] As Cohen well points out, the challenge was scarcely a new one: "Even in pre-
exilic times the Israelites had to determine the extent to which they could draw on
the riches of the cultures among which they lived" (*From the Maccabees to the Mishnah*, 38).

[4] See J. J. Collins, *Between Athens and Jerusalem: Jewish Identity in the Hellenistic Diaspora*
(New York: Crossroad, 1983) 175–94.

together; to locate points of contact from which one could forward
claims of compatibility. Inevitably, these endeavors led not only to
new interpretations of Judaism, but to distinctive treatments of Greek
philosophical ideas as well.

Given the importance of traditions of Mosaic legislation to Second
Temple Judaism in general, it is not surprising that the Stoic concept of a divinely ordained law provided one such point of contact.
From at least the first century of the Common Era, some Jewish
thinkers claimed that their nation's law, revealed to Moses by the
creator of the world, was in act a written expression of the Stoics'
natural law. Analogous claims would continue to be forwarded by
Christians, who, however, more often asserted that it was rather the
teaching of Jesus which gave verbal expression to natural law.[5] In
either case, what resulted were diverse presentations of the concept
of natural law that diverged variously and significantly from the theory as originally conceived. Two common and fundamental divergences are noteworthy at the outset. The very notion, first of all,
that the "right reason" which comprises natural law can find definitive
verbal expression in some set of ethical directives seems to have been
quite alien to the original Stoic idea.[6] Second, and perhaps more
important, is the fact that the origin of this law was no longer associated with the immanent deity of the Stoics. The author of this law
was now the transcendent god whose past interaction with humanity, and with the descendants of Abraham in particular, is recorded
in the Jewish scriptures, and whose future activity, at least in much
of the Christian literature, would include an eschatological judgment.

In short, what one finds in this literature are recognizably Stoic
ideas associated with concepts and discussed in terms which are utterly
foreign to Stoicism. This phenomenon greatly illuminates the treatment of the implanted *logos* in the Letter of James, and an examination of selected examples will be instructive. In addition, analysis
of several works which speak particularly of an "implanted" law or
logos in this context will confirm the findings of the preceding chapter.

---

[5] See, however, below in this chapter on the *Apostolic Constitutions*, and the following chapter on the Letter of James.
[6] See the introductory comments in Chapter Two, above. Note at the same time,
however, that Cicero is also moving in this direction.

Philo of Alexandria

The writings of Philo of Alexandria present the most well-known and obvious example of the Jewish appropriation of the Stoic theory of natural law. Philo's recurring use of patently Stoic terms and concepts leaves his indebtedness to Stoicism beyond doubt. Philo, however, is no Stoic. His general philosophical orientation is more Middle Platonic than Stoic,[7] and his discussion of natural law, in particular, shows strains of Neo-Pythagoreanism. Moreover, in Philo's writings, these various philosophical concepts have been filtered through a fundamental conviction that the writings of "Moses" represent an unparalleled expression of philosophical truth, of the "right reason" that the Stoics considered natural law. The end result is a quite distinctive treatment of the concept of natural law: one clearly rooted in, but also significantly different from, the early Stoic theory.

Philo and the Stoics

The Stoic correlation of law and "right reason" is fundamental in Philo's writings.[8] On more than one occasion, he offers a version of what we have seen to have been a standard Stoic definition of law as *logos* in its function of commanding and prohibiting.[9] Moreover, his comment at one point that "knowledge of the things we ought to do and of the things we ought not" (ἐπιστήμην . . . ὧν τε δεῖ ποιεῖν καὶ ὧν μή) is the special property of the "reasonable part" (μέρος λογικόν) of the human soul,[10] suggests that he, like Chrysippus and Cicero, used this definition of law in conjunction with a more general account of the workings of the human *logos*—albeit with a view of the soul that is quite at odds with the monistic psychology of the early Stoics.[11] For the Stoics, this definition concerned *logos* both as

---

[7] J. Dillon, *The Middle Platonists*, 139–83.

[8] Philo equates law specifically with ὀρθὸς λόγος in *Opif.* 143, *Ebr.* 142, *Prob. Lib.* 46–47, and *Agr.* 51, but his terminology is in general rather fluid. As Goodenough points out, "the word ὀρθός is frequently omitted and λόγος alone put in formulae where we know ὀρθὸς λόγος must have been understood by both Philo and his reader" (*By Light, Light: The Mystical Gospel of Hellenistic Judaism* [New Haven: Yale University Press, 1935] 56).

[9] See *Jos.* 29; *Praem. Poen.* 55; *Migr. Abr.* 130.

[10] *Leg. All.* 1.70. All translations of Philo's writings, unless otherwise noted, are taken from the LCL.

[11] Cf. Plutarch, *St. Rep.* 1037F; also Cicero, *De Leg.* 10. On the various divisions

a divine principle that pervades the cosmos as law of the World
City, and as the reason of the human sage, the citizen of the Cosmopolis. This basic conceptual framework, patently Stoic, surfaces
repeatedly in Philo's works.[12]

A particularly striking example is found in the treatise *On Joseph*,
where the notion of the world as a "Great City" is directly linked
to the Stoic definition of law:

> For this world is the Megalopolis and it is furnished with one consti-
> tution and one law: the *logos* of nature is that which commands what
> one must do, and that which prohibits what one must not do.[13]

The premise of a World City governed by *logos* is most prominent,
however, in his *On the Creation of the World*. Here we find, not surprisingly, that citizenship in Philo's City, as with that of the Stoics,
is limited to rational beings; to beings, that is, whose "constitution"
is also comprised by *logos*. This includes in the first place, again analogously with the Stoics, a constituency of divine beings: the λογικαὶ
καὶ θεῖαι φύσεις, such as the incorporeals and the stars, are citizens,
with God himself as ἄρχων τῆς μεγαλοπόλεως.[14] It also includes, of
course, the human being. More precisely, it is specifically the sage—
that is, the one whose constitution is defined by *right* reason—who
is the world citizen.[15] This becomes quite explicit as Philo explains
Adam's status as "world citizen":

> Now since every well-ordered State has a constitution, the citizen of
> the world enjoyed of necessity the same constitution as did the whole

---

of the soul espoused by Philo, see further Dillon, *The Middle Platonists*, 174–76. A
further hint of Philo's awareness of the implications of the Stoic psychology of action
for natural law might also be seen in *Opif.* 3, where he associates the universal law
with "the will of Nature" (τὸ βούλημα τῆς φύσεως). Cf. the use of the same phrase at
Epictetus, *Ench.* 26 and *SVF* 3.180, and further the discussion of Inwood, *Ethics and
Human Action*, 107–8. This passage from Philo, in fact, would seem to provide further
confirmation of Inwood's suggestion that the Stoics understood the law in this way.

[12] On the Cosmic City see *Mos.* 2.51; *Dec.* 53; *Spec. Leg.* 1.34; *Prov.* frag. 2.39;
Jos. 29–31; 69. On the "world citizen" see *Spec. Leg.* 2.45; *Migr. Abr.* 59; *Somn.*
1.243; *Conf. Ling.* 61; *Jos.* 69.

[13] *Jos.* 29: ἡ μὲν γὰρ μεγαλόπολις ὅδε ὁ κόσμος ἐστὶ καὶ μιᾷ χρῆται πολιτείᾳ καὶ
νόμῳ ἑνί· λόγος δέ ἐστι φύσεως προστακτικὸς μὲν ὧν πρακτέον, ἀπαγορευτικὸς δὲ ὧν
οὐ ποιητέον; translation mine.

[14] *Opif.* 143–144; cf. *De Leg.* 1.23 and *SVF* 2.528. On God as "ruler" of this City,
see *Dec.* 53, with which cf. *Spec. Leg.* 1.34, where humans are said to infer from the
order of the "Great City" of the world a ἡγεμών. Philo's god, however, is of course
distinct from the *logos*; see Dillon, *The Middle Platonists*, 155–58.

[15] See Diog. Laert. 7.33; cf. Cicero, *De Leg.* 1.23.

world: and this constitution is the right reason of nature (ὁ τῆς φύσεως ὀρθὸς λόγος), more properly called an "ordinance", or "dispensation", seeing it is a divine law . . .[16]

This description of Adam, in fact, assumes his idealization as "in body and soul, surpassing all that now are and all that have been before us," since God created him not from a material pattern, but μόνῳ . . . τῷ ἑαυτοῦ λόγῳ.[17] Thus while all humans, by virtue of their possession of *logos*, have the potential to live in accord with right reason and thus become world citizens,[18] it is "the man who observes the law" who is "constituted thereby a loyal citizen of the world (τοῦ νομίμου ἀνδρὸς εὐθὺς ὄντος κοσμοπολίτου), regulating his doings by the purpose and will of Nature (τὸ βούλημα τῆς φύσεως), in accordance with which the entire world itself also is administered."[19] In fact, the only other figure explicitly identified by Philo as a "world citizen" is Moses, the paradigm of the sage and lawgiver of the Jews.[20]

The Law of Nature and the Law of Moses

If Philo's indebtedness to the Stoics for his understanding of law is thus clear, his divergences from them are no less so. The most obvious of these can be correlated with his fundamental orientation toward Judaism. It is, undoubtedly, in no small part due to his

---

[16] *Opif.* 143: ἐπεὶ δὲ πᾶσα πόλις εὔνομος ἔχει πολιτείαν, ἀναγκαίως συνέβαινε τῷ κοσμοπολίτῃ χρῆσθαι πολιτείᾳ ᾗ καὶ σύμπας ὁ κόσμος· αὕτη δέ ἐστιν ὁ τῆς φύσεως ὀρθὸς λόγος, ὃς κυριωτέρᾳ κλήσει προσονομάζεται θεσμός, νόμος θεῖος ὤν . . .; I have altered the LCL translation of ὁ τῆς φύσεως ὀρθὸς λόγος as "nature's right relation" to make the reference to "right reason" more explicit. Note also in this connection *Abr.* 31, where Philo states that the "kin" of the sage are other virtuous people rather than those to whom he is tied by blood.

[17] *Opif.* 139–40; I have altered the translation of the LCL only to avoid the impression that Philo's language in 1.40 is gender specific.

[18] Cf., e.g., *Abr.* 5 where Moses is said to have included narratives concerning the patriarchs in his law so that "those who wish to live in accordance with the laws as they now stand have no difficult task, seeing that the first generations before any at all of the particular statutes was set in writing followed the unwritten law with perfect ease . . ."

[19] *Ibid.*; cf. *Mos.* 1.157 where it is specifically ὁ σπουδαῖος who is κοσμοπολίτης.

[20] E.g., *Mos.* 1.156; *Conf. Ling.* 106; cf. also *Quod Omn. Prob. Lib.* 44. On Philo's idealization of Moses, see esp. *Mos* 2.192 and *Ebr.* 94; further Goodenough, *By Light, Light,* 180–234. Winston characterizes Moses as Philo's "super sage" (*Logos and Mystical Theology in Philo of Alexandria* [Cincinnati: Hebrew Union College Press, 1985] 41). By the same token, one can safely assume that Abraham, Isaac and Jacob were also considered to be such given their status as as ἔμψυχοι νόμοι. See on this concept below, with note 36.

assumption of the Jewish god, for example, that he inclines away from the immanent Stoic deity and views the *logos* in relation to a transcendent, more platonic, god.[21] Of more direct relevance to the present study is his core conviction that the "right reason" which the Stoics equated with true law finds written expression in a law that Moses gave to the Jewish people. In the opening of his *On the Creation*, Philo lauds Moses's decision to preface his laws with an account of the world's creation. By doing so, says Philo, Moses indicated that "the world is in harmony with the Law, and the Law with the world."[22] Indeed, Moses thus implied that the one who observes his law "regulat[es] his doings by the purpose and will of Nature (τὸ βούλημα τῆς φύσεως), in accordance with which the entire world itself also is administered." It is precisely this one, therefore, who is the "world citizen."[23]

If Moses's law is thus in harmony with the *logos* that structures the cosmos, it can also be seen, from another vantage point, as a written expression of the *logos* of the human sage. On one hand, to be sure, Philo considers the "right reason" of the sage to stand over against all "lifeless" (ἄψυχοι) written laws:[24]

> right reason is an infallible law engraved not by this mortal or that and, therefore, perishable as he, nor on any parchment or slabs, and, therefore, soulless as they, but by immortal nature on the immortal mind, never to perish.[25]

Nonetheless, the "sacred books" of Moses's law, says Philo, are "likenesses and copies of the patterns enshrined in the soul, as also are the laws set before us in these books, which shew so clearly the said virtues."[26] That is to say, the commands of the law of Moses are,

---

[21] On Philo's *logos* see esp. Winston, *Logos and Mystical Theology*; also Dillon, *The Middle Platonists*, 158–61.

[22] *Opif.* 3: τοῦ κόσμου τῷ νόμῳ καὶ τοῦ νόμου τῷ κόσμῳ συνᾴδοντος.

[23] *Ibid.*

[24] On the "Higher Law" in Philo see Goodenough, *By Light, Light*, 48–71; also J. W. Martens, "Philo and the 'Higher' Law," *SBLSP* 30 (1991) 309–22.

[25] *Quod Omn. Prob. Lib.* 46: νόμος δὲ ἀψευδὴς ὁ ὀρθὸς λόγος, οὐχ ὑπὸ τοῦ δεῖνος ἢ τοῦ δεῖνος, θνητοῦ φθαρτός, ἐν χαρτιδίοις ἢ στήλαις, ἄψυχος ἀψύχοις, ἀλλ᾽ ὑπ᾽ ἀθανάτου φύσεως ἄφθαρτος ἐν ἀθανάτῳ διανοίᾳ τυπωθείς. On the immortal nature of the human διάνοια, see *Opif.* 135.

[26] *Mos.* 2.11; i.e., the four virtues chiefly required for legislation, all of which Moses alone possessed. Those especially crucial for the task of legislation are τὸ φιλάνθρωπον, τὸ φιλοδίκαιον, τὸ φιλάγαθον, and τὸ μισοπόνηρον (2.9). Note that Moses's trainer in the quest for virtue was ἐν ἑαυτῷ λογισμός, and his single goal

so to speak, "copies" (ὡς ἂν εἰκόνων) of the "originals" (ὡς ἂν ἀρχετύπους); copies, that is, of the "men who lived good and blame-less lives, whose virtues stand permanently enshrined in the most holy scriptures . . . for in these men we have laws endowed with life and reason (ἔμψυχοι καὶ λογικοὶ νόμοι)."[27] In short, while not, strictly speaking, identical to the "higher law," the law of the Jews stands in contrast to the ἄψυχοι νόμοι of all other peoples[28] as a written copy of the ἔμψυχοι νόμοι, the sages found particularly in Israel's past: Abraham, Isaac, Jacob and, above all, Moses himself.[29]

The Sage as ἔμψυχος νόμος

Philo's notion that the true law is the right reason of the sage—though obviously not his view that the Jewish patriarchs provide models of the sage!—is clearly rooted in the Stoic theory of law. One of his most characteristic expressions of this idea, the descrip-tion of the sage as ἔμψυχος νόμος, however, is not typical of Stoicism. As several scholars have pointed out, this terminology seems in fact to have been derived from Neo-Pythagorean, not Stoic, philosophy.[30]

---

was "the right reason of nature" (τὸν ὀρθὸν τῆς φύσεως λόγον), which alone is the beginning and font of the virtues" (*Mos* 1.48; cf. *Abr.* 6).

[27] *Abr.* 3–6; cf. *Abr.* 275–76; *Virt.* 194; *Mos.* 1.162.

[28] Though "right reason" is understood to be the "fountain head of all other laws" (τοῖς ἄλλοις πηγὴ νόμοις) in *Quod Omn. Prob. Lib.* 47, it is nonetheless assumed throughout Philo's writings that Moses's law alone presents the perfect written expres-sion of natural law. Cf. in this respect Justin's comparison, to be discussed below, of the "natural law" promulgated by Jesus with "the laws of men"; Justin's com-parison, though, assumes a developmental-historical understanding of the λόγος which would have been alien to Philo.

[29] Enos, Enoch and Noah, the first trio of patriarchs discussed by Philo, are of a lesser stature and are not called ἔμψυχοι νόμοι. So too Joseph, even in the more positive portrayal given him in *De Josepho*, nonetheless represents, as πολιτικός, an "addition" to the natural polity of the World City and is for this reason never called ἔμψυχος νόμος. Thus while Philo writes at *Jos.* 148 that "the πολιτικός takes a second place to the king," he makes it clear elsewhere that it is the king who is ἔμψυχος νόμος (*Mos.* 2.4); see further below. On Philo's ambivalent portrayal of Joseph, see E. R. Goodenough, *The Politics of Philo Judaeus: Practice and Theory* (New Haven: Yale University Press, 1938) 21–33, 46–63.

[30] See most fully E. R. Goodenough, "The Political Philosophy of Hellenistic Kingship," *Yale Classical Studies* 1 (1928) 55–102; also G. F. Chesnut, "The Ruler and the Logos in Neopythagorean, Middle Platonic, and Late Stoic Political Philosophy," *ANRW* 2.16.2 (1978) 1310–1332. The closest analogue in the Stoic sources is found in Seneca, *Ep.* 92, on which see Chesnut, "The Ruler and the Logos," 1324–26.

Stobaeus has preserved the fragments of several Neo-Pythagorean treatises on the subject of kingship in which the king (βασιλεύς), as opposed to the tyrant (τύραννος), is characterized as ἔμψυχος νόμος.[31] That Philo's use of this term bears some relation to this tradition is sufficiently clear from the fact that his fullest treatment of it occurs precisely in connection with a discussion of the king (βασιλεύς).

> It is a king's duty to command what is right and forbid what is wrong. But to command what should be done and to forbid what should not be done is the peculiar function of law; so that it follows at once that the king is a living law and the law a just king.[32]

What emerges from this passage, in fact, is a remarkable synthesis of Stoic and Neo-Pythagorean concepts. Philo, in a manner unparalleled in the Neo-Pythagorean fragments, clarifies the sense in which the king can be viewed as an ἔμψυχος νόμος by appealing to the Stoic definition of law: he is such inasmuch as he shares the law's "peculiar function" of commanding what is to be done and forbidding what is not.

Philo's "king," moreover, is not simply the literal (albeit idealized) monarch of the Neo-Pythagorean fragments. The "king" of Philo's writings, like that of the Stoics, is such simply by virtue of his status as sage, regardless of his possession of an actual dominion:[33]

> no one of the foolish (is) a king, even though he should be master of all the land and sea, but only the wise and God-loving man, even if he is without the equipment and resources through which he may obtain power with violence and force.[34]

---

[31] The passages are conveniently collected in Goodenough's "The Political Philosophy of Hellenistic Kingship."

[32] *Mos* 2.4: βασιλεῖ προσήκει προστάττειν ἃ χρὴ καὶ ἀπαγορεύειν ἃ μὴ χρή· πρόσταξις δὲ τῶν πρακτέων καὶ ἀπαγόρευσις τῶν οὐ πρακτέων ἴδιον νόμου, ὡς εὐθὺς εἶναι τὸν μὲν βασιλέα νόμον ἔμψυχον, τὸν δὲ νόμον βασιλέα δίκαιον. Cf. *Praem.* 53–55.

[33] Cf., e.g., Diog. Laert. 7.121f. The Neo-Pythagorean fragments on kingship also routinely insist that the king be characterized by virtue, justice, etc; indeed, the fragment ascribed to the Pythagorean Sthenidas of Locri asserts that the king must be a sage (see Goodenough, "The Political Philosophy of Hellenistic Kingship," 73–74). However, the chief contrast in the fragments generally is that between the king and the tyrant, not the sage and the fool, and there is no indication from the fragments that the sage, conversely, is *de facto* a king.

[34] *QG* 4.76. Philo makes this assertion in explicit disagreement with "some of those who philosophize." It is tempting to take this as an indication of his awareness that he is going beyond the Neo-Pythagorean theory of kingship in his second point—i.e., in the application of the title "king" to people who may never have any literal kingdom—but this is of course uncertain inasmuch as it is unclear which philosophers he has in mind.

Analogously with the offices of pilot, physician, or musician, king-ship, for Philo, resides in the mastery of the "certain kingly art" (τέχνη τις βασιλική); it does not depend on possession of the tools of the trade.[35] The titles sage, king and ἔμψυχος νόμος, in short, simply express different aspects of the same basic character type. And here again, characteristically, it is the "sages" of Moses's "sacred books"—whether literal kings or not—who embody the type.[36]

Conclusion: Philo on Natural Law

The presence of decidedly Stoic terms and concepts in Philo's treat-ment of natural law is quite clear. The definition of law as *logos* com-manding and prohibiting; the identification of the *logos* in question as both that which structures the cosmos and that of the human sage; the notions of "World City" and "world citizen"; the identification of the sage and the king; all these elements of Philo's writings are patently Stoic. His presentation of these ideas, however, is scarcely typical of the Stoics in every respect. Philo's treatment of these Stoic ideas is informed by his dependence on other traditions of discourse, whether Middle Platonic, Neo-Pythagorean, or Jewish, which are in any case alien to Stoicism. The result is a quite distinctive presen-tation of the Stoic correlation of *logos* and law.

4 MACCABEES

Like the writings of Philo, *4 Maccabees* abounds with terms and con-cepts derived from Greek philosophy. Its stated theme of reason's

---

[35] See further Goodenough, *Politics*, 91–93.

[36] On Adam as "king," see *Opif.* 148. On Moses as ἔμψυχος νόμος see *Mos.* 1.162, and further *Mos.* 1.158. Moses's role as king is the subject of the whole of book one of the *Life of Moses*; see esp. 1.334. Abraham is described as "king" in *QG* 4.76 and, along with Isaac and Jacob, as ἔμψυχος νόμος in *Abr.* 3–6. Note also that the multi-book work that had discussed him, Isaac and Jacob was given the alternate title *On the Unwritten Laws*, a designation intended to characterize the patriarchs themselves, as is clear from *Abr.* 3–6 and 276; on the equation of "unwritten law" and "animate law" in Philo, see Martens, "Philo and the 'Higher' Law."

Also significant in this connection, finally, is the fact that Joseph, as the type of the πολιτικός who takes "second place to the king," is characterized neither as "king" nor as ἔμψυχος νόμος despite his more literal rule; see *Jos.* 148. Goodenough observes that the Joseph of the *De Josepho*, "as a politician analogous to the Roman ruler of Egypt, is a highly admirable being, *almost* one of the νόμοι ἔμψυχοι, though distinctly lower than the patriarchs" ("Philo's Exposition of the Law and his De Vita Moses," *HTR* 26 [1933] 116, emphasis mine).

supremacy over the passions is indeed a "highly philosophical" (1:1, φιλοσοφώτατον) one.[37] To be sure, neither the depth of the author's philosophical knowledge nor the particular school of philosophy to which he is most indebted are as clear as is the case with Philo; but a substantial measure of Stoic influence is recognized on all accounts.[38] Most commonly cited in the latter connection are his association of (right)[39] reason with freedom and kingship,[40] his definition of wisdom,[41] his notion of the unity of humankind,[42] as well as his position on the equality of sins.[43]

-----

[37] As A. Dupont-Sommer recognizes, this opening characterization of the theme from the very start "donne, en quelque sorte, le ton: l'orateur est un philosophe, et c'est à des philosophes qu' il entend s'adresser" (*Le Quatrième Livre des Machabées: Introduction, Traduction et Notes* [Paris: Librairie Ancienne Honoré Champion, 1939] 88).

[38] See R. Renehan, "The Greek Philosophic Background of Fourth Maccabees," *Rheinisches Museum für Philologie* 115 (1972) 223–38, esp. 223–26 for a brief summary of the scholarly discussion, and 233–38 on Stoic influence in particular. Renehan suggests that *4 Maccabees* is directly dependent upon Posidonius. See further Dupont-Sommer, *Le Quatrième Livre des Machabées*, 55f; H. Anderson, "4 Maccabees: A New Translation and Introduction," *OTP* 2.538; U. Breitenstein, *Beobachtungen zu Sprache, Stil und Gedankengut des Vierten Makkabäerbuchs* (2d ed; Basel and Stuttgart: Schwabe & Co. Verlag, 1978) 159–61; H.-J. Klauck, *4 Makkabäerbuch* (JSHRZ 3.6; Gütersloh: Gerd Mohn, 1989) 665–66; D. A. deSilva, *4 Maccabees* (Guides to Apocrypha and Pseudepigrapha; Sheffield: Sheffield Academic Press, 1998) 13, 51–75. Even M. Hadas, who argues that the author is a Platonist, concedes that he also "knew Stoicism, of course, and at many points uses Stoic language and echoes Stoic views" (*The Third and Fourth Books of Maccabees* [New York: Harper & Bros., 1953] 116–118, esp. 117 n. 57).

[39] Note that λογισμός connotes not simply "reason" in *4 Maccabees*, but more specifically νοῦς μετὰ ὀρθοῦ λόγου προτιμῶν τὸν σοφίας βίον (*4 Macc* 1:15); see on this further below.

[40] *4 Macc* 14:2; see Dupont-Sommer, *Le Quatrième Livre des Machabées*, 56 and 137; Hadas, *The Third and Fourth Books of Maccabees*, 215; Breitenstein, *Beobachtungen*, 160; Klauck, *4 Makkabäerbuch*, 740. See further on kingship 2:23, where the one who lives by the law is said to "reign over a kingdom," and 7:10, where Eleazar is rhetorically addressed by the author as μέγιστε βασιλεῦ. See further on freedom 5:38 and 13:2.

[41] *4 Macc* 1:16:, "Wisdom . . . is knowledge of things divine and human, and their causes." See DuPont-Sommer, *Le Quatrième Livre des Machabées*, 34–35; Hadas, *The Third and Fourth Books of Maccabees*, 149; G. W. E. Nickelsburg, *Jewish Literature Between the Bible and the Mishnah* (Philadelphia: Fortress, 1987) 224; Breitenstein, *Beobachtungen*, 159; P. L. Redditt, "The Concept of *Nomos* in Fourth Maccabees," *CBQ* 45 (1983) 260. Note, however, the caveat of Renehan, who points out that this definition was a "philosophical commonplace": "The extant evidence suggests that, even if this definition of σοφία is Stoic in origin, nevertheless . . . it did not remain an *exclusively* Stoic definition" ("The Greek Philosophic Background," 228, 229).

[42] *4 Macc* 12:13; see Dupont-Sommer, *Le Quatrième Livre des Machabées*, 56; Hadas, *The Third and Fourth Books of Maccabees*, 208; Klauck, *4 Makkabäerbuch*, 735.

[43] *4 Macc* 5:19–21: "you must not regard it as a minor sin for us to eat unclean food; minor sins are just as weighty as great sins, for in each case the law is

If a familiarity with and respect for Greek philosophy in general and Stoicism in particular on the part of its author is thus obvious, one of the underlying concerns of *4 Maccabees* is nonetheless the challenge such thinking might pose to traditional Jewish piety. How can the Jew who accepts the fundamental premises of Greek philosophy continue to affirm the validity and importance of observing peculiarly Jewish customs?

The issue emerges with particular clarity as the martyrdom of the aged Eleazar during the persecution of Antiochus is recounted. In *4 Maccabees*, the story is recast to include an intellectual exchange between Antiochus and the "philosopher" Eleazar.[44] In an attempt to persuade Eleazar to eat pork in a symbolic act of apostasy, Antiochus offers a critique of Judaism from the perspective of the "enlightened" Greek.[45] The critique, in short, is that "the religion of the Jews" (ἡ Ιουδαίων θρησκεία) is not really a philosophy at all, and a "nonsensical" philosophy at best (5:7, 11). Two specific charges are leveled: that adherence to Judaism is not reasonable (5:11; cf. 5:22); and that the Jewish law is out of step with nature (5:8–9).[46]

---

despised." For a comparison with the relevant Stoic idea, see Dupont-Sommer, *Le Quatrième Livre des Machabées*, 55, 107, nn. 19–21; also Breitenstein, *Beobachtungen*, 159. According to Hadas, *4 Maccabees* "significantly diverges" from the Stoics in this matter by retaining a distinction between minor and great sins, though it is not altogether clear whether he believes this to be a *conscious* divergence; see *The Third and Fourth Books of Maccabees*, 172f, n. 21, and note further p. 173, n. 23. Redditt is more explicit: "the author seems to distance himself slightly from the Stoic notion that all errors are everywhere alike in severity" ("The Concept of *Nomos*," 254). Renehan, with whom, at least on this matter, I am in substantial agreement, remarks that "I myself cannot comprehend how the clear statement in verse 20 can be construed as anything but general agreement (intended or not) with the Stoic teaching"; see "The Greek Philosophic Background," 230, and further 229–31. The author's point, after all, is that all sins are ultimately *equally* serious. Cf. deSilva, *4 Maccabees*, 106–7.

[44] *4 Maccabees* 5; cf. 2 Macc 6:18–31, upon which *4 Maccabees* most likely depends (Hadas, *The Third & Fourth Books of Maccabees*, 92–95; Klauck, *4 Makkabäerbuch* 654–57; deSilva, *4 Maccabees*, 28–29). 2 Maccabees neither places Antiochus at the scene nor describes Eleazar as a "philosopher"; with respect to the latter, cf. *4 Macc* 5:7, 21; 7:7, 9, 21; and 5:4 in some manuscripts; also 8:1, on the seven brothers.

[45] *4 Macc* 6:21–22. Hadas characterizes Antiochus's critique as forwarded "on the basis of the Stoic philosophy which he [sc. Antiochus] assumes Eleazar follows" (*The Third & Fourth Books of Maccabees*, 170, n. 7); cf. Klauck, *4 Makkabäerbuch*, 710. Note, *pace* Hadas, that this assumption on the part of Antiochus is accurate; see below.

[46] These overlapping points are supplemented by two further arguments which are not, however, directed against Judaism *per se*: Eleazar's capitulation in this matter would be the expedient course of action (5:6, 10–12); and finally, even if Eleazar's piety should have some divine sanction, his transgression would be mitigated by the fact that it was committed under compulsion (5:13).

The author finds his solution to this challenge in the Stoic concept of a natural law. On the lips of Eleazar and throughout *4 Maccabees*, the claim is developed that the Torah accords with both "right reason" and human nature.

Human Reason and Jewish Law

It is clear from both Antiochus's critique and Eleazar's rebuttal that the underlying claim of Eleazar—and the author of *4 Maccabees*—is that adherence to the Torah is to be viewed not only as the "philosophy" of the Jews, but a philosophy that is supremely rational. Having first explained the necessity of fidelity to that law under any circumstances,[47] Eleazar begins to speak of life according to law as "our philosophy," correctly perceiving the basic thrust of Antiochus's argument: "You mock at our philosophy as though our living under it were contrary to reason."[48] He defends the reasonableness of his "philosophy" by asserting that the law trains its adherents in the virtues and, conversely, teaches control of the passions:

> [our philosophy] teaches us temperance so that we are in control of all our pleasures and desires;[49] and it gives us a thorough training in courage so that we willingly endure all hardship; and it teaches us justice so that whatever our different attitudes may be we retain a sense of balance; and it instructs us in piety so that we most highly reverence the only living God. Therefore, we do not eat unclean food ..."[50]

With Eleazar's claim that observance of the Jewish law leads to virtue and control of "pleasures and desires," we are immediately reminded of the author's central thesis: that reason should be master of the passions.[51] The Torah, that is, functions vis-à-vis the passions and

---

[47] *4 Macc* 5:16–21; cf. Antiochus's argument in 5:13.

[48] *4 Macc* 5:22: χλευάζεις δὲ ἡμῶν τὴν φιλοσοφίαν ὥσπερ οὐ μετὰ εὐλογιστίας ἐν αὐτῇ βιούντων. All translations of *4 Maccabees*, unless otherwise indicated, are taken from Anderson, "4 Maccabees."

[49] The early Stoics would not, of course, have spoken in terms of "control" of the passions, but rather in terms of their elimination; see further Long and Sedley, *The Hellenistic Philosophers*, 1.410–23. It is to be observed in this connection that the understanding of the passions in *4 Maccabees* is more in line with that of Posidonius and other detractors of the monistic psychology of the earlier Stoics; see, e.g., *4 Macc* 3:5 and 2:21. See further Renehan, "The Greek Philosophic Background," 226–27; deSilva, *4 Maccabees*, 52–54.

[50] *4 Macc* 5:23–25.

[51] For the association of pleasure and desire with the passions, see the author's discussion of the latter in 1:20–29.

the virtues precisely as does human reason.[52] In fact, he claims, just as the creator gave humanity an intellect as its "sacred guide," so too did he give a law to the intellect; thus, he says with a distinctly Stoic ring, the one who lives in accord with this law "shall reign over a kingdom that is temperate and just and good and brave."[53] The "divine law" protects reason in its struggle to maintain dominance over the passions;[54] reason, in fact, dominates the passions precisely "through the law" (διὰ τὸν νόμον).[55] The correlation of reason and law is such that the author can simply pass from ὁ λογισμός to ὁ νόμος as though the two are simply synonymous.[56] Indeed, Exod 20:17 can be cited as proof of reason's ability to dominate the passions: "Surely, then, since the Law tells us not to covet (μὴ ἐπιθυμεῖν), I should the much more readily persuade you that reason has the power to control the desires (τῶν ἐπιθυμιῶν)."[57]

The relationship between human reason and the Torah is spelled out systematically in 1:15–17, where λογισμός is defined.

> λογισμός, I suggest, is intellect selecting with right reason (νοῦς μετὰ ὀρθοῦ λόγου προτιμῶν) the life of wisdom. Wisdom, I submit, is knowledge of things divine and human, and of their causes. And this wisdom, I assume, is the culture we acquire from the Law (ἡ τοῦ νόμου παιδεία) through which we learn the things of God reverently and the things of men to our worldly advantage.[58]

In *4 Maccabees*'s usage, therefore, λογισμός denotes not merely "reason," but particularly the "right reason" that amounts to wisdom

---

[52] On the relation between the passions, the virtues and reason, see esp. *4 Macc* 1:2–4, 6, 13–30. Note that the verb κρατέω, used in 5:22 in connection with the Jewish philosophy's instruction in the domination of the pleasures and desires, is used routinely in *4 Maccabees* in connection with reason's control of the passions; see the index of Dupont-Sommer (*Le Quatrième Livre des Machabées*, 170), under κρατέω, for references.

[53] *4 Macc* 2:23: καθ᾽ ὅν πολιτευόμενος βασιλεύσει βασιλείαν σώφρονά τε καὶ δικαίαν καὶ ἀγαθὴν καὶ ἀνδρείαν; cf. Diog. Laert. 7.122.

[54] *4 Macc* 11:27.

[55] *4 Macc* 2:8, 14. Conversely, it is "through reason" (διὰ τὸν λογισμόν) that one is brought under the rule of law (2:9).

[56] Noted also by Dupont-Sommer, *Le Quatrième Livre des Machabées*, 38, 94, n. 10; Hadas, *The Third & Fourth Books of Maccabees*, 154, n. 10; Breitenstein, *Beobachtungen*, 171; Anderson, "4 Maccabees," 546, note b.

[57] *4 Macc* 2:6. This reasoning is to be understood in light of *4 Macc* 5:26, on which see below.

[58] Anderson's translation of νοῦς μετὰ ὀρθοῦ λόγου προτιμῶν in 1:15 as "the mind making a deliberate choice" is rather interpretive, and quite obscures the Stoic connection. Hadas's (*The Third and Fourth Books of Maccabees*, 149) and Redditt's ("The Concept of *Nomos*," 258) translation "correct judgment," is more appropriate, but still fails to make the Stoic reference explicit.

and virtue.[59] And this wisdom is nothing other than that which is taught in the Torah.[60] The upshot of this string of definitions is that observance of the law is, by definition, life in accord with "right reason"[61]—an association which is by now quite familiar from the Stoic sources.

It is no doubt this core conviction that has given rise to the author's choice of Jews martyred during the persecution of Antiochus as the chief exempla of his formal thesis that "pious reason is absolute master of the passions." Moreover, it is in this light that his peculiar and characteristic phrase "pious reason" is itself to be understood.[62] Like "right reason" itself, ultimately, piety too in *4 Maccabees* consists "einzig und allein in *Gesetzesgehorsam.*"[63] The treatise, that is, is not merely concerned with the ability of reason to master the passions; its interest lies, more precisely, in the mastery of the passions by right reason *specifically as it finds expression in the Torah.*[64]

Human Nature and Jewish Law

The other criticism of Judaism raised by Antiochus in his attempt to persuade Eleazar to eat pork is more immediately to the point: "Why should you abhor eating the excellent meat of this animal which nature has freely bestowed on us? . . . it is wrong to spurn nature's good gifts."[65] This providential and anthropocentric understanding of the existence of the pig echoes the Stoic view of the

---

[59] As opposed to the "weak reason" (τὸν ἀσθενῆ λογισμόν) of those who do not "with all their heart make piety their first concern," and who are thus unable to master their passions; see *4 Macc* 7:17–23.

[60] Note that the law, like wisdom itself, is also said to concern things both divine and human (1:16–17).

[61] Cf. Heidland, "λογίζομαι," 286: "The norm of λογισμός . . . is the Mosaic Law (2:6, 14). But for him this is identical with the principle of reason."

[62] *4 Macc* 1:1; 6:31; 7:16; 8:1; 13:1; 15:23; 16:1, 4. See further S. Lauer, "Eusebes Logismos in IV Macc," *JJS* 6 (1955) 170–71; R. B. Townshend, "The Fourth book of Maccabees," *APOT* 2.664, 666–67; Breitenstein, *Beobachtungen,* 168–71; Redditt, "The Concept of *Nomos,*" 258–59; deSilva, *4 Maccabees,* 54.

[63] Breitenstein, *Beobachtungen,* 171; emphasis his.

[64] Redditt describes the theme of reason's dominance over the passions as "only the formal and not the crucial focus of 4 Maccabeees," and finds the central issue, following Breitenstein, to be rather the importance of piety, which is to say obedience to the law ("The Concept of *Nomos,*" 249); cf. Breitenstein, *Beobachtungen,* 171. See also deSilva, *4 Maccabees,* 44: "obedience to the Torah is the primary concern, for which the philosophical thesis becomes a sort of cipher."

[65] *4 Macc* 5:8–9.

relation of human to non-human creation, and is in fact reminiscent of a sentiment found in Cicero's *De Legibus*:

> ... Nature has lavishly yielded such a wealth of things adapted to
> man's convenience and use that what she produces seems intended as
> a gift to us ... and this is true ... also of the animals; for it is clear
> that some of them have been created to be man's slaves, some to sup-
> ply him with their products, and others to serve as his food.[66]

Eleazar counters the point raised by Antiochus with his own argument from providence:

> Believing that God established the law, we know that the creator of
> the world, in giving us the law, conforms it to our nature (κατὰ φύσιν
> ἡμῖν συμπαθεῖ νομοθετῶν ὁ τοῦ κόσμου κτίστης). He has commanded us
> to eat whatever will be well suited to our souls (τὰ μὲν οἰκειωθησόμενα
> ἡμῶν ταῖς ψυχαῖς), and has forbidden us to eat food that is the reverse.[67]

Eleazar, in short, argues that it follows from the premises that (i)
God is creator of the world; (ii) God is the legislator of Jewish law;
and (iii) God is concerned for humanity, that the law God has legislated takes the nature of the human being into account. The dietary
restrictions contained in that law, therefore, must be considered as in
step with human nature.[68] Thus the Torah as presented in *4 Maccabees*

---

[66] *De Leg.* 1.25; cf. *De Nat. Deor.* 1.37; Philo *Opif.* 77; see further the references
cited by Kenter (*De Legibus*, 110), who describes this passage from Cicero as "specifically
Stoic."

[67] *4 Macc* 5:26.

[68] Cf. de Silva, *4 Maccabees*, 134. Redditt, "The Concept of *Nomos*," 256f, argues
that κατὰ φύσιν here refers to φύσις as the general world order rather than human
nature in particular. Against this, however, are the following considerations. First,
Chrysippus himself used this same phrase to denote human as well as cosmic nature
when speaking of "life in accord with nature" (Diog. Laert. 7.89). Second, such a
use of the term would be unique among its eight total appearances in *4 Maccabees*.
(Against Redditt [*ibid.*, 256], 5:8f clearly uses "nature," in a manner reminiscent of
the Stoics, with reference to the *deity* as the giver of gifts, not primarily "a structure in harmony with which men ought to live.") Third, and most importantly, it
is clear from 5:26 that the author regards biblical law in any case as enacted with
the nature of the human being in mind: God "has commanded us to to eat whatever will be well suited to our souls and has forbidden us to eat the reverse"; in
fact, the specific association of the law with τὰ μὲν οἰκειωθησόμενα ἡμῶν ταῖς ψυχαῖς
draws on the Stoic concept of οἰκείωσις (see below). Whether or not Redditt's claim
that there is "no grammatical warrant" for Hadas's apparent translation of the
dative ἡμῖν in *4 Macc* 5:8 as indicating possession is valid (though cf. Smyth, *Greek
Grammar*, §1480), it is not necessary to conclude that the nature in question is not
human nature: the phrase κατὰ φύσιν at the very least is intended to explain, in
Stoic terminology, what it means that God ἡμῖν συμπαθεῖ in giving the law.

can fairly be described as natural law—though, perhaps like the early Stoics themselves, the author never actually uses this term.

Dupont-Sommer saw in this equation of the law of Moses with the law of nature a concept similar to that found in Philo, and one rooted ultimately in the Stoic theory of law.[69] For Hadas, however, Eleazar's assertion that the law of Moses corresponds to the nature of the human being

> is not, as it has been taken to be, a mechanical synthesis of Judaism and Stoicism, but rather an affirmation of the one (the Law as divinely ordained) and a refutation of the other. Man is not to bring himself into harmony with an impersonal natural law; rather has the Law itself been designed to conform to and serve the nature of man, who is paramount, as the dietary regulations prove.[70]

Hadas thus understood Eleazar's response to Antiochus's argument regarding the relation between Jewish law and nature to consist in the point that "the Stoic principle [of life κατὰ φύσιν] can . . . not be invoked as an argument to disregard the dietary prescriptions of the law" since such prescriptions "are not necessarily in accord with the Stoic principle of living according to nature" to begin with.[71] Anderson echoes Hadas's sentiment regarding the difference between Eleazar and the Stoics:

> Whereas the Stoic thought of nature's sovereignty and man's need to adapt himself to nature's gifts and demands, the (Jewish) thought here is of the sovereignty of the creator God who graciously confers on man the Law that is adapted to man's needs and nature, the dietary regulations, for instance, being given to man as morally purifying.[72]

At least in the formulation given by Anderson, this contrast between the Stoic and Jewish understanding of law is based upon a rather transparently apologetic comparison of the "grace" centered Judaeo-Christian tradition with its Greco-Roman counterpart. In any case, the contrast is rooted in a fundamental misapprehension of the Stoic understanding of the goal as life κατὰ φύσιν. From the time of Chrysippus, the φύσις in accord with which one was to live was understood at least as much with respect to human nature as to

---

[69] Dupont-Sommer, *Le Quatrième Livre des Machabées*, 39–40; cf. deSilva, *4 Maccabees*, 109; cf. 134.

[70] Hadas, *The Third and Fourth Books of Maccabees*, 174 n. 25.

[71] *Ibid.*, n. 26.

[72] Anderson, "4 Maccabees," p. 550, note g.

cosmic Nature.[73] The Stoic reasoning in this matter is in fact quite analogous to that of Eleazar, depending as it does upon a belief in a providential creator. Given divine providence, the Stoics argued, it is unlikely that when creating an animal

> nature should estrange the living thing from itself or that she should leave the creature she has made without either estrangement from or affection for its own constitution (οὔτε γὰρ ἀλλοτριῶσαι εἰκὸς ἦν αὐτὸ (αὐτῷ) τὸ ζῷον, οὔτε ποιήσασαν αὐτό, μήτ' ἀλλοτριῶσαι μητ' οἰκειῶσαι). We are forced then to conclude that nature in constituting the animal made it near and dear to itself (οἰκειῶσαι πρὸς ἑαυτό); for so it comes to repel all that is injurious (τὰ βλάπτοντα) and give free access to all that is serviceable or akin to it (τὰ οἰκεῖα).[74]

In fact, this doctrine of οἰκείωσις, as we have seen, provided the starting point for all of Stoic ethics by ensuring that all animals, human and non-human, naturally strive to live κατὰ φύσιν, that is, in accord with *their own* natures. It is therefore quite striking that Eleazar alludes to this Stoic doctrine when countering Antiochus's charge that the Jewish law is out of step with nature: God, being both creator and lawgiver, "has commanded us to eat whatever will be well suited to our souls (τὰ οἰκειωθησόμενα ἡμῶν ταῖς ψυχαῖς), and has forbidden us to eat food that is the reverse" (5:26).[75]

Conclusion: Torah as Natural Law in 4 Maccabees

4 Maccabees opens with an exhortation to "give earnest attention to philosophy," which is itself described as an "indispensable branch of knowledge."[76] If indispensable, however, Greek philosophy is nonetheless secondary in importance to this work, the primary concern of which is to promote observance of the Torah. As David deSilva has put it: "the author uses Greek rhetorical forms and philosophical ideas in order to make being Jewish in a thoroughly Hellenized world both tenable and sensible."[77] The divinely ordained natural law is not, as for the Stoics, defined as "right reason"; rather, "right reason"

---

[73] Diog. Laert. 7.89. See further on this point Engberg-Pedersen, *The Stoic Theory of Oikeiosis, passim.*

[74] Diog. Laert. 7.85.

[75] So also Breitenstein, *Beobachtungen*, 160; Klauck, *4 Makkabäerbuch*, 713.

[76] *4 Macc* 1:1–2. I render τῇ φιλοσοφίᾳ more generically than Anderson's "to my philosophical exposition;" cf. the RSV.

[77] *4 Maccabees*, 11. deSilva provides a nice discussion of the social and cultural setting of the work in his chapter 2, esp. pp. 43–46.

is itself ultimately defined with reference to divine law—indeed, the law of the Jews. The ideal life which Greek philosophers in general characterized as virtue, and which the Stoics in particular conceived in terms of natural law is, according to *4 Maccabees*, prescribed in the Torah. Indeed, it is remarkable that appeal is made to the Torah's status as natural law particularly in connection with its proscription of pork: Jewish law does not correspond to natural law merely inasmuch as it reflects the Greek virtues, but in its legislation of peculiarly Jewish customs as well.[78] Thus can it be said that "the children of the Hebrews alone are invincible in defense of virtue."[79]

The fact that Greek philosophical concepts are used in *4 Maccabees* in the service of this larger Jewish agenda significantly impacts the terms of their presentation. We have already discussed the author's oft-noted predilection for the phrase "pious reason"; scarcely typical of the Stoic sources, this expression is apparently the coinage of an author interested in subordinating reason to the Torah. Dupont-Sommer has noted, too, the consistent use of the term λογισμός rather than the more typically Stoic λόγος or ὀρθὸς λόγος.[80] Certainly not owing to his lack of familiarity with the latter,[81] it is quite possible that the author consciously avoids the more usual Stoic terms in order to distance himself from certain aspects of Stoicism which he finds distasteful. In particular, he may have considered these terms to be too suggestive of a divine principle immanent in the world;

---

[78] Note, against Hadas (*The Third and Fourth Books of Maccabees*, 174 n. 25) and Klauck (*4 Makkabäerbuch*, 713), that the interpretation of the Jewish dietary restrictions in *4 Maccabees* differs significantly from that of *The Letter of Aristeas*. In *4 Maccabees*, the dietary prescriptions are *not* merely a symbolic, if nonetheless necessary, component of Jewish law; rather they correspond to the actual nature of the human being. Cf. Dupont-Sommer, *Le Quatrième Livre des Machabées*, 40–41.

[79] Though one might reasonably conclude that the author of *4 Maccabees*, if pressed, would argue for the corollary that all people, not merely Jews, should thus live in accord with Torah, there is no such "evangelistic" dimension to this work. His primary concern is to formulate a defense of Jewish customs in the face of the challenge posed by hellenistic philosophical conceptions; arguments for a subsequent proposition regarding obedience by non-Jews are apparently beyond the scope of his concern, and are in any case not explicitly formulated in *4 Maccabees*.

[80] *Le Quatrième Livre des Machabées*, 39–40.

[81] Indeed λογισμός is defined in terms of "right reason" from the outset (*4 Macc* 1:15). The only other reference to "right reason" in *4 Maccabees* comes in the wordplay of *4 Macc* 6:7, where it is said that Eleazar's λογισμός remained ὀρθός despite the "bending" of his body as Antiochus tried to force him to apostatize from the law under torture. Klauck recognizes this passage as "Reminiszenz an den stoischen Leitbegriff des ὀρθός λόγος" (*4 Makkabäerbuch*, 715).

notably, just as λογισμός suggests human intellectual activity in particular, there is in fact no hint of anything analogous to the cosmic dimension of the Stoic theory of law or *logos* in *4 Maccabees*.[82]

It must not be overlooked, finally, that the significance of the Torah is not in any case limited to its status as natural law in *4 Maccabees*. Alongside this more universalistic notion lies a distinct interest in the Torah's significance vis-à-vis the covenant which the creator made with Israel in particular.[83] The account of the events surrounding the persecution of Antiochus, in fact, has a positively deuteronomistic flavor. The peace the Jews enjoyed prior to the persecution was due to "their observance of the Law," and it was Jason's "disregard for the Law" which provoked the wrath of "Divine Justice" and the rise of the "arrogant and terrible" Antiochus, the instrument of vengeance.[84] The peace was restored only through the faithfulness of Eleazar and the anonymous mother and her seven sons, who "revived the observance of the Law in their land and repulsed their enemies' siege."[85] In *4 Maccabees*, the Stoic notion of natural law walks hand in hand with the Jewish notion of covenantal nomism.[86]

THE *APOSTOLIC CONSTITUTIONS*

Given the common synthesis of Greek and Jewish traditions evident in the early Christian literature in general, it is not surprising that Christian authors, too, attempted to incorporate the Stoic theory of natural law into their own religious thought. The *Apostolic Constitutions* provides an example that is of special interest for our purposes for two reasons. First of all, this work describes the natural law comprised by human reason as an "implanted law" (ἔμφυτος νόμος), and does so particularly from the same theoretical viewpoint that led to an analogous usage in the Greek source of Cicero's *De Legibus*: the "implanted law" is correlated with an innate endowment of "seeds of divine knowledge" (τὰ σπέρματα τῆς θεογνωσίας), also called

---

[82] Cf. Townshend, "The Fourth Book of Maccabees," 666; deSilva, *4 Maccabees*, 54.
[83] See deSilva, 133–37.
[84] *4 Macc* 3:20; 4:15–22.
[85] *4 Macc* 18:4.
[86] A similar tension between universalistic and covenantal notions of the law is found in Sirach; see L. G. Perdue, *Wisdom and Creation: The Theology of Wisdom Literature* (Nashville: Abingdon, 1994) 284–85.

"implanted knowledge," which consist particularly in the ability to
distinguish ethical contraries. This work thus provides important
confirmation of the interpretation of Cicero's use of the phrase
"implanted reason" offered in the preceding chapter. Secondly, the
Christian redactor of the *Apostolic Constitutions*, like Philo and the
author of *4 Maccabees*—and, as will be argued in the following chapter, like the author of the Letter of James—finds a written expression of natural law in the law of Moses.

The passages that are most critical for our purposes, however,
have often been considered as Jewish (i.e., non-Christian) in origin.
A few words must be said, therefore, regarding the source problem
surrounding these passages before we analyze the presentation of the
"implanted law" in the *Apostolic Constitutions*.

The Question of a Non-Christian Prayer Collection

The *Apostolic Constitutions* is a fourth century compilation and re-
editing of earlier works, only some of which are otherwise extant
today. Books 1–6 rely heavily on the *Didascalia*, while portions of
books 7 and 8 draw on the *Didache* and the *Apostolic Tradition* of
Hippolytus.[87] The bulk of the passages that are of interest to us
appear in books 7 and 8 in a collection of prayers of unknown origin. It has been widely agreed, since late in the 19th century, that
some or all of these prayers were not originally Christian, but rather
Jewish prayers slightly re-touched by a Christian hand.[88]

Evidence cited for the non-Christian origin of these prayers is of
three kinds: similarities to known Jewish prayers; the presence, more
generally, of Jewish ideas and themes; and traces of Christian redaction. Kaufmann Kohler, the first scholar to forward such a thesis,
concluded from a comparison of *AC* 7.33–38 with the Hebrew Seven
Benedictions that the former represents a Christian version of the
latter.[89] Wilhelm Bousset, apparently unaware of the work of Kohler,

---

[87] See D. A. Fiensy, *Prayers Alleged to be Jewish: An Examination of the Constitutiones Apostolorum* (BJS 65; Chico, CA: Scholars Press, 1985) 19–41, with his references to previous research; further R. H. Connolly, *Didascalia Apostolorum: The Syriac Version Translated and Accompanied by the Verona Latin Fragments, With an Introduction and Notes* (Oxford: Clarendon Press, 1929) xx–xxi.

[88] For a history of the discussion see Fiensy, *Prayers Alleged to be Jewish*, 1–17.

[89] K. Kohler, "Ueber die Ursprünge und Grundformen der synagogalen Liturgie. Eine Studie," *MGWJ* 37 (1893) 441–51, 489–97; *idem*, "The Origin and Composition of the Eighteen Benedictions with a Translation of the Corresponding Essene Prayers in the Apostolic Constitutions," *HUCA* 1 (1924) 410–25; repr. in *Contributions to the*

began his argument for the non-Christian origin of some of the prayers of *AC* 7 and 8 with a narrower comparison of *AC* 7.35 to the Hebrew Kedusha.[90] He then proceeded to point out the clear Christian redaction of the Sabbath prayer at *AC* 7.36.[91] In light of the precedent set by these two rather obvious instances of Christian redaction clustered together in *AC* 7, he went on to examine 7.37, 7.38, 7.34, and 7.33 more liberally, arguing primarily from the presence of Jewish features and the lack of distinctively Christian ones, and came ultimately to a conclusion quite similar to that of Kohler: "the entire prayer collection in the *Constitutions* 7.33–38 is borrowed from the synagogue."[92] He observed further the striking points of contact shared by 7.34 and the long prayer at 8.12, arguing that the two prayers represented distinct redactions of the same Jewish original.[93] Having established the non-Christian origin of this core of prayers, Bousset went on to argue a bit more cautiously for the similar origin of still more prayers from *AC* 7 and 8, based on both the presence of Jewish ideas and similarities in thought among the prayers themselves.[94] E. R. Goodenough worked to clarify the theological tendency in the prayers and, finding it at work in other sections of books 7 and 8, expanded the list of passages collected by Bousset still further.[95]

Scientific Study of Jewish Liturgy (ed. J. J. Petuchowski; New York: Ktav, 1970) 52–90. This line of argument has recently been developed by David Fiensy, who explicitly enumerates the points of contact that Kohler, apparently, felt were self-evident. Fiensy, however, rightly abandons Kohler's ascription of the original prayers to "Essenes." See *Prayers Alleged to be Jewish*, 129–34, 228–31.

[90] W. Bousset, "Eine jüdische Gebetssammlung im siebenten Buch der apostolischen Konstitutionen," *Nachrichten von der Königlichen Gesellschaft der Wissenschaften zu Göttingen: Philologisch-historische Klasse* [1915] 438–85; repr. in *idem, Religionsgeschichtliche Studien: Aufsätze zur Religionsgeschichte des Hellenistischen Zeitalters* (ed. A. F. Verheule; NovTSup 50; Leiden: E. J. Brill, 1979) 231–86; all references are to the reprinted edition. On *AC* 7.35, see pp. 231–38. Note that Bousset makes no reference to Kohler, nor is he aware of the similarities of *AC* 7.33–38 to the Seven Benedictions; cf. Fiensy, *Prayers Alleged to be Jewish*, 1.

[91] Bousset, "Eine jüdische Gebetssammlung," 238–41.

[92] *Ibid.*, 265: "Und so wäre denn nachgewiesen, daß die ganze Gebetssammlung in den Konstitutionen VII 33–38 der Synagoge entlehnt ist"; see pp. 241–65, noting also his interesting comparison of *AC* 7.38 with a prayer form described by Philo at *Spec. Leg.* 1.211 on pp. 243f.

[93] Eine jüdische Gebetssammlung," 244–259.

[94] *Ibid.*, 265 82.

[95] Goodenough (*By Light, Light*, 306–36), who was also apparently unaware of Kohler's work, expanded Bousset's collection to include also 7.26.1–3, 8.16.3, and 8.40.2–4; he further included 8.6.5–8 and 8.41.2–5 whereas Bousset suggested only 8.6.5 and 8.41.4–5.

The argument that *AC* 7.33–38 as a whole represents a Christian version of a Jewish prayer collection, especially in the form given it by Fiensy, is compelling. Fiensy demonstrates that the prayers in this section of the *Apostolic Constitutions* share not only similarities in order and content, but also a degree of verbal equivalence to the Hebrew Seven Benedictions. The argument from the rather obvious Christian redaction of the Sabbath prayer at 7.36 is likewise impressive, and can be taken as a confirmation of the hypothesis regarding 7.33–38.

Arguments based solely on the presence of Jewish ideas or the lack of distinctively Christian ones, however, are much less persuasive. The former arguments are dubious from the start given the broad interaction with Jewish traditions on the part of Christians in general, while the latter suffer from the circularity that results from the systematic excision of those distinctively Christian features that *are* present in the prayers as later additions.[96] Indeed, as Fiensy has pointed out, at least one of the "Jewish" elements of the prayers enumerated by Bousset is in fact characteristic of the Christian compiler's own redactional work.[97] It is precisely this failure to take into account the redactional tendencies of the compiler of the *Apostolic Constitutions*, as evidenced in his use of known sources, that is most problematic for the work of Bousset and Goodenough.[98] Such evidence is particularly important with respect to our present concern: the correlation of the Mosaic law with a law of nature innate in the human animal. Examination of the redactor's handling of *Didascalia* with an eye to this theme is quite instructive.

Characteristic of the *Didascalia*, the primary source for the first six books of the *Apostolic Constitutions*, is the notion that biblical law actually consists of two separate bodies of legislation:[99] the law properly

---

[96] In this connection one might note with Fiensy (*Prayers Alleged to be Jewish*, 148) that the caution that had characterized the work of Bousset in identifying originally Jewish prayers beyond 7.33–38 and 8.12 was entirely lost on Goodenough, who thought that Bousset's "fine methodology" had established with certainty the Jewish origin of all of these prayers; see *By Light, Light*, 306, 336.

[97] Fiensy, *Prayers Alleged to be Jewish*, 136f, referring to the assembling of lists of heroes from Israel's past.

[98] The introduction of this type of evidence into the discussion of the prayers is the chief contribution of Fiensy. A redactional analysis of *AC* 7.33 has also recently been offered by P. W. van der Horst, in a paper presented at the 1997 meeting of the *Society of Biblical Literature* entitled "The Jewish Prayers in the Apostolic Constitutions." I am grateful to Prof. van der Horst for giving me a copy of this paper, and was gratified to find that we are in substantial agreement on several key issues in the interpretation of the prayers.

[99] See the discussion of Connolly, *Didascalia*, lvii–lxix. All translations of the

so called, which is essentially the ten commandments,[100] and the
deuterosis, which consists primarily of the codes concerning temple
sacrifice and purity.[101] The latter, given to Israel only as a punishment for their idolatry at Sinai in the first place, is believed to have
been "abolished" by Christ. The former, on the other hand, is
"renewed and fulfilled and affirmed" by Christ.[102] Indeed, the law
properly so called "is life to them that keep it."[103] It is thus the
bishop's duty "before all" to "be a good discriminator between the
Law and the Second Legislation."[104]

This distinction within the Mosaic law is repeated in the first six
books of the *Apostolic Constitutions*, where the compiler draws on the
Didascalia. At the same time, however, several significant changes are
introduced. First of all, the redactor shows himself to be rather squeamish regarding the absolute abolition of the *deuterosis*: while he preserves
a number of the *Didascalia*'s statements that Christ took away its
commands, he repeatedly adds the stipulation "though not all of
them."[105] His understanding of the original purpose of the *deuterosis*,
similarly, is substantially less negative: God is now said to give Israel
the laws regarding sacrifice and purity not simply as punishment,
but to help them return "to that law which is sown by [God] into
the nature of all human beings" (ἐκεῖνον τὸν νόμον τὸν ὑπ᾽ ἐμοῦ τῇ

Didascalia are those of Connolly, and are cited according the page numbers of his
volume. I have also depended upon Connolly's edition of the Latin fragments of
this work. Translations of the *Apostolic Constitutions* are my own unless otherwise
noted, though for passages from books 7 and 8 I have drawn liberally upon the
translations of D. R. Darnell ("Hellenistic Synagogal Prayers," *OTP*, 677–97), Fiensy
(*Prayers Alleged to be Jewish*, 43–127), and Goodenough (*By Light, Light*, 306–36); see
also the translation in *ANF* 7.391–508. For both the *Didascalia* and the *Apostolic
Constitutions* I rely on the edition of F. X. Funk, *Didascalia et Constitutiones Apostolororm*
(Paderborn: Schoeningh, 1905), large sections of which are reprinted by Fiensy.

[100] The Latin characteristically speaks of *decalogus et iudicia*; the Syriac is consistently rendered by Connolly as "ten words and judgments" (Connolly, *Didascalia*,
14f and esp. 218f). Connolly (*ibid.*, lxvii) understands these "judgments" to refer to
the legislation given at Exod 21–23. Notably, the decalogue's Sabbath commandment is interpreted by the author of the *Didascalia* as a "type of the (final) rest,"
and is thus not generally to be observed by Christians; see Connolly, *Didascalia*,
233–38; cf. 190–92.

[101] Cf. the lists of the types of laws covered by the *deuterosis* in Connolly, *Didascalia*,
218, 222, and 252.

[102] This approach to biblical law is not uncommon in early Christian literature;
cf., e.g., Ptolemy's *Letter to Flora*; Irenaeus, *A. H.* 4.14–15; Ps.-Clem. *Rec.* 1.35–39;
and more generally H. Bietenhard, "Deuterosis," *RAC* 3 (1957) 842–49.

[103] See esp. Connolly, *Didascalia*, 218–230; see further his General Index under
"law" and "*Deuterosis*." On the law as "life," see *ibid.*, 228.

[104] *Ibid.*, 34.

[105] Cf. *AC* 1.6: εἰ καὶ μὴ πάντων; cf. 6.22.1 and 6.22.5: εἰ καὶ μὴ πάντα.

φύσει καταβληθέντα πᾶσιν ἀνθρώποις).[106] On the whole, one can fairly say that the redactor has a much more positive appraisal of the Torah—and not simply the ten commandments—than does his source. In fact, the whole notion of a *deuterosis* never surfaces at all in books seven and eight, when the redactor relies on other sources.[107]

On the other hand, the compiler's redactional additions to the *Didascalia* in books 1–6 do include several aspects of the treatment of the law found in books 7–8. That which the *Didascalia* considers the "law" properly so called is repeatedly identified as "natural law" (φυσικὸς νόμος).[108] Similarly, the patriarchs are described as having been "moved by natural law from themselves";[109] and this law is in fact said to be "sown" by God "into the nature of all human beings."[110] These redactional elements clearly anticipate the fuller discussion of that law variously described as ἔμφυτος or φυσικός in books 7 and 8.

The arguments of Bousset and Goodenough regarding the non-Christian origin of additional prayers from books 7 and 8 are considerably weakened when such characteristic concerns of the compiler of the *Apostolic Constitutions* are taken into account. Indeed, Goodenough

---

[106] *AC* 6.20.10.

[107] The fact that the law/*deuterosis* dichotomy that is so prominent in books 1–6 has been entirely left behind in books 7–8 is noteworthy. The only possible allusion to this doctrine in the latter books comes at 7.1.3, where *Didache*'s "way of life" is called φυσική, while the "way of death" is called "additional" (ἐπείσακτος). However, though on the face of it, the contrasting use of these two terms would seem to recall the compiler's treatment of the *Didascalia*'s law/*deuterosis* dichotomy (cf. *AC* 1.6.7–10 and 2.35.1), even this reference is quite problematic. For while the "way of life"—which is to say the "natural" way—is said to be the way "which the law also declares (7.2.1: καὶ ἔστιν αὕτη [sc. ἡ ὁδὸς τῆς ζωῆς], ἣν καὶ ὁ Νόμος διαγορεύει), the "way of death" is said to come not from God or Moses, as the *deuterosis* clearly does, but from the "adversary" (7.1.3: ἐξ ἐπιβουλῆς τοῦ ἀλλοτρίου; cf. 6.20, esp. 6.20.6–11). Compare in this connection the compiler's characteristic qualification of the *Didascalia*'s belief in Christ's abolition of the entire *deuterosis* (on which see immediately below). Certainly he would not wish to affirm that some elements of the "way of death" are still binding for Christians! Moreover, when the "way of death" is described at 7.14, there is no hint of the types of practices characteristic of the *deuterosis*; it is characterized, rather, simply by behaviors opposite to the "way of life."

[108] *AC* 1.6.8; 6.20.1–11; 6.22.5; 6.23.1; cf. 6.12.13 where the Noachide commands are described as "natural law." See in addition the redactional references to certain behaviors that are "contrary to nature," e.g., certain forms of sexual activity (*AC* 6.[28].1; 7.2.10) or not divorcing an adulterous wife (*AC* 6.14.4).

[109] *AC* 6.20.4: φυσικῷ δὲ νόμῳ κινηθέντας ἀφ᾽ ἑαυτῶν.

[110] *AC* 6.20.10: ἐκεῖνον τὸν νόμον τὸν ὑπ᾽ ἐμοῦ τῇ φύσει καταβληθέντα πᾶσιν ἀνθρώποις; the syntax here is difficult, but the intention is clear enough from the context of 6.20 and the thought of the *Constitutions* as a whole. See further below.

understood the conception of a natural law both innate in the human animal and written in the law of Moses to be one of the primary indications that the prayer collection originated in the context of the Jewish "Mystery" which he found attested above all in the writings of Philo of Alexandria.[111] So important was this element, in fact, that among the additions Goodenough made to Bousset's delineation of the collection was *AC* 7.26.1–3, which refers to the fact that God "sowed a law into the souls" of all human beings.[112] This statement, however, is a redactional addition to material taken from the *Didache*— a fact of which Goodenough was apparently unaware, and which considerably complicates his hypothesis.[113] Goodenough, moreover, reckoned neither with the references to the "natural law" which occur repeatedly as redactional elements in books 1–6, nor with the compiler's characteristic reluctance to endorse the *Didascalia*'s stark rejection of the *deuterosis*.[114] As noted above, Fiensy observed an analogous problem in the case of Bousset's singling out of the lists of Jewish heroes as distinctively Jewish elements of the prayers found in *AC* 7–8.

In sum, the redactor's clear interest in the association of biblical law with the law of nature, especially when coupled with his tendency to assemble lists of heroes from Jewish history, seriously compromises the arguments offered by Bousset and Goodenough for the non-Christian origin of many of these prayers. While *AC* 7.33–38, at least, almost certainly represents a Christian version of an originally non-Christian Jewish prayer collection, much of what Bousset

---

[111] Goodenough, *By Light, Light*, 348–50. What Goodenough saw as the chief indications of the Jewish "Mystery" in these prayers are just as easily understood as the simple incorporation of Greek philosophical ideas into Jewish or Christian thought. One should be careful not to confuse the two, as the Jewish (or Christian) adoption of Greek philosophical ideas—regardless of one's evaluation of Philo's philosophical and religious orientation—is, in and of itself, by no means necessarily suggestive of a "Mystery"; cf. in this respect the discussion of *4 Maccabees*, above.

[112] *AC* 7.26.3: νόμον κατεφύτευσας ἐν ταῖς ψυχαῖς ἡμῶν.

[113] Goodenough, *By Light, Light*, 334f; see Fiensy, *Prayers Alleged to be Jewish*, 22.

[114] Moreover, among the Greek philosophical terms which surface repeatedly in these prayers and which suggested to Goodenough the Jewish Mystery are several that are also characteristic of the author's redaction. Regarding πρόνοια (found in the prayers at *AC* 7.33.2; 7.34.5; 7.35.10; 7.39.2; 8.12.8, 30), Fiensy reports that "In every case where the word occurs in AC, where we can compare the AC with its source, the word has come from the compiler"; see *Prayers Alleged to be Jewish*, 169, and the passages listed on p. 204 n. 15. An examination of the term λογικός, particularly as descriptive of human as opposed to non-human animals, yields similar results (*ibid.*, 174, noting the passages listed on p. 204 n. 28).

and Goodenough found to be most distinctively "Jewish" about these
and the other prayers of *AC* 7–8 are in fact redactional elements
characteristic of the Christian compiler of the *Apostolic Constitutions*.[115]

It is possible, of course, that the redactor has taken over this association of the law of Moses with an innate natural law from an earlier prayer collection which was itself edited and incorporated into
his larger work.[116] One might find support for such a hypothesis in
the fact that a common source apparently underlies 7.34 and 8.12,
the latter of which presents the fullest account of this natural law.[117]
Certainly he got the idea from somewhere: it would seem rather
improbable that this fourth century compiler has come up with the
notion entirely on his own, especially since the incorporation of Stoic
ideas into conceptions of biblical law had long been accomplished.
Without further investigation, however, it can be assumed neither that
such a source existed, nor, if it did, that it was not itself a Christian
work. The prominence of this idea among the compiler's redactional
interests in any case warrants caution; it is clear in any event that
the ideas most characteristic of such a supposed source were also
characteristic of the redactor of the *Apostolic Constitutions* himself.[118]

Ultimately, whether these ideas come from a source—and whether
that source, further, was Christian or not—matters little for the present investigation. The philosophical concepts and terminology pre-

---

[115] So also Fiensy, *Prayers Alleged to be Jewish*, 143–44.

[116] van der Horst, who wrestles with a similar problem in the recurring phrase
"God of Abraham, Isaac and Jacob," formulates the difficulties in formulating such
hypotheses quite well: ". . . the formula 'God of Abraham, Isaac and Jacob' which
has such a close parallel in *Avoth* that it is generally taken to be part of the original Jewish prayer, was also *inserted twice into other texts by our compiler* (VII 26,3 and
VIII 40,3)! It could thus be argued that this formula is from the compiler's hand
as well, but in view of the parallel in *Avoth* it seems better not to do that. But the
matter does demonstrate painfully how difficult it is to separate tradition from redaction and how many uncertainties remain."

[117] This problem is deserving of more attention than can be given it in the present context. Neither does Fiensy go into this issue in detail; but it is interesting
that he finds the best parallels for such an underlying prayer in *Christian* sources;
see *Prayers Alleged to be Jewish*, 137–40.

[118] Cf. van der Horst, "The Jewish Prayers," who comments on *AC* 7.33.3 as
follows: ". . . the intervening words, 'by implanted knowledge and natural judgment
as well as through the teaching of the Law', reflect recurring motifs in the *AC*. The
words 'implanted' (ἔμφυτος) and 'natural' (φυσικός) belong to the compiler's favourites
in connection with the implanted law and natural knowledge, and his emphasis on
the value of the teaching(s) of the Law recurs throughout the *AC*."

date his work in any case, and the precedent for their incorporation into a theory of the Mosaic law had been established for centuries. Whatever his source for them, however, the Christian redactor
has made these ideas his own.

The Implanted Law and the Law of Moses

Scholarship on the prayers in books 7 and 8 of the *Apostolic Constitutions*
has been rather limited. What studies have been done have focused
primarily on the question of their possible Jewish origin, especially
in connection with the larger problem of the dependence of the early
Christians upon Jewish liturgical forms.[119] E. R. Goodenough, as far
as I have been able to determine, remains the only scholar who has
undertaken a detailed discussion of the religious thought of these
prayers.[120] As interesting as such a study might prove to be, a full
examination of the thought of the prayers would be out of place
here, taking us much too far afield from our present concern. I will
focus my attention, rather, on the more apposite issue of the "implanted
law" and its relation to the law of Moses.

As we have seen, in the first six books of the *Apostolic Constitutions*,
the compiler incorporated the idea of a "natural law" which was
"sown" by God into all humanity into the understanding of the
Mosaic law he took over from the *Didascalia*. He associated the natural
law particularly with what the latter considered the true law as
opposed to the prescriptions of the *deuterosis*. This notion of a natural law internal to the human being is articulated in more detail
in books 7 and 8. The fullest treatment appears in the hymn of
praise to God at 8.12.6–27, which cites in turn God's unique nature
(8.12.6–7), his role as providential creator (8.12.7–18), his special
concern for the human animal in general and the descendants of
Abraham—variously called "Hebrews" or "Israelites"—in particular
(8.12.19–26), culminating in a final praise of God to be pronounced

---

[119] See Fiensy, *Prayers Alleged to be Jewish*, 1–10.
[120] Goodenough, *By Light, Light*, ch. XI, "The Mystic Liturgy"; see esp. 336–58.
Fiensy limits his discussion of the "theology" of the prayers to his reconstruction of
the Jewish source lying behind 7.33–38, and thus does not deal with the ἔμφυτος
νόμος. His treatment in any case consists simply of a paragraph each on the topics "God," "Man," "Angels," "Eschatology," and "The Number Seven," and all
told covers less than two full pages; see *Prayers Alleged to be Jewish*, 231f.

by "all the people" together with the angelic hosts (8.12.27; cf. Isa
6:3).[121] The creation of the human being, narrated in 8.12.16–18, is
described as follows:

> And not only did you create the world, but you also made the world
> citizen (τὸν κοσμοπολίτην) within it, declaring him to be the ornament
> of the world (κόσμου κόσμον).[122] For you said to your Sophia,[123] "Let
> us make man according to our image and according to our likeness,
> and let them rule over the fish of the sea, and the birds of the air."[124]
> Therefore you made him out of an immortal soul and a dissoluble
> body, the former out of that which is not, and the latter out of the
> four elements.[125] And you gave to him, with respect to his soul, ra-
> tional discernment (τὴν λογικὴν διάγνωσιν), ability to distinguish piety
> and impiety (εὐσηβείας καὶ ἀσεβείας διάκρισιν), [and] observation of just
> and unjust (δικαίου καὶ ἀδίκου παρατήρησιν); and with respect to the
> body, you granted the five senses[126] and progressive motion.[127] For you,
> Almighty God, through Christ,[128] planted a paradise in Eden in the

---

[121] Goodenough (*By Light, Light*, 348) considered this prayer "our best guide to
the theology and philosophy" of the prayers.

[122] The phrase κόσμου κόσμον is found several times in the prayers (cf. 7.34.6;
8.9.8), and can be taken either with reference to the human as "microcosm" (so
Darnell, "Hellenistic Synagogue Prayers," 692; 679, note c) or as the "ornament of
world" (so Goodenough, *By Light, Light*, 348; Fiensy, *Prayers Alleged to Be Jewish*, 65,
n. 21) with some justification. The three translators I have just mentioned, while
naturally favoring one or the other, all seem to recognize both possibilities. The idea
that the human being is a "microcosm" of the universe is itself common enough
in Hellenistic thought and is possible here as well, perhaps referring to the creation
of the human body out of the four elements and its soul out of the stuff of the divine;
Fiensy, however, points out that this concept is usually denoted with another term
(*Prayers Alleged to be Jewish*, 65 n. 21). In favor of the translation as "ornament of
the world," on the other hand, is the fact that the creation of this "rational animal,
the citizen of the Cosmos," is understood to be the very "goal of creation" (*AC* 7.34.6).

[123] τῇ σῇ σοφίᾳ: Darnell translates this dative instrumentally, thus "by your
Wisdom"; it seems possible, however, that this is to be read in light of God's words
"Let *us* make man," which Philo also thought required explanation (see *Opif.* 72–75).
Goodenough (*By Light, Light*, 322) and Fiensy, (*Prayers Alleged to be Jewish*, 103) trans-
late it as I have.

[124] LXX Gen 1:26.

[125] Cf. Cicero, *De Leg.* 1.24: "For while the other elements of which man consists were derived from what is mortal, and are therefore fragile and perishable,
the soul was generated in us by God"; see further Philo, *Opif.* 135. On the phrase
ἐκ τοῦ μὴ ὄντος, see Goodenough, *By Light, Light*, 346–47.

[126] Cf. Cicero, *De Leg.* 1.26 who similarly pairs the gift of the senses with that
of the implanted preconceptions, but considers the former as endowments of the
mind, not the body. On the significance of the implanted preconceptions for this
passage from the *Apostolic Constitutions*, see below.

[127] τὴν μεταβατικὴν κίνησιν; the translation is Goodenough's.

[128] διὰ Χριστοῦ is of course believed to be an interpolation or an alteration of an
orignal διὰ λόγου by proponents of the view that this prayer was not originally Christian.

east,[129] sowing all sorts of edible plants, in order;[130] and into it, as if into an extravagant home, you led him; and in making him[131] you have given him an implanted law (νόμον ἔμφυτον), so that from within himself (οἴκοθεν καὶ παρ' ἑαυτοῦ), he should have the seeds of divine knowledge (τὰ σπέρματα τῆς θεογνωσίας).

The mention of the implanted law recalls the redactional reference, in *AC* 6.20, to the law sown by God into the nature of all human beings. Later in this prayer it is called simply "the natural law" (8.12.25) a phrase we have also found to be characteristic of the author's redaction in books 1–6. This implanted law is mentioned several other times in connection with the creation of the human animal in books 7–8. We have already seen one such instance in a redactional insertion into material taken over from the *Didache* in book 7, where God is said to have "created the world and the things in it through him [sc. Ἰησοῦ τοῦ παιδός σου], and planted a law in our souls."[132] Again, in a petitionary prayer using language quite similar to that of the two previous passages, it is said that God the creator "raised up the human as κόσμου κόσμος, and gave it both an implanted and a written law."[133] Finally, a reference to the "implanted knowledge" (ἔμφυτος γνῶσις) given to each human by God, being, as it is, reminiscent of 8.12.17–18, and coupled with "natural judgment" and "exhortation of the law," is also to be understood in connection with the giving of the implanted law.[134]

Like the "natural law" of *AC* 1–6, the implanted law of books 7–8 is also understood to have a written form: the law which God

---

[129] Cf. LXX Gen 2:8.

[130] κόσμῳ; translated according to Darnell.

[131] κἂν τῷ ποιεῖν: translated according to Goodenough and Fiensy. Cf. Darnell: "Indeed, you have given him an implanted law *to do*" (emphasis mine).

[132] *AC* 7.26.3: σὺ δέσποτα παντοκράτορ, ὁ θεὸς τῶν ὅλων, ἔκτισας τὸν κόσμον καὶ τὰ ἐν αὐτῷ δι᾽ αὐτοῦ, καὶ νόμον κατεφύτευσας ἐν ταῖς ψυχαῖς ἡμῶν; cf. also the redactional material in 6.20.10.

[133] *AC* 8.9.8: Παντοκράτορ θεὲ αἰώνιε, δέσποτα τῶν ὅλων, κτίστα καὶ πρύτανι τῶν πάντων, ὁ τὸν ἄνθρωπον κόσμου κόσμον ἀναδείξας διὰ Χριστοῦ καὶ νόμον δοὺς αὐτῷ ἔμφυτον καὶ γραπτόν.

[134] *AC* 7.33.3; cf. the "natural judgment" and " seeds of divine knowledge" which comprise the implanted law in 8.12.17–18. The phrase ἐκ τῆς τοῦ νόμου ὑποφωνήσεως, literally rendered "from the answer of the law," or perhaps, reading an objective genitive, "by their response to the law" (so Darnell, "Hellenistic Synogogal Prayers," 678), is difficult. There seems to be general agreement, however, that it is to be read in relation to the exhortations of the written law as opposed to the ἔμφυτος γνῶσις contained in the natural law. So Fiensy, *Prayers Alleged to be Jewish*, 51, n. 17; Goodenough, *By Light, Light*, 349; Darnell, "Hellenistic Synogagal Prayers," 675.

gave to the human is a νόμον ἔμφυτον καὶ γραπτόν.[135] The relationship between these two forms of the law is also clarified in the long
prayer in 8.12:

> But when men corrupted the natural law (τὸν φυσικὸν νόμον), at times
> considering the creation to be mere chance,[136] and at times honoring
> it more than they ought, comparing[137] it to you, the God of the uni-
> verse, you did not allow them to go astray, but rather raised up your
> holy servant Moses, through whom you gave the written law as an
> aid to the natural one (πρὸς βοήθειαν τοῦ φυσικοῦ τὸν γραπτὸν νόμον
> δέδωκας); and you showed the creation to be your work, and exposed
> the polytheistic error (τὴν . . . πολύθεον πλάνην).[138]

The notion that the written Mosaic law was given in order to "help"
the natural law is also found in a redactional alteration of a passage
from the *Didascalia* at *AC* 6.19.2, but there the "help" comes, owing
to the source material, specifically in the form of the ten commandments rather than the whole of biblical law.[139] Notably, there
is no hint of such a limitation in 8.12. As pointed out above, one
finds not even the vaguest allusion to the *Didascalia*'s characteristic
division of biblical law into the "law" proper and the *deuterosis* any-
where in books 7 and 8. In fact, as was also previously noted, the
redactor regards the laws regarding sacrifice and purity themselves
to have been a form of aid: they were given to correct a polytheistic
error,[140] in the hopes that Israel would return "to that law which is
sown by [God] into the nature of all human beings" (ἐκεῖνον τὸν νόμον
τὸν ὑπ' ἐμοῦ τῇ φύσει καταβληθέντα πᾶσιν ἀνθρώποις). This confusing
state of affairs serves only to underline the problem of the relation-

---

[135] *AC* 8.9.8.
[136] αὐτόματον, rendered by Fiensy as "an accident." Goodenough interprets it as
"self-caused," and Darnell as "happening without cause." The proper translation
would seem to depend upon the relation of this "error" to that mentioned subsequently (likening God to the world), and the determination of the particular philosophical theology which the author combats. The present translation suggests the
Epicureans might be in view. See below note 154 for a similar passage from Philo.
[137] συντατTόντων: so Darnell and Fiensy; Goodenough renders it "made it the
equivalent of thee."
[138] *AC* 18.12.25.
[139] *AC* 6.19.2: δέδωκεν νόμον ἁπλοῦν εἰς βοήθειαν τοῦ φυσικοῦ, καθαρόν, σωτήριον,
ἅγιον, ἐν ᾧ καὶ τὸ ἴδιον ὄνομα ἐγκατέθετο, τέλειον, ἀνελλειπῆ, δέκα λογίων πλήρη . . .;
cf. *Didascalia* 6.15.
[140] *AC* 6.20.10: τῆς πολυθέου πλάνης; cf. 8.12.25: τὴν πολύθεον πλάνην. Note,
however, that the "polytheistic error" of 6.20, given the context, concerns Israel's
worship of Baal, while that of 8.12 alludes to Greek philosophical doctrine.

ship between the understanding of the law of Moses found in books
1–6, which relies on the *Didascalia*, and that found in books 7–8, which
is more indicative of the compiler's own thought, whether derived
from a prior source or not.[141] Sufficiently clear in any case is the
fact that the redactor, similarly to Philo and the author of *4 Maccabees*,
understands Moses's law, however precisely interpreted, to be a written form of the implanted law given by God to all human beings.

Implanted Law as Human Reason

The *Apostolic Constitutions'* association of biblical law with a natural
law innate in the human animal, as for both *4 Maccabees* and Philo,
is ultimately rooted in the Stoic philosophy of law. A number of
points of contact at the level of detail were pointed out already in
the footnotes to the translation of 8.12.16–18 given above. A further hint of such influence is found in a redactional passage from
book 6 where, in connection with a discussion of the natural law,
the compiler, again like both the author of *4 Maccabees* and Philo,
interacts with a decidedly Stoic idea in his assertion that God "made
laws to cut out not the natural passions [themselves], but rather their
excess."[142] Stoic influence emerges most clearly, however, in the
prayers of books 7 and 8.

The account of the creation of the human animal found in the
long prayer of 8.12 begins with the description of the human as
"world citizen" (*AC* 8.12.16, κοσμοπολίτης), a title repeated in several of the prayers. This description of the human animal is by now
quite familiar from our earlier discussions of the Stoics and Philo:
the human is a "world citizen" by virtue of his or her possession of
logos which, in its ideal form as "right reason," constitutes the law
of the great Cosmic City. That the use of this designation in the
Apostolic Constitutions, too, bespeaks a similar set of assumptions cannot be doubted. In two of the three passages where the title "world
citizen" appears, it occurs in apposition to the characterization of

---

[141] This is clear from the fact that the redactor repeatedly attempts to integrate
into books 1–6 the natural law theory which he presents most fully in books 7–8,
while, conversely, the law/*deuterosis* distinction, so prominent in books 1–6 as a result
of his dependence upon the *Didascalia*, is not at all incorporated into books 7–8.

[142] 6.23.2: οὔτε δὲ τὰ φυσικὰ πάθη ἐκκόπτειν ἐνομοθέτησεν, ἀλλὰ τὴν τούτων ἀμετρίαν.
This statement is only intelligible as a rejection of the early Stoic understanding of
the passions.

the human as "the rational animal" (τὸ λογικὸν ζῷον).[143] It is in fact emphasized repeatedly throughout the *Apostolic Constitutions*, and particularly in books 7 and 8, that the human animal is λογικόν.[144] Thus when it is stated in the third passage containing this title that one who wishes to be initiated into the group must first understand, among other things, "why the human being was appointed world citizen" as well as "his/her own nature, of what sort it is," it is almost certainly the case that the "nature" intended here is the rational human nature.[145] The connection is further attested by the repeated characterization, in these same passages, of the human as κόσμου κόσμος, an ambiguous title that seems in any case to be related to the human animal's rational nature.[146]

The compiler never states categorically that the implanted law is to be identified with the human *logos*. Perhaps owing to the centrality of Moses's law to his purpose, he speaks directly of an ἔμφυτος νόμος rather than of an ἔμφυτος λόγος which is νόμος, as in the source of Cicero's *De Legibus* and the Letter of James. It is nonetheless quite clear that he understands the relationship between the two as being of the most intimate order; indeed, so much is already suggested by his characterization of the human animal as "world citizen." Moreover, the close association of human reason with both the implanted and the Mosaic law becomes quite explicit when it said that God "raised up the human [to be] the κόσμου κόσμος through Christ, and gave to it an implanted and written law so that it might live lawfully, as a rational [animal]" (καὶ νόμον δοὺς αὐτῷ ἔμφυτον καὶ γραπτὸν πρὸς τὸ ζῆν αὐτὸν ἐνθεσμῶς ὡς λογικόν). Given to the human both as an innate endowment and, later, in written form, God's law, as in *4 Maccabees*, provides the definitive guidelines for the rational life. The phrase ὡς λογικόν, moreover, must be seen

---

[143] *AC* 7.34.6; 8.41.4. It is noteworthy, too, that this latter description recalls the philosophical definitions of ἄνθρωπος as "a rational mortal animal"; cf. in this connection esp. 8.41.4, where the human animal is further defined as θνητός, thus echoing even more clearly the Stoic definition.

[144] For references see Fiensy, *Prayers Alleged to be Jewish*, 204, n. 28. Note, however, that while Fiensy does not indicate that any of the references in books 1–6 apply the term specifically to a "special characteristic of man," this is clearly the implication in several of these passages (see esp. 2.19.2; 6.10.2; 6.11.7). It is noteworthy that this designation is particularly prominent in the prayers of books 7 and 8.

[145] *AC* 7.39.2: παιδευέσθω ... δι' ὃ κοσμοπολίτης ὁ ἄνθρωπος κατέστη· ἐπιγινωσκέτω τὴν ἑαυτοῦ φύσιν, οἵα τις ὑπάρχει.

[146] *AC* 7.34.6; 8.9.8; 8.12.16. See further above, note 122.

in light of the repeated description of the human as "the rational animal": the law is given so that humans might live "as rational beings," which is to say in accord with their own nature, the definitive feature of which is reason.[147] Thus the repeated use of the term "natural law" (φυσικὸς νόμος).

The relationship—indeed, the implicit identification—of the implanted law with human reason is also apparent from the association of the former with "seeds of divine knowledge." In the long prayer of 8.12, the implanted law is said to have been given to Adam, the first rational animal, "in order that from his own self he should have the seeds of divine knowledge" (τὰ σπέρματα τῆς θεογνωσίας).[148] Elsewhere such "knowledge" (γνῶσις) is itself described as "implanted" (ἔμφυτος γνῶσις); and this "implanted knowledge" is closely associated both with law and with the gift of "natural judgment" (φυσικῆς κρίσεως) given by God to each human individual.[149] The significance of the latter is clarified more fully in the prayer of 8.12:

> And you gave to [the world citizen], with respect to the soul, rational discernment (τὴν λογικὴν διάγνωσιν), ability to distinguish piety and impiety (εὐσεβείας καὶ ἀσεβείας διάκρισιν), observation of just and unjust (δικαίου καὶ ἀδίκου παρατήρησιν) . . .[150]

"Rational discernment" or "natural judgment," then, specifically concerns the ability to distinguish ethical contraries—precisely the sort of knowledge that the Stoics discussed under the rubric of "implanted preconceptions." It is particularly noteworthy, then, that the reference to the "seeds of divine knowledge" here echoes the imagery used by both Cicero and Seneca to describe nothing other than these same implanted preconceptions. Moreover, the specific categories of knowledge singled out in 8.12.17—justice and piety (cf. belief in the deity)—are both explicitly associated with οἰκείωσις in the Stoic sources.[151]

---

[147] Cf. AC 7.39.2, where an understanding of one's "own nature," of one's status as "world citizen," and of "the judgment seats of different legislation" are all required of the initiate. The third element of this triad is generally understood as a reference to the innate and written law; see Goodenough, By Light, Light, 327, n. 111; 350; and Fiensy, Prayers Alleged to be Jewish, 145.

[148] AC 8.12.18.

[149] AC 7.33.3. On the phrase ἐκ τῆς τοῦ νόμου ὑποφωνήσεως, see above note 134.

[150] AC 8.12.17.

[151] See the discussion of the origins of the concept of justice and of belief in the deity in Chapter Two. The emphasis on piety here should also be viewed in relation to the prayer's account of the corruption of the natural law; see AC 8.12.25.

A further correspondence between the treatment of the "seeds of knowledge" in the *Apostolic Constitutions* and the Stoic implanted preconceptions can also be seen in connection with the theme of the corruption of this divine endowment. As we have seen, Cicero repeatedly emphasizes the inevitable corruption of these "seeds" and "sparks" of virtue and knowledge which results from mistaken human opinion and immoral behavior.[152] It is in connection with this theme that the author of the prayer, rather cleverly, finds a suitable entrée for the introduction of Moses's law into the Stoic theory: the implanted law, which in the *Apostolic Constitutions* is comprised of "seeds of divine knowledge," similarly gave way to the corruption caused by errant human beliefs, and was thus supplemented by God with the written law of Moses. It is noteworthy, nonetheless, that whereas Cicero thinks chiefly of mistaken conceptions of the good in this regard, the concern of the *Apostolic Constitutions* lies first and foremost with improper conceptions of the relation of the deity to the world:

> But when men corrupted the natural law, at times considering the creation to be mere chance (αὐτόματον), and at times honoring it more than they ought, comparing it to you, the God of the universe, you did not allow them to go astray, but rather raised up your holy servant Moses, through whom you gave the written law as an aid to the natural law . . .[153]

This notion that the law of Moses was given to correct mistaken notions of God's relation to the world is reminiscent of a similar sentiment found in Philo's *On the Creation of the World*, where "Moses's" view of this relationship is contrasted with that of those who hold "the world in admiration rather than the Maker of the world . . . while with impious falsehood they postulate in God a vast inactivity."[154] Here, however, the *Apostolic Constitutions* seems to have integrated critiques of the theology and cosmology of the Greeks into the familiar Stoic theme of the corruption of the "seeds of knowledge."

If it is thus clear that the "seeds of divine knowledge" and "implanted knowledge" of the *Apostolic Constitutions* are to be understood in light of the Stoic doctrine of implanted preconceptions, then this in turn confirms what has already emerged from a number of other con-

---

[152] See, e.g., *TD* 3.1–4; *De Leg.* 1.47.

[153] *AC* 8.12.25.

[154] Philo, *Opif.* 7; see further Goodenough, *By Light, Light*, 349–50. Dillon reads this complaint with reference to Aristotle and the Peripatetics (*The Middle Platonists*, 157).

siderations: the implanted law is nothing other than human reason. According to Cicero, the implanted preconceptions comprise the initial divine endowment that eventually develops first into the mature human *ratio*, and ultimately, ideally, into the *recta ratio* which is itself natural law. It is therefore quite striking that in the *Apostolic Constitutions*, the gift of the implanted law and that of the "seeds of divine knowledge" are one and the same: "And when you [sc. God] made him, you gave to him an implanted law (νόμον ἔμφυτον) so that from his own self he should have the seeds of divine knowledge."[155] The explanation, particularly in light of the many other points of contact with Stoicism in this prayer, is clear: the author has taken over the Stoic identification of natural law with human reason and utilized it, as had Philo and the author of *4 Maccabees* before him, in order to depict the law of Moses as a written expression of natural law.

Conclusion: Implanted Law in the Apostolic Constitutions

The *Apostolic Constitutions* exhibits an adaptation of the Stoic theory of law that is broadly similar to what is found in *4 Maccabees* and the writings of Philo. Once again, the deity associated with this law is identified as the god of the Jewish scriptures: the god who also appointed Abraham "heir of the world," delivered his descendants from Egypt and led them to victory over the Canaanites, and who has promised a resurrection of the dead.[156] And once again, accordingly, the claim is made that the law this god gave to Israel through Moses is a written expression of natural law.

Goodenough felt that the ἔμφυτος νόμος of the *Apostolic Constitutions* was "obviously a verbal variant of Philo's νόμος ἔμψυχος."[157] "Literally," he wrote, "the two terms express the same notion from slightly different angles. The Law could be said to have been 'implanted' within the Patriarchs, or they themselves could be regarded as that Law become animate."[158] This evaluation is accurate only in a very general sense and requires significant refinement. While Philo's use of the term ἔμψυχος νόμος is clearly informed by his dependence on the Stoic identification of the *logos* of the sage as natural law, the term itself derives from the Neo-Pythagorean theory of kingship, as

---

[155] *AC* 8.12.18.
[156] See esp. *AC* 8.12.20–26.
[157] Goodenough, *By Light, Light*, 325.
[158] *Ibid.*, n. 98.

Goodenough himself pointed out. The expression "implanted law,"
on the other hand, comes directly out of the Stoic theory itself. More
precisely, it is rooted in the theory that the "right reason" which
comprises natural law develops out of an initial divine endowment
of "implanted preconceptions." The ἔμφυτος νόμος of the *Apostolic
Constitutions* thus finds its closest analogue not in the νόμος ἔμψυχος
of Philo, but in the definition of law in terms of *ratio insita* in Cicero's
De Legibus, where the implanted preconceptions are similarly located
at the beginning of the developmental process that leads ultimately,
ideally, to natural law.[159]

LAW AND *LOGOS* AS "IMPLANTED"

Taken together, Cicero's *De Legibus* and the *Apostolic Constitutions*
provide strong evidence that the implanted preconceptions played
an important role in the Stoic identification of human reason as
natural law—a dimension of the theory that was in all probability
in place at least from the time of Chrysippus.[160] It is therefore quite
striking that both works use the term "implanted" not only with reference to the preconceptions, but as descriptive of the inchoate *logos*
or law itself that is comprised of these "seeds of knowledge." The
recurrence of this terminology is all the more striking given the similar correlation of "the implanted *logos*" and a "perfect law" in the
Letter of James. In fact, the use of analogous terminology in a number of other early Christian works that deal with natural law reveals
that this usage was more widespread than might initially appear to
be the case. The remainder of this chapter will establish this point
by briefly examining several such works. Along the way, we shall
continue to note how the incorporation of this Stoic concept into
worldviews alien to Stoicism influences the terms of its presentation.

---

[159] Horsley ("The Law of Nature in Philo and Cicero"), in arguing that Cicero
and Philo rely on the same source—namely Antiochus of Ascalon—for their theory of law, does not take the origin of Philo's characteristic term νόμος ἔμψυχος
into account. His thesis appears all the more tenuous when the *Apostolic Constitutions*
are brought into the comparison: more remarkable similarities exist, it seems to me,
between Cicero and the *Apostolic Constitutions* than between Cicero and Philo.

[160] Chrysippus defined law as the *logos* of the sage, the *logos* as a "collection of
conceptions and preconceptions," and worked with a doctrine of implanted preconceptions. It seems rather improbable that he would not have himself recognized
the import of this assortment of doctrines for his theory of law.

The Second Apology *of Justin Martyr*

In the *Second Apology* of Justin Martyr, the term ἔμφυτος is used both in connection with the Stoic doctrine of implanted preconceptions and to describe the less-than-complete *logos* common to all human beings.[161] The term appears twice in connection with Justin's well-known Logos theory.[162] In *App* 13.2, Justin expresses his wish to be considered only as a Christian despite his Platonic background

> not because the teachings of Plato are different from those of Christ, but because they are not in all respects similar, as neither are those of the others, the Stoics, and poets, and historians.[163]

He proceeds to explain this partial agreement of Greek and Christian thought:

> For each man [among those just mentioned] spoke well in proportion to his share of the divine spermatic *logos* (μέρους τοῦ σπερματικοῦ θείου λόγου), seeing what was related to it . . . For all the writers were able to see realities darkly by means of the implanted seed of the *logos* which was in them (διὰ τῆς ἐνούσης ἐμφύτου τοῦ λόγου σπορᾶς).[164]

In contrast to the mere "seed" of the divine *logos* possessed by such earlier great thinkers, the Christians have access to the complete *logos* by virtue of their knowledge of the teaching of Christ, who was himself its full embodiment. This contrast is made explicit elsewhere as Justin attributes the past persecutions of philosophers and the present Christian persecution to the same demonic source:

> And those of the Stoic school—since, so far as their moral teaching (τὸν ἠθικὸν λόγον) went, they were admirable, as were also the poets in some particulars, on account of the seed of reason implanted in every race of men (διὰ τὸ ἔμφυτον παντὶ γένει ἀνθρώπων σπέρμα τοῦ

---

[161] I follow throughout the recent Greek edition by M. Marcovich, *Iustini Martyris Apologiae pro Christianis* (Berlin and New York: de Gruyter, 1994). All translations, unless otherwise noted, are taken from *ANF*, vol. 1.

[162] For an excellent account of this theory, including the history of its interpretation, see R. Holte, "Logos Spermatikos. Christianity and Ancient Philosophy according to St. Justin's Apologies," *ST* 12 (1958) 109–68. Note also, however, the recent attempt by M. J. Edwards ("Justin's Logos and the Word of God," *Journal of Early Christian Studies* 3 [1995] 216–80) to downplay the importance of Greek philosophical thought for Justin's doctrine. On the relative importance of this theory for Justin's notion of the similarities between Christian and Greek thought, see Droge, *Homer or Moses*, 49–72, esp. 65–72.

[163] *App.* 13.2.

[164] *App.* 13.3, 5. I have slightly modified the translation of *ANF*.

λόγου)—were, we know, hated and put to death . . . For, as we inti-
mated, the devils have always effected, that all those who in any case
are zealous to live according to *logos* (κατὰ λόγον βιοῦν) and shun vice,
be hated. And it is no wonder if the devils are proved to cause those
to be much worse hated who live not according to a part only of the
spermatic *logos*, but by the knowledge and contemplation of the whole
logos, which is Christ (<οὐ> κατὰ σπερματικοῦ λόγου μέρος, ἀλλὰ κατὰ
τὴν τοῦ παντὸς λόγου, ὅ ἐστι Χριστοῦ).[165]

In both of these passages, the application of the term "implanted"
(ἔμφυτος) to the *logos* itself—more precisely, to the "seed" of the *logos*—
is analogous to its use in the *Apostolic Constitutions* and in Cicero's *De
Legibus*. Strikingly, Justin uses the term particularly with reference to
the divine, yet incomplete, *logos* that is implanted in all human beings.[166]
He emphasizes this incomplete state, moreover, by means of the
"seed" (σπορά, σπέρμα) metaphor that we have found to be commonly associated with the implanted preconceptions in the writings
of Cicero, Seneca, and the *Apostolic Constitutions*. The developmental
process that such language implies in these latter works, however,
has undergone a radical alteration in the context of Justin's presentation: the process by which the *logos* is completed has been removed
from the sphere of individual human development and projected
onto the stage of history. Maturation, so to speak, comes not through
an individual's own intellectual effort, but only as the *logos* is fully
revealed in the person and teaching of Jesus Christ. The result is a
starkly pessimistic view of the possibilities of human achievement
apart from Christianity. A life governed by right reason is positively
impossible without Christ.[167]

It is likely that Justin's use of the term "implanted" in this connection
is informed by an awareness of the intimate relationship between
the potential *logos* with which humans are born and the implanted
preconceptions.[168] The evidence, however, is limited. In addition to
his use of the "seed" imagery in this connection, it is noteworthy

---

[165] *App* 8.1–3. The translation of *ANF* has been slightly modified.
[166] Cf. in this respect Cicero's *ratio summa insita*.
[167] On the other hand, Justin's remarkable claim that certain great men of the
past like Socrates, Heraclitus and Abraham were Christians is likely also to be
understood in this context: the *logos* with which they lived in accord was indeed
Christ the divine *logos*. Nonetheless, they did not have access to its complete reve-
lation, which became available only with the historical appearance of Christ.
[168] So also Holte, "Logos Spermatikos," 136–40, who compares Justin with Cicero
in this respect.

that the type of knowledge associated with the "implanted seed of the *logos*" is characteristic of preconception according to the Stoics: the possession of this "partial" *logos* allowed pre-Christian thinkers to see τὰ ὄντα, but only "dimly" (ἀμυδρῶς).[169] That Justin was in fact acquainted with the Stoic doctrine of "natural conceptions" is clear from his *Dialogue with Trypho*, where he associates humankind's universal knowledge of "that which is always and universally just, as well as all righteousness," with τὰς φυσικὰς ἐννοίας, even blaming human failings in these areas on "education," "wicked customs," and "sinful institutions" in a manner reminiscent of Cicero.[170] Moreover, the only other use of the term ἔμφυτος in Justin's extant writings, found also in the *Second Apology*, appears in connection with a supposed universal human belief in the deity. Pointing out that his god, in contrast with the many gods of the Greco-Roman world, has no proper name, Justin explains that the simple title 'god' "is not a name, but rather an opinion of a matter difficult to expound implanted in the nature of human beings" (πράγματος δυσεξηγήτου ἔμφυτος τῇ φύσει τῶν ἀνθρώπων δόξα).[171] As we have seen, a universal human belief in the deity was counted among the implanted preconceptions at least by several later philosophers; it is particularly striking that Dio, too, speaks specifically of an implanted δόξα in this connection.[172]

While Justin's concern in the *Second Apology* lies elsewhere than with the theory of law, one can nonetheless catch glimpses of the significance of his understanding of the "implanted seed of the *logos*" for his understanding of law. According to Justin, human laws (τοὺς νόμους τῶν ἀνθρώπων) contain a mixture of correct and incorrect elements. The good elements apparently owe their existence to the

---

[169] *App* 13.5; cf. the similar characterization of the knowledge given directly to the human being by nature in the form of the "seeds of knowledge," e.g., in Seneca, *Ep.* 121.23.

[170] *Dial.* 93.1; cf. Cicero, *De Leg.* 1.47; *TD* 3.2.

[171] *App.* 6.3; translation mine. According to *App.* 6.2, "'Father' and 'God' and 'Creator' and 'Lord' and 'Master' are not names, but appellations derived from His good deeds and functions."

[172] Dio Chrysostom, 12.27; cf. further Seneca's reference to the *insita de dis* opinio (*Ep.* 117.6). Holte, apparently unaware of these parallels, considers Justin's use of the term δόξα in this context "unexpected," and incorrectly regards it as "an obvious undermining of the human πρόληψις θεοῦ" ("Logos Spermatikos," 139 n. 94 and 152). Why this term is used esp. in connection with the preconception of God is not immediately clear; cf., however, Cicero's comment in *De Leg.* 1.24: "there is no race either so highly civilized or so savage as not to know that it must believe in a god, even if it does not know in what sort of god it ought to believe." By the same token, preconceptions *by definition* are vague and ill defined.

share of the *logos* that all humans possess, while the latter are said to result from the meddling of wicked angels who "appointed laws conformable to their own wickedness."[173] This problem, says Justin, is overcome only with the appearance of Christ, who, as "right reason," resolves the confusion that exists between the various "laws of men" by showing that "not all opinions nor all doctrines are good, but that some are evil, while others are good."[174]

If Christ is himself "right reason," Justin can also describe his teaching as such. In fact, given Justin's knowledge of the common Stoic definition of law in terms of "right reason" in its function of commanding and prohibiting,[175] it is not surprising that he identifies Christ's teaching further with natural law. This emerges most clearly from an anecdote in *Second Apology* 2, where Justin relates the story of a woman who, having abandoned her former dissolute life when "she came to a knowledge of the teachings of Christ" tried to convince her husband to do the same. Having introduced him, too, to these teachings, she warned him that "there shall be punishment in eternal fire inflicted upon those who do not live temperately and conformably to right reason" (τοῖς οὐ σωφρόνως καὶ μετὰ λόγου ὀρθοῦ βιοῦσιν).[176] Justin informs us, however, that her husband, undaunted, continued in his pursuit of those pleasures which are "contrary to the law of nature" (παρὰ τὸν τῆς φύσεως νόμον), so that the woman was compelled to divorce him.[177] The phrases "teaching of Christ" (διδάγματα Χριστοῦ), "right reason" (ὀρθὸς λόγος), and "the law of nature" (ὁ τῆς φύσεως νόμος) are essentially interchangeable here. Thus can we understand Justin's repeated description of Christ as "the lawgiver," or even of Christ himself as the "new law."[178] Justin's Christ in this respect bears a limited resemblance to Philo's Moses:

---

[173] *App.* 9.3–4; cf. *App.* 13.3, 5; 8.1; 9.

[174] *App.* 9.3–4.

[175] Cf. his reference in *App.* 7.7 to "those men everywhere who have made laws and philosophized according to right reason, by their prescribing to do some things and refrain from others" (οἱ πανταχοῦ κατὰ λόγον τὸν ὀρθὸν νομοθετήσαντες καὶ φιλοσοφήσαντες ἄνθρωποι ἐκ τοῦ ὑπαγορεύειν τάδε μὲν πράττειν, τῶνδε δὲ ἀπέχεσθαι). Indeed, it would seem here that the commonness of this definition has led Justin to a momentary lapse, as he attributes to non-Christians the formulation of laws and philosophy according to *right* reason! In fact the only two references to the ὀρθὸς λόγος in the *Apologies* are made in association with νόμος; see in addition to *App.* 7.7, also *App* 2.1–5; 9.3–5; cf. further *Dial.* 141.1.

[176] *App.* 2.1–2.

[177] *App.* 2.3f.

[178] See, e.g., *Dial.* 12.2; 18.3; cf. *Dial.* 43.1.

as "right reason," he both embodied and gave verbal expression to the law of nature.

In sum. Justin, in a manner analogous to Cicero and the author of the *Apostolic Constitutions*, conceives of the initial endowment of the *logos* given to all of humanity as an "implanted seed." It is likely that Justin was himself aware that the roots of this terminology lie in the Stoic doctrine of implanted preconceptions; his use of such expressions is in any case clearly to be understood in light of this doctrine. Nonetheless, like the other authors examined in this chapter, and in a more radical fashion, Justin adapted the Stoic theory of natural law to accommodate a set of religious and historical convictions alien to Stoicism. All humans, he claimed, have always received an "implanted seed" of the *logos*; life in accord with "right reason," and thus natural law, however, became possible only comparatively recently, with the appearance in history of Jesus Christ. This theory allows Justin to explain the partial overlap between the law of nature and the laws of various nations, while at the same time securing possession of the whole natural law for Christians alone. Moreover, Justin integrates this philosophical theory into a worldview that includes wicked angels and fiery eschatological punishment for "those who do not live temperately and conformably to right reason." If such elements of Justin's theology highlight the fact that he cannot simply be classified as a Stoic, it is no less clear that concepts of Stoic origin form a significant component of his religious thought.

Methodius

A fragment from a work of Methodius preserved in the *Panarion* of Epiphanius provides an analogous instance of such an adaptation.[179] Interpreting Paul's discussion of his experience of inner conflict in Rom 7:14–25, Methodius explains:

> there are two kinds of thoughts (λογισμῶν) in us. The one kind arises from the desire (τὸ μὲν ἀπὸ τῆς ἐπιθυμίας) which lurks in the body, and

---

[179] The excerpt, from a work in which Methodius critiques Origen's view of the resurrection, is quite extensive, comprising *Pan.* 4.64.12–62. The particular passage which is most significant for our present purposes is *Pan.* 4.64.60–62. I cite the Greek text as found in K. Holl, *Epiphanius (Ancoratus und Panarion)*, vol. 2: *Panarion: Haer. 34–64* (GCS; Leipzig: Heinrichs, 1922). All translations, unless otherwise noted, are taken from F. Williams, *The Panarion of Epiphanius of Salamis: Books II and III (Sects 47–80, De Fide)* (NHMS 36; Leiden: Brill, 1994).

has been caused . . . by the inspiration of the material spirit. The other has come from our regard for the commandment, which we received to have as an innate natural law (τὸ δὲ ἀπὸ τοῦ κατὰ τὴν ἐντολήν, ὅν ἔμφυτον ἐλάβομεν ἔχειν καὶ φυσικὸν νόμον), and which urges and restores our thoughts to the good. Hence we "delight" [cf. Rom 7:22] in the law of God in our minds (τῇ μὲν νομοθεσίᾳ τοῦ θεοῦ)—this is what the "inner man" means—but with the desire that dwells in the flesh (τὴν ἐνοικοῦσαν ἐπιθυμίαν ἐν τῇ σαρκί) we delight in the law of the devil (τῇ δὲ νομοθεσίᾳ τοῦ διαβόλου). For the law which "warreth and opposeth the law of God" [cf. Rom 7:22]—that is, which opposes our impulse to the good (τῇ πρὸς τὸ ἀγαθὸν ὁρμῇ), the desire of our mind, is the law which is forever fostering lustful, material diversions to lawlessness, and is nothing but a temptation to pleasures (παντάπασι πρὸς ἡδονὰς ὢν ἑλκτικός).[180]

The "commandment" which Methodius identifies as the "implanted and natural law" (ἔμφυτον . . . καὶ φυσικὸν νόμον) is apparently God's command to Adam and Eve not to eat from the tree of the knowledge of good and evil.[181] Adam and Eve had lived briefly in freedom from irrational desire (ἄλογος ἐπιθυμία)—which, "with the enticing distractions of pleasures (ἑλκτίκαις ἡδονῶν)," leads to a lack of self control (ἀκρασία)[182]—and were thus free from sin[183] and death.[184] With an eye to Rom 7:7–12, however, he writes that they were "infected with desire" after God's commandment to them that they not eat of the tree of knowledge; "for once the commandment had been given, the devil got his opportunity to produce desire (ἡ ἐπιθυμία) in me through the commandment."[185] The result was that the "natural law within us" (ὁ ἐν ἡμῖν φυσικὸς νόμος) was weakened "from its defeat by the desire (ἐπιθυμία) in our bodies";[186] thus God sent his Son to condemn sin to destruction, so that "the requirement of the law of nature would be fulfilled."[187] The "gospel" (τὸ

---

[180] *Pan.* 60.5–6. I have altered the translation of Williams only by translating ἐλάβομεν more literally than his "we have been given," and by rendering τῇ . . . νομοθεσίᾳ τοῦ διαβόλου as "the law of the devil" in order to bring out the parallelism (cf. μέν . . . δέ) with τῇ μὲν νομοθεσίᾳ τοῦ θεου.

[181] Note the importance of this "commandment" for his general exposition of Rom 7:12; see *Pan.* 4.50.2ff, esp. 4.50.4–5.

[182] *Pan.* 4.55.2–3.

[183] *Pan.* 4.50.5; cf. 4.60.1.

[184] For Methodius's account of the origin of death see esp. *Pan.* 4.28–34; also 4.56.4–5.

[185] *Pan.* 4.56.1; cf. Rom 7:8. Methodius identifies Paul's personified "sin" with the devil; see *Pan.* 4.56.5.

[186] *Pan.* 4.62.11.

[187] *Pan.* 4.62.11: τὸ δικαίωμα τοῦ φυσικοῦ νόμου πληρωθῇ; cf. Rom 8:3–4 and further *Pan.* 4.62.10.

εὐαγγέλιον), as "the law of the Spirit of life" (cf. Rom 8:2), "is different from the other laws and was meant to foster obedience and the forgiveness of sins through its preaching"; it has "entirely conquered the sin which rules the flesh."[188] Nonetheless, "Christ did not come to announce the remaking or transformation of human nature into some other, but its change into its original nature before its fall (ὃ ἦν ἐξ ἀρχῆς πρὸ τοῦ ἐκπεσεῖν), when it was immortal."[189]

There are several obvious and significant differences between Methodius's "implanted natural law" and the Stoic view of natural law, owing above all to the former's dependence upon Paul and the myth of the fall from the book of Genesis. In the first place, the precise relationship between human reason and natural law is not altogether clear: while the human was from the start created as the "rational image" (τὸ ἄγαλμα τὸ λογικόν) of God,[190] the natural law was "implanted" only when God commanded Adam and Eve not to eat from the tree of knowledge. Moreover, given the role of the serpent in Genesis 3, Methodius introduces a demonic dimension to the Stoic opposition of reason and human desire: the latter, standing opposed to the law of God, represents the law of "the devil" (ὁ διάβολος; cf. ὁ πονηρός). In fact, in his attempt to make sense of Rom 7:23, Methodius speaks of the existence of three laws: the "law of the mind"—God's law—which corresponds to τὸ ἔμφυτον ἐν ἡμῖν ἀγαθόν; that of the devil, which is "at war with the law of the mind" (cf. Rom 7:23); and "the law of sin which dwells in the members," and "which corresponds to the sin that has become habitual in the flesh because of its lust (τῆς ἐπιθυμίας)."[191] With a stark view of the possibilities for human existence apart from Christianity reminiscent of Justin, Methodius believes that as a result of the transgression of Adam and Eve, fulfillment of the "requirement of the natural law" was impossible before the appearance of Jesus Christ, the son of God, in the flesh.[192] Moreover, as with Justin, transgression of the

---

[188] *Pan.* 4.62.13; cf. Rom 8:3–4.

[189] *Pan.* 4.41.6.

[190] *Pan.* 4.27.8. See further *Pan.* 4.26.1–27.4 on the creation of the human being, whom Methodius, like the author of the prayers from the *Apostolic Constitutions*, terms ὁ κόσμος τοῦ κόσμου (*Pan.* 4.27.8).

[191] *Pan.* 4.61.1–3.

[192] Indeed, according to Methodius, even after the appearance of Christ it is still impossible to fulfill the law of nature prior to the dissolution that comes with death. This point, too, seems to result from his dependence upon Romans; see esp. *Pan.* 4.36.4–5; cf. 4.56.10–59.6.

law of nature is given profound eschatological consequences: there will be a judgment by God "according to works and according to pursuits" (κατὰ τὰ ἔργα καὶ κατὰ τὰ ἐπιτηδεύματα),[193] and those who choose evil will face punishment.[194]

Despite the differences, however, the influence of the Stoic view of law on Methodius's interpretation of Romans and the myth of the fall is unmistakable.[195] Most significant in this respect for our present purposes is of course the notion of an "implanted natural law," given by God to Adam and Eve, which functions in opposition to human desire (ἐπιθυμία) and the pleasures (αἱ ἡδοναί). Methodius, notably, makes no explicit mention of implanted preconceptions or "seeds" or "sparks" of knowledge in this connection; still, several aspects of the fragment might suggest that he was, nonetheless, aware of this dimension of the theory. Both his description of virtue as οἰκεῖα and his reference to the wicked thoughts which first plagued humanity after the transgression of Adam and Eve as λογισμῶν ἀνοικείων would seem to suggest his familiarity with the Stoic doctrine of οἰκείωσις.[196] Similarly, his passing reference to the fact that "it is plain that the better and the worse (τὸ μέν βέλτιον τὸ δὲ χεῖρον) are within ourselves" might well be understood in this connection;[197] the language is in fact quite reminiscent of that used by Oecumenius and Theophylactus as they interpret the implanted *logos* of Jas 1:21.[198] Finally, it is tempting to suppose that it is precisely Methodius's awareness of the connection between these theories that underlies his somewhat unexpected correlation of the "implanting" of this law not with the creation of the human *per se*, but specifically with God's command regarding the tree of the knowledge of good and evil. Whatever the extent of his familiarity with the details of the original theory, however, Methodius's dependence on this philosophical tradition is plain.

---

[193] *Pan.* 4.49.9.

[194] See e.g. *Pan.* 4.36.4–5.

[195] In addition to evidence cited in this paragraph, see esp. the account of the creation in *Pan.* 4.26–27, in which God is said to have "brought all into being in good order like a great city, and regulated it τῷ λόγῳ" (4.26.1), as well as his description of the human being as ὁ κόσμος τοῦ κόσμου (4.27.8).

[196] *Pan.* 4.58.9; 4.60.2.

[197] *Pan.* 4.61.4.

[198] See above, Chapter One, and further immediately below.

Early Interpretation of James 1:21

Of particular interest to the present investigation are the interpretations of the phrase ἔμφυτος λόγος in early Christian commentaries on the Letter of James. James itself will be discussed in detail in the following chapters. Leaving aside for the moment the question of its precise relationship to this philosophical tradition, it is noteworthy in any case that the Greek catenae of Oecumenius and Theophylactus preserve an interpretation of Jas 1:21 which clearly assumes the theory at work in Cicero's *De Legibus* and the *Apostolic Constitutions*. Theophylactus interprets the phrase as follows: "he [sc. James] calls 'implanted *logos*' that owing to which we have become rational, able to distinguish the better and the worse" (Ἔμφυτον δὲ λόγον καλεῖ τὸν, καθ᾽ ὅν λογικοὶ γεγόναμεν, διακριτικοὶ τοῦ βελτίονος καὶ τοῦ χείρονος).[199] The same interpretation, with some minor variations, is offered by Oecumenius: Ἔμφυτον λόγον καλεῖ, τὸν διακριτικὸν τοῦ βελτίονος καὶ τοῦ χείρονος. Καθ᾽ ὅ καὶ λογικοί ἐσμεν καὶ λεγόμεθα.[200] Clearly these two works are drawing upon some common prior source[201] whose author was aware of the Greek philosophical tradition that has been reconstructed in the previous pages of this study. The "implanted *logos*" of Jas 1:21 is identified as human reason and, especially strikingly, associated particularly with the ability to distinguish ethical contraries—precisely, that is, the ability the Stoics attributed to οἰκείωσις and associated with the implanted preconceptions.

Still more impressive in this respect is the interpretation of the 12th century exegete Dionysius bar Salibi. Commenting upon the clause δέξασθε τὸν ἔμφυτον λόγον in Jas 1:21, Dionysius first paraphrases, and then explains:

> "Receive the word implanted in our nature." That is, he refers to natural law; for God implanted it into [our] nature, in order that it should love good things and have an aversion to bad things (*excipite verbum insitum naturae nostrae; h.e. legem naturalem innuit. In natura enim inseruit Deus, ut amet bona et odio habeat mala*).[202]

---

[199] MPG 125. 1145.
[200] MPG 119. 468.
[201] See above, Chapter One, esp. note 1.
[202] Sedlacek, *Dionysius Bar Salibi*, 91–92.

Dionysius, therefore, without comment or apology, simply identifies ὁ ἔμφυτος λόγος as a reference to natural law.[203] Moreover, similarly to the exegete whose interpretation of Jas 1:21 is preserved in the commentaries of Oecumenius and Theophylactus, he associates this law with the human tendency, "inserted" or "implanted" by God *in natura*,[204] to love good things and be averse to bad ones. Dionysius's combined association of the implanted *logos*, natural law, and the ability to distinguish ethical contraries is immediately intelligible in light of Cicero's *De Legibus* and the *Apostolic Constitutions*. It is clear that he, like the exegete followed by Oecumenius and Theophylactus, is interpreting Jas 1:21 in light of this apparently well-known philosophical tradition.

CONCLUSION

The purpose of this chapter has been twofold. Analysis of diverse Jewish and Christian adaptations of the Stoic theory of law has provided us with a model for apprehending those aspects of the treatment of the implanted *logos* in the Letter of James which are not typical of the Stoic sources. All of the works examined in this chapter clearly draw on the Stoic theory that human reason comprises a natural law. The authors of these works, however, are not Stoics. In each case, Stoic terms and concepts are fused with ideas that are entirely alien to Stoicism, and this, inevitably, has impacted their treatment. Similar in their correlation of human reason and natural law, these works nonetheless differ both from the early Stoics and from one another in the details and language of their presentation.

In the second place, this chapter has examined several works that use the term "implanted" (ἔμφυτος, *insitum*) to describe either reason itself or the law it comprises in order to confirm the findings of the previous chapter. The recurrence of this terminology in such otherwise disparate works admit of only one conclusion: each draws on a philosophical tradition that identifies human reason as natural law;

---

[203] Cf. his comments on "the perfect law of freedom" in Jas 1:25, which he also, not surprisingly, takes to be natural law.

[204] Note the absence of the limiting genitive *hominis*, and cf. in this respect Cicero *De Leg*. 1.18: *summa ratio insita in natura*. As in this passage from Cicero, it is nonetheless clear that it is specifically *human* nature that Dionysius has in mind here: cf. his paraphrase of ἔμφυτος λόγος as *verbum insitum naturae* nostrae.

that correlated the inchoate *logos* with which humans are born with implanted preconceptions; and which, accordingly, described either the *logos* or natural law itself as "implanted." The terminology of each of these works, in other words, is rooted in the Stoic theory of natural law.

The repeated appearance of this terminology in works as different in date, provenance and religious and philosophical orientation as Cicero's *De Legibus* (and its Greek source), the *Apostolic Constitutions*, Justin's *Second Apology* and the Methodius fragment suggest that this coinage was in fact rather widespread. Indeed, the theory was apparently common enough that both Dionysius bar Salibi and the Greek exegete whose work is preserved by Oecumenius and Theophylactus, with little apology or explanation, simply read the ἔμφυτος λόγος of Jas 1:21 in light of it. And this, as we shall see in the following chapters, is precisely how it should be read.

CHAPTER FOUR

THE IMPLANTED *LOGOS* AND THE LAW OF FREEDOM

According to Stoic theory, the inchoate *logos* with which humans are born, and which in its perfect form as "right reason" is natural law, consists in an endowment of implanted preconceptions (ἔμφυτοι προλήψεις). As is plain from the various works examined in the previous chapters, the term "implanted" came to be used of the *logos* or natural law itself in this connection by at least the first century B.C.E. The Letter of James, which equates "the implanted *logos*" (ὁ ἔμφυτος λόγος) with a "perfect law," "the law of freedom" (1:21–25; cf. 2:12), provides another example of this usage.

While dependence on the Stoics has often been cited in connection with James's association of law and freedom, his correlation of the "law of freedom" with the implanted *logos* has received much less attention in this respect.[1] For those majority who have (rightly) read James as a Christian composition, the notion of a *logos* which "saves souls" has seemed a rather obvious reference to the Christian Gospel; the Stoics, on the other hand, scarcely spoke of human reason in this way, nor as something which could be "heard and done" or "received." According to this line of interpretation, then, comparison with the Stoic sources is essentially irrelevant for understanding James's "implanted *logos*": the way that James talks about this *logos*, it is said, indicates that he is, at the very most, parroting a Stoic term that he either wholly misunderstands or has filled with an entirely new meaning.

Such differences between James and the Stoic sources are indeed quite significant. But the facile that conclusion the author of James either does not depend on Stoic thought at all, or that he at most uses a philosophical term with a sense entirely different from its original usage, betrays a much too simplistic approach to the complex problem of the merger of Jewish, Greek and Christian traditions in the early Christian literature. Justin differs quite significantly from Cicero

---

[1] On past interpretation of Jas 1:21, see Chapter One.

and the Stoics with respect to his claim that, while all humans are
endowed with an "implanted seed of the *logos*," life in accord with
"right reason" and thus "natural law" became possible only after the
life and death of Jesus of Nazareth in first century Palestine. His
dependence on Stoic concepts is patent nonetheless; nor is it by any
means obvious that this divergence results from his failure to "understand" the Stoic theory as originally conceived. As seen in the previous
chapter, such differences are not the exception in works that fuse
Stoic concepts with ideas alien to Stoicism, but the rule.

James's language of "hearing and doing" the *logos* is in fact quite
instructive in this respect. This pair finds a certain analogue in the
common Greek pairing of word and deed, speech and action.[2] Use
of the phrase "*logos*-doer" (ποιητὴς λόγου) in this context, however, is
hardly typical of the Stoics. Indeed, as has often been observed, this
phrase would most likely conjure up images of an orator or poet in
classical Greek usage. James's use of ποιέω to denote a carrying out
of *logos* in the sense of obedience is a semitism;[3] it is thus in the
Jewish and Christian literature that one finds the "word and deed"
theme expressed in terms of "hearing and doing." The pair is often
used, in fact, particularly with reference to the law, as by Paul: "it
is not the hearers of the law (οἱ ἀκροαταὶ νόμου) who are righteous
in God's sight, but the doers of the law (οἱ ποιηταὶ νόμου) who will
be justified."[4] Similarly, James himself elsewhere speaks directly of
the "doer of law" (ποιητὴς νόμου) rather than, as in 1:22, the "doer"
of the *logos* which is also law.[5] If, then, James's notion that the
implanted *logos* can be "heard" and "done" thus derives ultimately
from Jewish rather than Stoic usage, his use of this language nonetheless confirms that, quite like the Stoics, *he conceives of the* logos *precisely as a law.*[6] That is to say, this passage simultaneously points to
a significant similarity and a significant difference between James and
those who originally coined the expression "implanted *logos*." Both
associate it with the perfect law, but in James the understanding of

---

[2] Johnson, *Letter of James*, 206–7.
[3] This point has often been made in the commentaries; see, e.g., Ropes, *St. James*,
175; Dibelius, *James*, 114; Johnson, *Letter of James*, 206; also Ludwig, *Wort als Gesetz*,
164. See further the following note.
[4] Rom 2:13. For further instances of "hearing and doing," see, e.g., LXX Deut
30:8 20; Ezek 33:30–32; Sir 3:1; Matt 7:24–27 par. Luke 6:46–49; further Ropes,
St. James, 174–75; Fabris, *Legge*, 63–64; Klein, *Ein vollkommenes Werk*, 124f.
[5] Jas 4:11; cf. 1 Macc 2:67: τοὺς ποιητὰς τοῦ νόμου.
[6] See further on this point below, under the heading "Implanted *Logos* and the
Perfect Law of Freedom."

that law is informed by Jewish and Christian tradition. As in the works examined in the previous chapter, the divine law conceived by the Stoics, according to James, was legislated by the creator of the Jewish scriptures, the only true "lawgiver" (4:12).[7] And if James assumes that this *logos* can be "heard"—and, in some sense, "received" (cf. 1:21, δέξασθε)—this suggests only that he, like other Jewish and Christian authors who adapted the Stoic theory of natural law for their own purposes, understands it, though internal to the human individual, to have some external form as well.[8]

The extent of James's familiarity with the niceties of the philosophical theories which gave rise to phrases like ὁ ἔμφυτος λόγος is less clear than is the case with the *Apostolic Constitutions*, Justin, or even Methodius. He makes no mention of implanted preconceptions in this connection, nor is there any explicit indication that he uses the expression to denote specifically a potential *logos*.[9] That he has, nonetheless, at least a general grasp of the term's original significance is immediately clear from the fact that he, too, associates it precisely with divine law—a law, indeed, that is "perfect" and "of freedom."[10] One cannot simply conclude from the author's use of "un-Stoic" language in this connection, therefore, that he wholly misunderstands the original significance of the expression, much less that he is not ultimately indebted to the philosophers in this respect at all.[11]

---

[7] Jas 4:12: εἷς ἐστιν [ὁ] νομοθέτης. As has often been noted, it is not always possible to tell whether the author of James is referring to God or Jesus Christ, esp. when he simply uses the title κύριος as, e.g., in 5:7–8, 14, 15. That the "lawgiver" in question is God rather than Jesus Christ is clear, however, from the allusion in Jas 4:12 (εἷς ἐστιν [ὁ] νομοθέτης) to Deut 6:4 (LXX: κύριος ὁ θεὸς ἡμῶν κύριος εἷς ἐστιν); cf. further in this respect Jas 2:19: σὺ πιστεύεις ὅτι εἷς ἐστιν ὁ θεός, καλῶς ποιεῖς. See further Ropes, *St. James*, 275; Dibelius, *James*, 229; Johnson, *Letter of James*, 294; and Klein, *Ein vollkommenes Werk*, 163–65, who rightly correlates God's role as "lawgiver" with the "implanting" of the *logos*. In fact, as will be argued below, the "law of freedom" is nothing other than the law which God himself, according to the Jewish scriptures, gave through Moses.

[8] The command δέξασθε τὸν ἔμφυτον λόγον is equally difficult on any interpretation of the *logos*. Whether conceived as something inborn in all humans or inserted later in only a specific group, it is nonetheless *already* "implanted"—and thus the apparent contradiction. See further on this problem below, under the heading "Implanted *Logos* in light of the Torah and Judgment."

[9] Note, however, that mere possession of this *logos* ensures neither that one lives in accord with it nor, subsequently, "salvation."

[10] See immediately below, under the heading "Implanted *Logos* and the Perfect Law of Freedom." As we shall see in the following chapter, moreover, this *logos* functions particularly in opposition to human desire (ἐπιθυμία) and the pleasures (αἱ ἡδοναί).

[11] Of course, whether the author's acquaintance with this expression was mediated

This is as true of his notion that the implanted *logos* "saves souls" as it is of his assumption that it can be "heard and done." In fact, in a passage which is, incidentally, reminiscent of James in several respects, Philo writes similarly of the importance of the dominance of reason over that part of the soul which is the seat of anger: "For then is the soul saved (ἡ ψυχὴ σῴζεται), when the seat of anger (ὁ θυμός) is steered by reason (ὑπὸ λόγου) as by a charioteer . . ."[12] Such language of "saving souls" does not seem to have been typical of the Stoics; on the other hand, neither can Philo, nor especially the eschatologically oriented author of James, be fairly described as typical Stoics. To be sure, it is by no means clear that "saving souls" means the same thing in Philo's *Allegorical Interpretation* as it does in the Letter of James; but what this example from Philo does show is that the use of such language does not necessarily result from "misunderstanding" or a use of philosophical concepts with a meaning entirely unrelated to their original sense. The interesting question, in any event, is how a concept of "saving souls" came to be associated by Philo and—more importantly for our purposes—by James, with a Stoic concept of *logos*. And if, on the face of it, James's eschatological orientation seems more incompatible with Stoicism than Philo's mysticism, one need only recall that the Christians Justin and Methodius both thought eschatological punishment awaited those who did not live in accord with natural law.

The Letter of James is indebted to the Stoics for its equation of "the implanted *logos*" with a perfect law. The elements of James's presentation of this concept that differ from the Stoics, though, are just as illuminative of its role in his religious imagination as are the similarities. Special attention must therefore be given to several questions that arise with the observation of apparent differences between

---

by other Jewish or Christian sources who drew on the Greek philosophers or results from a direct dependence upon the works of Greek philosophers themselves is purely a matter of speculation. The ultimate provenance of the concept of an implanted *logos* which represents the perfect law is in any case Greek philosophy. Similar questions can be raised with respect to the other usages of the letter which are typical of Greco-Roman literature, e.g., the metaphors of the bridle and the rudder in James 3.

[12] *Leg. All.* 3.137: τότε γὰρ ἡ ψυχὴ σῴζεται, ὅταν καὶ ὁ θυμὸς ἡνιοχηθῇ ὑπὸ λόγου; my translation. (The LCL translation of Colson, by rendering ὁ θυμὸς ἡνιοχηθῇ ὑπὸ λόγου as "when the seat of anger has received reason as its charioteer," might—in the present context—give the false impression that this passage is also similar to James with respect to the latter's expression δέξασθε τὸν ἔμφυτον λόγον.) For discussion of *Leg. All.* 3.114–37 see below pp. 201f and 227f.

James's understanding of the implanted *logos* and Stoic discussions of human reason. If the notion that it can be "heard" and, in some sense, "received" assumes that it has some external form, what does the author consider this latter to be? What, that is, is the referent of the "perfect law of freedom"? In what sense is the implanted *logos* understood to be that "which is able to save your souls"? What, further, is the relation of this *logos* to the "*logos* of truth" by which "God gave birth to us" according to 1:18? When, and in whom, does James imagine the ἔμφυτος λόγος to have been "implanted"?

The relationship between the implanted *logos* and the "*logos* of truth" will be taken up in Chapter Five. The present chapter will focus on James's correlation of the implanted *logos* with the "perfect law of freedom." After a closer examination of this correlation itself, it will be argued that James, like Philo, *4 Maccabees* and the *Apostolic Constitutions*, finds a written expression of the implanted *logos* in the Torah.

IMPLANTED *LOGOS* AND THE PERFECT LAW OF FREEDOM

Jas 1:19b contains a three-part admonition: "let each person be quick to hear, slow to speak, and slow to anger."[13] Each of the elements of this admonition is elaborated over 1:20–27, and the phrase "implanted *logos*" occurs as its last element, "slow to anger" (βραδὺς εἰς ὀργήν), is being explained.[14]

---

[13] The exact admonition of 1:19b is not, to my knowledge, attested elsewhere in ancient literature. Cf. however the remarkably similar grouping of speech, hearing and anger in the advice regarding the "best way to excercise authority" in Lucian *Demon.* 51: Ἀόργητος, ἔφη, καὶ ὀλίγα μὲν λαλῶν, πολλὰ δὲ ἀκούων. This would seem to suggest that James is at least following a traditional association of the three, whether or not he has himself formulated the particular admonition of 1:19b.

[14] On 1:19–27 as structured around the saying of 1:19b, see Dibelius, *James*, 108–23, esp. 108–9; cf. Fabris, *Legge*, 55–56. Note, however, that I disagree with Dibelius in several points of detail, the most important of which, in this context, concerns 1:21 itself. The contrast of ἐν πραΰτητι in 1:21 with the ὀργή of 1:20, particularly considering the use of διό to join these verses, seems to me to indicate that 1:21 is to be viewed primarily as part of the elaboration of the theme "slow to anger"; thus, to paraphrase: "anger doesn't produce righteousness; therefore, set aside all evil and receive the implanted *logos* with humility." Dibelius, while recognizing the contrast between "anger" and "humility," nonetheless views this verse as a part of the elaboration of "slow to hear," albeit as "the transition to that theme" (*ibid.*, 112; cf. 108–9). So also Fabris, who consequently considers the author's use of the strong conjunction διό to be somewhat less than appropriate: "Il verso 21 presenta una nuova esigenza, come conseguenza, διό, di quello che precede, anche se il nesso causale con il verso 20 sembra sproporzionato" (*Legge*, 56).

For human anger (ὀργή) does not work God's righteousness. Therefore, setting aside all filth and evil excess (περισσείαν κακίας),[15] receive with humility the implanted *logos* (τὸν ἔμφυτον λόγον) which is able to save your souls (1:20–21).[16]

This *logos*, however, also receives emphasis in the immediately subsequent elaboration of the admonition's first element, "quick to hear" (ταχὺς εἰς τὸ ἀκοῦσαι), which consists of a contrast between two types of "hearer" (ἀκροατής) of the *logos*:

> And (δέ)[17] become *logos*-doers and not merely hearers who deceive themselves. For if someone is a *logos*-hearer and not a doer, this one is like a man who looks at the face of his birth in a mirror; for he looks at himself and departs, and immediately forgets what sort he is (ὁποῖος ἦν).[18] But the one who looks into the perfect law which is of freedom and remains becomes not a forgetful hearer but a deed-doer; this one will be blessed in his or her doing (1:22–25).

The expression "*logos*-doer" with this sense, as mentioned above, is a semitism, and such a pairing of "hearing" and "doing" is in fact common in Jewish and Christian ethical instruction. In this instance, the need to "become *logos*-doers and not merely hearers" is explained by likening the latter type of hearer to one who looks into a mirror, and contrasting his or her behavior in this respect to that which is typical of the doer.[19]

---

[15] Cf. Johnson, *Letter of James*, 201: "excess of evil"; Ropes, *St. James*, 171: "'excrescent wickedness', 'superfluity of naughtiness'"; Dibelius, *James*, "profuse wickedness"; NRSV: "rank growth of wickedness." On the options for translating περισσεία in particular see esp. Mayor, *Epistle of St. James*, 67–68. I take the phrase περισσείαν κακίας as a genitive of quality on the model of ἀκροατὴς ἐπιλησμονῆς (Jas 1:25), κριταὶ διαλογισμῶν πονηρῶν (2:4) and, perhaps, ὁ κόσμος τῆς ἀδικίας (3:6), ἐν πραΰτητι σοφίας (3:13) and ἡ εὐχὴ τῆς πίστεως (5:15); see further BDF §165. In this case, desire—which, as we shall see, is the opposite of *logos*; which is associated with impurity (cf. 1:21, ῥυπαρία) in 4:8 (in contrast to "humility"!) and elsewhere; and which is linked with [τὰ] κακά in 1:13—would be thought of in terms of an "excess" or "rank growth." Cf. in this respect esp. *4 Macc* 1:29; also *AC* 6.23.2; further Inwood, *Ethics and Human Action in Early Stoicism*, ch. 3, esp. 155–73.

[16] On ἐν πραΰτητι as modifying δέξασθε in particular, see below p. 189. This phrase, which sets up a contrast with ὀργή (cf. 1:19, 20), may however have been positioned so that it can modify both ἀποθέμενοι and δέξασθε; cf. in this respect the phrase ὑπὸ τῆς ἐπιθυμίας in 1:14, which can (and should?) be read with both πειράζεται and ἐξελκόμενος καὶ δελεαζόμενος.

[17] On the force of δέ here, see below p. 189, note 200.

[18] On the sense of this clause, see p. 142, note 26.

[19] My gender inclusive language does not reflect the author's use of the gender

James's mirror metaphor has been subject to a number of different, and often very exacting, interpretations.[20] It has been argued variously that he intends to liken the law to a mirror,[21] to set up a contrast between the law and a mirror,[22] or that he intends no such comparison or contrast at all.[23] In addition, great significance is often attached to the use of different verbs of "seeing" in 1:23–24 (κατανοέω) and 1:25 (παρακύπτω) in the service of one or another of these interpretations.[24]

The least likely by far of the three general positions regarding the relationship between the law and the mirror is that which finds a contrast between them. It is clear from the elaboration as a whole that the self-deception characteristic of the "mere hearers" (1:22) lies not in their attention to some deficient *logos*, but in their overestimation of "hearing," and subsequent failure to respond appropriately to, the *logos* which "saves souls" (cf. 1:21). That is to say, the distinction between the "mere hearer" and the "doer" lies not in the object of, but rather in the actions subsequent to, their respective "hearing." Thus the self-deception: the former does indeed "hear" that "which is able to save souls," but "blessedness" consists in "doing" (ποίησις), not merely "hearing."[25] The sudden (and subtle) injection

---

exclusive ἀνήρ for the purposes of this simile (1:23). ἀνήρ was perhaps chosen over ἄνθρωπος for the sake of a vivid illustration; cf. however the use of ἀνήρ also in 1:8, 12 and 3:2.

[20] See already the critical comments of Dibelius on this matter in *James*, 115. The most recent and, to my knowledge, most extensive treatment is that of L. T. Johnson, "The Mirror of Remembrance (James 1:22–25)," *CBQ* 50 (1988) 632–45.

[21] So, e.g., Mayor, *St. James*, 72; Johnson, "Mirror." So also apparently Ropes, who observes that Philo, in *Vit. Cont.* 10 §78, "compares the law (ἡ νομοθεσία) to a mirror for the rational soul (ἡ λογικὴ ψυχή), in a manner which recalls James's figure" (*St. James*, 176). Ropes, however, does not interpret the implanted *logos* as human reason; his point, apparently, is rather that both writers consider the law to be a mirror of the soul.

[22] So Laws, *Epistle of James*, 85–86.

[23] So Dibelius, *James*, 115; Blackman, *Epistle of James*, 64.

[24] Thus Laws, who argues that the author intends to set up a contrast between the *logos* and a mirror, suggests that παρακύπτω suggests a mere glance while κατανοέω suggests a more careful consideration; the author thus implies that just a quick look in the *logos* is sufficient, while even close study of the image in the far inferior literal mirror is futile (*Epistle of James*, 86). It is indicative of the confusion surrounding the meaning of this simile that Johnson, who argues that the author intends to liken the *logos* to a mirror, argues precisely the opposite: that παρακύπτω suggests a more steady "gaze" while κατανοέω connotes a more transitory "noticing" or "fleeting glance"! See Johnson, *Letter of James*, 207–9. On the significance of the use of these different terms, see below, note 30.

[25] Cf. Dibelius, *James*, 114: "Merely hearing is equivalent to self-deception so long as one believes that even then the word can still 'save'."

of a distinction between the objects of the respective hearers' attention would only serve to distract one from what is clearly the root issue: the implanted *logos* which is "able to save your souls" must not only be "heard," but "done" as well.

On the other hand, it is quite possible, indeed probable, that the simile implies that the author understood the law to function in some sense as a mirror.[26] This would in fact be consistent with the use of mirror imagery by Greco-Roman moralists, as Johnson has shown,[27] while Dibelius's view that the mirror appears in this passage merely as a result of a popular correspondence between mirrors and forgetting finds little support in the ancient literature.[28] Nonetheless, the remarkable divergence in the interpretation of this passage results precisely from the fact that this particular comparison is in any case not pursued. Rather, the only comparison that is explicit in the text is that drawn between the *logos*-hearer who is *not* also a doer and one who looks into a mirror. The comparison itself, moreover, is formulated specifically on the basis of three actions shared by these two types: the mere hearer is like a man who looks at his face in a mirror inasmuch as (s)he too [i] looks at him/herself, [ii] departs,

---

[26] Note in this case the peculiar use of the phrase τὸ πρόσωπον τῆς γενέσεως αὐτοῦ to describe that which is seen in the mirror. Assuming such a comparison is at work, τῆς γενέσεως might simply connote the "natural" face seen in a mirror (as opposed to the psychic reality reflected in the law of freedom); so, e.g., Johnson, "Mirror of Rembrance," 634. However, given the author's notion that "God gave birth (ἀπεκύησεν) to us" by means of *logos*—a birth which he has just mentioned in 1:18—it might be taken more literally as "the face of one's birth," and thus as an allusion to the fact that the law reflects the *logos* that was was involved in "our" birth. Cf. in this respect Hort, *Epistle of St. James*, 39: "The γένεσις is his birth strictly, in antithesis to his later degeneracy; but the face is the invisible face, the reflexion of God's image in humanity"; cf. Sidebottom, *James, Jude and 2 Peter*, 35. Note also in this connection Jas 3:9: τοὺς ἀνθρώπους τοὺς καθ' ὁμοίωσιν θεοῦ γεγονότας. If this is in fact the case, then ὁποῖος ἦν (Jas 1:24) would most likely refer to the nature of the human being as λογική; cf. in this case AC 7.39.2: "Let him [sc. the one who is to be baptized] learn the order of a distinguished creation, the sequence of providence ... why the world came to be and why man was appointed a world citizen. Let him understand his own nature, of what sort it is (ἐπιγινωσκέτω τὴν ἑαυτοῦ φύσιν, οἵα τις ὑπάρχει)"; see further on this passage p. 118, above. Note also in this connection Philo, *Vit. Cont.* 78, where the law (ἡ νομοθεσία) is said to represent a mirror for the rational soul (ἡ λογικὴ ψυχή).

[27] See Johnson, "Mirror," 636–41.

[28] Cf. Dibelius, *James*, 115 with n. 115. Ludwig argues that the theme of "forgetfulness" in connection with the law is to be understood in light of the Jewish literature in particular (*Wort als Gesetz*, 168–69).

and [iii] immediately forgets what (s)he has seen (1:24).[29] Whether or not the use of a verb of "looking" in 1:25 implies a continuation of the mirror simile—and thus a further, if only implicit, likening of the hearer who *is* a "doer," too, to one who looks into a mirror— it is precisely these three actions which provide the basis for the comparison that is the chief concern of the passage: that of the "mere hearer" and the "doer." The *looking, departing,* and *forgetting* of the mere hearer (1:24) are inevitably to be compared with the *looking, remaining,* and *not forgetting* of the doer (1:25).[30]

Though that which one has "heard" and not forgotten in 1:25 is understood to be that which was "seen" in the "perfect law of free- dom," the elaboration as a whole, as pointed out above, assumes that both types of "hearer" in fact "hear" the same *logos.* The cru- cial difference between the "mere hearer" and the "hearer" who is also a "doer" lies in their actions subsequent to "hearing," not in the object of their perception. The force of the comparison thus indi- cates that "hearing the *logos*" and "looking into the perfect law of freedom" are equivalent actions. Indeed, it is through constant atten- tion to the perfect law of freedom that one becomes a "*logos*-doer."[31] As has been recognized by the majority of James's interpreters,

---

[29] Note esp. the use of γάρ in 1:24: the mere hearer "is like a man looking at the face of his birth [or: natural face] in a mirror, *for* he looks at himself and departs and immediately forgets . . ." (I translate all of the verbs—perfect and aorist— of 1:24 with the present on the understanding that they all function essentially as gnomic aorists; see BDF §344; cf. Mußner, *Der Jakobusbrief*, 105 n. 8. Ropes's view that the perfect ἀπελήλυθεν is used "because of reference to a lasting state" [see *St. James*, 176–77] seems to me weak in light of the fact that the real "lasting state" with which the author is concerned is that of forgetfulness. The perfect is perhaps used above all for the sake of euphony [cf. ἀπελήλυθεν with ἐπελάθετο], as Dibelius suggests [*James*, 115 n. 41].)

[30] In fact, the use of a verb of "looking" at the beginning of 1:25 may be intended above all to make the comparison in terms of this series of three actions all the more explicit; cf. the somewhat different view of Dibelius, *James*, 116. It should also be noted, however, that the "law of freedom" is in fact a written law (see on this point below), and to this extent the use of a verb of "looking" is quite natural. In this connection, I find quite interesting a suggestion made by H. D. Betz, in a sem- inar on James at the University of Chicago, that παρακύπτω (lit., "stoop," "bend over") might suggest a reading posture. One should not in any case, with Johnson, see in παρακύπτω a *contrast* with κατανοέω: the latter does not generally connote a "hasty glance" but, on the contrary, "contemplation" or considered reflection; see the entries for κατανοέω in BAGD and LSJ.

[31] In 1:25, the ideal type is described as a ποιητὴς ἔργου, but clearly not in dis- tinction to the "*logos*-doer." On the relation of "doing" *logos* to "doing" ἔργα, see Chapter Five, under the heading "*Logos* and *Erga.*"

regardless of their divergent interpretations of the relationship assumed to exist between the *logos* and the mirror, the ease with which the author moves from *logos* to law in 1:21–25 indicates that "implanted *logos*" and "perfect law of freedom" are functionally equivalent terms.[32]

As has been argued at length in the previous two chapters, this equation of implanted *logos* and law is rooted in Stoic philosophy. While James, despite the interpretations of Theophylactus, Oecumenius and Dionysius bar Salibi, makes no mention of anything analogous to implanted preconceptions in this connection, the similarity of his equation of law and ἔμφυτος λόγος to Cicero's definition of natural law in terms of *ratio insita*, the association of human reason with an ἔμφυτος νόμος in the *Apostolic Constitutions*, the relationship between natural law and an ἔμφυτος σπορὰ τοῦ λόγου assumed by Justin Martyr, and the ἔμφυτος φυσικὸς νόμος of Methodius, can scarcely be dismissed as mere coincidence. James has not, alone among these authors, formulated this equation entirely apart from Stoic influence. The understanding of law in the Letter of James, as in these diverse works, has been informed by the Stoic theory of natural law.

James's peculiarly lavish description of the law as one that is both "perfect" and "of freedom" is striking in this connection.[33] One finds limited analogies for these individual epithets in other ancient literature, but their combination here is extraordinary, and creates a quite emphatic effect.[34] Both, moreover, are best understood in light of the correlation of this law with ὁ ἔμφυτος λόγος.

---

[32] In fact, many authors speak in terms of identity in this connection: see, e.g., Kühl, *Die Stellung des Jakobusbriefes*, 18–26; Ropes, *St. James*, 173; Dibelius, *James*, 116; Blackman, *Epistle of James*, 67; Mußner, *Der Jakobusbrief*, 107; Fabris, *Legge*, 154 and *passim*; Martin, *James*, 51; Vouga, *L'Epître de Saint Jacques*, 65; Ludwig, *Wort als Gesetz*, 18 and *passim*; Klein, *Ein vollkommenes Werk*, 135–44, 152–53; Tsuji, *Glaube*, 108–10. Others are more reticent in this respect, but posit a very close relation between the law of freedom and the implanted *logos* nonetheless. See, e.g., Cadoux, *The Thought of St. James*, 74–76; Laws, *Epistle of James*, 79; Hoppe, *Der theologische Hintergrund*, 94–95; Johnson, *Letter of James*, 214. My own view is closer to these latter authors: the "perfect law of freedom" represents a written expression of the implanted *logos*; while the two are thus functionally equivalent, they are not, strictly speaking, identical. See further on this below.

[33] Jas 1:25, νόμον τέλειον τὸν τῆς ἐλευθερίας; cf. 2:12, νόμος ἐλευθερίας.

[34] For a suggestion regarding the rhetorical context in which James's emphatic glorification of the law is to be understood, see the concluding chapter of this study.

The Law of Freedom

As has often been pointed out, the concern for "freedom," both in itself and in connection with law, are characteristically Greek, and typical of the Stoics in particular, whose paradox that "only the sage is free" was well known in antiquity.[35] Fabris was well aware of the Greek and especially Stoic precedents for James's association of law and freedom.[36] Nonetheless, on the basis of the presence of clearly Jewish and Christian traditions in the context in which the expression "law of freedom" is found in James, he concluded that it was necessary to explain the expression entirely without recourse to the Greek sources.[37] The logic of this conclusion, however, is quite problematic. As has been pointed out in our discussion of the implanted *logos* itself, such an interpretation fails to account for the possibility that the thought of James, like that of many other Christian authors of his period, represents a fusion of Hellenistic, Jewish and Christian concepts.

Fabris's attempt to explain the repeated use of the expression "law of freedom" in James "on the basis of some supposedly pure OT and Jewish background" is not persuasive in any case.[38] The primary "freedom" treated in the Hebrew scriptures is that social state

---

[35] For a discussion of the development of the Greek concept of freedom, see M. Pohlenz, *Freedom in Greek Life and Thought: The History of an Ideal* (Dordrecht-Holland: D. Reidel; New York: The Humanities Press, 1966); H. Schlier, "ἐλεύθερος, κτλ.," *TDNT* 2.487–96; H. D. Betz, *Paul's Concept of Freedom in the Context of Hellenistic Discussions about the Possibilities of Human Freedom* (Protocol of the 26th Colloquy of the Center for Hermeneutical Studies in Hellenistic and Modern Culture; Berkeley: The Center for Hermeneutical Studies in Hellenistic and Modern Culture, 1977); F. S. Jones, "Freedom," *ABD* 2.855–59. For the Stoic interest in and understanding of freedom, see esp. Diog. Laert. 7.121 and 7.32–33; Cicero, *Paradoxa Stoicorum* 5; Epictetus, *Diss.* 4.1; Philo, *Every Good Man is Free*; further Schlier, "ἐλεύθερος," 493–96; and Dibelius, *James*, 116–17.

[36] Fabris, *Legge*, 33–42.

[37] See ch. 3 of Fabris, *Legge*, and esp. p. 81: "È precisamente questo carattere biblico e giudaico del contesto delle formule di Giacomo che esclude l'ambiente greco e stoico come matrice delle nozioni di Giacomo." Fabris leaves himself some flexibility when he goes on to assert that the "somiglianze esterne" between the language of James and the Greek sources would allow at most the hypothesis that the author of James has infused Greek terminology with an entirely new meaning. His openness to this possiblity is somewhat puzzling inasmuch as he elsewhere makes the methodological point that a determination of the origin of an expression is decisive for its interpretation (see, e.g., *Legge*, 13, 32). He does not in any case seem to take this possibility seriously, as it is not discussed further. See further on Fabris above, Chapter One.

[38] Jones, "Freedom," 858, explicitly against Fabris.

opposed to literal slavery,[39] and the use of the term ἐλευθερία and its cognates in the LXX,[40] as well as the usage in later Jewish literature,[41] is largely consistent in this respect. It is not likely accidental, therefore, that one begins to find a clear and explicit interest in freedom as an abstract value in Jewish thought only from the Hasmonean and early Roman periods: in 1 and 2 Maccabees;[42] in the writings of Philo and Josephus;[43] on the coins minted during the revolts from Rome;[44] perhaps in the eschatological expectations of 4

---

[39] Cf. the comments of Jones, "Freedom," 855.

[40] ἐλευθερία is nearly always used in the LXX with reference to a social state of individuals, whether with reference to nobility (e.g., 1 Kgdms 17:25; 3 Kgdms 20:8, 11; 2 Esdr 23:17) or, most often, in opposition to literal slavery (e.g., Exod 21:2, 5, 26, 27; Lev 19:20; Deut 15:12, 13, 18; 21:14). It is telling in this connection that, in contrast to the usual format for entries in *TDNT*, Schlier's article on ἐλεύθερος, κτλ. does not even include a section on the Jewish literature; see *TDNT* 2.487–502.

[41] A.-M. Denis, *Concordance Grecque des Pseudépigraphes d'Ancien Testament* (Louvain-la-Neuve: Université catholique de Louvain, 1987) contains only twelve entries for cognates of ἐλευθερία, seven of which occur in the *Testaments of the Twelve Patriarchs*, three in the *Letter of Aristeas*, and one each in the *Testament of Abraham* (Recension A) and the *Apocalypse of Sedrach*. Again, the majority of these occur in connection with the social institution of slavery or literal captivity (*T. Jud.* 21:7; *T. Naph.* 1:10; *T. Jos.* 1:5; 13:6; 14:1; *T. Abr.* A 19:7; *Ep. Arist.* 27; 37); though cf. the use of ἐλευθέριος in *Ep. Arist.* 246. On *T. Jud.* 4:3, see the immediately following note; on *Apoc. Sedr.* 8:12; *T. Ben.* 10:8; and *4 Ezra* 13:25–26, 29 and 7:96–98, note 45.

[42] Both 1 & 2 Maccabees depict the Maccabean revolt in terms of a quest for the freedom of Jerusalem (1 Macc 2:11; 14:25; 2 Macc 2:22; 9:13). Perhaps significantly, one such instance occurs in a letter purportedly from the hellenistic king Demetrius, which officially grants freedom to Jerusalem (1 Macc 15:7). Cf. *T. Jud.* 4:3, where Judah and his brothers are said to have "liberated" (ἠ-/ἐλευθερώσαμεν) Hebron. For an earlier, but somewhat different, use of "freedom" as a political concept, see 1 Esdr 4:49.

[43] According to Jones, discussion of the Exodus under the rubric of freedom such as is posited by Fabris first occurs in the writings of Philo and Josephus ("Freedom," 856). Jones points out that Josephus also depicts both the Maccabean revolt and the first revolt against Rome in terms of a struggle for "freedom," commenting that "it is not least in this point that Josephus is indebted to Greek and Roman historiography" ("Freedom," 856).

[44] See Fabris, *Legge*, 93, who must refer to the coins minted during the first revolt to demonstrate that the term חרות ("freedom")—which is not found in biblical literature—was even known in the first century CE. Note further in this connection that B. Kanel suggests that the shift from the legend "freedom (חרת, חרות) of Zion" on the coins of the second and third years of the first revolt, to "for the redemption (לגאלה) of Zion" in the fourth year, has a religious significance: "Redemption seems to infer Messianic hopes current among the adherents of Bar Gioras . . . The era 'Freedom of Zion' had probably implied only political freedom" ("Ancient Jewish Coins and their Historical Importance," *BA* 26 [1963] 57). So too, the shift from "redemption" in the first year of the second revolt to "freedom" in the second year: noting that in the papyri, the followers of Simon bar Kosiba continue in the second year to date documents with reference to "the redemption of Israel through

Ezra and the *Testaments of the Twelve Patriarchs*;[45] and, finally, in a few passages from the rabbinic literature.[46]

Fabris's conclusion that "[i]l rapporto tra legge e libertà non è . . . un fatto isolato nell'ambiente biblico e giudaico, ma una struttura portante" based on the myth of the Exodus is in any case considerably

---

Simon bar Kosiba, Prince of Israel," Kanel suggests that "the majority of the Rabbis opposed the claim of Simon to be styled 'Prince of Israel' . . . as well as the assumption held by Rabbi Akiba that Simon was the redeemer of Israel; therefore in the second year of the revolt the terminology on the coins was changed to claim only political freedom" (*ibid.*, 62). A similar interpretation is offered by Y. Meshorer, *Ancient Jewish Coinage. Vol. II: Herod the Great through Bar Cochba* (Dix Hills, NY: Amphora, 1982) 122–23, 150–52. If such a line of argument as these authors propose is in fact correct, it tells quite strongly against Fabris's contention that "freedom" and divine redemption go hand in the hand in ancient Jewish thought!

[45] See *T. Ben.* 10:8 (b) which, however, is clearly from a Christian hand: "and the Lord will first of all judge Israel for their wrongs toward him, for they did not believe God arrived in flesh [as] liberator" (ὅτι παραγενάμενον θεὸν ἐν σαρκὶ ἐλευθερωτὴν οὐκ ἐπίστευσαν); cited according to M. de Jonge, et al., *The Testaments of the Twelve Patriarchs: A Critical Edition of the Greek Text* (PVTG 1; Leiden: Brill, 1978). R. H. Charles bracketed the entire clause as an interpolation, and the key term ἐλευθερωτήν, which apparently occurs only in ms. b, was placed in the margin of his critical edition; see *The Greek Versions of the Testaments of the Twelve Patriarchs. Edited from Nine MSS together with the Variants of the Armenian and Slavonic Versions and Some Hebrew Fragments* (repr. ed.; Oxford: Oxford University Press; Hildesheim: Georg Olms Verlagsbuchhandlung, 1960) 229. H. C. Kee, who generally follows the edition of Charles, omits the clause altogether ("Testaments of the Twelve Patriarchs," *OTP* 1.828).

Cf. also *4 Ezra* 13:25–26, where it is said either that the Messiah (so the Latin), or God through the Messiah (so most versions; cf. 13:29), "will liberate his [sc. God's] creation" (*liberabit creaturam suam*). This is echoed in 13:29, with God as its subject even in the Latin, and with human beings in particular as its object: "Behold, the days are coming when the Most High will begin to deliver those who are on the earth (*quando incipiet Altissimus liberare eos qui super terram sunt*)" (the translation is based on that of M. E. Stone, *Fourth Ezra: A Commentary on the Book of Fourth Ezra* [Hermeneia; Minneapolis: Fortress, 1990] 392; I cite the Latin text as found in A. F. J. Klijn, *Der lateinische Text der Apokalypse des Esra* [TU 131; Berlin: Akademie Verlag, 1983]). See further 7:96–98, where those who have "kept the ways of the Most High," after their death but before they reach their final heavenly destination, will "see the straits and great toil from which they have been delivered (*angustum et <labore> plenum quo liberati sunt*), and the spaciousness (*spatiosum*) which they are to receive and enjoy in immortality" (the translation is again based on Stone, *4 Ezra*, 237). Stone points out that this passage is to be understood in light of the discussion of the "narrow road" which leads to the inheritance in *4 Ezra* 7:3–13 (*ibid.*, 244); that is, what they are "delivered" or "liberated" from is the exceedingly difficult journey toward Israel's "portion." Cf. further *4 Ezra* 7:101.

Note too, finally, *Apoc. Sedr.* 8:12 (= 8:10 in S. Agourides, "Apocalypse of Sedrach," *OTP* 1.611), where the seer requests God to "free the human being from punishment" (ἐλευθέρωσον τὸν ἄνθρωπον ἐκ τὴν κόλασιν), i.e., esp. eschatological punishment; the Greek text is cited according to O. Wahl, *Apocalypsis Esdrae. Apocalypsis Sedrach. Visio Beati Esdrae* (PVTG 4; Leiden: Brill, 1977).

[46] See Fabris, *Legge*, 84–103, 113–21, 130–31.

overdrawn.[47] As Jones has pointed out, "[t]hough the redemption of Israel from slavery in Egypt is cited in support for the manumission of Hebrew slaves in the 7th year (Deut 15:15), the OT does not develop a theology of freedom on the basis of the Exodus."[48] In fact, the interpretation of the Exodus under the rubric of "freedom" is first evident in the writings of Philo and Josephus.[49] In any event, while the association of law and freedom (or disobedience and slavery) is occasionally made in the rabbinic literature,[50] a direct link between the two in a manner comparable to James's "law of freedom" is rarely found elsewhere in the Jewish sources.[51] To be sure, given the combination of the Greek interest in freedom and the dynamics of covenantal thought, the ingredients for the formulation of a direct connection between obedience to the law and freedom were in place by the hellenistic period; however, there is little evidence to support the thesis that this was a widespread Jewish sentiment—let alone one that emerged entirely apart from Greek influence.[52]

It is therefore striking that Philo and the author of *4 Maccabees*, each of whom *are* clearly indebted to the Stoic understanding of law,

---

[47] *Legge*, 113. Cf. the similar judgment regarding Fabris in Klein, *Ein vollkommenes Werk*, 140 n. 120. Note that even with respect to the key evidence provided by the interpretation of Exod 32:16 (according to which חָרוּת ["engraved"] is given the alternative vocalization חֵרוּת ["freedom"]), the rabbis disagreed regarding the significance of the "freedom" in question, i.e., whether it was best understood with reference to the exile, the angel of death, or suffering; see *Legge*, 84. Moreover, the interpretation of this passage in *m. 'Avot* 6:2 has no clear connection to the Exodus myth, and seems, in fact, to envision an individual rather than a corporate freedom; cf. Jones, "Freedom," 856, who describes this passage as "[m]uch closer to the Stoic understanding of (internal) freedom."

[48] Jones, "Freedom," 855; perhaps with an eye to Fabris: cf. *Legge*, 97–98.

[49] See above note 43.

[50] See Fabris, *Legge*, 84–103, and further 113–21. See also, however, note 47 above.

[51] Certainly, given the circumstances in which the Maccabean revolt arose, the desired "freedom" was largely that to live and worship in accord with Jewish law; see, e.g., 2 Macc 2:22; cf. 1 Macc 2:6–13; 15:7. This, however, is quite different from the notion that the law itself guarantees freedom.

[52] Johnson argues that "the idea [apparently, "that obedience to the law renders a person free"] is widespread enough . . . to make any direct dependence on Stoic ideas [on the part of the author of James] unnecessary" (*Letter of James*, 209). The signficance of the implicit distinction between "direct" and "indirect" dependence on Stoic ideas on the part of James here is not altogether clear; whatever the case, of "the examples from Jewish literature" which Johnson cites in support of his position, at least two of the three writings (Philo, *That Every Good Man is Free* and *4 Maccabees*) are obviously indebted to Stoicism in this respect.

both explicitly associate the law with freedom.[53] For the Stoics, ἐλευθερία was defined in terms of "living as one wishes,"[54] which is to say, to be subject neither to hindrance (κωλῦσαι) nor compulsion (ἀναγκάσαι),[55] and thus, in a word, to be the sole master of one-self.[56] Such freedom is impossible if one longs for things which are not entirely under his or her own control, because one thereby renders oneself subject to hindrance or compulsion.[57] If, on the other hand, one conforms one's will and aims entirely to those of God, everything will of necessity happen as one wishes; therefore, one will by definition be free. Thus Epictetus:

> But I have never been hindered (ἐκωλύθην) in the exercise of my will, nor have I ever been been subjected to compulsion (ἠναγκάσθην) against my will. And how is this possible? I have submitted my impulse (μοῦ τὴν ὁρμήν)[58] unto God ... He wills that I should choose (ὁρμᾶν) some-thing; it is my will too. He wills that I should aim for (ὀρέγεσθαι)[59] something, it is my will too. He wills that I should get something, it is my wish too. He does not will it; I do not wish it.[60]

True freedom, therefore, "is not acquired by satisfying yourself with what you desire, but by destroying your desire" (οὐ ... ἐκπληρώσει τῶν ἐπιθυμουμένων ... ἀλλὰ ἀνασκευῇ τῆς ἐπιθυμίας).[61] Indeed, desire and the other passions are the ultimate source of the soul's slavery. In the words of Philo, "if the soul is driven by desire (ἐπιθυμίας), or enticed by pleasure (ἡδονῆς), or diverted from its course by fear

---

[53] Cf. the discussion of these works by Fabris, *Legge*, 37–42.

[54] Epictetus, *Diss.* 4.1.1: ἐλεύθερός ἐστιν ὁ ζῶν ὡς βούλεται; cf. Cicero, *Par.* 5.34: *Quid est enim libertas? potestas vivendi ut velis*; Philo, *Quod. Omn. Prob. Lib.* 59: ζῆν ὡς βούλεται. This expression already had a substantial history in Greek thought; see Pohlenz, *Freedom*, 48 and 186 n. 50.

[55] Epictetus, *Diss.* 4.1.1; Philo, *Quod. Omn. Prob. Lib.* 60; cf. Cicero, *Par.* 5.34.

[56] Cf. αὐτοπραγία (Diog. Laert. 7.121; Philo, *Quod Omn. Prob. Lib.* 21); αὐτεξούσιος (Epictetus, *Diss.* 4.1.56, 62); αὐτόνομος (*Diss.* 4.1.56).

[57] See esp. Epictetus, *Diss.* 4.1.62–84. Cf. Philo's discussion of the endurance of torture by Zeno the Eleatic and Anaxarchus in *Quod Omn. Prob. Lib.* 105–109 (cf. Diog. Laert. 9.27, 59).

[58] Cf. Oldfather: "my freedom of choice." On the Stoic understanding of ὁρμή, see above, pp. 37f.

[59] I alter the translation of Oldfather, who renders ὀρέγεσθαι "desire." Such a translation might create a certain confusion given the common use of this English term to translate ἐπιθυμεῖν and its cognates, which connote something quite different; cf. e.g. *Diss.* 4.1.175, which is cited immediately below. On the Stoic understanding of ὄρεξις, see further Inwood, *Ethics and Human Action*, 114–26 and 224–42, esp. 235–37.

[60] Cf. Epictetus, *Diss.* 4.1.89.

[61] Epictetus, *Diss.* 4.1.175.

(φόβῳ), or shrunken by grief (λύπῃ), or helpless in the grip of anger (ὀργῆς), it enslaves itself and makes him whose soul it is a slave to a host of masters."[62] Freedom consists, rather, in obedience to God.[63] Specifically, says Philo, this entails living in accord with "right reason," the true divine law:

> just as with cities, those which lie under an oligarchy or tyranny suffer enslavement, because they have cruel and severe masters, who keep them in subjection under their sway, while those which have laws to care for and protect them are free,[64] so, too, with men. Those in whom anger (ὀργή) or desire (ἐπιθυμία) or any other passion (τι ἄλλο πάθος), or, again, any insidious vice (κακία) holds sway, are entirely enslaved, while all whose life is regulated by law are free (ὅσοι δὲ μετὰ νόμου ζῶσιν, ἐλεύθεροι). And right reason is an infallible law (νόμος δὲ ἀψευδὴς ὁ ὀρθὸς λόγος) engraved . . . by immortal nature on the immortal mind, never to perish. So, one may well wonder at the short-sightedness of those who . . . deny that right reason, which is the fountainhead of all other law, can impart freedom to the wise, who obey all that it prescribes or forbids.[65]

Thus, too, can the author of *4 Maccabees* extol the reasoning faculties (λογισμοί) of the seven brothers as "freest of the free" (ἐλευθέρων ἐλευθερώτατοι) in light of their ability to overcome their passions and remain faithful to the law, despite the tortures of Antiochus Epiphanes.[66]

To be sure, the fact that James shows no interest in "freedom" apart from his obvious desire to associate it with law prohibits one from drawing any decisive conclusions regarding his understanding of the concept, or even how, precisely, he conceived of its relation to law.[67] On the other hand, that he describes as νόμος ἐλευθερίας

---

[62] Philo, *Quod Omn. Prob. Lib.* 159; cf. 17–18; see further Cicero, *Paradoxica Stoicorum* 5, *passim*.

[63] Cf. Seneca, *De Vita Beata* 15.7: *deo parere libertas est*; further Epictetus, *Diss.* 4.1.91–110.

[64] Philo here alludes to the associaton of law and freedom found in Greek political thought; see on this Schlier, "ἐλεύθερος," 488–92.

[65] Philo, *Quod Omn. Prob. Lib.* 45–47 (with a clear allusion to the Stoic definition of law); cf. 62. See also Epictetus, *Diss.* 4.1.158, where Diogenes is said to be free because he did not consider his body to be his own, because he needed nothing (οὐδὲν δέομαι), and because "the law (ὁ νόμος), and nothing else, is everything" to him.

[66] *4 Macc* 14:2; cf. in this respect Philo's discussion of Zeno the Eleatic and Anaxarchus (see above note 57); and further Epictetus, *Diss.* 4.1.90, 172. On the parallel use of the phrase βασιλέων βασιλικώτεροι in this connection in *4 Maccabees*, see immediately below.

[67] Conversely, the author speaks of "slavery" only in a positive sense, when describing himself (or his literary persona) as θεοῦ καὶ κυρίου Ἰησοῦ Χιριστοῦ δοῦλος (Jas 1:1). Presumably, he understands such "slavery" to be anything but opposed to ἐλευθερία.

precisely that law which he equates with the implanted *logos* is scarcely coincidental,[68] and is at the very least suggestive of his understanding of the term. In fact, the *logos* of James, as we shall see in the following chapter, functions above all in opposition to desire (ἐπιθυμία) and the pleasures (αἱ ἡδοναί); indeed, James's admonitions to "receive" the implanted *logos* and to become a "*logos*-doer" by giving constant attention to the "law of freedom" come on the heels of an argument that human individuals, not God, are responsible for temptation, and is coupled, further, with a charge to lay aside all vice (κακία),[69] and anger (ὀργή) in particular.[70] What is clear in any case is that the author is obviously eager to associate the law with "freedom"; and his equation of it with "the implanted *logos*" is a move that immediately warrants this association.[71]

---

[68] So also the *libertatis lex* of Irenaeus (*A. H.* 4.34.4) which, though identified with "the word of God, preached by the apostles," includes the "natural precepts" which were *ab initio infixa . . . hominibus*; these, according to Irenaeus, were given to Israel in the form of the decalogue, and brought to fulfillment by Christ (*A. H.* 4.15.1; see further 4.16). Note also the connection assumed between freedom and rationality in, e.g., *A. H.* 4.4.3; cf. 4.2.4. At the same time, however, the "freedom" which is characteristic of this "law" is opposed to the "slavery" which characterizes the remainder of Jewish law (e.g., *A. H.* 4.9.1–2; 4.13.4), which was imposed, at least in part, as a result of Israel's proclivities toward idolatry (*A. H.* 4.14–15); this polemical use of the concept of "freedom" is somewhat reminiscent of Gal 4:21–5:1. See further on Irenaeus's notion of natural law W. R. Schoedel, "The Appeal to Nature in Graeco-Roman and Early Christian Thought" (Ph. D. diss., University of Chicago, 1963) 435–43.

Note in this connection Davids's formulation of the problem of the "law of freedom" in James: ". . . unless one finds specific Stoic concepts (such as natural law or passionless life) [in James] it is more likely that he [sc. the author of James] is still within a Jewish Christian world" (*Epistle of James*, 99). In fact, the author of James not only draws on the Stoic equation of law and ἔμφυτος λόγος, but understands this λόγος to function above all in opposition to ἐπιθυμία and αἱ ἡδοναί; on this latter point, see Chapter Five. Whatever the case, Davids's assumption of a sharp dichotomy between the concept of freedom in the "Jewish Christian world" and in Greek thought is problematic.

[69] On the meaning of κακία here, see the remarks of Johnson, *Letter of James*, 201.

[70] Cf. in this respect Philo, *Quod Omn. Prob. Lib.* 45–47, cited above. (On the relation of Jas 1:21 to 1:20 and 1:13–18, see below.) Cf. the comment of Reicke, *The Epistles of James, Peter, and Jude*, 23–24: "[The expression 'law of liberty'] may have been inspired by the Stoic ideal of freedom, according to which men ought to strive for independence from every passion of the soul, such as anger, fear, etc. Freedom of this kind is of interest here since in vss. 19–21 the author admonishes his readers to shun wrath and all evil passions."

[71] It is of course possible that the author's interest in "freedom" works on more than one level; cf. in this respect Irenaeus's *libertatis lex* and above note 68. This possiblity is at least implicitly recognized, for example, by Dibelius, who interprets James's "law of freedom" in light of both Stoic concepts and a supposed freedom from "the burden of ritualism" on the part of Christians who found, in the teaching

The Perfect Law

Similarly, while a certain analogy for James's description of his law as "perfect" is found in LXX Ps 18:8 (ὁ νόμος τοῦ κυρίου ἄμωμος),[72] the epithet τέλειος, too, is best understood in light of the equation of the law with the implanted *logos*.[73] The apologetic comparison with other (imperfect) laws which this description implies is characteristic of ancient treatments of natural law. Zeno himself, in his *Republic*, had envisioned a state in which the different local systems of justice (ἰδίοις δικαίοις) were replaced by the κοινὸς νόμος.[74] Similarly, Philo contrasts "right reason" with the laws of Solon and Lycurgus: it is "engraved not by this mortal or that and, therefore, perishable as he, nor on parchment or slabs, and, therefore, soulless as they, but by immortal nature on the immortal mind, never to perish." It is, in short, an "infallible" or "trustworthy" law (νόμος ἀψευδής).[75] Justin, too, contrasts the conflicting human laws (τοὺς νόμους τῶν ἀνθρώπων), each of which contains some mix of proper and improper elements, to the "right reason" of Christ, which dispelled the confusion engendered by this diversity by presenting the true law, the law of nature.[76]

In fact, the theme of perfection emerges elsewhere in James particularly in association with *logos* and the resistance of desire. The "perfect man" (τέλειος ἀνήρ) is identified explicitly as one who does not stumble ἐν λόγῳ (3:2)—a phrase which surely intends a reference to speech, but speech, more specifically, in its relation to the implanted *logos*. The definition of such a τέλειος as one who is able to "bridle

---

of Jesus, "a new law"; see *James*, 116–20. On the author's interest in freedom, see the Conclusion of this study.

[72] Cf. MT Ps 19:8: תמימה. Cf. further the similar description of the law of the Jews, owing to its supposed divine origin, as "pure" or "without contamination" (ἀκέραιον) in *Ep. Arist.* 31. Note, however, that in this latter passage the law is also described as "most philosophical" (φιλοσοφωτέραν); cf. in this respect the presentation of the law of Moses in *4 Maccabees* as the "philosophy" of the Jews (see above, Chapter Three). While Ps.-Aristeas, unlike the author of the latter work, stops short of identifying Jewish law with natural law, it is the implication of the work as a whole—and of this passage in particular—that it represents the Jewish "philosophy," and one which ranks among the best of the Greek philosophies, not least owing to its divine origin.

[73] In what follows I assume the discussion of perfection found in the following chapter, under the heading "τέλειος."

[74] *SVF* 1.262; on this passage see further above, pp. 32f.

[75] *Quod Omn. Prob. Lib.* 46; the translation of ἀψευδής as "infallible" is Colson's. Note that despite Philo's disparaging reference to "parchment" and "slabs" here, the equation of the law of Moses with natural law is nonetheless assumed throughout his writings; see, e.g., *Opif.* 3, and above, Chapter Three.

[76] *App.* 9.3–4.

his whole body" (Jas 3:2) is in fact reminiscent of the complete self-mastery which, for the Stoic, comprises the true freedom of the sage. And while the failure to resist the temptation of desire (ἐπιθυμία) results in "sin," the endurance of such temptation—and thus the "doing" of *logos*—is said to manifest itself in a "perfect deed" (τέλειον ἔργον).[77]

The Royal Law

A word should also be said in this connection regarding the use of the phrase "royal law" (νόμος βασιλικός) in Jas 2:8. The problem of the significance of the epithet "royal" here is complicated by the fact that, ultimately, it is not entirely clear whether it is used to describe "the whole law" (cf. 2:10), that is, the "perfect law of freedom," or to describe Lev 19:18 in particular. If, as is more likely, the former is the case,[78] it is noteworthy that this association, too, has good Greek and Stoic precedents.[79] Of particular interest in the present context is *4 Macc* 14:2, where the reasoning faculties (λογισμοί) of the seven brothers, whose dominance of the passions is such that they can resist the tortures ordered by the "tyrant" (not βασιλεύς! cf. *4 Macc* 5:1, 14, 27) Antiochus and thus avoid apostasy from the law, are lauded as both ἐλευθέρων ἐλευθερώτατοι ("freest of the free") and βασιλέων βασιλικώτεροι ("more royal than kings"). One might note further in this connection Philo's view that the sage will "hold that nothing is more royal than virtue (βασιλικώτερον οὐδὲν ἀρετῆς)," and will thus "not fear the orders of others whom they regard as subordinates"; literal kings, on the other hand, are "more often in the position of the sheep than of the shepherd" since they are caught "in the snares of pleasure" (πάγαις ἡδονῆς).[80] Understood in this light, the law of James would be described as "royal" inasmuch as obedience

---

[77] Jas 1:2–4; cf. 1:13–15, and further 1:25: it is through constant attention to the "perfect law" that one becomes a "deed-doer." See further on this point Chapter Five, under the heading "*Logos and Erga.*"

[78] I am inclined to agree with scholars such as Ropes, Dibelius, Fabris, Wachob and Johnson—against those like Kühl, Hort, Mußner, Laws and Ludwig—that the νόμος βασιλικός refers to "the whole law," i.e., to the "perfect law of freedom," esp. as the nine other occurrences of νόμος in James (four of which occur in 2:8–12) clearly refer to the law as a whole.

[79] See Meyer, *Rätsel*, 150–53; Fabris, *Legge*, 44–46; see further above, p. 94f on Philo.

[80] Philo, *Quod Omn. Prob.* 154 and 31.

to it renders one "kingly," just as obedience to the "perfect law of freedom" renders one "perfect" and "free." At the same time, there is likely some connection between the description of the law as royal in 2:8 and the reference to the "kingdom" (βασιλεία) God promised "to those who love him" in 2:5.[81] The two, however, are not mutually exclusive options; indeed, the adjective may have been attractive to the author precisely because it works on more than one level.[82]

Conclusion: James and the Stoics on Law

The understanding of law in the Letter of James is indebted to Stoic philosophy. James's use of the terms "implanted *logos*" and law as functional equivalents derives from the Stoic identification of human reason as a divinely given natural law. His lavish description of this law as one that is both "perfect" and "of freedom" is also best understood in light of the Stoics.

Like the various works examined in the previous chapter, however, James's presentation of these philosophical ideas is also informed by his adherence to traditions and historical convictions alien to Stoicism; ideas and beliefs with which the Stoic understanding of the *logos* innate in each human individual was not originally associated. This is evident particularly where the author speaks of the implanted *logos* with language that is more typical of Jewish and Christian than Stoic literature. James's notions that this *logos* can be "heard" and, in some sense, "received" in particular suggest that he, like the Jewish and Christian authors examined in the previous chapter, assumes that this *logos* has some external, verbal form. How does he conceive of that form? What is the "perfect law which is of freedom"?

THE LAW OF FREEDOM AND THE TORAH

The "perfect law of freedom" that James correlates with the implanted *logos* in 1:21–25 is referred to with a more abbreviated expression in 2:12, where the "brothers and sisters" are warned that they should

---

[81] Cf. Johnson, *Letter of James*, 230. Note especially in this connection that the phrase τοῖς ἀγαπῶσιν αὐτόν, used here to designate those to whom the kingdom was promised, is a formulaic expression typically used in Jewish literature with reference to those who are faithful to God's law. See below, p. 166.

[82] Cf. in this respect the author's use of the expression "law of freedom," on which see, in this connection, the Conclusion of this study.

"speak (λαλεῖτε) and act (ποιεῖτε) as those about to be judged by the law of freedom" (διὰ νόμου ἐλευθερίας). The references to speech and particularly "doing" in connection with the law of freedom in this admonition echo the general treatment of these themes in 1:19–26.[83] In 2:12, however, the author has a specific type of speech and action in mind: the warning appears at the conclusion of an extended admonition against "acts of partiality" (2:1–13). In fact, the warning of 2:12 comes right on the heels of an argument intended to prove that showing partiality is a transgression of the law (2:8–11).[84] If, then, this warning is to make any sense in its context, the "law of freedom" by which the "brothers and sisters" will ultimately be judged must be the same law which excludes acts of partiality. Jas 2:8–11 thus emerges as a critical passage for determining which law, precisely, is referred to as the "perfect law of freedom"; indeed, as the only passage in the entire work in which the author explicitly identifies commands included in this law, it is *the* critical passage in this respect.[85]

Despite Dibelius's claim that "in his ritual and moral injunctions the author does not have the Mosaic law in mind at all," but rather Christianity itself "as a new law," it is clear from the outset that the "perfect law of freedom" bears some significant relation to the Torah.[86] The love command is quoted in 2:8 with specific reference to its context within the Torah (κατὰ τὴν γραφήν). Similarly, the fact that the LXX order is followed when reference is made to the law's commands regarding murder and adultery suggests that here, too, it is

---

[83] The difficulty in using the same English term to translate ποιέω and its cognates idiomatically throughout the letter should not obscure the fact that the same Greek verb is being used in 2:12 as in 1:22–25. The connection between 2:12 and James 1 is also recognized, e.g., by Ropes, *St. James*, 201.

[84] See further below.

[85] Both Dibelius and Fabris view Jas 1:27, where the author defines characteristics of "pure and undefiled religion," as being significant in this respect as well; see Dibelius, *James*, 116; and Fabris, *Legge*, 64–66, 73, 160–65 (though cf. further 176). However, while Jas 1:27 is undoubtedly revealing of issues which are especially important to the author, it does not address the question of the precise commands which the law of freedom contains in the same way as does Jas 2:8–12.

[86] Dibelius, *James*, 18 and 119; see further 116–20. Dibelius felt that both the expression "law of freedom" and the author's silence on matters such as circumcision, diet and the Sabbath were decisive in this respect. He describes the content of this "new law" as "Jesus's words as well as the ethics which developed from them or were contained in his words" (*ibid.*, 119). Note also, however, that Dibelius himself elsewhere suggests that "core" of the "new Christian law" was "the ethical teaching of the old Jewish law" (*ibid.*, 143).

particularly the *scriptural* commands which are view.[87] The precise
relation of the "law of freedom" to the Torah, however, is obscured
by several factors. First, it is not immediately clear if it is specifically
a scriptural command that is at stake in connection with the main
concern of the passage, acts of partiality. The Torah does contain
several such prohibitions (Lev 19:15; Deut 16:19; cf. Deut 1:16–17),
but some interpreters remain skeptical as to whether James intends
a reference to the *biblical* command in particular as opposed to some
more general prohibition of partiality, as found elsewhere in traditional Christian instruction.[88] Second, the love command mentioned
in Jas 2:8, of course, receives special emphasis in a number of
Christian works as a (or even the) central command of Jewish law.
Thus a number of exegetes have argued that, while the author does
have a scriptural prohibition in mind in 2:1–13, the argument of
2:8–11 assumes that showing partiality is a transgression not simply
because it is prohibited by the Torah, but, more specifically, because
it is excluded by the love command.[89] According to Luke Timothy
Johnson, for example, the author of James regards the Torah (and
the Jewish scriptures generally) as something which only lays out
concrete examples of what the "law of love" requires.[90] Evaluation

---

[87] D. Deppe, *The Sayings of Jesus in the Epistle of James* (Chelsea: MI: Bookcrafters,
1989) 35–36; W. H. Wachob, "'The Rich in Faith' and 'the Poor in Spirit': The
socio-rhetorical function of a saying of Jesus in the epistle of James" (Ph.D. Diss.,
Emory University, 1993) 213–23, 273–79. LXX Deut 5:17–18 reverses the MT
order of these two commands; LXX Exod 20:13–15 likewises places the adultery
command before that concerning murder, and in addition places the prohibition of
stealing between them. To be sure, the author of James's use of μή plus the aor.
subj. for these commands is different from both LXX Exod 20:13, 15 and Deut
5:17–18; but cf. Mark 10:19 par. Luke 18:20.

[88] C. Burchard seems to consider it to be equally plausible that this prohibition
is merely part of the nebulous mass of paraenetic material available to early Christians
("Nächstenliebegebot, Dekalog und Gesetz in Jak 2, 8–11," *Die Hebraische Bibel und
ihre zweifache Nachgeschichte: Festschrift für Rolf Rendtorff zum 65. Geburtstag* [ed. E. Blum
et al.; Neukirchen-Vluyn: Neukirchener, 1990] 27); Davids considers an explicit reference to a biblical command by James to be no more than "an attractive hypothesis" (*James*, 115). Dibelius, on the other hand, sees the influence of Lev 19:15 as
the result of the author's dependence upon a supposed "Jewish paraenesis which
dealt with partiality in the context of its treatment of love on the basis of Lev 19"
(*James*, 142); in this respect he nears the later position of L. T. Johnson, "The Use
of Leviticus 19 in the Letter of James," *JBL* 101 (1982) 391–401.

[89] See in greatest detail Wachob, "Rich in Faith," 197–223, esp. 198–212.

[90] See esp. Johnson, "The Use of Leviticus 19." Johnson's understanding of the
author of James's approach to the Torah is also well illustrated in *idem*, "Mirror of
Rembrance," 641–45. Note in this connection that Johnson apparently considers

of the author's understanding of the relation of "love of neighbor" to the partiality command on one hand, and to "the whole law" (2:10) on the other, are thus critical for determining his general approach to the Torah. Third, the letter is silent on issues such as diet, ritual purification, the calendar and circumcision. Given this silence, one can do little more than speculate on their role in the author's view of law; and the conclusions one draws from this silence will likely depend as much or more upon one's understanding of the place of such Jewish practices in emerging Christianity in general as upon interpretation of James itself. Nonetheless, given the importance of these matters in the formation of groups within the Christian movement, this question deserves at least some attention. These three issues will be dealt with in turn.

Acts of Partiality in 2:1–13

Jas 2:1–13, as a coherent argument against the practice of partiality, represents a discrete section within James.[91] In 2:1 the audience is instructed not to "have the faith" of Jesus Christ together "with acts of partiality" (ἐν προσωπολημψίαις).[92] What "partiality" entails is

---

the author of James to have understood the Jewish scriptures in general (however precisely his "canon" may or may not have been defined) to represent the "law of freedom": of the several "models for imitation" which he finds in James, only one (Abraham) is actually found in the Torah (contrast Rahab, Elijah and Job); see esp. "Mirror of Rembrance," 641–42.

[91] Thus, e.g., does Dibelius refer to it as "A Treatise on Partiality" (*James*, 124); cf. Chaine, *Saint Jacques*, 39: "Ne faire pas acception de personnnes"; Hauck, *Die Kirchenbriefe*, 14–16: "Keine Verachtung der Armen"; Mußner, *Der Jakobusbrief*, 114: "Personenkult und kommende Gericht"; Cantinat, *Les Epîtres*, 119: "Réprobation de la partialité"; Fabris, *Legge*, 66 (cf. 165): "Parenesi contro il favoritismo"; Davids, *Epistle of James*, 105: "No Partiality is Allowable." See further Burchard, "Nächstenliebegebot," 520ff; and esp. the recent analyses of 2:1–13 in light of ancient rhetoric by Wachob ("The Rich in Faith") and D. F. Watson ("James 2 in Light of Greco-Roman Schemes of Argumentation," *NTS* 39 [1993] 94–121, esp. 102–108). While Johnson recognizes that Jas 2:8–13 "is not in the least a transition to another topic than that pursued in 2:1–7" (*Letter of James*, 235), he nonetheless presents James 2 as "a single argument" made up of three discrete sections: 2:1–7; 8–13; 14–26 (*ibid.*, 218–19). Johnson is certainly correct to emphasize the overarching unity of James 2 (see on this also Watson, "James 2," and further below, the Conclusion of this study); however, his separation of the chapter into three sections gives the impression that 2:8–13 and 2:1–7 are no more closely related to each other than they are to 2:14–26, while in fact they form, together, a single argument against the practice of partiality. See further on this below.

[92] On the precise force of the phrase ἐν προσωπολημψίαις as "a designation of accompanying circumstance," see Dibelius, *James*, 126 n. 9. For the phrase ἔχειν πίστις, cf. Jas 2:14, 18.

illustrated in an example, framed as an accusatory rhetorical question, which contrasts the deference shown to a wealthy man with the disrespectful treatment of a poor man as both enter a "synagogue" (2:2–4, συναγωγή).[93] After a further series of rhetorical questions intended to reveal that such behavior disregards both the precedent set by God's treatment of the poor (2:5b–6a) and the audience's own social experience at the hands of the wealthy (2:6b, 7), the author proceeds to argue more formally that such behavior is a transgression of the law (2:8–11, esp. 2:9).[94] In 2:8–9, showing partiality and thus transgressing the law are juxtaposed with fulfilling the "royal law" by loving one's neighbor as oneself. The love command is quoted from the LXX, and cited with specific reference to its scriptural context (2:8, κατὰ τὴν γραφήν). It is therefore striking that within the Torah, just prior to the command regarding love of neighbor (Lev 19:18), one finds a prohibition of partiality (Lev 19:15):

> You shall not render an unjust judgment; you shall not be partial to the poor (LXX: οὐ λήμψῃ πρόσωπον πτωχοῦ), or defer to the great: with justice you shall judge your neighbor.

A number of interpreters have thus concluded that the argument from the law in 2:8–11 is made with the prohibition of partiality as found in the Torah in mind.[95] The citation of the love command specifically as "scripture" would thus serve to point to the written context of Lev 19:18, where one also finds an injunction against partiality.

---

[93] Against, e.g., Spitta, *Der Brief des Jakobus*, 61 n. 3, the image of these two "going into" (εἰσέρχομαι εἰς) the συναγωγή and then being seated suggests that the term is used of the meeting place of the assembly rather than the assembly itself. (Cf. the use of ἐκκλησία with the latter meaning in Jas 5:14.) The author's use of this term is interesting given other aspects of the work which seem to suggest a self-understanding which is not formulated over-against "Judaism," e.g., the address of the letter to "the twelve tribes," on which see the preliminary remarks in M. A. Jackson-McCabe, "A Letter to the Twelve Tribes in the Diaspora: Wisdom and 'Apocalyptic' Eschatology in James" (*SBLSP* 35 [1996]) 510–15. It is, however, by no means decisive in this respect: as Dibelius points out, even Marcionite Christians could use συναγωγή as a term of self-reference, whether with respect to their meeting place or the community itself; see Dibelius, *James*, 132–34.

[94] Cf. Burchard, "Nächstenliebegebot," 524f. "Sprache und Sache wechseln [in 2:8–11]. Statt rhetorischen Fragen Argumentation mit wenn und weil, allgemeine moralische Urteile auf Grund von Normen statt Kennzeichen von Personengruppen."

[95] Spitta, *Der Brief des Jakobus*, 66–69; Ropes, *St. James*, 199; Mußner, *Der Jakobusbrief*, 124; Laws, *Epistle of James*, 114; Ludwig, *Wort als Gesetz*, 172; Johnson, "The Use of Leviticus 19," 393; *idem, Letter of James*, 231; cf. Martin, *James*, 64, 68; and Klein, *Ein vollkommmenes Werk*, 148 n. 171.

This much is in fact confirmed by a comparison of the author's illustration of "acts of partiality" in 2:2–3 with other ancient treatments of the theme. Immediately following the initial admonition against such acts in 2:1, the author offers an example of the type of behavior he has in mind in order to explain the relevance of this exhortation for his audience:

> My brothers and sisters, do not hold the faith of our glorious Lord Jesus Christ[96] with acts of partiality (ἐν προσωπολημψίαις). For if into your synagogue should come a man with gold rings and brilliant clothes, and at the same time a poor man in filthy clothes should enter, but you look to the one wearing the brilliant clothes and you say, "you sit here, in an honored place" (καλῶς),[97] while to the poor man you say, "you stand there" or "sit beneath my footstool", have you not made distinctions among yourselves[98] and become judges who reason evilly?[99]

---

[96] On the somewhat awkward τοῦ κυρίου ἡμῶν Ἰησοῦ Χριστοῦ τῆς δόξης, see esp. Dibelius, *James*, 126–28; more recently, Wachob, "The Rich in Faith," 148–59.

[97] Ropes sought to account for this adverb by hypothesizing a conversational use of this term analogous to the English "please" (*St. James*, 190). Regardless of any such convention, its primary effect in James is to contrast the "honor" shown to the rich man in the seat given him with the "dishonor" shown to the poor man; note in this respect 2:6a: by acting in this way, the addressees have "dishonored the poor" (ὑμεῖς δὲ ἠτιμάσατε τὸν πτωχόν). Cf. Wachob, "The Rich in Faith," 167, 190–92. It is also likely that the much discussed invitation to the poor man to sit ὑπὸ τὸ ὑποπόδιον μου ("under my footstool") in 2:3 is to be regarded less as realistic dialogue than as an hyperbole which makes the point regarding the humiliation of the poor man painfully clear; cf. the use of the image of the footstool in LXX Ps 109:1 (= Ps 110:1). Cf. Ward, "Communal Concern," 94f.

[98] On the problems in the interpretation of οὐ διεκρίθητε ἐν ἑαυτοῖς, see Dibelius, *James*, 136–37, and further R. B. Ward, "Partiality in the Assembly: James 2:2–4," *HTR* 62 (1969) 87–97. Some have found the use of διακρίνεσθαι in 1:6 to be decisive, and thus translate the clause in light of the theme of division within individual human beings which is so prominent in the letter (cf., e.g., the figure of the δίψυχος in 1:8, 4:8); so, e.g., Mayor, *Epistle of St. James*, 85: "Are you not divided in yourselves?, *i.e.*, guilty of διψυχία." In fact, Dibelius's objection to this, viz., that the example of 2:2–3 does not concern a wavering between "the world" and God (*James*, 136–37), seems to me to be quite off the mark: such a courting of the rich to the dishonor of the poor might be taken to signify precisely that lack of faith in the providence of God against which the author rails in James 1 and 4:1–6 (see the discussion of these passages below, in Chapter Five). At the same time, however, given the association of partiality with "judgment" and making unjust distinctions between people on the basis of their social status, it seems likely that the connotation of "judging" or "making distinctions" is foremost on the author's mind. Mitton suggests that the author plays on both senses of the verb (*Epistle of James*, 84); cf. in this respect the author's use of διαλογισμῶν in 2:4, on which see the following note.

[99] The characterization of those who show partiality as those with "evil reasonings" (διαλογισμῶν πονηρῶν) is noteworthy, for, as we have seen, the law which

This example, as definitive of the type of behavior that the author has in mind, is fundamental to the elaboration as a whole: it is an example of the "partiality" (προσωπολημψία) that, he will argue, renders one a transgressor of the law.[100]

The nominal and verbal forms of προσωπολημψία, not evident prior to their occurrence in several Christian works of the first and second centuries, are compound forms of the expression πρόσωπον λαμβάνειν, with this, in turn, being a rather literal translation of the Hebrew נשׂא פנים.[101] As used in the Hebrew Bible and LXX, these expressions do not necessarily carry a negative connotation.[102] Such a connotation is frequent, however, in judicial contexts, often implying particularly—as in Lev 19:15—a subversion of justice.[103] It is this negative usage which becomes most prominent in later Jewish and Christian literature, whether or not the term is associated with a formal judicial setting.[104]

In conformity to this later usage, προσωπολημψία carries a clearly negative connotation in Jas 2:1–13. Here it is flatly stated that faith is not to be held ἐν προσωπολημψίαις (2:1), and that those who act in this way "work sin, being convicted by the law as transgressors" (2:9). Typical, too, is the application of the concept particularly to the disparate treatment of people on the basis of their socio-economic standing;[105] and the characterization of those who act in this manner as "judges," moreover, recalls the common judicial associations of the term.[106]

---

such people thereby transgress (see 2:8–12) is itself equated with ὁ ἔμφυτος λόγος. There may in fact be a pun at work here, for διαλογισμός, as Ward points out ("Partiality," 94 n. 32), can also have the more technical legal sense of "verdict"; see BAGD, διαλογισμός §1. The audience would thus be characterized both as judges who "reason evilly" and "judges with evil verdicts." Such wordplay is by no means unknown to this author; cf., e.g., his description, in 2:20, of ἡ πίστις χωρὶς τῶν ἔργων as ἀργή: it is "useless," but more literally ἀ-εργός.

[100] Cf. Wachob, "Rich in Faith," 199 n. 163. This point will become clearer in what follows.

[101] E. Lohse, "πρόσωπον, κτλ.," TDNT 6. 779–80. On the use of such expressions in the Jewish and Christian literature, see further Ward, "Communal Concern," 41–77.

[102] Davids, Epistle of James, 105–6.

[103] Cf. Deut 1:16–17; Deut 16:18–20; 2 Chron 19:5–7; Prov 18:5.

[104] The term is explicitly connected with a (divine or human) judicial setting in Sir 35:14–16; PssSol 2:18; Rom 2:11; Did. 4:3; Ep. Barn. 4:12; 1 Pet 1:17; such a setting also seems to be implied in Col 3:25 (cf. Eph 6:9); Pol. Phil. 6:1. This association is less clear in Sir 4:22, 27; Gal 2:6; Luke 20:21 (cf. Mark 12:14 par. Matt 22:16); Jude 16; 1 Clem 1:3; Acts 10:34.

[105] Cf. Lev 19:15; Deut 1:16–17; Eph 6:9; cf. Deut 10:17; Sir 35:14–16.

[106] While the author does use judicial language here, it is doubtful that he has a formal judicial setting in mind; see further on this below, note 118.

The use of the term with reference particularly to disparate seating arrangements, on the other hand, is not widespread. Analogies are found, however, in the rabbinic literature.[107] R. B. Ward has pointed out that rabbinic interpretation of the instructions for judging outlined in the Torah included, in a manner similar to Jas 2:2–4, the formulation of hypothetical examples to illustrate partiality.[108] In one tradition of interpretation, a rich and a poor person are characterized, as in James, by means of an extravagant contrast of their clothing:

> How do we know that, if two come to court, one clothed in rags and the other in fine raiment worth a hundred manehs, they should say to him [sc. the rich man], "Either dress like him, or dress him like you?"[109]

The proof-text cited in this connection is Exod 23:7, but the words which are to be spoken to the rich man in such a situation are elsewhere attributed to R. Ishmael in connection with the interpretation of Deut 16:19, one of the biblical injunctions against partiality.[110] The similar contrast in the descriptions of the clothing of the rich and poor man in James and this rabbinic tradition is, of itself, not particularly remarkable: such stylized descriptions of the rich and the poor are not uncommon in ancient literature generally.[111] More striking, however, is the tradition of interpretation which reads the biblical injunctions against partiality particularly as prohibiting judges from inviting a rich litigant to sit while forcing a poor one to remain standing. In one passage, this tradition is connected with the interpretation of Deut 1:17 and attributed to R. Meir:

---

[107] Ropes (*St. James*, 190–91) has pointed to similar examples from the *Didascalia Apostolorum* 12 (= *Apostolic Constitutions* 2.58) and some later Christian church orders; perhaps the oldest of these is the Ethiopic *Statutes of the Apostles*, where instructions are given to a presbyter regarding the reception of wealthy or poor people who come into a Christian gathering. It is possible, as Dibelius (*James*, 134f n. 62) and Mußner (*Der Jakobusbrief*, 118f n. 5) assume, that such instructions depend upon James, though Ropes and Ward ("Communal Concern," 81 n. 4) are skeptical. James is in any case more similar to the rabbinic examples than to these; see on this below, esp. note 116.

[108] Ward, "Partiality," 89–91. For what follows I depend upon Ward's findings. Note, however, that his primary concern is to identify the social situation envisioned in Jas 2:2–4, not to establish the author's interest in the biblical command concerning partiality in particular.

[109] *b. Shebu.* 31a, as cited by Ward, "Partiality," 89f.

[110] Ward, "Partiality," 89, referring to *Deut. R., Shofetim* V, 6.

[111] See H. D. Betz, *Lukian von Samosata und das Neue Testament: Religionsgeschichtliche und Paränetische Parallelen. Ein Beitrag zum Corpus Hellenisticum Novi Testamenti* (TU 76; Berlin: Akademie Verlag, 1961) 197–98. Note also the close verbal similarities between Jas 2:2–3 and Philo *Jos.* 105: "Then they put on him a bright and clean raiment instead of his filthy prison clothes" (ἀντὶ ῥυπώσης λαμπρὰν ἐσθῆτα ἀντιδοδόντες).

> Rabbi Meir used to say: Why does the verse say, Ye shall hear the small and great alike (Deut 1:17)? So that one of the litigants shall not be kept standing and the other sit . . .[112]

This tradition is elsewhere presented as a saying handed down by R. Judah, and mentioned in connection with the interpretation of Lev 19:15:

> R. Judah said, I heard that if they please to seat the two, they may sit. What is forbidden? One shall not stand and the other sit.[113]

Ward also points to additional passages in which the interpretation regarding standing and sitting and that regarding clothing are found side by side.[114]

As is clear from these passages, the formulation of examples illustrating partiality as manifest in disparate seating arrangements made for rich and poor was an element of an oral tradition of interpretation of the Torah's partiality commands.[115] It is therefore quite striking that the author of James, too, goes on to condemn those "judges" who express partiality in this way as transgressors of the law; this point, in fact, will constitute the climax of his admonition against partiality.[116] Moreover, his specific reference to the written context of the love command in this connection, as he contrasts its fulfillment to showing partiality in 2:8–9, serves to point the reader toward a section of the scriptural law in which partiality is expressly prohibited (Lev 19:15; cf. Lev 19:18)—a passage, in fact, which the rabbis interpreted by means of examples quite similar to his own.

---

[112] *'Abot R. Nat.* 1:10, as cited by Ward, "Partiality," 90. Note that a prohibition of partiality immediately precedes the command to "hear the small and great alike" in Deut 1:17 (LXX: οὐκ ἐπιγνώσῃ πρόσωπον ἐν κρίσει).

[113] *Sipra, Kedoshim Perek* 4:4; cited by Ward, "Partiality," 90, who identifies the R. Judah in question as ben El'ai.

[114] See Ward, "Partiality," 90.

[115] The first certain attestation of this tradition of interpretation comes in the third generation of Tannaites (i.e., ca. 130–60 CE); note, however, that R. Judah may himself be passing on earlier tradition (cf. "I heard . . ."). For the dates of R. Judah and R. Meir, see H. L. Strack and G. Stemberger, *Introduction to the Talmud and Midrash* (2d printing, with emendations and updates; Minneapolis: Fortress, 1996) 75–77.

[116] Both with respect to its reference to the law and to its characterization of the transgressors as "judges" (perhaps even as judges with "evil verdicts") in this connection, Jas 2:1–13 is more similar to the rabbinic examples than those found in the later church orders and in the *Didascalia* and *Apostolic Constitutions* (on which see above, note 107).

The peculiar similarity between Jas 2:1–13 and these rabbinic passages, as Ward recognized, is best explained in terms of a common dependence upon a shared tradition of biblical interpretation.[117]

Whether the author of James, like the rabbis, presupposes a formal judicial setting, or, as is more likely, a more general liturgical one,[118] the admonition of 2:1–13 is made particularly with the biblical prohibition of partiality in mind. Among all of the instruction given in the Letter of James, then, the only commands explicitly attributed to the "law of freedom" are all from the Torah. It is

---

[117] Note also that the author of James, like R. Meir and R. Judah, is concerned specifically with giving preferential treatment to the rich over against the poor, while Lev 19:15 addresses deference to the powerful (δυνάστης) *or* poor (πτωχός).

Ward does not explore the question of the genetic relationship between Jas 2:2–3 and this rabbinic exegetical tradition in detail, for his interests lie elsewhere; and indeed, there is little in the way of evidence to discuss beyond the similarities themselves. Note, however, his comment that "It is possible that the author [of James], informed by judicial tradition, composed the example with relative freedom . . . Nevertheless, the formal similarity between the example in James and the rabbinic instructions do not allow us to speak simply of 'free composition'" (Ward, "Partiality," 97 n. 38); cf. "Communal Concern," 97: Jas 2:2–3 is "informed by judicial tradition."

[118] It is the thesis of Ward that the example of Jas 2:2–4, like the similar examples in the rabbinic literature, assumes a formal judicial setting, and he has won a significant following in this respect; see, e.g., Davids, *Epistle of James*, 105–11; Martin, *James*, 61–64; and Wachob, "The Rich in Faith," 166–69, and further his fifth chapter, "The Social and Cultural Texture of James 2:1–13." It seems more likely to me, however, that the author of James applies this tradition of legal interpretation, originally associated particularly with formal judicial proceedings, to the more general ancient practice of expressing social status through seating arrangements in public or private gatherings. That is to say, Wachob both correctly identifies the stasis of 2:1–13 as one of definition ("The Rich in Faith," 365–71) and rightly emphasizes that the argument is to be understood in light of ancient patronage (*ibid.*, esp. 383–94); but in my view what the author attempts to do is to present the commonplace ancient practice of reflecting disparate social status through seating arrangements in public (or semi-public) gatherings—not merely in formal judicial hearings—under the rubric of "partiality" and "unjust judging." I would suggest, in short, that the author of James applies a traditional interpretation of Lev 19:15, which saw partiality as being reflected particularly in disparate seating arrangements given to the wealthy and poor in formal judicial proceedings, to a situation which he finds current in Christian assemblies, in which the wealthy are given the seats of honor by virtue of their wealth and/or patronage. When the "brothers and sisters" engage in such practices, he argues, they have become "unjust judges," and thus transgressors against the biblical prohibition of partiality. Viewed from this perspective, Jas 2:1–13 appears as a quite radical critique of a system of patronage which was largely taken for granted in the ancient Mediterranean world. See further the recent study by J. S. Kloppenborg, "Status und Wohltätigkeit bei Paulus und Jakobus," *Von Jesus zum Christus: Christologische Studien. Festgabe für Paul Hoffmann zum 65. Geburtstag* (ed. R. Hoppe and U. Busse; BZNW 93; Berlin and New York: de Gruyter, 1998) 127–54. I am grateful to Prof. Kloppenborg for providing me with a copy of this article.

therefore quite clear that the author assumes, at the very least, a close relationship between the scriptural law and the law of freedom—and thus between the Torah and the implanted *logos*. Indeed, his juxtaposition of loving one's neighbor "according to the scripture" (κατὰ τὴν γραφήν; cf. Lev 9:18) and showing partiality (cf. Lev 19:15) assumes the written context of these commands within this law.[119] This casts strong doubt upon the "new law" interpretation of the law of freedom, at least as formulated by Dibelius. What begins to emerge as a more likely possibility is rather a particular interpretation of the Torah itself.[120] In this connection, the import of the reference to Lev 19:18 in Jas 2:8 becomes crucial. Johnson, for example, has recently argued that this command represents *the* central command of the law in James's view, with the rest of the Torah serving primarily as a privileged pool of examples that illustrate the ways in which it is to be concretely observed.[121] Does James in fact interpret the law entirely through the lens of the love command? Is showing partiality wrong particularly because it is a transgression of the love command, or simply because it is prohibited in the Torah?

---

[119] On the significance of this juxtaposition, as well as the εἰ μέντοι . . . εἰ δέ construction which makes it clear, see below.

[120] Cf. Ropes's view, based on James's description of his law as one which is "perfect" and "of liberty," that "he conceived of Christianity as a law, including and fulfilling the old one." Ropes goes on to speak of a "new law" in this connection (*St. James*, 178–79). Ropes elsewhere speaks of this law as "the Jewish law as understood by Christians" (*ibid.*, 167), with "the ten commandments and other precepts of the O. T." holding "a chief place . . . however much they may or may not be supplemented by other teaching and by Christian interpretation" (*St. James*, 30). On this latter description, at least, the sense in which this represents a "new law" is not immediately clear—as Ropes himself apparently recognized, as suggested by his use of sanitary pips with the phrase "new law." After all, divergent interpretations of the Torah were an important factor in the formation of Jewish groups, but one does not normally speak of the "new law," for example, of the Dead Sea Sect, the Sadducees or the Pharisees.

[121] See above, note 90. See esp. "The Use of Leviticus 19," 400 (emphasis his): "keeping the law of love involves observing the *commandments* explicated by the Decalogue (2:11) and Lev 19:12–18 in their entirety . . . Breaking the prohibition against partiality is breaking the law of love, for that prohibition is one of its explications." See also Wachob, "The Rich in Faith," 268–69: "[Lev 19:15] is not simply a precept from the written law but a rhetorical judgment that is based on the scripture recited in Jas 2:8, the written summary of the whole law. Hence the injunction against partiality in Lev 19:15 is effectively reinterpreted by our author as the opposite of 'loving one's neighbor as oneself'."

Partiality, Love of Neighbor, and the "Whole Law"

Love of neighbor, of course, receives special emphasis in a number of early Christian works. Of particular interest in connection with Jas 2:8–11 are those instances in which Lev 19:18 is accorded some special status specifically among the other commands of the law.[122] Love of neighbor, paired with love of God (Deut 6:5), is so elevated in each of the synoptic gospels. In Luke, Jesus agrees when a legal expert singles out these two commands from all that is "written in the law" as the particular requirements for inheriting "eternal life" (Luke 10:25–28). Conversely, Mark tells of a scribe's approval when Jesus ranks Deut 6:4–5 and Lev 19:18 as first and second, respectively, of all the commandments; and when the scribe then suggests that these two are more important than demands of the sacrificial cult in particular, Jesus declares that he is "not far from the kingdom of God" (Mark 12:28–34). The Jesus of Matthew similarly names Deut 6:5 as "the greatest and first commandment," and Lev 19:18 the "second," when a Pharisaic legal expert asks him "which commandment in the law is the greatest" (Matt 22:34–39). Matthew's Jesus then adds that these two commands are those upon which "the whole law (ὅλος ὁ νόμος)[123] and the prophets hang" (Matt 22:40). So too Paul, somewhat like Matthew's Jesus, accords love of neighbor a summarizing function vis-à-vis "the entire law." Quite unlike the former, however, Paul considers this command alone to be an adequate summary in this respect: "The . . . entire law (ὁ . . . πᾶς νόμος) is fulfilled in a single word, in 'you will love your neighbor as yourself'" (Gal 5:14).[124]

---

[122] As opposed, for example, to the general emphasis on love found in the Johannine epistles, where no explicit connection to scriptural law is made.

[123] I follow the text as rendered in the 26th edition of Nestle-Aland, *Novum Testamentum Graece*; note, however, that ὅλος is omitted in some mss.

[124] In the context of Galatians, the force of this statement seems to me to be more pointed than the NRSV translation of πεπλήρωται as "is summed up" suggests: Paul implies not merely that love of neighbor is an apt summary of the law, but that loving one's neighbor is in fact equivalent to fulfilling "the whole law." Cf. Rom 13:8: ὁ . . . ἀγαπῶν τὸν ἕτερον νόμον πεπλήρωκεν; and further the nuanced discussion in H. D. Betz, *Galatians: A Commentary on Paul's Letter to the Churches in Galatia* (Hermeneia; Philadelphia: Fortress, 1979) 274–76. This, perhaps, represents another significant difference between Paul and Matthew's Jesus, for it is not at all clear that the latter would agree that his summary has this implication.

The formulation of such summaries was not a peculiarly Christian phenomenon; nor, as the passages from Mark and Luke examined above already suggest, was the placement of emphasis particularly on love of God and/or love of one's fellow human being in this connection. Love of God, while not, to my knowledge, explicitly cited as a summary of the law, is routinely used in Jewish literature as a shorthand expression for living in accord with the law.[125] In fact, the repeated references in James to the eschatological rewards promised by God "to those who love him" (1:12; 2:5: τοῖς ἀγαπῶσιν αὐτόν) echoes a common designation of those who maintain the covenant by keeping God's commands, and to whom God will therefore remain faithful. Such usage is found already in the decalogue's prohibition of idolatry as found in Exod 20:5–6 and Deut 5:9–10: "I the Lord your God am a jealous God, punishing children for the iniquity of parents, to the third and fourth generation of those who reject me, but showing steadfast love to the thousandth generation of those who love me (LXX: τοῖς ἀγαπῶσίν με) and keep my commandments."[126] The precise phrase τοῖς ἀγαπῶσιν αὐτόν itself, in fact, is found repeatedly in such contexts.[127] Paul's notion that "the entire law" is fulfilled through love of neighbor, on the other hand, might be compared with Hillel's reported view: "What is hateful to you, do not to your neighbor: that is the whole law (זו היא כל התורה כולה), while the rest is commentary thereof."[128] More similar to the synoptics in this respect, finally, is Philo's division of Moses's law under the two great headings (κεφάλια) of duty to God (τὸ πρὸς θεόν), specified as εὐσέβεια and ὁσιότης, and to one's fellow human being (τὸ πρὸς ἀνθρώπους), specified as φιλανθρωπία and δικαιοσύνη, "each of them splitting up into multiform branches, all highly laud-

---

[125] See Ludwig *Wort als Gesetz*, 144–50, esp. 144–46. Note, however, that some of the passages discussed by Ludwig are not entirely to the point; a number of them, for example, speak of love of the commands themselves rather than love of God in the form of obedience to the commands of his law (e.g. Ps 119:47, 48, 127, 159, 166–68).

[126] Cf. Deut 30:16, 20.

[127] Deut 7:9; 2 Esdr 11:5 (= Neh 1:5); *Pss. Sol.* 14:1–2; cf. further LXX Dan 9:4, where the object of the phrase is second-person, being directly addressed to God.

[128] *b. Shabb.* 31a; the translation is that of H. Freedman, *Shabbath: Hebrew-English Edition of the Babylonian Talmud* (2 vols.; London; Jerusalem; New York: Soncino, 1972). See further I. Abrahams, *Studies in Pharisaism and the Gospels. First and Second Series* (repr. in Library of Biblical Studies; ed. H. M. Orlinsky with a prolegomenon by M. S. Enslin; New York: Ktav, 1967 [= 1917–1924]) 1. 18–29; I cite the Hebrew as found on p. 23.

able."[129] Thus for Philo the first table of the decalogue concerns τὰ ἱερώτατα and the second τὰ πρὸς ἀνθρώπους δίκαια,[130] with these two tables, in turn, presenting the "genera" or "headings" under which the "special laws" which make up the remainder of the law can be classified.[131]

Such summaries, moreover, functioned differently for different authors. While figures such as Hillel or Philo might have been inclined to agree with Paul that "the [commandments] 'you shall not commit adultery', 'you shall not kill', 'you shall not steal', 'you shall not covet', and any other commandment is summed up (ἀνακεφαλαιοῦται) in this word, 'you will love your neighbor as yourself,'" it is by no means clear that they would have given unqualified assent to Paul's subsequent inference[132] that "one who loves another has fulfilled (πεπλήρωκεν) the law" (Rom 13:8–9), that "love is therefore the fulfilling of law" (Rom 13:10). To the extent that Paul's view of the summarizing function of the love command is advanced with an eye to his more general position on the importance of circumcision, etc.,[133] Hillel and Philo would surely have chafed at the claim. Philo elsewhere rails against so-called "extreme allegorists" who, having recognized (correctly, according to Philo!) the symbolic nature of the laws, neglect their literal sense and thus their observance "as though they had become disembodied souls."[134] And if the "whole law" was for Hillel only "commentary" on his version of the golden rule, it was a "commentary" whose details nonetheless demanded careful attention and exacting interpretation—tasks to which he, in large measure, devoted his life. The identification of basic principles in

---

[129] *De Spec. Leg.* 2.63. Cf. in this respect the double command "Love the Lord and your neighbor" in *T. Iss.* 5:2, which follows on a still more general instruction to "keep the law of God" (5:1); here, however, it is not explicitly said that love of God and of neighbor are understood to sum up "keeping the law of God." Given the questions surrounding the literary history of the *Testaments* generally, it is not altogether clear in any case whether this constitutes non-Christian evidence.

[130] *De Dec.* 106; cf. the superscript to *De Specialibus Legibus*. Note also Philo's explanation in *De Dec.* 107 of the fact that the fifth commandment, despite this schema, concerns honoring one's parents.

[131] *De Spec. Leg.* 1.1: τὰ γένη ... τῶν ἐν εἴδει νόμων; cf. *De Dec.* 175: κεφάλαια ... τῶν ἐν εἴδει νόμων.

[132] Note esp. that Rom 13:9, with its post-positive γάρ, is presented as an explanation of 13:8b—a logical connection which the NRSV quite obscures.

[133] It is noteworthy that Paul mentions the summarizing function of the love command only in Galatians and Romans, i.e., in those letters in which he was most preoccupied with the question of Jewish customs.

[134] Philo, *Mig. Abr.* 89–93.

terms of which the law of Moses could be summarized was made
by these figures with heuristic, not reductionistic, intentions.

The reference in Jas 2:8 to fulfilling "the royal law according to
the scripture, 'you will love your neighbor as yourself'" is undoubtedly to be understood in light of the emphasis placed on love of
one's fellow human beings in the Jewish and Christian literature,
and more particularly on the emphasis placed on Lev 19:18 by early
Christians. Comparison of James with this literature, however, requires
attention to two distinct questions. Does the author of James understand the love command to be a summary of the Torah? And if so,
what are the implications of this fact for his understanding of the
other commands which this law contains?[135]

In Jas 2:8–9, loving one's neighbor and showing partiality are contrasted by means of an εἰ μέντοι . . . εἰ δέ construction:

> εἰ μέντοι νόμον τελεῖτε βασιλικὸν κατὰ τὴν γραφήν· ἀγαπήσεις τὸν πλησίον
> σου ὡς σεαυτόν, καλῶς ποιεῖτε· εἰ δὲ προσωπολημπτεῖτε, ἁμαρτίαν ἐργάζεσθε
> ἐλεγχόμενοι ὑπὸ τοῦ νόμου ὡς παραβάται.[136]

These verses are critical for understanding the author's view of the
love command vis-à-vis the law as a whole and its other commands.
Isolated from their context, however, they can and have been taken
to support a variety of interpretations. There are two chief ambiguities which complicate interpretation. First, it is unclear whether
the "royal law" refers to the whole of the "law of freedom" or to
Lev 19:18 in particular.[137] Second, and more important for our purposes, is the relation of the condition of 2:8 to that of 2:9: taken by
themselves, these verses can be construed either as a statement of
opposite or of simultaneous conditions. Thus while the majority of
interpreters have argued that the author juxtaposes loving one's neighbor and showing partiality because he views the latter as a transgression of the love command,[138] a number of scholars have understood

---

[135] The mere categorization of James as a Christian writing is not, of course,
sufficient grounds for concluding that he would have been more similar to Paul
than to Philo or Hillel with respect to his understanding of the implications of such
a summary for the other commands of the law. As is clear from a variety of sources
(including Galatians and Romans themselves), Paul's stance on the question of the
law was anything but ubiquitous in early Christianity.

[136] For the textual situation as regards 2:8–9, see B. Aland *et al.*, *Novum Testamentum
Graecum. Editio Critica Maior. IV: Catholic Letters. Installment 1: James* (Stuttgart: Deutsche
Bibelgesellschaft, 1997) 1. 31–32.

[137] For a sampling of advocates of each position see Klein, *Ein vollkommenes Werk*,
147 with notes 157 and 158.

[138] Thus the vast majority of interpreters, whether or not they consider the author

him to be arguing that those who show partiality, even if they love their neighbor, are transgressors of the law nonetheless.[139] Given these ambiguities, the author's view of the relation of the love command to the biblical prohibition of partiality and, by implication, to the "whole law," can only be determined in conjunction with an analysis of the larger argument from the law presented in 2:8–11.

The argument of 2:8–11

However one interprets 2:8–9, it is clear that 2:10–11 is meant to explain the charge that those who show partiality are "convicted by the law as transgressors."[140] Immediately after this latter charge, the author states a more general principle which justifies it: "for (γάρ) whoever keeps the whole law (ὅλον τὸν νόμον), but stumbles in one [respect], has become liable for all of it (πάντων ἔνοχος)."[141] As we have seen, phrases analogous to James's ὅλον τὸν νόμον are used in connection with summaries of the law by Paul (Gal 5:14, ὁ πᾶς νόμος) and Hillel (b. Shabb. 31a, כל התורה כולה), while precisely the same phrase is found in at least some manuscripts of Matthew (Matt 22:40, ὅλος ὁ νόμος), whether with reference to loving one's neighbor as oneself (Paul), the golden rule (Hillel), or a combination of Deut 6:5 and Lev 19:18 (Matthew). It is therefore striking that if—as is clearly the case—the second half of the complex condition of 2:10 (stumbling in one respect) refers back to the condition of 2:9 (showing partiality), the first half of the complex condition of 2:10 (keeping "the whole law") corresponds to the condition of 2:8 (fulfilling the "royal law" according to Lev 19:18). In short: fulfilling "the royal law according to the scripture 'you will love your neighbor as yourself'" in Jas 2:8–9 corresponds with keeping "the whole law" in Jas 2:10.[142] This correspondence is not likely to be coincidental. On the

---

to have Lev 19:15 in mind. See in most detail the recent analysis of Wachob, "The Rich in Faith," 197–212.

[139] So Spitta, Der Brief des Jakobus, 66–69; Kühl, Die Stellung des Jakobusbriefes, 4–11; Ludwig, Wort als Gesetz, 171–75.

[140] Note esp. the repeated use of γάρ in 2:10 and 2:11; cf. Wachob, "The Rich in Faith," 212–23.

[141] For the sense of πάντων ἔνοχος see Ropes, St. James, 200: "This is a rhetorical way of saying that he is a transgressor of 'the law as a whole' (παραβάτης νόμου, v. 11), not of all the precepts in it." Nonetheless, note in this connection that while the neuter ἑνί cannot refer to an implied (feminine) ἐντολή, it is clear from the context of 2:8–11—and particularly from 2:11, which is intended to explain 2:10 (note again the use of γάρ)—that the author here thinks of "one" and "all" of the law's commands.

[142] See the graphic depiction of this structural parallel below, on p. 172.

contrary, it strongly suggests that the author is aware of the use of Lev 19:18 as a summary of "the whole law." The reference to the "royal law" in this connection supports this conclusion whether it describes the love command in particular or, more likely, "the whole law":[143] if the "royal law" connotes "the whole law," 2:8 apparently refers to "fulfilling the whole law" by loving one's neighbor as one-self; and if the "royal law" refers specifically to the love command, this lavish description denotes its special importance relative to the law's other commands. Either way, the verse clearly indicates that Lev 19:18 is accorded some special status among the other commands of the law; and given the corresponding reference to keeping "the whole law" in 2:10, it can safely be concluded from the argument of 2:8–11 that the author is aware of the use of "love of neighbor" as a summary of "the whole law."

On the other hand, given this correspondence between 2:8 and 2:10a, and 2:9 and 2:10b–c, respectively, 2:8–9 are clearly to be understood, like 2:10, as positing simultaneous rather than opposite conditions. That is, despite the allusion to the love command's summary function, the author formulates a condition in which one *both* (i) "keeps the whole law," that is, by loving one's neighbor as one-self *and* (ii) "stumbles in one respect," that is, by showing partiality. The result is rather paradoxical—as, indeed, is 2:10 itself.[144] Nonetheless, the subsequent explanation of 2:10 confirms that this is in fact the case; for the defense of 2:10 in 2:11 also assumes a condition in which one command is kept while another is broken. The warrant for 2:10 is presented as follows:

ὁ γὰρ εἰπών· μὴ μοιχεύσῃς, εἶπεν καί· μὴ φονεύσῃς· εἰ δὲ οὐ μοιχεύεις, φονεύεις δέ, γέγονας παραβάτης νόμου.[145]

The first half of this verse identifies the basis for the general principle that "stumbling in one respect" renders one "liable for the law as a whole" (2:10). Citing, by way of example, two additional com-

---

[143] See above, note 78.

[144] The condition envisioned in Jas 2:10, in which one "keeps the whole law" while failing with respect to one of its elements is, strictly speaking, impossible. According to Johnson, "[i]t must be that someone *tries to keep* the whole law, since the condition of not keeping each part shows that the translation 'whoever keeps the whole law' is impossible" (*Letter of James*, 232). This latter view, however, fails to recognize the irony of the passage, on which see below.

[145] The only substantive variant in this verse is the replacement of παραβάτης with ἀποστάτης in 𝔓[74] and A.

mands (murder and adultery), the author grounds this principle in the various commands' common source, whether conceived as the law or the lawgiver himself.[146] He then proceeds, in the latter half of the verse, to formulate a condition parallel to that of 2:10 using these newly introduced commands. A condition, that is, of simultaneous obedience to the adultery command and disobedience to the murder command is posited in order to demonstrate more forcefully the specific claim that such a condition results in one's status as a transgressor of the law: no one, it is assumed, would deny that a murderer who has not committed adultery is any less a law-breaker![147]

The entire argument of 2:10–11, then, is predicated on the assumption of a condition of simultaneous obedience and disobedience which renders one a transgressor of the law. The argument moves from specific commands (love of neighbor and partiality in 2:8–9), to the statement of a general principle (2:10), and back to specific commands (adultery and murder in 2:11) in order to support the claim that showing partiality—even, paradoxically, if one "keeps the whole law" by loving one's neighbor—renders one a transgressor of the law. The correspondences between the two conditional statements of 2:8–9 and the complex conditions of 2:10 and 2:11 are in fact quite striking:[148]

---

[146] While the author of James elsewhere refers to scripture itself as "speaking" (cf. 2:23; 4:5, 6) the aorist forms seem to suggest that it is the "lawgiver" (cf. 4:12) that is the implied subject; so Mußner, *Der Jakobusbrief*, 125; Laws, *Epistle of James*, 114; Davids, *Epistle of James*, 117; Burchard, "Nächstenliebegebot," 519; Johnson, *Letter of James*, 232; Wachob, "The Rich in Faith," 218f.

In contrast to the position argued here, namely, that the principle of 2:10 is based upon the common origin of all the commands, Fabris contends that the author argues that "stumbling in one respect" is to become liable for "the whole" precisely inasmuch as the latter is summed up in the command of love of neighbor. This argument, however, as Fabris himself acknowledges (*Legge*, 172), is simply not in the text. Fabris's interpretation is rather a function of the problematic assumption of a single "New Testament" view of the love command which he brings to the text: "Questo precetto dell'amore del prossimo, secondo la tradizione parenetica del N.T., non è solo il più importante di tutti, ma è la sintesi ed il compimento di tutte le prescrizioni della legge" (*ibid.*, 171).

[147] Laws, who finds this section of James "curiously inept" since murder and adultery were "so generally accepted that assent to them would hardly be seen to entail assent to the Jewish Law and everything contained in it" (*Epistle of James*, 113), has missed the point of 2:11b entirely. The argument is effective precisely because these commands were "so generally accepted"!

[148] Note further that, as Wachob points out ("The Rich in Faith," 219, 222), the conditional statements of 2:8–9 and 2:11 are both present simple conditionals, while 2:10—as the general principle which undergirds both the judgment of 2:8–9 and 2:11—is formulated as a conditional relative sentence which functions as a future more vivid condition (see on this latter point *ibid.*, 214f).

2:8–9	2:10	2:11b
εἰ μέντοι	ὅστις γὰρ	εἰ δὲ
νόμον τελεῖτε βασιλικὸν κατὰ τὴν γραφήν· ἀγαπήσεις τὸν πλησίον σου ὡς σεαυτόν,	ὅλον τὸν νόμον τηρήσῃ	οὐ μοιχεύεις
καλῶς ποιεῖτε·		
εἰ δὲ προσωπολημπτεῖτε,	πταίσῃ δὲ ἐν ἑνί,	φονεύεις δέ,
ἁμαρτίαν ἐργάζεσθε ἐλεγχόμενοι ὑπὸ τοῦ νόμου ὡς παραβάται.	γέγονεν πάντων ἔνοχος.	γέγονας παραβάτης νόμου.

Given the fact that the juxtaposition of fulfilling the royal law according to Lev 19:18 with breaking the partiality command of Lev 19:15 in 2:8–9 corresponds to that of keeping "the whole law" with "stumbling in one respect" in 2:10; and given, further, that both the general principle which forms the basis for the judgment of 2:9 and the demonstration of the viability of that principle in 2:11 assume a condition of simultaneous obedience and disobedience; it can only be concluded that 2:8–9, too, are intended as positing simultaneous rather than formally opposite conditions.[149]

The upshot of this analysis is that James assumes, at least for the sake of argument, the use of the love command as a summary of "the whole law." Nonetheless, he presents for consideration a situation in which the love command is kept while another of the law's commands—namely, that prohibiting partiality—is broken; and he concludes that the subject of such a condition is a "transgressor of the law" despite his or her attention to the summarizing command of Lev 19:18.[150] The citation of the latter specifically within its writ-

---

[149] Against Wachob, it is scarcely an "immediate inference" from the simple juxtaposition of 2:8 and 2:9 that showing partiality is an offense against the love command ("The Rich in Faith," 208). On this logic, one might also assert that it is an "immediate inference" from 2:11 that committing murder is an offense against the adultery prohibition.

[150] To be sure, the author's primary concern lies with socio-economic matters rather than with legislation regarding diet or ritual purity; see on this below, under the heading "The Law of Freedom and the Torah." Nonetheless, it is clear from the logic of the argument presented in 2:8–11 that he considers the love command,

ten context is quite effective in this respect.[151] Unlike Paul, for example, who refers to love of neighbor more generally as a "word" which summarizes the whole law (Gal 5:14; Rom 13:9), the love command is cited explicitly κατὰ τὴν γραφήν: the command to love one's neighbor in Lev 19:18 is thus presented as one (albeit one important) command alongside others—including the prohibition of partiality (cf. Lev 19:15!)—within the written law.

In fact, the apparent tension between obeying a command that summarizes "the whole law" while at the same time breaking another command of that law is captured perfectly in the paradoxical statement of 2:10. Obeying "the whole law" while stumbling with respect to one of its commands is, strictly speaking, impossible. However, when 2:10 is viewed as a more general restatement of 2:8–9, the paradox is somewhat mitigated: keeping the "whole law," in this context, is actually a reference to obeying a particular command of

---

regardless of its summarizing function, to be one command among others within the Torah. Already in 1905, Kühl characterized the failure of exegetes to recognize this fact as "eine der merkwürdigsten Erscheinungen in der Geschichte der Exegese." His attempt to account for this is quite telling: "Ich kann mir das nur aus der begreiflichen Scheu erklären, *innerhalb des neuen Testamentes unterchristliche Anschauungen* von dem Werte des Gesetzes für den Christen und von der Bedeutung des Liebesgebotes im Zusammenhange mit der Frage nach der Erfüllung des Gesetzes konstatieren zu müssen" (*Die Stellung des Jakobusbriefes*, 10; emphasis added). It is likely that such a general notion that "love of neighbor" lies at the very heart of Christianity is responsible for the tension, observed already by Meyer (*Rätsel*, 149 and n. 6), in Dibelius's assessment of the understanding of the love command in James: on one hand, it "is not considered in our passage to be the chief commandment, in the sense of the famous saying of Jesus," but is rather "one commandment alongside others" (though, it is to be noted, within a new Christian law, not the "old" Jewish one); at the same time, however, this "Christian law," *as a Christian law*, "is not obeyed by being ever so careful in tiny matters, but rather by fulfilling the great commandment of love" (Dibelius, *James*, 142, 144)! Note also that Dibelius himself describes the author's remarkably hostile statements regarding "the rich" as "sub-Christian" (*unterchristlichen*); see *James*, 49 (= *Der Brief des Jakobus*, 49). In this connection, it is hardly coincidental that Spitta (*Der Brief des Jakobus*, 66–69) and Meyer (*Rätsel*, 149–50)—each of whom understood James to have originally been a non-Christian Jewish writing—both argued that its author did *not* consider loving one's neighbor to be tantamount to fulfilling "the whole law." The fact that these competing interpretations can be correlated with opposing general classifications of James as "Christian" or "Jewish" suggests that the issue here is not simply the text of James: equally critical for interpretation are the assumptions regarding the nature of "Christianity" and its relation to "Judaism" which one brings to the text.

[151] If the "royal law" does in fact refer to the "whole law" as suggested above, then 2:8 is to be understood as an ironic statement of the view that one can fulfill the "whole law" simply by loving one's neighbor—an irony which emerges in any case in 2:10. See further on the ironic aspects of this passage immediately below.

the law, namely, Lev 19:18. The paradoxical quality remains nonetheless, lending, indeed, a rather derisive tone to the argument: there is an unmistakable irony in the author's allusion in 2:10 to keeping "the whole law" by fulfilling the love command given his larger point that one can love one's neighbor as oneself and yet still be exposed by the law as a transgressor.[152] While aware of the use of "love of neighbor" as a summary of "the whole law," the author himself is at best wary of this summary, at least to the extent that it might lead one to neglect other specific points of the law. Regardless of its possible summarizing function, "loving one's neighbor as oneself" is not, without further ado, simply equivalent to fulfilling the whole law in the Letter of James.

From a structural point of view, the primary difference between 2:8–9 and the conditionals of 2:10 and 2:11 is that while the latter two present single, complex conditional statements, 2:8–9 consists of two formally distinct conditions. Jas 2:8, that is, contains its own apodosis: "you do well" (καλῶς ποιεῖτε). Even this difference, though, strongly supports interpreting 2:8–9 as presenting simultaneous conditions, and reading a certain irony in the author's treatment of the love command as a summary of "the whole law." For this same "commendation," differing only in number, appears with an unmistakable sarcasm in the immediately following—and closely related[153]— discussion of πίστις and ἔργα: you who "believe that 'God is one'," the author says, "do well" (καλῶς ποιεῖς); but no more so than the demons who also believe this "and shudder" (2:19)!

It is particularly striking that while this "commendation" is given in Jas 2:8 to those who "love their neighbor" in accord with Lev 19:18, it is directed in 2:19 to those who believe that "God is one," a passage which echoes the Shema as found in Deut 6:4–9: ἄκουε, Ἰσραηλ· κύριος ὁ θεὸς ἡμῶν κύριος εἷς ἐστιν . . . (LXX Deut 6:4).[154]

---

[152] That is, the author grants for the sake of argument the claim of his imagined audience that they have observed the commandment in which "the whole law" is fulfilled by loving their neighbor as themselves. Nonetheless, he argues, they are *still* lawbreakers if they disregard other commands of the law, e.g., Lev 19:15. In short, while granting that love of neighbor might serve in some sense as a summary of "the whole law," the author pointedly critiques the notion that one actually fulfills the whole law simply by loving one's neighbor as oneself. Put in the terms of the distinction drawn above on pp. 167f, the author concedes the heuristic use of this summary while rejecting the reductionistic one.

[153] See on this point the concluding chapter of this study.

[154] Dibelius, *James*, 159; Cantinat, *Les Épitres de Saint Jacques et de Saint Jude*, 147; Davids, *Epistle of James*, 125; Martin, *James*, 89; cf. Johnson, *Letter of James*, 240.

Lev 19:18 and this passage from Deuteronomy, which follows the statement that "God is one" with an injunction to love him (Deut 6:5), are of course precisely those two passages singled out in the synoptic gospels as the two most important passages of the law.[155] Though seldom noted in the commentaries,[156] this correspondence between Jas 2:8 and 2:19 goes a long way toward clarifying the author's interest in the love command in 2:8–11. Given the emphasis placed on love of neighbor particularly in connection with summaries of the law in Jewish and especially Christian literature, it is no more necessary to suppose that the reference to Lev 19:18 in 2:8 implies that some "opponents" have defended behaving in the manner described in 2:2–3 by claiming that they had thereby sought to "love" the wealthy man[157] any more than it is necessary to assume that 2:19 reflects a situation in which some actual interlocutor has appealed to his belief that "God is one" to defend his extraordinarily callous treatment of the poor as narrated in 2:15–16. Nor is it the case that the author wishes to deny the importance of Lev 19:18 or Deut 6:4ff., or even the possibility that they might, together or separately, represent in some sense an adequate summation of that which is required for "life" or entrance into the "kingdom."[158] Rather, the author singles out Lev 19:18 in 2:8 and alludes to Deut 6:4ff in 2:19 because he is concerned that an eschatological confidence based on attention to these general principles might lead to neglect of other elements of the law which are, ultimately, of equal importance.[159] Faith that "God is one" is crucial,[160] but cannot, of itself,

---

[155] See esp. Mark 12:29–30, which includes Deut 6:4 in its citation; Matthew and Luke both omit Deut 6:4 in this connection, and cite the command to love God in Deut 6:5 immediately.

[156] This is apparently a consequence of the failure to recognize the irony in the author's treatment of Lev 19:18 in 2:8–11. Indeed, where the repetition of the clause καλῶς ποιεῖτε, -εῖς in 2:8 and 2:19 is noted at all by those who argue that showing partiality is a transgression of the love command, it is generally only to point out that the phrase is used ironically in the latter, but not in the former! See Mayor, *Epistle of St. James*, 91; also Johnson, *Letter of James*, 231.

[157] So, e.g., Spitta, *Der Brief des Jakobus*, 66–69; Kühl, *Die Stellung*, 4–11; Ropes, *St. James*, 197.

[158] The repeated designation of those for whom God's promises of "life" (1:12; cf. Luke 10:25–28) and "kingdom" (2:5; cf. Mark 12:28–34) will be fulfilled as "those who love him" would seem to suggest that he himself finds "love of God," at least, to be an apt summary. See above p. 166 on the use of this phrase in other literature. The issue in 2:8–11 is not, however, merely one of competing summaries.

[159] All commands, after all, come from God; cf. Jas 2:10–11. Cf. Kühl, *Die Stellung*, 10f; Ropes, *St. James*, 197.

[160] Note that the author himself elsewhere invokes this belief—indeed, likely Deut

"save" (cf. 2:14); so too, those who "love their neighbor" do well, but this, of itself, does not ensure that they will not ultimately be "convicted by the law as transgressors" (2:10). Summary or not, merely to love one's neighbor is not necessarily to "keep the whole law." Attention to this command alone, therefore, is not sufficient grounds for confidence in the face of a coming judgment which will be executed by the standard of the whole "law of freedom" (2:12, διὰ νόμου ἐλευθερίας), and one which will be, potentially, "merciless" (2:13).

The Law of Freedom and the Torah

That it is the Torah which the author of James describes as the "perfect law of freedom" emerges with clarity from his argument that those who show partiality are transgressors of the law (Jas 2:8–11). All four of the commands explicitly identified as elements of the law in this passage—and indeed, in the letter as a whole—are commands of the Torah. He follows the LXX order when citing, as words of the law or of God the "lawgiver" (cf. 4:12), the prohibitions of murder and adultery; and he draws upon a tradition of legal interpretation associated with the biblical prohibition of partiality in order to provide an example of the type of behavior he feels Lev 19:15 excludes. More tellingly still, his references to love of neighbor and partiality in 2:8–9 assume the written context of these commands within the Torah: aware that "love of neighbor" is used as a summary of "the whole law," the author effectively locates this command within its scriptural context, thus identifying it as one command alongside others within a larger body of law—and particularly alongside that which prohibits partiality, his chief concern. Obedience to each of these commands is equally important given the fact that both stem from the same source, whether conceived as the law or, which is the implication in any case, the lawgiver himself. Regardless of its summarizing function, therefore, adherence to the love command alone will not suffice for success at the eschatological judgment, for this judgment will be executed by the lawgiver in accordance with the whole of the "law of freedom" (2:12; cf. 4:12).

Scriptural law—that is, the various bodies of legislation that were gathered together and identified as a law given by God through

---

6:4ff itself—when arguing for the necessity of "doing" rather than "judging" the law (4:12): εἷς ἐστιν [ὁ] νομοθέτης καὶ κριτὴς ὁ δυνάμενος σῶσαι καὶ ἀπολέσαι.

Moses—was (and is), of course, subject to a variety of interpretations. Differing interpretations of this law were one important factor, albeit among others, in the formation of distinct Jewish and Christian groups.[161] One cannot, therefore, make facile conclusions regarding the author's interpretation of particular aspects of this body of legislation based simply on his general allegiance to it. Indeed, of the four commands of this law that he explicitly cites, the only ones to which he devotes any extended attention are the prohibition of partiality and the love command. Interestingly, both in connection with the former and in the statement of his general legal principle that "whoever keeps the whole law but stumbles in one respect has become liable for all" (2:10), one finds similarities to rabbinic tradition.[162] One ought not, however, draw any sweeping conclusions from these isolated examples. Little more than his adherence to this general principle, his related insistence that obedience to the love command does not of itself constitute keeping "the whole law," and his particular interest in social and economic matters[163] can be determined regarding his general approach to the Torah.

The distinction between the written body of legislation and its interpretation at the hands of different individuals or groups takes on a particular importance with respect to those aspects of Jewish law whose interpretation proved most divisive in early Christianity, that is, the legislation concerning the cult, purity, diet, the calendar, and circumcision. The author's silence with respect to these aspects of the law would seem to indicate, at least, that they are not among his foremost concerns.[164] On the other hand, there is little in the letter which suggests that he rejected these parts of the law outright.

---

[161] See, e.g., E. P. Sanders, *Judaism: Practice and Belief 63 BCE–66 CE* (London: SCM; Philadelphia: Trinity Press International, 1992) 13–29 and Part III: "Groups and Parties." Sanders's omission of, e.g., the Jerusalem Christians from this discussion is perhaps indicative of a more general—and quite problematic—scholarly tendency to view the terms "Christianity" and "Judaism" as contrastive categories even within the earliest period of the former's emergence.

[162] On the author's treatment of partiality, see above pp. 161ff; on the basic legal principle of 2:10, see the passages assembled by Dibelius, *James*, 144. Interestingly, some (beginning with Augustine) have also pointed out the similarity between Jas 2:10 and the Stoic principle of the unity of virtue; see esp. M. O'Rourke Boyle, "The Stoic Paradox of James 2:10," *NTS* 31 (1985) 611–17.

[163] See further on this immediately below.

[164] It is not at all clear, for example, to what extent the command "purify (καθαρίσατε) hands," coupled with that to "sanctify (ἁγνίσατε) hearts" in Jas 4:8, is meant literally. What is clear in any case is that the only "impurity" for which the author shows any explicit concern is that which results from the pursuit of one's

His basic legal principle that stumbling with respect to even one command of the law renders one a "law-breaker" is formulated with no such stipulation. He shows no interest in the allegorical interpretation employed to this end, for example, in *Epistle of Barnabas*; nor is anything analogous to a *deuterosis* theory clearly at work in his letter.[165] While his description of the law as both "perfect" and "of freedom" has often been taken as an indication that these aspects of the law were no longer binding,[166] we have already seen examples of Jewish authors who, also influenced by the Stoic concept of law, could describe the Torah similarly quite apart from any such view.[167] The mere fact that the author of James was Christian, of course, is hardly decisive in this respect. There was no single "Christian" position on such matters, and it is by no means clear that those who held a more conservative position with respect to them could not themselves have made apologetic use of the Stoic theory. The author's obvious interest in associating the law with "freedom" (ἐλευθερία), in fact, can just as easily be explained as a reaction to Paul's polem-

---

desires or the failure to control one's tongue. Thus do the commands of 4:8, given to "sinners" and δίψυχοι, respectively, follow the charge that such people's *pursuit of the pleasures* makes them enemies of God and, conversely, constitutes "friendship with the world" (4:1–6); see Chapter Five under the heading "Desire and the Gifts of God in 4:1–6," and on James's understanding of the δίψυχος in particular under the heading "ὁλόκληρος." Note, too, that it is the "tongue" above all else which leads to impurity; on this notion, see Chapter Five under the heading "τέλειος." It is in light of this association of "impurity" with "the world" and "the tongue" that one should understand the author's definition of "pure and undefiled religion" (θρησκεία καθαρὰ καὶ ἀμίαντος) as keeping oneself "unstained (ἄσπιλον) from the world" (1:27); note, in fact, that this follows immediately upon the statement that the religion (θρησκεία) of one who fails to "bridle" one's tongue is "useless" (1:26). On the use of purity language in James, see further see Seitz, "James and the Law," 481–83.

[165] As is the case, e.g., with Irenaeus (see above, note 68), who also, incidentally, interpreted certain aspects of Jewish law allegorically (*A. H.* 4.11.4; 4.14.3). See further on the *deuterosis* theory the discussion of the *Apostolic Constitutions* in Chapter Three.

[166] So, most recently, Tsuji, *Glaube*, 110–15.

[167] Cf. Ropes, *St. James*, 178: "there is no ground for the common affirmation that this phrase implies a sublimated, spiritualised view of the Jewish law, which, it is said, would have been impossible for a faithful Jew." Ropes, however, assumes that "[t]he use of the phrase by a Christian implies that he conceived Christianity as a law, including and fulfilling (Mt. 5:17) the old one." I find no evidence in James, however, that the author had any concept of an "old" law, nor that he conceived of "Christianity" as a "new" law which—as, presumably, in the conception of Ropes (cf. p. 179)—stood over against the law of "Judaism"; cf. Klein, *Ein vollkommenes Werk*, 137. It is in any case problematic to draw conclusions regarding a given early author's view of the law purely on the basis of his/her status as a "Christian."

ical association of it with "slavery"[168] as on the assumption that the communities for which he wrote, as a "liberated Diaspora Judaism," "no longer had to bear the burden of ritualism."[169] Indeed, the view of the love command against which the author argues in 2:8–11 is particularly reminiscent of Paul's peculiar notion that, since "'you shall not commit adultery', 'you shall not murder' (οὐ μοιχεύσεις, οὐ φονεύσεις; cf. Jas 2:11!), 'you shall not steal', 'you shall not covet', and any other command is summed up (ἀνακεφαλαιοῦται) in 'you shall love your neighbor as yourself'," it is the case that "the one who loves another has fulfilled the law" (Rom 13:8–9).[170] Moreover, the immediately following, and closely related section 2:14–26, despite the protestations of some scholars, is almost certainly to be understood in light of Paul's notion of salvation by faith apart from works.[171]

To be sure, the author's silence on the law's commands in such areas as purity, diet and the calendar is significant, and all the more so if he does intend to interact with Paul, whose association of the law with slavery rather than freedom, whose principle of "faith apart from works," and whose view of the love command, were all formulated especially with such issues in mind. It is in fact clear from the letter as a whole, and particularly from 2:1–13 and 2:14–26 themselves, that the author of James is concerned above all with social and economic issues. To the extent that he does interact with Paul, then, it cannot be doubted that his primary concern regarding a pauline formulation such as πίστις χωρὶς ἔργων is its possible implications for Christian attention to socio-economic matters rather than adherence to the legislation regarding diet, the calendar, or circumcision by Jewish or non-Jewish Christians.[172] While it might fairly

---

[168] I.e., as opposed to ἐλευθερία; see esp. Gal 4:21–5:1, and further the Conclusion to this study.

[169] Dibelius, *James*, 119.

[170] Cf. Ludwig, *Wort als Gesetz*, 184–87.

[171] Against, most recently, T. Penner, *The Epistle of James and Eschatology: Re-reading an Ancient Christian Letter* (JSNTSup 121; Sheffield: Sheffield Academic Press, 1996) 47–74; and Johnson, *Letter of James*, on which see my review in *JR* 78 (1998) 102–4. On this point, see further the Conclusion to this study.

[172] Cf. in this respect the very early caricature of Paul's thought, reported by Paul himself in Rom 3:8: "Let us do evil so that good may come." It is by no means clear that τὰ κακά refer specifically to the "evils" of disregard for circumcision or Jewish dietary customs. Whatever might have been the understanding of the law of those who formulated this caricature, the critique assumes a much more generalized understanding of Paul's theological principles—or at least a concern regarding the implications of his basic principles for Christian ethics in general.

be concluded from his silence on these matters that the author of
James was not among those who insisted on the necessity of circumcision for non-Jewish adherents to the Christian movement, the
question of whether he advocated the continuation of such practices
by *Jewish* members of the movement is more difficult to answer in
light of the following considerations.

The debate regarding the observance of Jewish customs by non-
Jewish Christians in which Paul was embroiled seems to have arisen
in connection with a specific circumstance within the Christian movement: the increasing number of non-Jewish adherents to the movement gave rise to questions regarding (i) the conditions which should
govern interaction between Jewish and non-Jewish adherents, particularly in the social context of shared meals; and, perhaps as a
consequence, (ii) the extent to which non-Jewish group members
should live according to Jewish customs.[173] The nature of this problem admits of a variety of solutions. At one pole is a position of
complete adherence, even by non-Jews, to (some interpretation of)
the law; so, apparently, the so-called "false brothers" of Gal 2:4 and
the "Pharisaic Christians" in the narrative of Acts 15:1, 5. At the
other pole, no restrictions whatsoever were incumbent on non-Jews,
whether or not Christian Jews themselves continued to live by them;
so, apparently, Paul himself, and perhaps Peter before the incident
at Antioch (Gal 2:11–12). In between these two poles one can conceive of more moderate positions, such as no shared meals between
Jewish and non-Jewish Christians unless some degree of non-Jewish
observance obtained, at least in the context of common meals; so,

---

[173] Such a generative context is reflected in Galatians 2; cf. Acts 10–11 and 15,
where Peter's (reluctant) decision to share a meal with non-Jews prompts a debate
about circumcision, resulting in a "decree" from James and the Jerusalem church
on the requirements for non-Jews in this respect. The issues behind the controversy
in Antioch recounted by Paul in Galatians 2 are notoriously murky; it seems rather
clear, however, that the issue was related to Jewish dietary restrictions. If this is
true, it appears that the simple connection of eating and circumcision made by the
author of Luke-Acts—despite the impression left from reading Galatians, in which
Paul recounts this incident before launching into an argument against the practice
of circumcision—reflects a non-Jewish perspective on the issues: a Jewish concern
for biblical purity regulations is viewed more simplistically as a Jewish reluctance
to eat with those who aren't circumcised. See, however, E. P. Sanders, "Jewish
Association with Gentiles and Galatians 2:11–14," *The Conversation Continues: Studies
in Paul and John in Honor of J. Louis Martyn* (ed. R. T. Fortna and B. R. Gaventa;
Nashville: Abingdon, 1990) 170–88, who tends toward the view that no specific law
was at issue in Antioch, with the conflict resulting rather from James's more general
concern for "Peter's reputation" if he consorted too closely, too often, with non-Jews.

it would seem, the "men from James," and ultimately, apparently, virtually all of the Christian Jews in Antioch after their arrival (Gal 2:12–13).[174] In fact, the evidence from the first centuries of the movement indicates that no one position was agreed upon by all interested parties, Acts 15 and 16:4 notwithstanding. While the bulk of the extant early Christian literature—preserved by later "orthodox" copyists!—reflects a more liberal position, it is clear from the scattered reports of a number of early authors that Christians continued to disagree on such matters. Though the details of such reports are often confused, it cannot be doubted that some Christians continued to assume the importance of observance of Jewish customs well beyond the first century.[175] In a particularly interesting passage from the *Dialogue with Trypho*, in fact, Justin distinguishes between two types of such Christians: those who observe Jewish customs and would further "compel those Gentiles who believe in Christ to live in all respects according to the law given by Moses, or choose not to associate so intimately with them," and those who continue to observe the law themselves, but who do *not* require non-Jewish members of the movement to do the same.[176]

There is in any case little reason to suppose that the religious concerns of those Christians who assumed the enduring validity of the Torah as law—regardless of their position on the matter of non-Jewish observance—revolved around the cult, purity, circumcision or diet. The fact that our primary evidence for such Christians are passages from Paul's letters which deal specifically with disagreements

---

[174] It is by no means clear from this passage that all of the Christian Jews in Antioch suddenly decided that the non-observant gentile Christians there could no longer be considered members of the movement. More likely, the issue was simply one of the implications of their non-observance for the interaction of Jews and non-Jews in the context of shared meals. Note also the "mediating" positions on Jewish dietary restrictions reflected in Acts 15:28–29, as well as in *Did.* 6:2–3: "For if thou canst bear the whole yoke of the Lord, thou wilt be perfect, but if thou canst not, do what thou canst. And concerning food, bear what though canst, but keep strictly from that which is offered to idols, for it is the worship of dead gods." Note that even Paul proved to be somewhat squeamish on the subject of food that had been involved in sacrifices to other gods (1 Cor 10:14–22; though cf. 8:1–13).

[175] See, e.g., the discussion of G. Strecker, "On the Problem of Jewish Christianity," in W. Bauer, *Orthodoxy and Heresy in Earliest Christianity* (2d German ed., with added appendices, by G. Strecker; ET ed. by R. A. Kraft and G. Krodel; Philadelphia: Fortress, 1971) 241–85 (Appendix 1).

[176] Justin *Dial.* 47; note that while Justin feels that the latter will "be saved," and thus interacts with them, he reports that other non-Jewish Christians disagreed with him on this matter.

on these issues has almost certainly distorted our picture of their religious motivations.[177] In fact, there are several indications that social and economic issues were paramount for at least some such Christians. Paul himself reports that the very leaders in Jerusalem whose misgivings regarding eating with non-Jews would later infuriate him initially (and quite possibly continually)[178] made only one stipulation regarding Paul's quest to secure non-Jewish adherents to the movement: they asked "only" that they "remember the poor" (Gal 2: 10, μόνον τῶν πτωχῶν ἵνα μνημονεύωμεν), resulting in Paul's on-going collection for Jerusalem from his non-Jewish churches (Gal 2:10).[179] Such a socio-economic interest is of course found throughout the synoptic gospels, and is particularly prominent in the synoptic sayings source, where οἱ πτωχοί—as, perhaps, among the Jerusalem Christians (cf. Gal 2:10; Rom 15:25)—seems to be used as a self-designation for members of the movement.[180] Such a self-designation

---

[177] Dibelius's interpretation of the Letter of James, e.g., seems to be informed by an approach to early Christianity which assumes only two basic forms of the movement for which "the break with Judaism was not accomplished in the radical fashion with which we are familiar from the Pauline Letters" (*James*, 119, with specific reference to the group I've numbered [i]): (i) a "liberated Diaspora Judaism," in which Christians "were no longer bound to the letter of the Old Testament" and thus "no longer had to bear the burden of ritualism" (*ibid.*); and (ii) "the advocates of a strict ritualistic praxis" characterized as a "hidebound Jewish-Christian piety," of which James the brother of Jesus and "the people from James" of Galatians 2 are taken to be representative (*ibid.*, 17).

[178] Paul accuses Peter (and, by implication, apparently every other Christian Jew at Antioch except himself!) of refusing to eat with non-Jews after "certain people from James" arrived (Gal 2:11–13)—which, of course, implies that these latter also had misgivings about eating with non-Jews, at least under the circumstances obtaining at Antioch. The extent to which those "certain people from James" attempted to force non-Jews into living in accord with Jewish customs, however, is by no means clear. Note particularly that Paul's characterization of Peter as "compelling the gentiles to live like Jews (ἰουδαΐζειν)" is not obviously based on anything more than his withdrawal from common meals. It is not clear, that is, whether the issue in Antioch was one of gentile participation in the movement *per se*, or the extent of the participation in the movement by non-observant adherents.

[179] Note that the (evidently) uncircumcised Titus (cf. Gal 2:3!) was himself engaged in this collection according to 2 Cor 8:16, 23.

[180] J. S. Kloppenborg, *The Formation of Q: Trajectories in Ancient Christian Wisdom Collections* (Studies in Antiquity and Christianity; Philadelphia: Fortress, 1987) 240–41. On the question of the relation of "the poor" of Gal 2:10 to the Jerusalem Christians, see Betz, *Galatians*, 102; further L. E. Keck, "The Poor Among the Saints in the New Testament," *ZNW* 56 (1965) 100–29; *idem*, "The Poor Among the Saints in Jewish Christianity and Qumran," *ZNW* 57 (1966) 54–78. Keck is skeptical regarding the use of "the poor" as a title among the early Jerusalem Christians.

The theme of poverty and wealth also receives special emphasis in Luke-Acts,

is also evident centuries later, notably, on the part of a group of Christians notorious for their continued adherence to the Torah, the "Ebionites," though our scant evidence for this group obscures the extent to which this name reflected their chief concerns.[181] It is worth noting, too, that what little evidence we have, apart from Paul, for those Christians who continued to live by Jewish customs also suggests a particular emphasis on social relations. Thus the cultic instruction preserved in Matthew's sermon, for example, assumes participation in the Jewish cult, but subordinates it to social concerns: "Therefore, when you bring your gift-offering (to be placed) on the altar, and there you remember that your brother has something against you, leave your gift there in front of the altar, and first go and become reconciled with your brother, and then come (back) and offer your gift."[182] One can also compare in this respect the following "woe" proclaimed against the Pharisees (and scribes, according to Matthew) in the synoptic sayings source:[183]

> Luke 11:42: But woe to you Pharisees! for you tithe mint and rue and every herb, and neglect the justice and love of God; these [latter] you ought to have done, without neglecting the others.

---

where it emerges with a vehemence rivalled only by *1 Enoch* and the Letter of James among the ancient Jewish and Christian literature; see G. W. E. Nickelsburg, "Riches, the Rich and God's Judgment in *1 Enoch* 92–105 and the Gospel According to Luke," *NTS* 25 (1979) 324–44. The parable of Lazarus and the rich man, for example, preserved only in Luke, envisions a post-mortem reversal in which a wealthy man is punished in Hades, apparently for no other crime than living in luxury while ignoring the poor man laying at his gate. The impoverished Lazarus, on the other hand, receives comfort "with Abraham" after his death (Luke 16:19–31; note esp. 16:25). It is of particular interest in the present connection that this story assumes an interpretation of "Moses and the prophets" according to which the problematic nature of such behavior should be perfectly clear (Luke 16:29–31). Notably, such socio-economic interests are associated in the second book of Luke's work particularly with the Christians at Jerusalem, who are also portrayed as continuing in their adherence to Jewish religious practices and who are, indeed, as a group, "zealous for the law" (Acts 2:44–47; 4:32–5:11; cf. 21:20).

[181] See, e.g., the recent and concise survey of the evidence in S. Goranson, "Ebionites," *ABD* 2.260–61; further Keck, "The Poor Among the Saints in Jewish Christianity and Qumran," 55–66.

[182] Matt 5:23–24, cited according to the translation of H. D. Betz, *The Sermon on the Mount: A Commentary on the Sermon on the Mount, including the Sermon on the Plain (Matthew 5:3–7:27 and Luke 6:20–49)* (Hermeneia; Philadelphia: Fortress, 1995) 198; see further Betz's comments in *ibid.*, 222–26.

[183] Cited according to the translation of J. S. Kloppenborg, *Q Parallels: Synopsis, Critical Notes & Concordance* (Foundations & Facets; Sonoma, CA: Polebridge, 1988) 113.

Matt 23:23: Woe to you, scribes and Pharisees, hypocrites! for you tithe mint and dill and cumin, and leave aside weightier matters of the law, justice and mercy and faithfulness; these [latter] you ought to have done, without leaving aside the others.

James's concern with socio-economic issues, too, is of course patent. "Pure religion" is boiled down to an active concern for "widows and orphans" and avoiding the impurity of "the world" (Jas 1:27).[184] While arguing for the necessity of ἔργα in addition to πίστις, he formulates as an example the callous treatment of "a brother or sister" who "is naked and lacking daily food" (2:15–16). Similarly, his admonition against acts of partiality, the crowning point of which warns that it is a transgression of the law by which people will ultimately be judged, is concerned specifically with dishonoring the poor while honoring the rich sheerly on the basis of wealth (2:2–4, 6). Interestingly, he, too, apparently uses "the poor" as a self-designation:[185] it is specifically "the poor" (οἱ πτωχοί) whom God "chose" (ἐξελέξατο) to be "rich in faith" and "inheritors of the kingdom which he promised to those who love him" (2:5).[186] On the other hand, he assumes a pattern of behavior on the part of "the rich" (οἱ πλούσιοι) which involves oppression, legal suits and blasphemy (2:6–7). These rich, the author warns with a searing irony, can expect a "day of slaughter" for which their luxurious living is "fattening them" (5:1–6). The author of James ultimately expects an eschatological reversal which will remedy the present circumstances: the humble will be exalted and the rich humiliated (Jas 1:12; cf. 5:1).[187] This, apparently, will be effected at the *parousia* of Jesus Christ.[188]

---

[184] On "impurity" in James, see above, note 164.

[185] So, e.g., Dibelius, *James*, 44: "Ja[me]s can express his sympathy with the poor with so little reserve because for him being poor and being Christian were coincidental concepts, not only by virtue of his archaizing dependence on the literature [sc. the Jewish literature dealing with "the poor"], but also by virtue of his own personal conviction."

[186] More precisely, οἱ πτωχοὶ τῷ κόσμῳ, i.e., "poor in the eyes of the world." Note the subsequent description of them as πλούσιοι ἐν πίστει: in actuality they are "rich" in the sense which matters most. This somewhat peculiar phrase is undoubtedly to be understood in light of the author's negative portrayal of "the world" as fundamentally opposed to God (4:4), and a source of impurity, the avoidance of which gets at the very heart of his understanding of true religion (1:27). See further on "the world" in James, L. T. Johnson, "Friendship with the World/Friendship with God: A Study of Discipleship in James," *Discipleship in the New Testament* (ed. with an introduction by F. F. Segovia; Philadelphia: Fortress, 1985) 166–83.

[187] Cf. Luke 16:19–31, on which see above, note 180.

[188] See Jas 5:7, 9, noting especially the οὖν that joins 5:7 to 5:6. On the "parou-

To point out such similarities, of course, is not necessarily to argue that the Letter of James originated among Jerusalem Christians or among second century Ebionites, much less that it represents an authentic writing of James the brother of Jesus.[189] It is only to point out that the question of its author's position regarding matters of diet, purity, cult and circumcision is much more complex than is often thought to be the case. Even if, as is most likely, the author's position regarding the relation of the love command to the "whole law" and his discussion of πίστις and ἔργα in Jas 2:14–26 are to be understood in light of pauline formulations, it is not clear what conclusions are to be drawn from the fact that he does not feel compelled to lay out his own position on those aspects of the Torah which most rankled Paul. While this, along with his characteristic emphasis on socio-economic concerns, surely does indicate what aspects of the law mattered most to him, he is apparently not altogether different in this respect from a number of Christians who themselves continued to follow Jewish customs. Such Christians could and did hold a variety of positions regarding issues like diet and circumcision; and some, at least, while continuing to live in accord with Jewish customs themselves, did not require such of non-Jews.[190] In short, firm conclusions regarding the position of the author on such matters require more information regarding him and his intended audience than we currently possess. While it is clear that James's law is the Torah, the question of his interpretation of those aspects of it which legislate matters such as purity, diet, circumcision and the calendar must remain open.[191]

---

sia of the Lord" in James, see Jackson-McCabe, "A Letter to the Twelve Tribes," 509–10; Johnson, *Letter of James*, 313–14.

[189] Such questions are difficult, perhaps impossible, to answer with any degree of certainty given the paucity of information in James regarding its origin, not to mention the meager evidence for the "historical James," the Jerusalem church, and the Ebionites.

[190] Cf., e.g., Acts 21:17–26: the problem is that Paul teaches *Jews* who live among non-Jews not to live in accord with the law.

[191] Cf. Wachob, "The Rich in Faith," 291 n. 94: "Whatever the author may or may not have thought about the so-called cultic ordinances of the law, matters like circumcision and dietary ordinances, we do not know." Note that while Wachob refers to Seitz, "James and the Law," in this connection, Seitz himself is inclined to the view that the "law of freedom," though representing "the 'old' law" to be sure, means "only the decalogue together with such ethical precepts as love of neighbor"; the author of James "simply ignores" issues of diet and cirumcision when using the expression "the whole law." See "James and the Law," 484–85.

IMPLANTED *LOGOS* IN LIGHT OF THE TORAH AND JUDGMENT

The expression ἔμφυτος λόγος was coined as a term for human reason by Greek philosophers, particularly in connection with the Stoic theory that human reason comprises a divinely given natural law internal to the human animal. That the author of James speaks of "the implanted *logos*" in 1:21 with at least a general grasp of its original significance is clear from the fact that he equates it with a "perfect law of freedom." Significantly, however, he also speaks of this *logos* in ways which are not typical of Stoic tradition. In a manner reminiscent, rather, of Jewish and Christian literature, he considers it to be something which can (and must) be both "heard" and "done," which "is able to save your souls," and which can, in some sense, be "received." These differences reflect the fact that in James, as in the other Jewish and Christian writings examined in the previous chapter, the Stoic concept of law has been fused with a set of religious and historical convictions alien to Stoicism. Given the obvious indications of the author's dependence upon Jewish and Christian traditions throughout the letter, such differences are hardly surprising. Nor are they by any means insignificant: the aspects of the treatment of the implanted *logos* in James which diverge from its treatment in Greek philosophical discussion are just as illuminative of the author's understanding of it and its role in his religious thought as the respects in which it is similar to them.

Of particular importance in this respect is the fact that the author of James, again like Philo, Justin, and the authors of *4 Maccabees* and the *Apostolic Constitutions*, assumes that this *logos* has an external, verbal form. The "perfect law of freedom" is in fact the Torah, however precisely interpreted by the author. It is in light of this identification that James's peculiar notion that the *logos* can be "heard" and "done" is to be understood; for while scarcely typical of Stoic discussions of natural law, such a pairing of "hearing and doing" is not uncommon in Jewish discussions of the Torah. In a manner which recalls Romans 2:13, the author of James insists that one must not only be a "hearer" of the *logos*, but a "doer" of it as well. Merely to "hear" it is to "deceive (παρα-λογιζόμενοι) oneself," for it is precisely "through doing" (ἐν τῇ ποιήσει) that one will become "blessed" (1:22, 25). One becomes such a "*logos*-doer" through constant attention to the "perfect law of freedom," which is to say, to the Torah.

James's emphasis on becoming a "doer" of the law (cf. 4:12)—and thus of the *logos*—acquires a particular urgency in light of the eschatological dimension of the letter. The *parousia* of Jesus Christ will entail judgment (5:8–9), executed in accord with the law by the divine lawgiver himself; and it will be, potentially, "merciless" (2:12–13; 4:12). Aware of the idea that "love of neighbor" represents a summary of "the whole law," he cautions against an eschatological confidence based on attention to this one general command: summary or not, Lev 19:18 is still one command among many within the law; transgressing any of the others, even if one "loves one's neighbor," can still render one liable to judgment.[192] In a manner reminiscent of his earlier warning regarding the self-deception of those who do not "do" the *logos*, he thus admonishes the "brothers and sisters" to speak and "do" (ποιεῖτε; more idiomatically: "act") "as those about to be judged by means of the law of freedom" (2:12).[193] This expectation of an eschatological judgment by the law goes a long way toward clarifying the author's description of the implanted *logos* as that "which is able to save (τὸν δυνάμενον σῶσαι) your souls" (1:21). Indeed, it is in his capacity as "lawgiver and

---

[192] This is not to say that James envisions a judgment that will of necessity proceed as a wooden accounting of one's transgressions of the law. Jas 2:13, in fact, points to an "escape clause": showing mercy to others will mean receiving mercy at the judgment. A similar notion is found both in the Matthean parable of the unmerciful servant (Matt 18:23–35), and esp. in Rabban Yohanan ben Zakkai's reported response to a companion's grief at the destruction of the temple, and thus of the mechanism for Israel's atonement: "Do not grieve. We have another atonement as effective as this. And what it is? It is acts of lovingkindness, as it is said: 'I desire mercy and not sacrifice'" ('*Abot R. Nat.* 6; cited as found in A. F. Segal, *Rebecca's Children: Judaism and Christianity in the Roman World* [Cambridge, MA: Harvard University Press, 1986] 131). In James, this notion can be correlated particularly with the author's emphatic concern for the socially and economically disadvantaged; see esp. 1:27; 2:1–13; 2:15–16; 5:1–6. Interestingly, he does not simply equate such a concern with the general notion of "love of neighbor." His notion that mercy "boasts over judgment," more specifically, is to be understood in light of the critique, implicit in Jas 2:1–13, of a social system in which tokens of honor are granted on the basis of wealth and/or patronage. The argument of 2:13 does not assume that one who "shows partiality" as defined in 2:2–4—perhaps by courting (or rewarding) a wealthy patron by granting him, rather than a beggar, an honorable seat in the synagogue—is violating the command of "love of neighbor." The argument, rather, is that they are violating the partiality command by acting as "unjust judges" of the rich and poor.

[193] Again, despite his wariness regarding the use of the love command as a summary of the law, his emphasis lies above all on socio-economic issues. See above all the construal of "pure religion" as concern for widows and orphans in 1:27.

judge" that James's god himself is described as one "who is able to save" (ὁ δυνάμενος σῶσαι)—and to destroy (4:12).[194]

Somewhat more difficult to interpret is the author's notion that the implanted *logos* can in some sense be "received." I must insist at the outset that the command δέξασθε τὸν ἔμφυτον λόγον (1:21) is equally problematic on any interpretation of the *logos*. The essential difficulty of the passage is the fact that the author commands his audience to "receive" something that is already "implanted." Whether, therefore, the *logos* is understood to have been so "implanted" in all humans from the time when God created them, or only more recently in a select group of people who consciously sought it, the apparent contradiction remains. Of itself, therefore, this command no more excludes interpreting James's ἔμφυτος λόγος in light of Stoic ideas, as has frequently been argued,[195] than it excludes reading it in light of an already implanted "gospel."

It is obvious in any case that the command ἐν πραΰτητι δέξασθε τὸν ἔμφυτον λόγον is not intended to connote a "reception" analogous to the initial "implanting" of the *logos*.[196] Even beyond the clear assumption in 1:21 that the *logos* is already "implanted" in those who are to "receive" it, it emerges from the letter as a whole that the author aims to induce in his intended audience something more appropriately characterized as "repentance" than as "conversion."[197] It is plain from 1:22–25 in particular that James assumes an audi-

---

[194] The soteriological significance of the *logos* in the religious thought of James will be taken up more fully in the following chapter.

[195] See Chapter One.

[196] Cf. Dibelius, *James*, 114.

[197] See esp. the conclusion of the letter, where the concern is that any who have "wandered from the truth" (cf. 1:18, λόγος ἀληθείας) be "turned back" (5:19–20). See also 4:1–10, where the author reminds his audience that their friendship with the world is incompatible with their (presumably desired!) friendship with God; points out that they are acting as "adulteresses" and as though "scripture speaks in vain"; and ultimately urges a posture of repentance upon them (4:7–10). In this respect, Johnson's use of the term "conversion" in connection with the aim of the letter as a whole, and with that of this latter section in particular, is not particularly helpful. Such a description apparently results from his classification of the work as "protreptic"; cf. esp. *Letter of James*, 16–24 with his description of 3:13–4:10 as a "Call to Conversion" (*ibid.*, 267). Regardless of the merits of this generic classification (on which see esp. the discussion of Wachob, "Rich in Faith," 98–122), it is clear from the letter as a whole that the author presupposes that his intended audience already has some manner of "faith" (cf. Klein, *Ein vollkommenes Werk*, 47). To this extent, "conversion" seems an inappropriate paradigm for characterizing the rhetorical aim of the letter.

ence whose current "hearing" of the *logos* is such that they might be deceived regarding its implications for their eschatological status. Given the context of 1:21 within the elaboration of the admonition to be "slow to anger," the emphasis of the command seems to lie particularly on the *manner* in which this *logos* is "received"—namely, "with meekness" (ἐν πραΰτητι), since anger (ὀργή) "does not produce God's righteousness" (1:20)—rather than with the "receiving" *per se*.[198] The "receiving" itself, that is, is simply assumed, much as the "hearing" of the *logos* is assumed in 1:22–25. The "receiving" of *logos* in 1:21 must in any case be understood more on the analogy of the "hearing" of 1:22–25 than the "implanting" of 1:21; and δέχομαι can in fact be used with a sense of "give ear to," or "hear."[199] Indeed, so understood, the transition from 1:21 to the discussion of "hearing and doing" in 1:22–25 appears all the more natural: "receive the implanted *logos* with humility . . . and (δέ)[200] become *logos*-doers, and not merely hearers who deceive themselves."

On the other hand, a number of authors have sought to account for James's peculiar command to "receive" something which is already

---

[198] Note in this connection esp. the use of διό to join 1:20 to 1:21: "anger does not effect the righteousness of God . . . therefore . . . receive the implanted *logos* with humility." Note also in this connection that whereas the (implied) command to "lay aside all filth" is paired with that to receive the *logos* with humility in 1:21, the call to "cleanse hands" and "purify hearts"—which follows a discussion of the origins of social strife (cf. ὀργή)—is paired with an injunction to "humble oneself" before God in 4:8–9. See further on this latter passage Chapter Five, under the heading "Desire and the Gifts of God in 4:1–6."

[199] See LSJ, δέχομαι, §I.3: "simply, *to give ear to, hear*"; cf. also §I.2: "of mental reception, *take, accept* without complaint." Again, the author of James certainly assumes that his audience, on at least some level, "accepts" the *logos*: thus the problem of "self-deception" (1:22). What concerns him is a perceived incongruity between this "acceptance" and their "doing."

[200] It is not immediately clear whether the δέ of 1:22 should be read with an adversative or a conjunctive, explanatory force; on the common use of the latter see BAGD, δέ §2. If the former, the "hearing" connotation of the "receiving" of 1:21 emerges with partiular clarity: "receive the λόγος; but don't just hear it, *do* it." If the latter, it implies rather that 1:22–25 broaches from a more general perspective the same point which the discussion of anger in 1:20–21 addresses: "receive the λόγος with humility; that is, hear it and do it." Mere "receiving" or "hearing," in other words, is not sufficient, but must be accompanied by a particular type of behavior which can be characterized as "humility" and which consists in "doing"; cf. in this case 2:14–26, and esp. 3:13, δειξάτω ἐκ τῆς καλῆς ἀναστροφῆς τὰ ἔργα αὐτοῦ ἐν πραΰτητι σοφίας, and further the discussion in Chapter Five under the heading "*Logos* and *Erga*." Given these latter passages and the emphasis on ἐν πραΰτητι rather than the command to "receive" the λόγος *per se* in Jas 1:21, it seems to me better to interpret it with an explanatory force.

"implanted" by arguing that the author is drawing on a fixed early Christian expression, δέχεσθαι τὸν λόγον.[201] Such expressions are found particularly in Acts and the pauline letters, and refer consistently to an initial acceptance of the Christian proclamation, the "gospel."[202] Since the author of James cannot in any case be using the phrase with reference to an *initial* acceptance of the *logos* (i.e., the "implanting" itself), such interpreters apparently understand him to be using an expression which connotes "conversion" with reference to an on-going "acceptance" of the now (i.e., post-conversion) implanted *logos*.[203] Indeed, it is often noted that James had just referred, in 1:18, to the fact that God "gave birth to us by means of a *logos* of truth (λόγῳ ἀληθείας) so that we are a sort of 'first fruits' of his creatures." Not only is this verse as a whole reminiscent of the notion, found in a variety of early Christian works, that members of the movement have been "reborn" or have experienced a "new creation," but the phrase λόγος ἀληθείας is itself used with clear reference to "the gospel" in several pauline letters.[204]

Now it must be pointed out at once that James's ἔμφυτος λόγος is first and foremost a law—indeed, an internal law which finds written expression in the Torah—and not a "gospel" in the usual sense of that term as a narrative proclamation.[205] However, one might

---

[201] See Chapter One.

[202] Note esp. the use of this expression with reference to a past "reception" or "acceptance": 1 Thess 1:6, "in spite of persecution you received (δεξάμενοι) the word with joy inspired by the Holy Spirit"; 2:13, "when you received (παραλαβόντες) the word of God that you heard from us, you accepted (ἐδέξασθε) it not as a human word but as what it really is, God's word . . ."; Acts 8:14, "Now when the apostles at Jerusalem heard that Samaria had accepted (δέδεκται) the word of God . . ." (with reference to Acts 8:4–13); Acts 11:1, "Now the apostles and the believers who were in Judea heard that the Gentiles had also accepted (ἐδέξαντο) the word of God . . ." (with reference to the conversion of Cornelius and his household in Acts 10). Cf. further Luke 8:13, where παραδέχονται (cf. Mark 4:16, λαμβάνουσιν; but also 4:20, παραδέχονται) is used in the explanation of the parable of the sower.

[203] Note that Dibelius suggests that the clause "receive the word" was a fixed expression used "simply as a periphrasis for the Christian life," despite the fact that all of the examples he cites in support of such a usage employ the phrase with respect to an *initial* acceptance of the "word"; see *James*, 114. Cf. Mußner, *Der Jakobusbrief*, 101: "Nehmt das euch bei der Taufe einst eingepflanzte Wort wirklich, in aller Konsequenz und vor allem ἐν πραΰτητι an . . ."

[204] For this line of argument see Chapter One; for a discussion of the evidence, see Chapter Five, esp. pp. 193–95.

[205] On Paul's use of the term "gospel" as a shorthand expression for his soteriological narrative, see M. M. Mitchell, "Rhetorical Shorthand in Pauline Argumentation: The Functions of 'the Gospel' in the Corinthian Correspondence," *Gospel in Paul: Studies in Corinthians, Galatians and Romans for Richard N. Longenecker* (ed. L. A.

compare in this respect 1 Pet 1:23–25, where a notion of the "word" (λόγος, ῥῆμα) as proclaimed "gospel" seems to be merged with a more mystical conception of an "imperishable seed" (σπορὰ φθαρτή) through which Christians have been "reborn" (ἀναγεγεννημένοι), and which entails a certain type of behavior.[206] A notion that some "rebirth" has been experienced by individual members of the Christian movement as a result of the insertion into them of some divine substance, the possession of which carries ethical consequences, is of course not uncommon in the early Christian literature. One thinks immediately of the "spirit" of the pauline corpus and of Acts, or the spirit/*logos* of the johannine epistles.[207] One might argue, therefore, that James simply conceives of an analogous divine substance in Stoic terms, as ἔμφυτος λόγος: a *logos*, that is, which is "implanted" by God in a select group of people in connection with a *new* creation rather than in all human beings at the *initial* creation,[208] and whose associated ethic—quite unlike, however, the johannine and especially pauline epistles—is understood to coincide with the Torah. One might think in this connection of the prophecy of Jer 31:31–35 (= LXX Jer 38:31–34), where the deity promises a future era for Israel in which "I will put my law within them, and I will write it on their hearts." Fabris, in fact, has argued that the author of James assumes that this prophecy has been fulfilled particularly among his own group ("the twelve tribes"), which is living in "the last days" (5:3).[209]

Jervis and P. Richardson; JSNTSup 108; Sheffield: Sheffield Academic Press, 1994) 63–88. Note also that it is the "word" of the Christian proclamation which is "received" in the various passages of Acts: cf. Acts 8:14 with 8:4; and Acts 11:1 with Acts 10, esp. 10:36–43.

[206] Cf. Dibelius, *James*, 105 n. 185, noting, however, that Dibelius rejects the idea that James has any such mystical notion in mind. The types of behaviors which are to characterize such "newborns" in 1 Peter are described collectively as τὸ λογικὸν ἄδολον γάλα. The term λογικόν is surely intended to play on the "word" (1:25: ῥῆμα; 1:23: λόγος) through which they have been born, and thus to indicate that the "milk" upon which they are to feed is to be λογικόν in the sense of "appropriate to that *logos*." It is noteworthy, however, that both this term and the description of the *logos* as an "imperishable seed" are reminiscent of the *logos* of contemporary philosophical discussion.

[207] See, e.g., the comparisons drawn by Fabris, *Legge*, ch. 6.

[208] Note in this connection that the *logos* concept of the johannine epistles seems to be informed by the Logos myth found in the opening of the Fourth Gospel, or at least something very closely approximating it. See esp. 1 John 1:1–4, and further R. Schnackenburg, *The Johannine Epistles: Introduction and Commentary* (New York: Crossroad, 1992) 49–69, esp. 50: "One may say that the opening of the letter [sc. 1 John] presumes the Gospel Prologue or the Logos hymn embedded in it."

[209] See on Fabris above, Chapter One. Note, however, that he understands the law in question to be a new "messianic law" rather than the Torah.

This line of interpretation, however, is most doubtful. While James does contain allusions to several scriptural prophecies,[210] Jer 31:31–35 and the other passages cited by Fabris in this connection are not among them. More importantly, though the term ἔμφυτος alone is not a decisive indication that the *logos* of James is "innate," the more specific concept of an ἔμφυτος λόγος or νόμος consistently denotes something given to all people at God's *initial* creation of humanity elsewhere in the ancient literature, including the Christian literature. Justin's adaptation of the Stoic concept of law is particularly significant in this respect; for while he held that "right reason" or "natural law" became available to humanity only after the earthly appearance of Jesus Christ, he nonetheless spoke of the "implanted seed of the *logos*," specifically with reference to that portion of the natural law that all humans have always possessed. Without some clear indication that the author of James conceived of ἔμφυτος λόγος differently in this respect, then, one should be most hesitant to assume that such a re-definition has taken place. In fact, the author's reference to God's "giving birth" to "us" by means of the "*logos* of truth"— which *logos*, we shall see shortly, is to be identified with "the implanted *logos*"—gives no such indication that what is imagined is a *re*-birth. Indeed, in the context of Jas 1:13–18, this statement is best understood with reference to God's initial creation of all humanity. Examination of Jas 1:13–18 in the following chapter will shed light not only on this issue, but will further illuminate, more generally, how *logos* functions in the religious thought of James.

---

[210] Cf. esp. Jas 1:10–11 with LXX Isa 40:6b–8, and Jas 5:5 with LXX Jer 12:3; see further D. Deppe, *The Sayings of Jesus*, 42–49.

CHAPTER FIVE

LOGOS AND DESIRE

A few lines prior to the mention of the implanted *logos* in Jas 1:21, reference is made to a "*logos* of truth" (λόγος ἀληθείας) through which God "gave birth to us, so that we are a sort of 'first fruits' of his creatures" (Jas 1:18). This statement has been seen by some interpreters as providing decisive confirmation that the *logos* that, according to James, "saves souls" is in fact "the Gospel."[1]

The expression λόγος ἀληθείας is found in several other works of the Christian canon, differing only in case or in the use of a definite article:[2] 2 Cor 6:7 (λόγῳ ἀληθείας), Col 1:5 (τῷ λόγῳ τῆς ἀληθείας), Eph 1:13 (τὸν λόγον τῆς ἀληθείας) and 2 Tim 2:15 (τὸν λόγον τῆς ἀληθείας). Colossians and Ephesians use this phrase with explicit reference to "the Gospel" (τὸ εὐαγγέλιον), and such an identification is also clearly implied in 2 Timothy.[3] Joseph Mayor concluded from this collection of passages that the phrase λόγος ἀληθείας was "a *vox technica* of early Christianity,"[4] but this conclusion overstates the evidence. It is to be noted in the first place that all of the latter references appear in pauline or pseudo-pauline writings; one should be cautious in making generalizing conclusions regarding "early

---

[1] See Chapter One.

[2] No great weight should be placed on the lack of the definite article in identifying the referent of the λόγος ἀληθείας of Jas 1:18. As will be argued below, and as virtually all agree, it is the same λόγος as that described in 1:21 as ὁ ἔμφυτος λόγος. Compare in this respect the inconsistent use of the definite article in connection with νόμος in James: see 1:25; 2:8, 9, 10, 11, 12; and 4:11.

[3] Note that just after ps.-Paul's words of encouragement to "Timothy" to be "a worker who has no need to be ashamed, rightly explaining τὸν λόγον τῆς ἀληθείας" (2:15), he refers to those "who have swerved from τὴν ἀλήθειαν by claiming that the resurrection has already taken place" (2:18). This implies that the "right" explanation of τὸν λόγον τῆς ἀληθείας entails a proper understanding of the resurrection; and this resurrection lies at the heart of "the gospel" of which ps.-Paul himself claims to be a "teacher" (1:11), and of which he, too, is "not ashamed" (1:12, οὐκ ἐπαισχύνομαι); see 2:8, and cf. 1:8–14.

[4] Mayor cites several other passages in the course of his discussion of the phrase λόγος ἀληθείας, but it is apparently these which he has in mind when he refers to "the N.T. quotations" which show that "λόγος ἀληθείας is a *vox technica*"; see *St. James*, 63.

Christianity" on the basis of evidence found in this limited corpus. Indeed, analogous phrases do occur in other Jewish and Christian literature with different meanings.[5] Even within the pauline literature itself, in fact, the extent to which we are dealing with a univocal "technical term" is far from clear. That Paul uses the phrase in 2 Cor 6:7—its only occurrence in the undoubted letters of Paul— with reference to the gospel is by no means obvious. Found among a list of attributes that, Paul says, characterize his ministry (including, among other things, the fact that he has acted with kindness, patience and "genuine love"), the phrase might well be understood more generally as connoting "truthful speech."[6] Moreover, the association of ὁ λόγος τῆς ἀληθείας with "the gospel" in both Colossians and Ephesians falsely inflates the evidence for the fixity of this expression, for in this case the similarity is most likely to be explained by *literary* dependence, not independent attestation of a pauline, much less an early Christian, "technical term."[7]

The strong impression that this assembly of passages might at first create is significantly tempered through these considerations, and

---

[5] Spitta had already pointed to LXX Ps 118:43, a passage which is often understood with reference to the law; see Laws, *James*, 76; also Johnson, *Letter of James*, 198. Particularly interesting for our purposes is Clement of Alexandria, *Strom* 1.13, where the phrase is used in connection with a concept somewhat reminiscent of Justin's *logos* theory: "Since, therefore, truth (τῆς ἀληθείας) is one . . . just as the Bacchanites tore asunder the limbs of Pentheus, so the sects both of barbarian and Hellenic philosophy have done with truth, and each vaunts as the whole truth (τὴν ἀλήθειαν) the portion which has fallen to its lot. But all, in my opinion, are illuminated by the dawn of Light. Let all, therefore, both Greeks and barbarians, who have aspired after the truth (τἀληθοῦς)—both those who possess not a little, and those who have any portion—produce whatever they have of the word of truth (τοῦ τῆς ἀληθείας λόγου)" (text in MPG 8.753–56; translation in *ANF* 2.313). Cf. also *T. Gad* 3:1; *Odes Sol.* 8:8; Philo, *Somn.* 1.23.

[6] So the NRSV. Such a more general claim of honest and straightforward speech would, of course, include Paul's preaching of "the gospel"; the question, however, is whether the phrase λόγος ἀληθείας referred only and specifically to the latter. Note in this connection Paul's need to address the Corinthians' evident dissatisfaction with his apparently vacillating travel plans (2 Cor 1:15–2:17); see esp. 2 Cor 1:18, ὁ λόγος ἡμῶν ὁ πρὸς ὑμᾶς οὐκ ἔστιν ναὶ καὶ οὔ. Cf. in this respect the use of the phrase ἐν λόγοις ἀληθείας with a more general reference to speech in *Pss. Sol.* 16:10; see further the λόγον ἀληθείας of LXX Ps 118:43, in which, too, there is some ambiguity. It should not be forgotten, in this connection, that the phrase λόγος ἀληθείας does not appear elsewhere in any of the undisputed letters of Paul.

[7] For a concise sketch of the problem of the relation of Ephesians to Colossians, see R. Schnackenburg, *Ephesians: A Commentary* (Edinburgh: T&T Clark, 1991) 30–33. Note also Tsuji's suggestion that the very fact that the "word of truth" is explicitly identified as "the gospel" in these works suggests that the two were *not* obviously synonymous (*Glaube*, 68).

Mayor's conclusion has in fact found few adherents.[8] Most interpreters have rightly concluded that the securest guide for identifying the particular referent of the "*logos* of truth" of Jas 1:18 is the
context in which the phrase occurs in James itself.[9] This discussion
has centered largely on the question of whether the divine "birthing"
mentioned in 1:18 is to be interpreted with reference to the creation
of humanity in general or to a new creation of Christians in particular, and it has been characterized by significant disagreement.[10]

To be sure, the issue of when, and with respect to whom, the
"birth" of 1:18 is imagined to have occurred is an important consideration in the identification and interpretation of James's "*logos* of
truth." Equally important, however, is the question of its relation to
the implanted *logos* and, more generally, its role in the religious
thought of the letter. This latter question, in particular, has received
surprisingly little attention. The primary concern of this chapter,
then, is to elucidate the function of the *logos*, to which James refers
variously as "*logos* of truth" or "the implanted *logos*,"[11] in the thought
of James. We shall see that this *logos*, like its counterparts in the works
examined previously in this study, functions primarily in opposition

---

[8] As far as I have noted, J. B. Adamson is alone among recent authors in his
affirmation of Mayor's view; see *James: The Man and His Message*, 397. Cf. the
significantly watered-down version of this thesis in Davids, *Epistle of James*, 89: "in
the NT . . . while never becoming a univocally technical term, the word of truth
does frequently mean the gospel."

[9] See esp. Dibelius, *James*, 103–107; and most recently the treatment of the problem in Ludwig, *Wort als Gesetz*, 151–57; Johnson, *Letter of James*, 197f and 205; and
Klein, *Ein vollkommenes Werk*, 129–34.

[10] Those arguing for a reference to the original creation of humanity in general
include Spitta, *Der Brief des Jakobus*, 45–47; Hort, *Epistle of St. James*, 31–35; Rendall,
The Epistle of St. James and Judaic Christianity, 63–65; Edsman, "Schöpferwille und
Geburt Jac 118" (though cf. *idem*, "Schöpfung und Wiedergeburt: Nochmals Jac.
1:18"); Cadoux, *The Thought of St. James*, 19–24; Elliott-Binns, "James 1.18: Creation
or Redemption?"; Frankemölle, *Der Brief des Jakobus*, 1.297–305; Tsuji, *Glaube*, 68–69.
Arguing for a reference to a new creation of Christians are Ropes, *St. James*, 165–68
(though seemingly with some hesitation); Dibelius, *James*, 103–107; Chaine, *L'Épître
de Saint Jacques*, 25–27; Mußner, *Der Jakobusbrief*, 92–97; Fabris, *Legge*, 134–42; Davids,
Epistle of James, 88–90; Martin, *James*, 39–41; Popkes, *Adressaten*, 146–51; Klein, *Ein
vollkommenes Werk*, 129–34. Johnson feels that "the most obvious way" to read the
phrase λόγος ἀληθείας in 1:18 is with reference to "the Gospel, that is, the Christian
proclamation"; he hastens to add, however, that "too great a distinction should not
be made between Gospel, Torah and the word of creation, since for James they
all represent gifts of God" (*Letter of James*, 214). Still less decisive are Sidebottom,
James, Jude and 2 Peter, 32–33; and Laws, *Epistle of James*, 75–78, cf. 83.

[11] On the identity of these *logoi*, see below pp. 214f.

to human desire (ἐπιθυμία) and the pleasures (αἱ ἡδοναί). Once again, however, James's presentation of this characteristic philosophical opposition of *logos* and desire is significantly impacted by his adherence to Jewish and Christian ideas. In James, this pair functions in the context of a worldview in which opposing supernatural beings, God and the Devil, vie to influence human behavior, and in which judgment by the divine lawgiver looms. *Logos* and desire, in short, function as the two mutually exclusive "ways" by which one might travel toward this eschatological judgment. "Implanted" at God's creation of the human being, James's *logos* is the common possession of humanity in general; it is not, in other words, "the Gospel."

Human Desire and the *Logos* of Truth

It is widely recognized that Jas 1:13–18 represents a discrete argumentative section in James, the central concern of which is stated in 1:13a: "no one who is tempted (πειραζόμενος)[12] is to say 'I am tempted (πειράζομαι) by God.'"[13] The author insists that God, unlike

---

[12] The root πειραζ- can connote both "temptation" arising from within and "tests" arising from without. Dibelius, who sought to drive a wedge between 1:2–4, 1:12, and 1:13–15 in the service of his thesis that the various sayings and sections of James were simply strung together on the basis of catchword connections, argued that while this root is clearly used with the former sense in 1:13–14, it is used with the latter sense in 1:2–4 and 1:12. According to Dibelius, then, the link between 1:12 and 1:13 is merely a superficial catchword connection (*James*, 69–71). To draw such a hard distinction between the "external" and "internal" aspects of the term, however, is misleading, particularly in the context of James; see further on this below. I have been unable to locate an English term which adequately reflects both dimensions of the Greek, and thus often leave the term untranslated in what follows.

[13] See, e.g., the heading for this section chosen by Dibelius: "The source of temptations" (*James*, 90); cf. Chaine: "Origine de la Tentation" (*L'Epître de Saint Jacques*, 18); Marty: "Origene humaine de toute tentation" (*L'Epître de Jacques*, 30); Windisch: "Die 'Versuchung' zum Bösen kommt aus uns selbst, alles Gute kommt von Gott" (*Die katholischen Briefe*, 8); Sidebottom: "God's Innocence" (*James, Jude and 2 Peter*, 30); Mußner: "Die Theodizee" (*Der Jakobusbrief*, 86); cf. also Klein, *Ein vollkommenes Werk*, 39.

A number of scholars, emphasizing the connection between 1:12 and 1:13 which Dibelius denied (see the preceding note), consider this section to begin at 1:12: so Reicke, *The Epistles*, 16–17; Laws, *Epistle of James*, 66–78; Davids, *Epistle of James*, 79–83; Perkins, *First and Second Peter, James and Jude*, 100–101; cf. Martin, *James*, 28–35. As will become clear in this chapter, I agree that there is an important connection between 1:12 and 1:13. Nonetheless, I would emphasize that 1:12, echoing much of the language of 1:2–4, forms, with the latter, something of an *inclusio* around the difficult 1:5–8 and 1:9–11. See below, note 95; further Ropes, *St. James*, 150; Dibelius, *James*, 69–71, 88; Johnson, *Letter of James*, 189; and see the comments of Klein, *Ein vollkommes Werk*, 43–45, 82–85.

humans, has nothing whatsoever to do with πειρασμός: he neither experiences it himself, nor does he cause others to experience it.[14] It is rather, according to James, an individual's own desire which is the true source of πειρασμός.[15] The experience is described in terms of both abduction and seduction: "each person is tempted by his or her own desire, being dragged off (ἐξελκόμενος) and seduced (δελεαζόμενος) [by them]" (1:14).[16] The imagery of seduction in particular is developed as the author personifies the principles in order to describe vividly the results of giving in to desire: "then desire (ἡ ἐπιθυμία), having conceived, bears sin; and sin (ἡ ἁμαρτία), when it reaches maturity, gives birth to death (θάνατον)" (1:15). The explanation of the origin of πειρασμός in 1:13–15, therefore, serves not only to exculpate God from the human experience of temptation, but from sin and, particularly remarkably, "death" as well.[17] Conversely,

---

[14] Jas 1:13b: ὁ γὰρ θεὸς ἀπείραστος ἐστιν κακῶν, πειράζει δὲ αὐτὸς οὐδένα. On the translation of ἀπείραστος, see esp. Mayor, *Epistle of St. James*, 51–53; on the philosophical character of the term see Klein, *Ein vollkommenes Werk*, 86. The claim of Jas 1:13b is quite remarkable. Note in the first place its apparent contradiction of the Jewish scriptures, indeed, of a passage to which the author of James will later refer: cf. Jas 2:21 with LXX Gen 22:1–19 (esp. 22:1, ὁ θεὸς ἐπείραζεν τὸν Αβρααμ). One might also contrast it with the Lord's Prayer, Matt 6:13 (cf. Luke 11:4; *Did.* 8:2): καὶ μὴ εἰσενέγκῃς ἡμᾶς εἰς πειρασμόν, on which see further Betz, *The Sermon on the Mount*, 405–13. According to Johnson (*Letter of James*, 203), in fact, Jas 1:13 exercised the early interpreters of James even more than its apparent contradiction of Paul in 2:14–26. Dibelius explains James's claim with reference to a wider trend toward dissociating God with human failings in the Jewish thought of the Hellenistic period (*James*, 90–91). He cites, for example, *Jubilees*'s account of Abraham's sacrifice of Isaac—the most intense, perhaps, in Abraham's series of "trials"—in which Mastema is identified as the ultimate inspiration for this particular test (17:16; cf. 17:9, 12); nonetheless, in *Jubilees* it is still God who does the actual "testing" in this case, as, apparently, in the earlier "tests": see *Jub.* 17:17–18 and 18:1ff. Whatever the case, the remarkable position of James on this matter is likely to be correlated more specifically with his view that πειρασμός, by definition, is caused by desire (ἐπιθυμία): this latter is understood to be entirely opposed to God's will (see below), and is therefore, apparently, wholly alien to God's nature; thus too, then, is πειρασμός.

[15] The problem of the origin of desire itself, on the other hand, is not addressed.

[16] Note that ὑπὸ τῆς ἰδίας ἐπιθυμίας is positioned so that it can modify both πειράζεται and ἐξελκόμενος καὶ δελεαζόμενος. As Dibelius points out, the verb δελεάζειν, while "found elsewhere in the New Testament only in 2 Petr 2:14, 18, is frequently used by Philo precisely in connection with desire" (*James*, 93). Further, Mayor cites a number of passages from hellenistic moralists like Philo, Epictetus and Plutarch in which this term, as in Jas 1:13, is "combined with ἕλκω or its cognates" (*St. James*, 54).

[17] An allusion to Genesis 3 at this point in James has often been noted. Cf. also, however, Wis 1:12–16; 2:23–24; the death in question here is not death of body, but of soul (3:1–4). Similarly, the author of James is concerned less with natural death than with eschatological death: even the "righteous" are subject to "death"

it places responsibility for escaping this deadly progression squarely and emphatically upon the shoulders of each human individual: the entire sequence is set in motion by a given person's own desire.[18]

The references to the *logos* of truth by means of which God "gave birth to us" in Jas 1:16–18 and, subsequently, to "the implanted *logos* which is able to save your souls" in 1:19–27, follow this account of the origin of πειρασμός, sin and death in human desire in 1:14–15. Uncovering the logic of the connection between 1:14–15 and 1:16–18 and, further, between 1:13–18 as a whole and 1:19–27, greatly illuminates the role of the *logos* in the thought of James.

The significance of 1:16–18 within the larger argument of 1:13–18 is typically construed as follows.[19] The admonition of 1:16, μὴ πλανᾶσθε, is translated "do not be deceived," and the "deception" in question is understood with reference to the position that the author has rejected, i.e., that God is the ultimate source of πειρασμός, sin and death.[20] Jas 1:17 is then interpreted as a terse—and incomplete—argument in support of the contrary view: from the premises (i) all good things come from God and (ii) God does not change, the author expects the reader to infer that no evil comes from God. The reference to the fact that God "gave birth to us by means of a *logos* of truth," on this interpretation, is taken to offer further proof of premise (i) by highlighting God's greatest act of beneficence, whether understood as his creation of humanity in general, his gift of salvation to Christians, or some combination of these.[21]

---

in the mundane sense; see esp. 5:6 (with which cf. Wis 2:12–20); on the other hand, those who endure, surely including those such as "the righteous" of 5:6, are nonetheless promised "life" (1:12). Note also in this respect Jas 1:21: ὁ ἔμφυτος λόγος is able to save τὰς ψυχὰς ὑμῶν.

[18] Jas 1:14: ἕκαστος . . . πειράζεται ὑπὸ τῆς ἰδίας ἐπιθυμίας.

[19] See, e.g., Spitta, *Der Brief des Jakobus*, 39–47; Ropes, *St. James*, 158–68; Dibelius, *James*, 70, 99–107; Chaine, *L'Épître de Saint Jacques*, 18–27; Cantinat, *Les Épîtres*, 89–98; Laws, *Epistle of James*, 72–78; Davids, *Epistle of James*, 85–90; Perkins, *First and Second Peter, James, and Jude*, 100–103. So also, apparently Klein; cf. *Ein vollkommenes Werk*, 44, 87–88, 129, 158. Cf. further Reicke, *The Epistles of James, Peter, and Jude*, 16–18, and Mußner, *Der Jakobusbrief*, 89–97, neither of whom, however, emphasize that 1:18 is a proof of God's goodness.

[20] Mußner's translation of μὴ πλανᾶσθε as "Laßt euch nicht verführen" would seem to relate this verse back to 1:14–15; cf. his comment on 1:14: "Die Begierde ist eine verführerische, unheimliche Macht" (*Der Jakobusbrief*, 88). However, neither this specific connection nor the more general image of *Verführung* are developed in his discussion of 1:16 itself, which is rather interpreted with reference to a mistaken idea (cf. 1:13) that God is the cause of πειρασμοί and sin (*ibid.*, 90).

[21] E.g., Johnson, *Letter of James*, 197: "God's creation of humans is taken to be the great demonstration of the conviction that he is the source of all good gifts";

This interpretation is questionable for a number of reasons. It is to be noted, first of all, that 1:18 has curiously little force if it functions merely to bolster the rather mundane premise that God is the source of good things. Certainly the more novel of the two premises—and indeed, the less self-evident from the Jewish scriptures—is that regarding the unchanging nature of God.[22] More importantly, as even the advocates of this interpretation are forced to concede, "the explicit negation which would be particularly important after vv 13ff" on this reading, namely, that God is not responsible for evil, "remains strangely unexpressed" in 1:16–18.[23] Aggravating this problem further is the fact that the argument assumed to be at work here is in any case invalid: it does not follow from the propositions (i) that God is the source of all good things and (ii) that God does not change, that God is not also the source of bad things.[24]

In fact, judging from Jas 1:17, which states that *every* (πᾶσα, πᾶν) good and perfect gift—not "*only*" good and perfect gifts—comes from God,[25] the "deception" against which the author warns here would seem first and foremost to concern the source of *good* things, not the

---

cf. Klein, *Ein vollkommenes Werk*, 66f. On the various views of the precise reference of the "birth" of Jas 1:18, see Chapter One and above note 10.

[22] Note, e.g., that Philo felt compelled to clarify this point when commenting on Gen 6:5–7 in *Deus Immut.* 21–22: "Perhaps some of those who are careless inquirers (lit.: "the unexamined"; τῶν ἀνεξετάστων) will suppose that the Lawgiver is hinting that the Creator repented of the creation of men when He beheld their impiety, and that this was the reason why He wished to destroy the whole race. Those who think thus may be sure that they make the sins of these men of old time seem light and trivial through the vastness of their own godlessness. For what greater impiety could there be than to suppose that the Unchangeable changes (τὸν ἄτρεπτον τρέπεσθαι)?" It is noteworthy, too, perhaps, that while one finds hints of it in the Jewish literature prior to the Hellenistic period (e.g., Mal 3:6), the notion that God is unchanging becomes emphasized in Jewish and Christian literature especially as a result of Greek philosophical influence.

[23] Dibelius, *James*, 99. Typically, Dibelius himself assumes that this deficiency in the supposed argument results from the author's combination here of two distinct "sayings" for his own novel purpose; cf. also in this respect Hauck, *Die Kirchenbriefe* (1949), 11; Klein, *Ein vollkommenes Werk*, 87 n. 275; and already Ropes, *St. James*, 159. This, however, is hardly an adequate explanation: if one grants (as Dibelius and these others do) that the author is in fact trying to make a point here, the oddity of his choice to leave that point unexpressed remains whether he has drawn upon an earlier source or not. Cf. Davids, *Epistle of James*, 88: "[According to 1:17, God] actually sends all good things and, since he is unchanging, could never send evil. But one notices that the argument could be more direct and clear."

[24] This was noted already by Hort (*Epistle of St. James*, 27) and Mayor (*Epistle of St. James*, 56).

[25] See Ropes, *Epistle of St. James*, 158; Dibelius, *James*, 99 n. 151.

origin of evil.[26] The connection of 1:16–18 to 1:13–15 must therefore be re-assessed. We will do well to begin by attempting to understand James's concern that his audience not be deceived regarding the fact that all good things come from God.

Acquiring "Good Gifts"

The characterization of God as the source of "gifts" is among the most prominent of James's properly theological conceptions,[27] and is closely linked to his understanding of prayer. The letter itself is largely framed by the treatment of these interrelated themes. In 1:5, the author writes of "the god who gives to all without reserve and without reproach" (τοῦ διδόντος θεοῦ πᾶσιν ἁπλῶς καὶ μὴ ὀνειδίζοντος), instructing anyone who "lacks wisdom" to ask (αἰτείτω) God, "and it will be given to him or her." Despite God's giving nature, however, his granting of such requests is not so automatic as this simple statement might suggest: the author immediately goes on to warn that one must, more specifically, "ask with faith, not at all doubting" (1:6, αἰτείτωδὲ ἐν πίστει μηδὲν διακρινόμενος), otherwise one cannot expect to "receive anything from the Lord" (1:7). This theme is revisited at the letter's end. In 5:13–16, the author emphasizes the importance of prayer in the case of misfortune and sickness, directly linking the healing of sickness to "the faithful prayer" (or: "the prayer of faith"; cf. ἡ εὐχὴ τῆς πίστεως). He then offers further encouragement in this respect by illustrating the power of such prayer with the example of Elijah, "a human being like us" who nonetheless withheld and subsequently restored rainfall through, it is assumed, his prayers.[28]

God's role as giver of gifts, the importance of asking God, and, more specifically, the importance of asking God *in the proper manner* also figure prominently in 4:1–6. Analysis of this section greatly illu-

---

[26] To be sure, the question of the origin of evil—or more accurately, the ultimate source of, and thus responsibility for the human experience of πειρασμός, sin and death—is the basic concern of 1:13–18. On the relation of 1:16–17 to this larger point, however, see below.

[27] So Johnson, writing of the concept of God in James: "Above all . . . it is James' characterization of God as gift-giver that is most important" (*Letter of James*, 86). As has often been noted, the view of God as gift-giver is typically hellenistic; see the passages listed, e.g., in Davids, *Epistle of James*, 86, and Johnson, *Letter of James*, 195. This emphasis also accords well with the author's characteristic concern for economic issues.

[28] Jas 5:16b–18; cf. 1 Kings 17:1 and 18:42, neither of which reports anything about Elijah *praying* regarding the rain.

minates the connection between James's concern to locate the origin of temptation, sin and death in desire in 1:13–15 and his reference to birth by means of *logos* in 1:18.

Desire and the Gifts of God in 4:1–6

Jas 4:1–6[29] begins as the author locates the origins of social strife (πόλεμοι and μάχαι) in "the pleasures that war in your members."[30] The proper punctuation of the lines following this in Jas 4:2 is notoriously difficult and has been the subject of much discussion. It is most likely, however, that the verse is to be understood as an explanation of the claim of 4:1, depicting killing as a result of frustrated desire, and—most tellingly—"battling and warring" as a result of a jealous striving for that which one does not possess. Thus:

> Whence come wars and whence come battles (πόθεν πόλεμοι και πόθεν μάχαι) among you? Is it not from within, out of your own pleasures that wage war among your members (ἐκ τῶν ἡδονῶν ὑμῶν τῶν στρατευομένων ἐν τοῖς μέλεσιν ὑμῶν)? You desire and you do not have, [so] you kill; and you are jealous and you are not able to obtain [that which you are jealous of], [so] you battle and war (μάχεσθε καὶ πολεμεῖτε).[31]

The logic here is quite similar to that which underlies Philo's discussion of the importance of reason dominating anger in a passage mentioned at the beginning of the previous chapter.

> When pleasure (ἡ ἡδονή) has the materials it needs to produce it, it haunts the belly and the parts below it. But when it is at a loss for these materials, it occupies the breast (τὰ στήθη) where wrath (ὁ θυμός) is; for lovers of pleasure (οἱ . . . φιλήδονοι) when deprived of their pleasures (τῶν ἡδονῶν) grow bitter and angry (ὀργίζονται καὶ παραπικραίονται).[32]

---

[29] The relation of 4:1–6 to what precedes and follows it is debated. Typically, 4:1–10 or 4:1–12 is regarded as a discrete section; however, as Johnson points out, 4:1–10 is closely related to 3:13–18 ("James 3:13–4:10 and the *Topos* ΠΕΡΙ ΦΘΟΝΟΥ," *NovT* 25 (1983) 327–47). Jas 4:1–6 can in any case be examined as an argumentative unit which concerns the proper and improper ways of attempting to acquire things, as will become clear shortly.

[30] Jas 4:1; for the sense in which ἐν τοῖς μέλεσιν is meant, cf. esp. the description of the tongue as the small "member" (3:5, μέλος) "among our members" (3:6, ἐν τοῖς μέλεσιν ἡμῶν).

[31] So also Mayor, *Epistle of St. James*, 134–37; Ropes, *St. James*, 254; Johnson, *Letter of James*, 277; cf. the NRSV. Dibelius's primary objection against this reading is its failure to account for the apparent harshness of the charge "you kill" (*James*, 217); but see now, however, Johnson's excellent study "James 3:13–4:10 and the *Topos* ΠΕΡΙ ΦΘΟΝΟΥ," and further below note 34.

[32] *Leg. All.* 3.114; Philo will go on say that "the soul is saved" only when reason (λόγος) dominates ὁ θυμός (*Leg. All.* 3.137).

In a manner reminiscent of James's preceding descriptions of "the wisdom from above" as "peaceful" (3:17, εἰρηνική; cf. 3:18) and the pleasures as "warring among your members" (4:1), Philo proceeds to characterize the pursuit of such baser drives as a circumstance in which "war (πόλεμος) prevails in the soul," with reason (λογισμόν), which "is in us not as a combative (μάχιμον) but as a peaceful (εἰρηναῖον) inmate," becoming a "prisoner of war" (*Leg. All.* 3.117).[33] In fact, such a causal connection between pleasure (ἡδονή) and anger as is made by Philo in this passage reflects a "logic of envy" which is commonplace among the Hellenistic moralists, as Johnson has well demonstrated.[34]

Following precisely such a logic, James locates the origin of social strife in the human pursuit of their own pleasures (4:1, ἡδοναί). More specifically, strife is thought to result from the fact that such a pursuit is precisely the *wrong* way to go about acquiring something: ἐπιθυμεῖτε καὶ οὐκ ἔχετε . . . οὐκ ἔχετε διὰ τὸ μὴ αἰτεῖσθαι ὑμᾶς (4:2). That is to say, τὸ αἰτεῖσθαι, not τὸ ἐπιθυμεῖν, is the way to obtain something. In fact, so opposed are the two that even one who "asks" cannot expect to receive anything if it is the object of his or her pleasures that is requested: αἰτεῖτε καὶ οὐ λαμβάνετε διότι κακῶς αἰτεῖσθε, ἵνα ἐν ταῖς ἡδοναῖς ὑμῶν δαπανήσητε (4:3).[35] Worse than vain, the pursuit of desire is likened to "friendship with the world," and thus "enmity with God" (4:4); indeed, it emerges subsequently that it represents a failure to "resist the Devil" (4:8).[36] The author thus reserves some of

---

[33] Note also Philo's emphasis in this connection on the importance of speech for healing anger (*Leg. All.* 3.124); see further on this below, pp. 227f.

[34] See Johnson, "James 3:13–4:10 and the *Topos* ΠΕΡΙ ΦΘΟΝΟΥ." As Johnson shows, the charge of 4:2, "you kill," when seen in this light, is far from surprising. On the contrary, "it fits the context perfectly, because in the *topos* on envy, murder is regarded as a logical concomitant of envy" (*idem, Letter of James,* 277). In this connection, one should particularly note Jas 5:6, where "the rich," who are the pre-eminent pleasure seekers in James (cf., e.g., 5:5), are charged with having "killed" (ἐφονεύσατε) the righteous"; note further the apparent echo of Jas 4:6 in Jas 5:6, on which see below p. 223.

[35] Cf. in this respect the author's logic in 1:5–8: though God is described as "the God who gives to all," it is nonetheless the case that the one who petitions God incorrectly should not expect to "receive anything from the Lord." Note that the author refers to both types of improper petitioners as δίψυχοι (1:8; 4:8); see further on this term below.

[36] For a similar synergy between human desires and God's angelic nemesis, see *The Testaments of the Twelve Patriachs,* esp. *T. Reu.* 4:7–11, and further Johnson, "James 3:13–4:10 and the *Topos* ΠΕΡΙ ΦΘΟΝΟΥ," 341–46.

his harshest invective for those who pursue their own desires, address-
ing them as "adulteresses" in the idiom of the biblical prophets (4:4).[37]

The host of exegetical problems involved in the interpretation of
4:5–6 have made this another of the letter's most controversial passages.[38] The question of whether the author here introduces a citation from some no longer extant "scripture" is not likely to be
definitively resolved barring the discovery of some ancient work,
dated earlier than James, which contains either some or all this passage.[39] Fortunately, this question is more important for the general
problem of the history of the canon than it is for the interpretation
of the passage itself. More critical with respect to the latter are the
subject of κατῴκισεν[40] in 4:5 and the punctuation of the verses.[41]

The neuter gender of τὸ πνεῦμα renders its syntax ambiguous: it
could be taken either as the subject or the object of ἐπιποθεῖ. If it
is taken to be the object, James would thus be implying that his
"adulterous" intended audience has underestimated the deity's jealousy (φθόνος) for them.[42] This reading, however, is most unlikely. In
the first place, that the author has chosen to emphasize the jealousy
of God in the context of a discussion which repeatedly treats "jealousy" (ζῆλος) as something entirely negative and opposed to God

---

[37] See the literature cited by Johnson, *Letter of James*, 278. Only the biting irony
of his (rhetorical) address to "the rich"—who, in James, are the pursuers of desire
and the "friends of the world" *par excellence*—is harsher. Cf. the rather less threat-
ening address of the foolish man in Jas 2:20, which is more reminiscent of diatribe.

[38] For discussion of the problems see the commentaries, esp. Mayor, *Epistle of St.
James*, 140–45 and Dibelius, *James*, 220–25; further S. Laws, "Does Scripture Speak
in Vain? A Reconsideration of James IV.5," *NTS* 20 (1973–74) 210–15; Johnson,
"James 3:13–4:10 and the *Topos* ΠΕΡΙ ΦΘΟΝΟΥ," 327–32; Klein, *Ein vollkommenes
Werk*, 111–15.

[39] See, however, the discussion below, with n. 59.

[40] The additional, textual problem of whether this or the intransitive κατῴκησεν
is to be read here is largely inconsequential for the interpretation of the passage:
whatever the case, the author would no doubt have assumed that it was God who
made πνεῦμα dwell in the human being.

[41] Dibelius raises the possibilty that the rhetorical question introduced in 4:5 ends
with πρὸς φθόνον, but ultimately argues that it runs through 4:5b, which is to be
understood as a citation (*James*, 220–23; cf. 207); cf. the NRSV. Laws argues that
4:5a and 4:5b are to be understood as two distinct rhetorical questions, and suggests that the "scripture" in question is an allusion to LXX Ps 83:3 ("Does Scripture
Speak in Vain?" esp. 214–15); cf. Johnson, *Letter of James*, 280. The 26th edition
of Nestle-Aland punctuates the passage with a colon after λέγει, and extends the
question (and apparently a supposed citation) through 4:6a.

[42] So, e.g., Ropes, *St. James*, 264–65; Dibelius, *James*, 224; Mußner, *Der Jakobusbrief*,
181f. This is the reading which I myself assumed in "A Letter to the Twelve Tribes,"
508 n. 35.

(3:14, 16; 4:2) is hardly plausible.⁴³ Moreover, while the motif of God's jealousy is, of course, not uncommon in the Jewish scriptures, the term ζῆλος is normally used in such contexts in Greek translations, and never, in any event, is φθόνος so used.⁴⁴ Indeed, "in Greek usage, *phthonos* is *always* a vice."⁴⁵ In light of these observations, it is *prima facie* likely that the author rather refers to the πνεῦμα⁴⁶ which resides within each of the "adulterers" among his audience. In fact, a characterization of the intended audience as longing for something "to the point of envy" (πρὸς φθόνον) accords quite well with the preceding depictions of them as people who are jealous (4:2, ζηλοῦτε; cf. 3:14, 16), who pursue desire (4:2, ἐπιθυμεῖτε), and thus at most petition God with the "evil motive" (κακῶς)⁴⁷ of pleasure.⁴⁸ The subsequent reference in 4:6 to the "greater gift" (μείζονα . . . χάριν), moreover, would seem to imply some comparison to a "lesser" gift; and this can be read as a comparison of that which God gives with the satisfaction of the pleasures for which the spirits of the imagined "adulteresses" vainly long.⁴⁹

---

⁴³ This seems to me to be a problem especially for those, like Dibelius, who advocate emending φονεύετε in 4:2 to φθονεύετε, for the author would thus be ascribing to God (cf. 4:5, φθόνον) the very behavior he condemns in his intended audience! Note also that the author understands "jealousy" (cf. ζηλοῦτε) to be the result of frustrated "desire" (cf. ἐπιθυμεῖτε) according to 4:2, and that God is not subject to temptation by ἐπιθυμία (cf. 1:13–14). Incidentally, it might be pointed out that, ironically, the "logic of envy" which Johnson describes applies quite well to the author's understanding of his god in any case: his "resistance" of such adulterous ones, at least in the case of the rich, will ultimately take the form of a brutal "day of slaughter" (cf. 5:5, on which see below)!

⁴⁴ Laws, *Epistle of James*, 177–78; cf. Johnson, *Letter of James*, 282, who considers the attribution of φθόνος to God to be "virtually impossible."

⁴⁵ Johnson, *Letter of James*, 281, emphasis his.

⁴⁶ This πνεῦμα is not analogous to the "holy spirit" referred to in the letters of Paul, but rather simply the life-giving human spirit; cf. Jas 2:26, and further Laws, "Does Scripture Speak in Vain," 212–13.

⁴⁷ As Johnson rightly notes, not simply "incorrectly" (*Letter of James*, 278); cf. esp. 1:13, where "evil" (cf. κακῶν) is associated with temptation by desire.

⁴⁸ Note that the entire discussion leading up to 4:5–6 has dealt with the "envy" which results from the pursuit of ἡδονή; see Johnson, "James 3:13–4:10 and the *Topos* ΠΕΡΙ ΦΘΟΝΟΥ."

⁴⁹ See further on this phrase below, note 61. The debate over the translation of χάρις as "gift" or "grace" owes more to comparisons of James with Paul than the logic of the passage itself. The following considerations seem to me to be decisive in favor of translating this, with Johnson (*Letter of James*, 282), as "gift." First, while the author does not show any overt interest in a pauline concept of "grace" elsewhere in his work (though cf. the comments of Mußner, *Der Jakobusbrief*, 96, and others on the use of βουληθείς in 1:18), he is very interested in God's role as giver of gifts. Second, and more importantly, 4:1–6 itself is concerned precisely with how one goes about acquiring things, contrasting a "vain" and "evil" way, i.e., pur-

It is obvious in any case that the two references to the fact that God "gives a gift" (δίδωσιν χάριν), one in a quotation from Proverbs and one immediately prior to that quotation, are to be understood in light of the preceding discussion of proper and improper ways of acquiring things. The citation of Prov 3:34, which makes a distinction between the "humble" to whom God "gives a gift" (δίδωσιν χάριν) and the "arrogant" whom he "resists," is intended as proof (διὸ λέγει) of the author's larger point regarding the evil and futility of pursuing one's own pleasures.[50] The "humble" of Prov 3:34, that is, are interpreted by James with reference to those who simply depend upon God for their needs; the "arrogant,"[51] on the other hand, are correlated with those "adulteresses" who either pursue their own pleasures and neglect to make requests of God,[52] or, just as bad, ask God in order that their desires might be sated. Indeed, in the mock address of 5:1–6, the author subsequently warns "the rich" (οἱ πλούσιοι)—whom he elsewhere contrasts with ὁ ταπεινός (1:9–11; cf. 4:6); who indulge themselves at the expense of others (5:4–5) and who, indeed, "kill" to this end (5:6, φονεύσατε; cf. 4:2); who are, in short, the pre-eminent "arrogant"[53]—that God ultimately will "resist" (ἀντιτάσσεται) them in a decisive and brutal manner.[54] Jas 4:1–6 is thus followed[55] by a call for repentance reminiscent of that which introduces the apostrophe to the rich in 5:1: those who seek to sate their own desires are to "lament and mourn and weep" (ταλαιπωρήσατε καὶ πενθήσατε καὶ κλαύσατε); they are, in short, to "*humble* themselves" (ταπεινώθητε) so that God might exalt (ὑψώσει) them.[56] Such "friends of the world" are to resist the Devil, who will thus "flee" from them, and draw near to God, who will thus draw near

---

suing one's own desires, with a "correct" and "effective" one, i.e., asking God, who has already been characterized as one "who gives to all generously and without grumbling" (1:5), and from whom comes "every good gift and every perfect present" (1:17).

[50] Cf. Johnson, "James 3:13–4:10 and the *Topos* ΠΕΡΙ ΦΘΟΝΟΥ," 346; *idem, Letter of James,* 283.

[51] For the association of φθόνος and ὑπερηφανία, see Johnson, "James 3:13–4:10 and the *Topos* ΠΕΡΙ ΦΘΟΝΟΥ," 335–36; *idem, Letter of James,* 283.

[52] Cf. Jas 4:13–15, where those who make their own plans—presumably business plans (cf. 4:13: "we will do business [ἐμπορευσόμεθα] and make a profit")—without deferring to the will of God are upbraided for their arrogance (ἀλαζονεία).

[53] Cf. Klein, *Ein vollkommenes Werk,* 115.

[54] Cf. Jas 4:6 with 5:6, and further 1:9–11. See L. A. Schökel, "James 5,2 [sic] and 4,6," *Bib* 54 (1973) 73–76; Davids, *Epistle of James,* 180; Johnson, *Letter of James,* 305; Penner, *Epistle of James and Eschatology,* 155.

[55] Note the use of οὖν in 4:7.

[56] Cf. Jas 4:9, 10 with 5:1; see further 1:9–11.

to them (4:7–8).⁵⁷ They are "sinners" (ἁμαρτωλοί) who must cleanse their hands; δίψυχοι who must "purify" (ἁγνίσατε) their hearts.⁵⁸

As the fact that the subject of the clause διὸ [ἡ γραφή] λέγει must be supplied from 4:5 already suggests, therefore, the charge that those who pursue an adulterous "friendship with the world" are acting as though "scripture speaks in vain" is issued with Prov 3:34 in mind, whether or not it is also made with reference to some now lost work, cited in 4:5(–6a).⁵⁹ Accordingly, it seems to me that Jas 4:5–6 is best punctuated as follows:

> Or do you think the scripture speaks in vain? The spirit which he [i.e., God] made to dwell in us longs to the point of envy (πρὸς φθόνον), but he [i.e., God] gives a greater gift. Therefore it says . . .

What is clear in any case is that the author imagines two ways in which one can go about acquiring things. The proper and effective way, emphasized also in the opening and closing sections of the letter, is simply to ask "the god who gives to all without reserve and without reproach" (1:5); more precisely, to ask him humbly, entirely apart from any intention of sating one's own desires. The improper way, conversely, is to attempt to sate one's desires, whether through petitions to God or not. To engage in the arrogant pursuit of one's own desires is to become an "enemy of God" and thus, ironically, to alienate the "gift-giver," whose gifts are reserved for the humble.

Desire and the Gifts of God in 1:13–18

Immediately following the claim, in Jas 1:13–15, that the chain of temptation, sin and death originates with an individual's own desire rather than from God, James states that "every good gift and every

---

⁵⁷ As has often been noted, these admonitions and promises find close analogies in the *Testaments of the Twelve Patriarchs*; see Dibelius, *James*, 226.

⁵⁸ Cf. Jas 1:8, where the one who does not ask God ἐν πίστει is similarly described as δίψυχος, ἀκατάστατος ἐν πάσαις ταῖς ὁδοῖς αὐτοῦ. Note further in this connection the association of ἀκαταστασία with an "earthly" and "demonic" wisdom in 3:16, while the "wisdom from above" is "in the first place" (πρῶτον) "pure" (3:17, ἁγνή).

⁵⁹ This latter possibility, however, seems to me to be an unnecessary hypothesis in light of the importance of Prov 3:34 to the passage. While it is possible that the author combines two quotations here (a coupling, one might suggest, facilitated by the occurrence in both of the phrase δίδωσιν χάριν), it seems more likely that the question in 4:5, "do you think scripture speaks in vain," simply anticipates the διὸ λέγει which introduces the citation of Prov 3:34; as pointed out, the subject of διὸ λέγει must in any case be supplied from 4:5. Less plausible still is Laws's suggestion that the author alludes here to LXX Ps 83:3 ("Does Scripture Speak in Vain?" 214f).

perfect present"[60] is "from above" (ἄνωθεν), i.e., from God. The connection between these two statements is greatly illuminated by the emphasis on God's role as the source of good things throughout the letter, and by 4:1–6 in particular. All truly good things, according to James, come from God; and it is by asking him rather than pursuing one's own desires that one can receive these gifts. On his view, scripture itself teaches that God "gives a gift" only to the humble, while resisting those who arrogantly pursue their own desires.[61] Succumbing to desire, in short, represents a mistaken understanding of how (truly) good things can be obtained: one must depend humbly, simply and wholly upon God. The pursuit of one's own desires, while enticing, will ultimately achieve nothing good, only sin and death.

---

[60] As has long been noted, πᾶσα δόσις ἀγαθή καὶ πᾶν δώρημα τέλειον forms a hexameter. H. Greeven has argued, on the supposition that this line must therefore be a quotation of an earlier saying, that Jas 1:17 actually consists of two sentences: a traditional statement and its explanation. Greeven thus paraphrases the verse as follows: "'Jede Gabe ist gut, und jedes Geschenk ist vollkommen'. Und warum? Weil es von oben stammt, herabkommt vom Vater des Lichts . . ." ("Jede Gabe ist gut," 13). Greeven, however, does not seem to have won a significant following on this point; see, e.g., the subsequent translations of Mußner (*Der Jakobusbrief*, 84), Cantinat (*Les Epîtres*, 90), Laws (*Epistle of James*, 72), Johnson (*Letter of James*, 173); see further Klein, *Ein vollkommenes Werk*, 66–67. Davids suggests that even if the hexameter was proverbial, it is altered in James so that "every good gift and every perfect present" is now the subject of ἄνωθέν ἐστιν (*Epistle of James*, 86). In fact, whereas the author's interest in establishing that all good things come from God is readily understandable in the context of 1:13–18 (see immediately below), it is difficult to see why he should suddenly feel compelled to defend the claim that all "gifts" are good or perfect.

The significance to be accorded to the use of two different phrases in connection with God's beneficence (i.e., δόσις ἀγαθή and δώρημα τέλειον) has also been the subject of some discussion. Some read here a distinction between the act of giving (δόσις) and the gift itself (δώρημα); see Mayor, *Epistle of St. James*, 56–58; Hort, *Epistle of St. James*, 28; more recently Johnson, *Letter of James*, 195. Ropes, on the other hand, argued that "there is no special distinction intended, the repetition being solely for rhetorical effect" (*St. James*, 159); see also H. Greeven, "Jede Gabe ist gut, Jak. 1,17," *TZ* 14 (1958) 1–13; Cantinat, *Les Epîtres*, 91; Davids, *Epistle of James*, 86; cf. Dibelius, *James*, 100. The issue is in any case not crucial for understanding the author's basic point, on which see below.

[61] Note that there is a certain tension between the author's view of God and his perception of his present economic realities: cf. Jas 1:7 and 4:2–3 with the wealth of the wicked "rich" (e.g., 5:2–3). This tension, perhaps, underlies his notion of the "greater gift" in 4:6: the material luxuries of "the rich" are not in fact the truly good gifts, but only fleeting material possessions which ultimately work to their disadvantage; cf. in this connection James's use of phrases πλούσιοι ἐν πίστει and πτωχοὶ τῷ κόσμῳ (2:5). If this is the case, the tension is apparently resolved by means of an imagined eschatological reversal of the present fortunes of "the humble," or "poor," and "the rich": despite their current oppression at the hands of "the rich," the former will ultimately be the inheritors of the promised kingdom.

In fact, the correlation drawn between desire and sin in 1:13–15 is also implied in 4:1–10, where those who pursue desire (cf. 4:2: ἐπιθυμεῖτε) are addressed as "sinners" (ἁμαρτωλοί) who need to "cleanse their hands" (4:8). A connection between desire and death, too, is evident in the latter passage, which locates the origin of "wars and battles" and "killing" in the pleasures (4:1–3).[62] The "death" which is of foremost concern in 1:14–15, however, is not that which those who pursue desire will inflict upon others; rather, it is the eschatological one which they themselves, or more precisely their "souls,"[63] will experience as a result of their sin.[64] Thus does James contrast the "death" (θάνατος) which results from giving in to πειρασμός in 1:14–15 with the "crown of life" (τὸν στέφανον τῆς ζωῆς) promised, in the immediately preceding macarism, to those who endure πειρασμός (1:12).[65]

The Two Ways and the Wandering Children of God

A concern for the eschatological "death" resulting from sin also emerges in the letter's concluding instruction, which presents the association of deception, sin and death made in 1:13–16 under the rubric of a "two ways" ethic (5:19–20).[66] The two ways are characterized by "truth" (ἡ ἀλήθεια) and "deception" (πλάνη), respectively.[67] The "sinner" (ἁμαρτωλός) is imagined to be travelling on the "way" or "path" (ὁδός) which is characterized by "deception" (πλάνη), and which ends in death (θάνατος). This is portrayed as πλανᾶσθαι ἀπὸ τῆς ἀληθείας,[68] a characterization which simultaneously exploits

---

[62] Johnson, in fact, understands Jas 4:2 to explain the logic behind 1:14–15; see *Letter of James*, 276, citing Laws, *Epistle of James*, 172. Cf. also in this connection Jas 5:6, where it is said that "the rich," the pre-eminent devotees of desire, are charged with "killing the righteous."

[63] See 1:21 and 5:20. Note also that "the righteous"—who, no doubt, will receive "the crown of life"—can nonetheless be (and have been!) "killed" by the enemies of God (5:6).

[64] Note that "the rich" not only "kill" (5:6), but will themselves soon face a "day of slaughter" for which their indulgent lifestyle has served to "fatten" them (5:5).

[65] On the relation of the πειρασμός in 1:12 to that of 1:13–15, see below pp. 221f.

[66] Cf. Klein, *Ein vollkommenes Werk*, 85.

[67] Cf. the use of ἀλήθεια and πλάνη as descriptive of the "two spirits" in *T. Jud.* 20:1; 1 John 4:6; cf. 1QS 3:18–19.

[68] Some mss read ἀπὸ τῆς ὁδοῦ ἀληθείας or τῆς ὁδοῦ τῆς ἀληθείας in Jas 5:19, thus explicitly identifying "the truth" as a way. Even if the work of later editors, however, these readings only make explict what is clearly implicit in any case: the author envisions two opposing "ways" which humans can travel, one characterized by "truth" (ἀλήθεια) and the other by "deception" (πλάνη). Similarly, whether the phrase

both the spatial and cognitive aspects of πλανάω: while the contrast set up between ἡ ἀλήθεια and πλάνη suggests that the "sinner" is "*deceived* from the truth," the portrayal of such a one as traveling the wrong path and needing to be "turned back" (ἐπιστρέφω) presents him or her as having "*wandered* from the truth."[69] One who turns the wandering "sinner" from the "way" characterized by "deception" and back to "the truth" will, in effect, "cover a multitude of sins (ἁμαρτιῶν)" and "save his or her soul from death" (σώσει ψυχὴν αὐτου ἐκ θανάτου).[70]

It is difficult to render πλανηθῆ ἀπὸ τῆς ἀληθείας (5:20) in English in a way which preserves both its spatial and its cognitive connotations. The translator is faced with a similar problem in Jas 1:16–18 where, once again, both aspects of the term πλανάω are operative. Here, the god who is the source of every good gift is not described simply as such, but as "the Father of Lights, with whom there is no alteration or shadow of change" (1:17, τοῦ πατρὸς τῶν φώτων, παρ' ᾧ οὐκ ἔνι παραλλαγὴ ἢ τροπῆς ἀποσκίασμα).[71] While it is not immediately clear what (if any) particular astrological phenomena the author has in mind in 1:17,[72] the contrast between the deity and the "lights" he created vis-à-vis such "changes," at least, is obvious.[73] Further, the fact that the author proceeds to point out that this

---

ἐκ πλάνης ὁδοῦ αὐτοῦ is translated "from his or her way of error" or "from the error of his or her way," the basic idea of a "way" characterized by error is clear.

[69] Cf. Johnson, *Letter of James*, 337; further Dibelius, *James*, 257 n. 94, who notes that "'[t]o wander' (πλανᾶσθαι) occurs frequently in conjunction with 'way'," citing several relevant passages.

[70] Jas 5:20; the reference to "covering a multitude of sins" is an allusion to Prov 10:12. Against Fabris, *Legge*, 69 n. 58, the "sins" which will be "covered" and the "soul" which will thereby be "saved from death" are most naturally read as those of the "sinner" whose deception leads him or her to death, not as those of ὁ ἐπιστρέψας. See further Johnson, *Letter of James*, 338–39.

[71] I simply cite the text as given in B. Aland *et al.*, *Novum Testamentum Graecum. Editio Critica Maior* IV, Installment 1, 1.13–14. On the severe textual problems here, see the discussions of Ropes, *St. James*, 162–64; and Dibelius, *James*, 100–102.

[72] On the astronomical connotations of παραλλαγή and τροπῆς ἀποσκίασμα, see the commentaries and the relevant entries in BAGD. That the author had specific astrological phenomena in mind here, however, must be considered most doubtful. Indeed, judging from the profound textual confusion surrounding this passage, his terminology in any case confounded early copyists. In fact, his primary interest here, as I will argue below, is in the (apparent) deviations from the normally quite regular movements of the heavenly "lights."

[73] It is therefore most doubtful that one should detect in this line a special concern to associate God with "light" (as opposed to "darkness") as suggested, e.g., by Ropes, *St. James*, 160f; cf. Mußner, *Der Jakobusbrief*, 91. Indeed, the "lights" are introduced here above all because of their association with change, in which respect they are contrasted with God; cf. the comments of Dibelius, *James*, 102.

same "Father" also "gave birth to us" suggests both an additional comparison between "us" and the "lights" (who are both offspring of God), and an analogous contrast between "the Father" and "us." Such a contrast between God and humans has in fact already been drawn in 1:13–15 and is, indeed, the essential point of the argument: while humans experience πειρασμός, God cannot be held responsible for this because he, unlike them, is ἀπείραστος. The implication, then, is that the "changes" evident among the "lights" but not reflective of the nature of their "father" are in some sense comparable to the πειρασμοί experienced by human beings but not by the god who "gave birth" to them.[74]

The command which precedes the reference to God as the unchanging "Father of Lights," μὴ πλανᾶσθε, is particularly suggestive in this respect. While the regular movements of the astral bodies was commonly emphasized in antiquity,[75] it was the perceived *irregularities* in

---

[74] Laws seems to sense this connection as well: "While heavenly bodies can be seen to change, then, either through their own movement or when shadows are cast upon them by the movement of others, God is both himself unchangeable and unaffected by change in anything outside himself (as in v. 13 he is both untempted and untempting)" (*Epistle of James*, 74). Laws suggests a comparison with Philo's contrast between God's unchanging nature and the observable movements in the heavens which he created. In *De Cherub.* 87–90, e.g., pointing out that "sabbath" means "rest" (ἀνάπαυσις), and commenting upon the fact that "Moses" often calls the sabbath "God's sabbath," Philo contrasts God and his creation in this way: God is the "one thing among that which exists (ἐν τοῖς οὖσιν; cf. Colson: "in the universe") which rests (ἀναπαυόμενον)." Philo singles out the astral bodies as the strongest case for purposes of the contrast: even these "are not self mastering and move and revolve continually," and can thus be said to "suffer" while God is ἄτρεπτος and ἀμετάβλητος (*De Cherub.* 88, 89). Elsewhere Philo speaks of this general contrast between God and his various creations in terms of the latter being by nature "subject to becoming (ἐν γενέσει) and constant change" (*Opif.* 12; cf. *Leg. All.* 2.33). More illuminating for James, however, is Philo's awareness that the concept of "unchangeableness" can be used in another sense, in terms of which the ideal human being can be compared, not contrasted, with the deity. Reacting to those who would infer from Gen 6:5–7 that "the Creator repented of the creation of men when He beheld their impiety," Philo writes:

> For what greater impiety could there be than to suppose that the Unchangeable changes? Indeed some maintain that even among men vacillation of mind and judgment is not universal; for those who study philosophy in guilelessness and purity, it is held, gain from their knowledge this as their chief reward, that they do not change with changing circumstances but with unbending steadfastness and firm constancy take in hand all that it behoves them to do (*Deus. Immut.* 22).

Such a one is described as ὁ τέλειος in §23; cf. his description of Moses—and ὁ σοφός and ὁ σπουδαῖος in general—in *Gigant.* 48, esp. the comment that "neither is virtue subject to movement nor the good man to change, but both are stayed on the firm foundation of right reason."

[75] Cicero, e.g., reports Cleanthes's view that "uniform motion and revolution of the heavens" and "the varied groupings and ordered beauty of the sun, moon and

the movement of some "stars" which led to their designation as πλανῆται, or "wanderers." These astral "wanderers" were the subject of a popular Jewish (and subsequently Christian) myth, which explained the supposed anomalies in terms of certain stars' rebellious deviations from the courses which were laid out for them by God. The earliest reference to this myth in the extant Jewish literature is perhaps found in our present *1 Enoch*,[76] in which the Watchers are identified as "stars" whose downfall, as it were, was precipitated by their illicit desire for the daughters of "the sons of men": "the angels, the children of heaven, saw them and desired (ἐπεθύμησαν) them" (*1 Enoch* 6:2).[77] In any case, these "wandering stars" became paradigmatic examples of those who disregard God's commands[78] for later writers, many of whom do clearly identify them with the Watchers. The author of the Letter of Jude, for example, likens a group of Christian "intruders" who "defile the flesh, reject authority and slander the glorious ones" to the ἀστέρες πλανῆται, whom he further identifies as the Watchers.[79] Clement of Alexandria speaks analogously of the Carpocratians:

---

stars" was "the most potent" of the four causes of the (supposed) universality of human belief in the gods (*De Nat. Deor.* 2.15); see further *De Nat. Deor.* 2.49–56, which includes a discussion of the stars "which are falsely called planets or wandering [stars]" (*quae falso vocantur errantes*). Cf. *1 Enoch* 2:1, and further the account of the laws governing the astral movements in the so-called "Astronomical Book" (*1 Enoch* 72–82).

[76] *1 Enoch* 18:9–19. Note, however, that the rebellious stars are not explicitly identified as "wanderers" in *1 Enoch*.

[77] The translation is that of E. Isaac, "1 (Ethiopic Apocalypse of) Enoch," *OTP* 1.15; for the Greek fragment of this passage see M. Black, *Apocalypsis Henochi Graece* (PVTG 3; Leiden: Brill, 1970) 21. There is disagreement regarding the identification of the Watchers with the rebellious stars in *1 Enoch* itself; note esp. that while the latter are seven in number (18:13), the former are said to number two hundred (6:6). See further M. Black, *The Book of Enoch or 1 Enoch: A New English Edition with Commentary and Textual Notes* (in consultation with J. C. VanderKam, with an appendix on the "Astronomical" Chapters [72–82] by O. Neugebauer; SVTP 7; Leiden: Brill, 1985) 160. Whatever the case regarding *1 Enoch* 1–36, an understanding of the Watchers as rebellious stars is clear at least in the so-called "Animal Apocalypse"; see *1 Enoch* 86, with Collins, *The Apocalyptic Imagination*, 54.

[78] Note in this connection *1 Enoch* 18:15: "And the stars which roll over upon the fire, they are the ones which have transgressed the commandments of God"; cf. the enumeration of such commandments in *1 Enoch* 72–82 which, however, does not discuss the "planets."

[79] Jude 8, 13; cf. 6–7. The charge that they "defile the flesh" in particular seems to hark back to the myth of the Watchers; cf. esp. the reference to the Watchers' pursuit of σὰρξ ἑτέρα in Jude 7; further R. Bauckham, *Jude, 2 Peter* (WBC 50; Waco: Word, 1983) 56. Note also the further play on the πλαν- root in this connection, as the Christian "intruders" are said to abandon themselves τῇ πλάνῃ τοῦ Βαλαάμ (Jude 11). See further Bauckham, *Jude*, 50–55 and 89–92.

these are the "wandering stars" (ἀστέρες πλανῆται) referred to in the prophecy,[80] who wander from the narrow road of the commandments (οἱ ἀπὸ τῆς τῶν ἐντολῶν ὁδοῦ . . . πλανώμενοι) into a boundless abyss of the carnal and bodily sins . . . [B]oasting that they are free, they have become slaves to servile desires (ἐπιθυμίων).[81]

A passage from Theophilus's *To Autolycus* is also noteworthy in this connection:

> The disposition of the stars, too, contains a type of the arrangement and order of the righteous and pious, and of those who keep the law and commandments of God (τῶν . . . τηρούντων τὸν νόμον καὶ τὰς ἐντολὰς θεοῦ). For the brilliant and bright stars are an imitation of the prophets, and therefore they remain fixed, not declining, nor passing from place to place. And those which hold the second place in brightness, are types of the people of the righteous. And those, again, which change their position, and flee from place to place, which are also called planets (οἱ καὶ πλάνητες καλούμενοι), they too are a type of the men who have wandered from God, abandoning his law and commandments (τῶν ἀφισταμένων ἀνθρώπων ἀπὸ τοῦ θεοῦ, καταλιπόντων τὸν νόμον καὶ τὰ προστάγματα αὐτοῦ).[82]

A final passage, from the *Testament of Naphtali*, in which the sons of the patriarch are urged not to become like Sodom "which departed from the order of its nature" (ἥτις ἐνήλλαξε τάξιν φύσεως αὐτῆς) is also instructive:

> Sun, moon, and stars (ἥλιος καὶ σελήνη καὶ ἀστέρες) do not alter their order; thus you should not alter the Law of God (νόμον θεοῦ) by the disorder of your actions. The gentiles, because they have wandered astray (πλανηθέντα) and forsook the Lord, have changed the order, and have devoted themselves to stones and sticks, patterning themselves after wandering spirits (πνεύμασι πλάνης)[83] . . . Likewise the Watchers departed from the order of their nature (τάξιν φύσεως αὐτῶν) . . .[84]

---

[80] An apparent reference to Jude 13; see on this point M. Smith, *Clement of Alexandria and a Secret Gospel of Mark* (Cambridge, MA: Harvard University Press, 1973) 8.

[81] *Letter to Theodorus*, 1.3–7. The text and translation are those of M. Smith, *Clement of Alexandria and a Secret Gospel of Mark*, 446–52; cf. the commentary on pp. 8–10, where the paradigmatic use of the "planets" elsewhere in Clement's writings is noted. The "carnal and bodily sin" again likely reflects an identification with the Watchers.

[82] *Ad Aut.* 2.15. The text is found in MPG 6.1077; the translation is that of *ANF* 2.115.

[83] So Kee; cf. H. W. Hollander and M. de Jonge, *The Testaments of the Twelve Patriarchs: A Commentary* (SVTP 8; Leiden: Brill, 1985) 306: "spirits of deceit." The divergence in the two translations highlights once again the difficulty in preserving the Greek word-play with πλάνη and its cognates.

[84] *T.Naph* 3:2–5; I have slightly revised the translation of H. C. Kee, "Testaments

This passage does not explicitly mention, at least as such, the ἀστέρες πλανῆται, and indeed seems to suggest that "stars" by definition "do not alter their order." The astronomical context, however, and particularly the analogy drawn from the Watchers, suggests that the "wandering spirits"[85] after whom "the nations" patterned themselves are to be understood as "wandering" astral bodies. Previously in the *Testaments*, moreover, the Watchers were associated particularly with illicit desire, which is thus here apparently assumed to be the underlying cause of their "wandering."[86]

Sandwiched between a claim that human temptation, sin and death stem from desire rather than God and a reference to the astral "lights" whose changes do not reflect their creator's character, the admonition μὴ πλανᾶσθε in Jas 1:16 is to be understood in light of this common use of the astral "wanderers" as paradigmatic examples of rebellion from God's law as a result of illicit desire. The allusion to this myth is in fact quite apposite in the context of the author's argument in 1:13–18, providing a parallel example in the service of the point made in 1:13–15. Though God is the "father" of the "lights," any wandering on their part reflects not his nature, but represents, on the contrary, a deviation from the path which God had marked out for them. So too, though God is our "father,"[87] the human experience of πειρασμός does not reflect God's nature—for he is ἀπείραστος—but rather stems from each individual's own desire.

---

of the Twelve Patriarchs," *OTP* 1.812, which obscures the fact that the "nature" in question is specifically that of the Watchers themselves. For the Greek text, see M. de Jonge, *The Testaments of the Twelve Patriarchs: A Critical Edition of the Greek Text*; cf. *idem, Testamenta XII Patriarchum: Edited according to Cambridge University Library MS Ff I.24 fol. 203a–262b, with Short Notes* (PVTG; Leiden: Brill, 1964). See further on this passage Hollander and de Jonge, *The Testaments of the Twelve Patriarchs: A Commentary*, 305–308.

[85] See above, note 83.

[86] Cf. *T. Reu.* 5:6. Note also in this connection the link between the Watchers and Sodom in this passage, which is, in fact, not uncommon; cf. Jude 6–7, and the comment of Hollander and de Jonge, *The Testaments of the Twelve Patriarchs: A Commentary*, 307–308.

[87] Note that while the peculiar use of the verb ἀπεκύησεν in 1:18 suggests a maternal, rather than paternal, image of God, its natural subject is the πατὴρ τῶν φώτων of 1:17; cf. further the description of God as "the Father" in 1:27 and 3:9, the latter of which uses the term—as, clearly, in 1:17—with reference to God's role as creator: "with it [sc. the tongue] we bless the Lord and Father, and with it we curse the human beings who were made according to the likeness of God." As has often been pointed out, this verb was likely used in 1:18 mainly to effect some manner of contrast with sin's "birthing" (ἀποκύει) of "death" in 1:15; so, e.g., Mayor, *Epistle of St. James*, 62; Mußner, *Der Jakobusbrief*, 93; Davids, *Epistle of James*, 89; Vouga, *L'Epître de Saint Jacques*, 15; Johnson, *Letter of James*, 197.

λόγος ἀληθείας *and* ἔμφυτος λόγος

God, according to James, is not the source of temptation. It is rather one's own desires that tempt one to stray from God's will and onto the path of sin and death. The Father's will for "us," James goes on to say, far from tempting people to pursue desire, is expressed in the fact that he "gave birth to us by means of a *logos* of truth so that we are a sort of 'first fruits' of his creatures."[88] If, as Dibelius rightly remarks, "the divine will to provide salvation is stressed" here,[89] this strongly suggests that the *logos* of truth stands in opposition to desire, as the way which leads to "life" rather than "death."

In fact, it is in the immediately following elaboration of the admonition "let each person be quick to hear, slow to speak and slow to anger" that the author refers to "the implanted *logos* which is able to save your souls." That these two *logoi* are indeed one and the same cannot be doubted. As we have seen, the phrase ἔμφυτος λόγος itself, like the reference to the "birth" by means of *logos* in 1:18, is an image of divine creation.[90] More striking still is the fact that, just as the "way" of deception, sin and death in 5:19–20 corresponds to the failure to resist desire in 1:14–15, so do the two primary characteristics of the opposite way enumerated in the conclusion—that is, "truth" (5:19, ἡ ἀλήθεια) and its ability to "save souls from death" (cf. 5:20, σώσει ψυχὴν αὐτοῦ ἐκ θανάτου)—correspond, respectively, to the descriptions of *logos* in 1:18 and 1:21: the *logos* by which God "gave birth to us so that we are the 'first fruits' of his creations" is "of truth" (1:18, ἀληθείας), while the implanted *logos* is identified as that "which is able to save your souls" (1:21, τὸν δυνάμενον σῶσαι τὰς ψυχὰς ὑμῶν).

The connection of 1:19–27 to 1:13–18 itself further confirms that the λόγος ἀληθείας and ὁ ἔμφυτος λόγος are one and the same,[91] and

---

[88] Jas 1:18; the use of quotation marks around "first fruits" is meant to reflect what I take to be the deliberate employment of metaphorical language by James (note the use of τινα). Interestingly, the same usage is found in Philo, who describes Israel as "set apart out of the whole human race as a kind of first fruits (τις ἀπαρχή) to the Maker and Father" (*Spec. Leg.* 4.180). For the sense in which this birth renders "us" "first fruits" in James, see below p. 237.

[89] Dibelius, *James*, 103; "this can be seen," he continues, "from the position of 'having willed' (βουληθείς)."

[90] See further on this creation below, under the heading "Birth by *Logos*."

[91] The identification of λόγος ἀληθείας and ὁ ἔμφυτος λόγος is widely assumed; see above, Chapter One. Even Dibelius, who objected in principle to interpreting 1:21 in light of 1:18 given his literary approach to the letter, ultimately identified both as "the gospel."

that this *logos* represents the "way" contrary to desire, i.e., the way which leads to "life." As we have seen, Jas 1:19–27 represents a discrete section within the first chapter of James: Jas 1:19b presents a three part admonition, each element of which is elaborated in 1:20–27. Its connection with 1:13–18, however, is clear nonetheless. Depending upon whether one takes ἴστε as an indicative or an imperative, 1:19a refers to what has preceded either as a reminder ("you know this") or, more generally, as something of which the audience should in any case be aware ("know this!").[92] Whatever the case, the use of ἴτε . . . δέ to introduce the admonition "let each person be quick to hear, slow to speak, and slow to anger" implies that this latter represents an ethical inference drawn from what has preceded, whether 1:13–18 as a whole or 1:18 in particular.[93] It is therefore striking, given the reference to the birth of "us" by means of the "*logos* of truth" in 1:18, that "the implanted *logos*" is central to the elaboration of 1:19b: since human anger doesn't produce God's righteousness, it is to be received "with humility" (1:21); though one is to be "quick to hear," one must not merely "hear" the *logos*, but "do" it as well (1:22–23); and while the *logos* is not explicitly mentioned when the author explains being "slow to speak" in terms of "bridling the tongue" (1:26, χαλιναγωγῶν γλῶσσαν), it emerges when this theme is revisited in James 3 that "bridling the tongue" is nothing other than not "stumbling" ἐν λόγῳ (3:2)—a phrase that certainly refers to speech, but speech particularly in its relation to the implanted *logos*.[94] In short, knowledge that an individual's own desire is the ultimate source of temptation, that giving in to temptation leads to sin and death, and, perhaps most especially, that God "gave birth to us by means of a *logos* of truth," should give rise to a particular type of behavior vis-à-vis the implanted *logos* which is "able to save souls."

Conclusion

The reference to the "*logos* of truth" by which God "gave birth to us" is made in the context of an argument that locates the origin of temptation, sin and death in human desire rather than with

---

[92] The reading ὥστε, while also strongly attested, is likely a later scribal attempt to solidify the transition from 1:18 to 1:19–26.

[93] So also Johnson, *Letter of James*, 199; cf. Klein, *Ein vollkommenes Werk*, 44, 133. Dibelius's characteristic rejection of any coherent connection between 1:18 and 1:19–26 results more from his general literary approach to the letter than to exegesis of this particular passage; see *James*, 109.

[94] See below, pp. 224–30.

God. A distinction is drawn between God and humanity: God, unlike human beings, neither tempts nor is himself tempted. The true source of temptation, rather, is each individual's own desire. Playing, as in 5:19–20, on both of the common connotations of the verb πλανάω, the author warns his audience, μὴ πλανᾶσθε: they are not to be "deceived" by the allure of desire and thus induced to "wander" in sin toward death. Despite its seductive allure, nothing that is truly good will be achieved by giving in to desire. "Every good gift and every perfect present" comes from God. His "gifts" are reserved for those that humbly depend upon him, while he "resists" those who arrogantly pursue their own desires.

In the same way that any "wandering" on the part of the astral "lights" is not reflective of the nature of their "Father" who created them, so too, God is not responsible when humans "wander" onto the path of sin and death, despite the fact that he "gave birth" to "us." Indeed, far from tempting people to pursue desire, God "gave birth to us" by means of *logos*; he "implanted" within us, that is, the *logos* whose primary characteristics of "truth" and the ability to "save souls" stand diametrically opposed to the deception and death of desire. Knowledge of this fact should lead one to resist the "desire" which leads to death, and "do," rather, the *logos* "which is able to save souls."

LOGOS AND ERGA

The antithetical relationship between *logos* and desire in James is underscored by the series of contrastive terms associated with each. They are portrayed as two "ways," with desire characterized above all by "deception" (1:16; 5:19–20, πλάνη) and *logos* by "truth" (1:18; 5:19, ἀλήθεια). The path of desire leads to "death" (1:15, θάνατος), while the *logos* is able to "save souls" from death (1:21; cf. 5:20: σώσει ψυχὴν . . . ἐκ θανάτου). Each "way," moreover, is characterized by its own particular category of behavior. Just as succumbing to desire results in "sin" (1:15, ἁμαρτία; cf. 5:20, ἁμαρτωλόν), so too does "doing" *logos* produce a particular type of action, namely an *ergon*: "the one who looks into the perfect law which is of freedom and remains" and thus becomes a "*logos*-doer" becomes, more specifically, a ποιητὴς ἔργου (1:25). Analyzing James's emphasis on "works" from the perspective of his view of *logos* and desire as "two ways," in fact, sheds a good deal of light on this controversial topic.

The role of *erga* as counterpart to sin within the ethical and soteriological thought of James emerges most clearly through a comparison of 1:2–4, 12[95] with 1:14–15. In Jas 1:2–4, the author insists that the "endurance" (ὑπομονή) produced (ideally) by πειρασμός must "have a perfect work (ἔργον τέλειον) in order that you might be perfect, whole, and lacking in nothing." The somewhat peculiar phrase ἔργον τέλειον has been variously interpreted.[96] Dibelius took it to be a rather pleonastic anticipation of the subsequent clause, ἵνα ἦτε τέλειοι καὶ ὁλόκληροι ἐν μηδενὶ λειπόμενοι. The latter, therefore, while "formally . . . dependent upon the imperative" ἡ δὲ ὑπομονὴ ἔργον τέλειον ἐχέτω, is "in thought parallel to it"; thus: "*You* are that perfect work."[97] This interpretation, however, treating 1:4 as a whole simply as the climactic element of a concatenation after the manner of Rom 5:3–5 and 1 Pet 1:6–7, utterly takes the teeth out of the imperative ἐχέτω.[98] Others have taken the phrase with reference to

---

[95] Jas 1:12, picking up the key theme of enduring πειρασμός, forms an *inclusio* with 1:2–4 (cf. esp. 1:2, πειρασμοῖς with 1:12, πειρασμόν; 1:3, 4, ὑπομονή(-ν) with 1:12, ὑπομένει; and 1:3, δοκίμιον with 1:12, δόκιμος). The problem of the logical development of the intervening verses—i.e., from 1:5–8 to 1:9–11—is among the most challenging problems in the interpretation of the letter, and is Dibelius's strongest case for reading James as a collection of disparate traditions; cf. the comments of Johnson, *Letter of James*, 174–76. Dibelius himself nonetheless recognized the resumptive character of 1:12 (*James*, 88). However one construes the precise logical connection both between Jas 1:5–8 and 1:9–11, and between what precedes and follows them, it should be stressed that these sections address issues which are not only of fundamental concern to the letter as a whole, but closely related to one another: the proper way of acquiring things (namely, from God through prayer [1:5–8]), and the coming eschatological reversal of the rich and humble (1:9–11). For recent attempts to discern the precise progression of thought in these verses, see Hoppe, *Der Theologische Hintergrund des Jakobusbriefes*, 18–44; Klein, *Ein vollkommenes Werk*, 92–100; Johnson, *Letter of James*, 182–84, 189–91; cf. Tsuji, *Glaube*, 64–67.

[96] Klein, approaching Jas 1:2–4 as a traditional *gradatio* (cf. Rom 5:3–5 and 1 Pet 1:6–7), but finding no prior use of the phrase ἔργον τέλειον in ancient literature, considers the latter, at least, to have been coined by the author of James himself (*Ein vollkommenes Werk*, 54). Indeed, it is Klein's view that this expression represents a summation of the overarching interest of the author of James: "Das 'vollkommene Werk' ist die Forderung, in der die verschieden Mahnreden des Jakobusbriefes ihr Zentrum haben" (*ibid.*, 12). For a discussion of the past interpretation of the phrase, see *ibid.*, 54–56.

[97] Dibelius, *James*, 74; emphasis his; followed by Mußner, *Der Jakobusbrief*, 66f; P. J. Hartin, *James and the Q Sayings of Jesus* (JSNTSup 47; Sheffield: JSOT Press, 1991) 85.

[98] Klein, *Ein vollkommenes Werk*, 55. Dibelius, who of course emphasizes the traditional nature of this passage, reduces the significance of the imperative to the level of form, attributing the "obscurity of the expression" to "the intention of the author to let the concatenation end, not with a declarative statement, but rather with an admonition; for such is in accord with the paraenetic character of his

the "complete" endurance that those experiencing πειρασμός must achieve; thus: "let [endurance] have its full effect."⁹⁹ This reading is accurate as far as it goes, but it remains too general. It too, like the preceding one, overlooks the significance of the appearance of a command to "have an *ergon*" in the opening admonition of a work whose emphasis on the soteriological importance of *erga* has become infamous.

The reference to the "perfect *ergon*" that endurance is to "have" is in fact quite consistent with the treatment of the theme of *erga* elsewhere in the letter. An abstract noun is used as the subject of ἔχειν ἔργα again in 2:17, though there the subject is faith itself rather than the endurance produced by the *testing* of faith as in 1:2–4.¹⁰⁰ Though "faith" is the nominal subject, the issue, of course, is nonetheless the significance of a person "having faith" (πίστιν . . . ἔχειν) if (s)he does not also "have" (ἔχῃ) *erga*, as is clear from 2:14.¹⁰¹ James's view of the matter is well known: "faith, if it does not have *erga*, is dead" (2:17). Such a πίστις χωρὶς ἔργων, he puns, is ἀ-εργον, "useless" (2:21; cf. 2:26): it cannot effect "righteousness" (2:24),¹⁰² nor is it "able to save" (2:14, δύναται . . . σῶσαι). Indeed, it is clear from the challenge posed to the "foolish" interlocutor in 2:18 that the author understands *erga* to be the tangible manifestation of a living faith:¹⁰³ "show me your faith apart from *erga*, and I will show you, out of my *erga*, my faith."¹⁰⁴

---

writing" (*James*, 74). The similarities between Jas 1:2–4, Rom 5:3–5 and 1 Pet 1:6–7 are indeed noteworthy; such similarities, however, should serve to underline, not obscure, the peculiar use of the imperative in Jas 1:4.

⁹⁹ So Mayor, *Epistle of St. James*, 36; cf. Martin, *James*, 16: "Let endurance yield its complete work."

¹⁰⁰ On τὸ δοκίμιον in Jas 1:4 as "the instrument or means by which a man is tested (δοκιμάζεται) and proved (δόκιμος)," see Mayor, *Epistle of St. James*, 34–35; more recently Klein, *Ein vollkommenes Werk*, 47.

¹⁰¹ Klein, *Ein vollkommenes Werk*, 55.

¹⁰² Indeed, with further wordplay, the author writes that in the case of Abraham's offering of Isaac, faith "worked with" (συν-ήργει) ἔργα to accomplish righteousness (2:22). It might be noted, in light of the association of faith and *erga* with πειρασμός in 1:2–4, that Abraham's sacrifice of Isaac is commonly presented as one—and sometimes the last and greatest—of a series of "tests" endured by the patriarch; see *Jub.* 17:15–18:19, and the additional literature discussed by Dibelius, *James*, 168–70. Note also that Sir 44:20 and 1 Macc 2:52 both speak of Abraham's being found faithful ἐν πειρασμῷ. See further on this point Klein, *Ein vollkommenes Werk*, 73–74.

¹⁰³ Contrast Jas 2:17, 26: faith without works is "dead."

¹⁰⁴ Jas 2:18 is another well-known crux in the interpretation of James; for a convenient description of the problem and its various solutions, see S. McKnight, "James 2:18a: The Unidentifiable Interlocutor," *WTJ* 52 (1990) 355–64, esp. 355–59. To my mind, it is the solution proposed by H. Neitzel ("Eine alte crux interpretum im Jakobusbrief 2, 18," *ZNW* 73 [1982] 286–93) and advocated by Klein (*Ein voll-*

A challenge quite similar to that posed to the one who says (s)he has faith in 2:18 is offered to any who claim to possess wisdom in 3:13:[105] whoever is "wise and understanding"[106] is to "show (δειξάτω) from a good manner of living his or her *erga* with wisdom's humility (or: "wise humility"; cf. ἐν πραΰτητι σοφίας)." It emerges from this passage that the two "ways" which the author imagines in 5:19–20 can also be conceived as two opposing "wisdoms": one which is "earthly" (ἐπίγειος), "psychic" (ψυχική) and "demonic" (δαιμονιώδης) and one which is "from above" (ἄνωθεν), that is, from God (cf. 1:17). Here again, each of these "wisdoms" has its own characteristic set of actions, conceived as manifestations of one's inner state. The jealousy and social discord (ζῆλος καὶ ἐριθεία) which, along with instability (ἀκαταστασία) and "every foul deed" (πᾶν φαῦλον πρᾶγμα), are the hallmark features of "earthly" wisdom, arise from and are reflections of "your pleasures which fight among your members."[107] Thus one whose pursuit of pleasure reveals him or her to be a "friend of the world" and near to the Devil (4:4, 8) manifests, in a corresponding manner, at best a wisdom which is "earthly" and "demonic." The "wisdom from above," on the other hand, is the ethic that corresponds to the law laid down by God, and characterizes those who are friends of God.[108] Not surprisingly, it is associated particularly closely with "humility" (cf. 3:13: ἐν πραΰτητι σοφίας).[109] It is characterized as "peaceful" (3:17, εἰρηνική; cf. 3:18) rather than by discord, and by "good fruits" rather than "every foul

---

kommenes Werk, 70–72) and others (see *ibid.*, 72 n. 184) which is the most satisfying. On this interpretation, the rebuttal of the τις consists only in σὺ πίστιν ἔχεις, and is read interrogatively; thus: "But someone will say, 'do you have faith?' And I [will say], 'I have works. Show me your faith apart from works, and I will show my faith from my works'." It is generally agreed in any case that the "show me your faith" sentence is to be understood as a statement in the voice of the author himself; see McKnight, "James 2:18a," 360.

[105] It is evident from the reprimand not to "boast" and lie κατὰ τῆς ἀληθείας in 3:14 that the author has in mind one who would make oneself out to be σοφὸς καὶ ἐπιστήμων while not exhibiting proper ethical behavior, just as he deals with "someone" (τις) who claims (λέγει) to have faith but does not have ἔργα in 2:14–26.

[106] For the use of the phrase σοφὸς καὶ ἐπιστήμων, cf. esp. Deut 1:13, 15, where it applies to the leaders of Israel's tribes (cf. Jas 1:1!).

[107] Jas 4:1; cf. esp. 4:2, ζηλοῦτε, with 3:14 and 3:16, ζῆλος. See further on ἀκαταστασία below, pp. 229ff. Note also in this connection the author's assumption of a sort of "unity of vices" in 3:16: where there is ζῆλος καὶ ἐριθεία, there is ἀκαταστασία and πᾶν φαῦλον πρᾶγμα; cf. with this the legal principle stated in Jas 2:10, on which see O'Rourke Boyle, "The Stoic Paradox of James 2:10."

[108] Klein, *Ein vollkommenes Werk*, 154–61; cf. Johnson, *Letter of James*, 287.

[109] Cf. esp. 1:21: ἐν πραΰτητι δέξασθε τὸν ἔμφυτον λόγον. Note further the general emphasis on humility elsewhere in the letter: 1:9–11; 4:6, 9–10; 5:1.

deed" (3:16–17). In short, it manifests itself in *erga* (3:13)—a term
which, interestingly, is consistently used by the author with a positive sense of "good works" rather than its usual neutral sense of
"works."[110] Thus the challenge of 3:13: one's inner state necessarily
manifests itself externally; it is simply not possible to have wisdom—
that is, the "wisdom from above"—without also having *erga*.

In both 2:14–26 (esp. 2:18) and 3:13, then, *erga* emerge as the
necessary external manifestations of an inner disposition thought of
variously as "the wisdom from above," or a living, which is to say
soteriologically efficacious, faith. The thought is quite similar in
1:2–4.[111] Here the author is concerned specifically with πειρασμός,
which is understood to be "the testing of faith" (1:3, τὸ δοκίμιον . . .
τῆς πίστεως). Such a test of one's faith, he suggests, is to be viewed
positively, for it represents the opportunity to achieve the "endurance"
(ὑπομονήν) which, it is subsequently pointed out, will lead ultimately
to "blessedness" and "the crown of life" (1:3; 1:12).[112] Like faith itself,
however, the endurance that can result from the "testing of faith"
in a situation of πειρασμός must also "have a perfect *ergon*"; it must
manifest itself, that is, in a good work.[113] The "perfect work" that
results from the endurance of πειρασμός contrasts with the "sin"

---

[110] See 1:4, 25; 2:14–26; 3:13. Thus my hesitance to render this term simply as
"works" or "deeds." Cf. the use of πρᾶγμα as the corresponding negative generic
term in 3:16, and ἁμαρτία in, e.g., 1:15. James's consistently positive use of the term
ἔργα is likely to be correlated with his interest in refuting a position that ἡ πίστις
χωρὶς τῶν ἔργων can "save" (Jas 2:14–26).

[111] Cf. Johnson, *Letter of James*, 178; also Ropes, *St. James*, 137. Klein considers
2:14–16 "als Verteidigung des Themas von 1,2–4 gegen eine andere Auffassung
des Verhältnisses von Glauben und Werken" (*Ein vollkommenes Werk*, 69). He too,
therefore, interprets the τέλειον ἔργον with reference to "das konkrete Tun," but
presses for an interpretation of the singular ἔργον in the collective sense of "das
'Lebenswerk' eines Menschen," i.e., that which one will ultimately have to show
for oneself at the eschatological judgment (*Ein vollkommenes Werk*, 55–56). Though
Klein can cite analogies from other early Christian works, such a usage of ἔργον
would be peculiar in James (cf. esp. the use of the singular in 1:25). More importantly, this interpretation seems to me to underestimate the extent of the contrast
between failing in a given instance of πειρασμός and thus effecting "sin" (1:14–15)
and enduring in such a circumstance and having an ἔργον (1:2–4).

[112] Cf. further 5:11: "We consider as blessed (μακαρίζομεν) those who endure
(τοὺς ὑπομείναντας)," citing as examples "the prophets who spoke in the name of
the Lord" and Job. On the sense in which the prophets can be considered models of endurance, cf. Matt 5:12 par. Luke 6:23; Matt 23:29–36 par. Luke 11:47–51;
Matt 23:37 par. Luke 13:34.

[113] Note that in the immediately following 1:5ff, the problem addressed is one in
which someone lacks wisdom—which wisdom, as we have seen, manifests itself in
erga (3:13), just as does a soteriologically efficacious faith.

(ἁμαρτία) produced when one succumbs to πειρασμός (1:15), just as the "death" to which such a failure leads contrasts with the "crown of life" received by the one who endures (1:15; cf. 1:12).[114] The description of such an *ergon* as "perfect" (τέλειον), besides serving this contrastive purpose, anticipates the consistently positive use of the term ἔργα throughout the remainder of the letter.

In sum, an action which results from the pursuit of one's own desire—like that which results from transgressing the "law of freedom" (2:9)—is described as "sin" (1:13, ἁμαρτία), just as those who pursue pleasure and travel the way of death are "sinners" (ἁμαρτωλοί, -ov, 4:8; 5:20). The one who does *erga*, in contrast, is one whose constant attention to "the perfect law of freedom" renders him or her not a "forgetful hearer" of the *logos* that "saves souls," but a "hearer" who is also a "doer." As we have seen, while this *logos* is "able to save (δυνάμενον σῶσαι) your souls," it is only through "doing" that one becomes so "blessed" (1:25; cf. 1:12). Thus too, faith is not "able to save" (δύναται . . . σῶσαι) apart from *erga* (2:14): faith itself, like the "endurance" which its "testing" is to produce, must "have *erga*" if it is to be soteriologically effectual. For the author of James, in short, human actions—whether "good fruits" (3:17) or "foul deeds" (3:16)—are concrete and necessary manifestations of one's inner disposition. *Erga* are inseparably linked to *logos* and the "wisdom from above," just as the jealousy, strife and, more generally, "sin" which arise from desire inevitably signal the presence of that wisdom which is "earthly" and "demonic" (3:13–18).

ENDURING TEMPTATION

A contrast emerges in Jas 1:2–4, 12 and 1:14–15 between the significance of enduring πειρασμός and that of the failure to so endure.[115] Endurance of any given instance of the diverse πειρασμοί humans face will manifest itself in a "perfect work" and will ultimately be rewarded by "the crown of life," while the failure to withstand πειρασμός results in "sin," and places one on the path toward "death." This contrast renders questionable the view, popular

---

[114] Cf. Klein, *Ein vollkommenes Werk*, 85.

[115] Cf. Klein, *Ein vollkommenes Werk*, 45: "V. 13–18 nimmt dann nicht auf V. 12 allein Bezug, sondern ebenso auf V. 2–4, wofür auch die ähnliche Gestaltung spricht (Kettenreihen in V. 3f und V. 14f)."

particularly in the wake of Dibelius's enormously influential commentary, that the term πειρασμός is used in 1:2–4, 12 and 1:14–15 with entirely different referents. Dibelius argued that "the temtpations whose origins are discussed in 1:13–15 are not the 'trials' in 1:2 over which one is supposed to rejoice; while these must be dangers from without, 1:13–15 deals with dangers of the inner life"; indeed, "the seduction by the lusts in vv 13–15 has nothing whatsoever to do with the afflictions in v 12 [and 1:2–4]."[116] This position owes more to Dibelius's general literary evaluation of the letter as a "treasury" of unrelated traditions of diverse origins, linked at most by catchword connection, than it does to any consistent distinction drawn between "dangers from without" and "dangers of the inner life" in the ancient literature. The author of *4 Maccabees*, for example, considered the quite external torture suffered by the Jewish martyrs at the hands of Antiochus to be the ultimate proof of reason's dominance over the passions.[117] The πειρασμοί of Jas 1:2–4 are in any case said to be "diverse" (ποικίλοι), and thus include a range of experiences. Jas 1:13–15 speaks not to a different set of (also diverse?) πειρασμοί, but seeks rather to locate the ultimate cause of all the various forms of πειρασμός in human desire. Indeed, for the author of James it is the desire for some perceived external desideratum that opens the door to the pleasures which war within the individual: the power of desire lies precisely in its ability to deceive one that some "good gift" can be obtained through its pursuit.[118] In fact, the promise in 1:4 that those who endure πειρασμοί will be "perfect and whole, lacking in nothing" (τέλειοι καὶ ὁλόκληροι ἐν μηδενὶ λειπόμενοι), far from being a redundant and platitudinous string of synonyms,[119] enumerates the specific results of enduring the temptation of desire as presented throughout the letter.

---

[116] Dibelius, *James*, 71, 90; Jas 1:12, on the other hand, "obviously belongs to the theme touched upon in 1:2–4" (*ibid.*, 88). Dibelius is criticized by Klein, *Ein vollkommenes Werk*, 46–47 and 82–85.

[117] On *4 Maccabees*, see Chapter Three. Cf. further p. 150 n. 66.

[118] See on this above, pp. 200–207. By way of illustration of this connection between "external" circumstances and "internal" struggles, one might imagine a situation in which a wealthy landowner withholds the wages owed to a laborer (cf. Jas 5:4). The resulting economic strain on the laborer might lead to a "test of faith" vis-à-vis God's providence, and to questions regarding the wisdom of relying solely upon prayer for acquiring needed things. Note in this connection, in fact, the author's characteristic concern for economic issues.

[119] So, in effect, Dibelius, *James*, 74.

ὁλόκληρος

According to Dibelius, while the term ὁλόκληρος "properly designates the external intactness of the physical body, or some other similar concrete notion," the author of James "quite obviously" uses it with a more abstract sense of "blameless."[120] Its more usual connotation of "wholeness,"[121] however, is in fact quite appropriate in the context of James. As we have seen, those who give in to desire become subject to an inner division which the author characterizes as "your passions warring within your members" (4:1). Particularly significant in this connection is his description of such people as δίψυχοι who must "cleanse their hearts" (4:8)—presumably of the pleasures whose wars inevitably spill over into inter-human relationships.[122] James's characteristic use of the term δίψυχος, "double-souled," to describe those whose faith in God's providence wavers (1:6–8), or who indulge their warring pleasures (4:8),[123] is in fact quite vivid and concrete given his assumption of a fundamental opposition between the implanted *logos* and human desire within the individual.[124]

---

[120] *Ibid.*

[121] See W. Foerster, κλῆρος, κτλ., *TDNT* 3.766–67.

[122] Cf. with the demand that δίψυχοι "purify" (ἀγνίσατε) their hearts (4:8) also the description of the "wisdom from above" as "above all ἀγνή" (3:17). Note in addition the typical contrast between διψυχία on one hand and purity and wholeness in other early Christian literature; see O. J. F. Seitz, "Antecedents and Signification of the Term ΔΙΨΥΧΟΣ," *JBL* 66 (1947) 211–19.

[123] These characteristics of the δίψυχος are two sides of a coin: it is a lack of faith in God's providence which opens the door to the temptation of seeking the satisfaction of one's own desires.

[124] The origins of the concept of the δίψυχος—which term is not found prior to James, the *Shepherd of Hermas, 1 & 2 Clement* and the *Epistle of Barnabas*—are often sought in Jewish thought, esp. in the concept of the good and evil "inclinations"; see esp. Seitz's series of articles on the term: "Relationship of the Shepherd of Hermas to the Epistle of James," *JBL* 63 (1944) 131–40; "Antecedents and Signification of the Term ΔΙΨΥΧΟΣ"; and "Afterthoughts on the Term 'Dipsychos'," *NTS* 4 (1957–58) 327–34; also W. I. Wolverton, "The Double-Minded Man in the Light of Essene Psychology," *ATR* 38 (1956) 166–75; cf. Tsuji, *Glaube*, 102f. See against this view and in favor of Greek philosophical influence, however, Ropes, *Epistle of St. James*, 156; more recently Klein, *Ein vollkommenes Werk*, 90–91, who, moreover, raises the possiblity that the rabbinic concept itself was influenced by Greek thought. Whatever the case, one can say at the very least that the concept takes on a distinctly "philosophical" coloring in James, where ἐπιθυμία functions primarily in opposition to ὁ ἔμφυτος λόγος. Cf. in this respect the *Testaments of the Twelve Patriarchs*: a contrast between ἁπλότης and being διπρόσωπος which recalls James figures prominently in this work, the "two spirits" ethic of which is informed by Stoic ethics. See further H. C. Kee, "The Ethical Dimensions of the Testaments of the XII as a Clue to their Provenance," *NTS* 24 (1978) 259–70; and for a broad yet concise

τέλειος

The sense in which one who endures πειρασμός will be "perfect" (τέλειος), on the other hand, is best understood in light of 3:2, where the "perfect man" (τέλειος ἀνήρ) is described as one who is "able to bridle his whole body."[125] Given James's characteristic emphasis on *erga*, this identification of the τέλειος specifically as one who does not fail with respect to speech—who does not "stumble," that is, ἐν λόγῳ (3:2)—is quite remarkable.[126] In 1:4 the promise of perfection depends on an endurance of πειρασμός which manifests itself in a "perfect *ergon*." Moreover, both this definition of the "perfect man" in 3:2 and James's general discussion of the tongue are found precisely between two passages which insist on the critical importance of *erga*: 2:14–26 and 3:13. How, then, can he say that "perfection" results from controlling one's speech?

Behind James's identification of the τέλειος as one who is perfect in speech lies an important presupposition regarding the tongue's relation to the rest of the body. The tongue, it is said, is "set up" (καθίσταται) among our members (Jas 3:6).[127] The use of καθίστημι in this context has at times been considered a curiosity, for it is a verb which often connotes the conferring of authority.[128] Seen within the wider context of James 3, though, the choice of this term is entirely appropriate. In 3:4, this "small member" (cf. 3:5, μικρὸν μέλος) among our other "members" (cf. 3:6, ἐν τοῖς μέλεσιν ἡμῶν) is

---

comparison of the two works, Johnson, *The Letter of James*, 43–46; *idem*, "James 3:13–4:10 and the *Topos* ΠΕΡΙ ΦΘΟΝΟΥ," 341–47.

[125] The theme of perfection in James is discussed at length by P. J. du Plessis, *ΤΕΛΕΙΟΣ: The Idea of Perfection in the New Testament* (Kampen: Kok, 1959) 233–40; P. J. Hartin, "Call to Be Perfect through Suffering (James 1,2–4). The Concept of Perfection in the Epistle of James and the Sermon on the Mount," *Bib* 77 (1996) 477–92; and most recently by Klein, *Ein vollkommenes Werk*, 54–81. Note that Klein interprets Jas 3:2 in light of 1:4 (esp. ἐν μηδενὶ λειπόμενοι) rather than, as here, 1:4 in light of 3:2; see *ibid.*, 79.

[126] Equally remarkable is the fact that the apparent oddity of this identification in the context of James generally goes entirely without notice in the commentaries. A welcome exception in this respect is Johnson, *The Letter of James*, 256: "The use of *teleios* ('perfect') is somewhat startling . . . Can James seriously think that 'perfection in speech' can make a person perfect?"

[127] On the notoriously difficult Jas 3:6, see the discussion of Dibelius, *James*, 193–98. Whatever its relation to ὁ κόσμος τῆς ἀδικίας, however, it is clear that ἡ γλῶσσα is the subject of καθίστημι.

[128] See the entry on καθίστημι in BAGD: doubt is expressed there regarding the correctness of the text of James at this point, despite the fact that the manuscripts are quite consistent in this respect.

likened to the rudder of a ship.[129] Control of one's speech, therefore, is critical for controlling "the whole body." The tongue can
taint "the whole body" (3:6, ἡ σπιλοῦσα ὅλον τὸ σῶμα); thus, just as
one places bridles into horses' mouths in order to lead their "whole
body" (3:3, ὅλον τὸ σῶμα), so too, one who does not "stumble" ἐν
λόγῳ is "able to bridle [his or her] whole body" (3:2, ὅλον τὸ σῶμα).[130]

The close connection assumed by the author between control of
speech and control of the whole body is remarkable. Baker's recent
and quite extensive monograph on "personal speech ethics" in James
fails to locate any good precedents for the notion, and thus sheds
little new light on this aspect of James 3.[131] The connection, however, is quite well understood in light of the close relationship between
human reason (λόγος) and speech posited by the Stoics[132]—who of
course considered the perfect self control envisioned here by the
author of James to be enjoyed only by those who lived in accord
with "right reason." Particularly noteworthy in this connection is the
image of the helmsman in Jas 3:4. The tongue is likened to a ship's
rudder, which is said to guide the ship in accord with the ὁρμή of
the one steering it (τοῦ εὐθύνοντος).[133] While rare in the earliest

---

[129] As has often been observed, the figures of ships and rudders (3:4) and horses
and bridle (3:3) are commonplace among the hellenistic moralists, and often used
precisely in connection with speech; see esp. the discussion and references in Dibelius,
James, 186–90, and further D. F. Watson, "The Rhetoric of James 3:1–12 and a
Classical Pattern of Argumentation," *NovT* 35 (1993) 58.

[130] Jas 3:2–3; cf. further 1:26, where the author speaks of "bridling the tongue."
Klein considers the term χαλιναγωγεῖν, which is found only in these passages of
James in the NT, to be of Stoic origin; see *Ein vollkommenes Werk*, 78 and n. 224.

[131] W. R. Baker, *Personal Speech-Ethics in the Epistle of James* (WUNT 2/68; Tübingen:
Mohr [Siebeck], 1995) esp. 123–38. J. L. P. Wolmarans points in the direction of
Stoicism in his "The Tongue Guiding the Body: The Anthropological Presuppositions
of James 3:1–12," *Neotestamentica* 26 (1992) 523–30. However, he thinks primarily of
a view of "'the word' as the steering mechanism of an audience," as expressed in
Plutarch, *Quomodo adolescens poetas* 33. Noting that "[t]his passage views 'the word'
as the steering mechanism of an audience, and not the tongue as the steering mechanism of the body, as James has it," Wolmarans concludes that "James either misunderstood Stoic teaching in this regard, or, more probably, understood it creatively"
(*ibid.*, 528). L. T. Johnson notes that "the best parallel to James' assertion concerning
the 'perfection' of someone who controls speech" is found in Philo, *Post. C.* 88 and
Migr. Abr. 73, but does not elucidate this comparison; see "Taciturnity and True
Religion: James 1:26–27," *Greeks, Romans, and Christians: Essays in Honor of Abraham
J. Malherbe* (ed. D. L. Balch *et al.*; Minneapolis: Fortress, 1990) 329–39, esp. 330
n. 9; and cf. *idem*, *Letter of James*, 256. For discussion of these passages, see below.

[132] This aspect of Stoic thought deserves fuller attention than can be given to it
here. At present, I simply sketch the direction in which a more systematic investigation might proceed.

[133] Note Philo's frequent use of the term εὐθύνω in this connection, e.g., in *Abr.*

Christian literature, the term ὁρμή is "common in classical Greek writers,"[134] and played a crucial role in the Stoic theory of action. For the Stoics, ὁρμή denotes the "impulse" with which all action ultimately originates, and which, in rational animals, takes the form of verbal (though of course not spoken) commands issued by one's *logos*.[135] If one's *logos* is not "right" (ὀρθός), the commands it issues will not conform to those of the divine law, and one's resulting actions, therefore, will not be characterized by virtue.[136]

The relation of uttered speech to the internal speech of the *logos* was considered to be of the most intimate order. Philo speaks on numerous occasions of the "two-fold" nature of *logos* in this connection, drawing on the Stoic distinction between ἐνδιάθετος and προφορικὸς λόγος.[137] The former is located in the commanding faculty (τὸ ἡγεμονικόν) and the latter in "the tongue and mouth and the rest of the vocal organism" (γλῶττα καὶ στόμα καὶ ἡ ἄλλη πᾶσα φωνῆς ὀργανοποιία).[138] The relationship between the two is conceived, in a manner reminiscent of Jas 3:11, as one of "spring" (πηγή) and "outflow."[139] The two divisions of speech are such, however, that one can have strengths with respect to one of them, but not in the other: "the so-called sophists," for example, "have shown great ability in expounding themes, and yet been most evil thinkers," while others "reason excellently, but find speech a bad interpreter of thought."[140] Perfection (ἡ τελειότης), according to Philo, depends "on both divisions of *logos*, the reason which suggests the ideas with clearness (καθαρῶς), and the speech which gives unfailing (ἀπταίστως)

70; *Leg. All.* 3.224; also *Conf. Ling.* 115, where the image of the helmsman, moreover, is used in combination with that of charioteer. See the additional passages cited in G. Mayer, *Index Philoneus* (Berlin and New York: de Gruyter, 1974) *s.v.* It is perhaps noteworthy that this term is found elsewhere in the NT only in John 1:23, and here in a "quotation" of Isa 40:3 (though cf. LXX Isa 40:3).

[134] Ropes, *St. James*, 230, who also notes that the term does not appear in James's sense in the LXX.

[135] On the Stoic understanding of ὁρμή, see B. Inwood, *Ethics and Human Action in Early Stoicism*, and above, pp. 37f.

[136] Note that a—indeed, perhaps *the*—key issue is the recognition of what is "good" in the true Stoic sense of the term; see Chapter Two, and cf. in this light the discussion of 1:16–17 above.

[137] See esp. *Mos.* 2.127–130 and *Migr. Abr.* 70–73.

[138] *Mos.* 2.127; cf. *Migr. Abr.* 71, where διανοία rather than τὸ ἡγεμονικόν is given as the realm of ἐνδιάθετος λόγος.

[139] *Migr. Abr.* 71; *Mos.* 127; see also *Somn.* 2.281, and also the description of speech as the "interpreter" of thought in *Migr. Abr.* 72, with which cf. Cicero, *De Leg.* 30.

[140] *Migr. Abr.* 72; an analogous critique of the sophists is found at *Post. C.* 86.

expression to them."[141] That is to say, it is the one who manages to bring "speech (λόγον) into harmony with intent (διανοίᾳ), and intent with deed (ἔργῳ)" who is to be considered τέλειος.[142]

So intimately related are these two aspects of *logos* that Philo elsewhere identifies control of speech as the key for putting "the whole soul" (τὴν ὅλην ψυχήν) at rest. Interpreting Exod 28:30, Philo asserts that "the Sacred Word knowing how strong is the impulse (ὁρμή) of either passion, of both high spirit (θυμοῦ) and lust (ἐπιθυμίας), puts a curb on each of them, by setting over them reason (τὸν λόγον) as a charioteer and pilot" (*Leg. All.* 3.118). He thus interprets the "oracle" (τὸ λόγιον) referred to in LXX Exod 28:30 as "the organ of speech, which is the uttered word," pointing out that the description of it as "the oracle of judgment" shows that Moses thinks particularly of the spoken word which is "well tested and examined" rather than one simply "spoken at random."[143] Having identified the Urim and the Thummim as the two virtues of this word, namely clearness and truthfulness,[144] he goes on to discuss the importance of controlling one's speech:

> It says, then, that the tested word, having the virtues which are peculiarly its own, was enthroned upon the breast (Aaron's namely), that is, upon the spirited element (τοῦ θύμου), that it might first of all be guided by reason (λόγῳ), and not injured by its own irrationality; in the next place by clearness, for it is not the nature of anger to be a friend of clearness. Do we not see in those who are enraged how not their understanding (ἡ διανοία) only but their words (τὰ ῥήματα)[145] also are full of disturbance and confusion? ... It must be guided in the third place by truthfulness, for together with its other faults anger has this one also as peculiarly its own, that of lying. As a matter of experience, of those who give way to this passion, hardly one speaks the truth.... *These are the antidotes for the region of anger* (τοῦ θυμικοῦ μέρους): *reason* (λόγος), *clearness of speech* (σαφήνεια λόγου), *truth of speech* (ἀλήθεια αὐτοῦ). For the three are virtually one, since reason, accompanied by the two virtues of truthfulness and distinctness, acts as a healer of anger, that sore sickness of the soul ... If high spirit (ὁ θυμός) be trained in this manner ... it will not only rid itself of much ferment, but will *render the whole soul* (τὴν ὅλην ψυχήν) *gentle.*[146]

---

[141] *Migr. Abr.* 73.

[142] *Poster. C.* 88; on the use of διανοία in this connection, see above note 138.

[143] *Leg. All.* 3.119.

[144] *Leg. All.* 3.120.

[145] For this distinction cf. esp. *Migr. Abr.* 71; cf. further *Leg. All.* 3.120ff.

[146] *Leg. All.* 3.123–24, 28.

Though Philo stops short of explicitly equating control of the tongue with control of "the whole body" (ὅλον τὸ σῶμα), his view that truthfulness and clarity of speech is the starting point in rendering gentle "the whole soul" (τὴν ὅλην ψυχήν) presents a much closer approximation of the thought of James than any of the other comparative materials which have previously been adduced in this respect. For Philo, this view is based on the Stoic distinction between ἐνδιάθετος and προφορικὸς λόγος, the latter of which is located in the tongue and the other organs of speech.

If the author of James's view that one whose speech is perfect is himself or herself τέλειος seems, on the face of it, rather starkly at odds with both the emphasis on *erga* that characterizes the letter in general[147] and the promise of perfection to the one whose endurance of πειρασμός manifests itself in a "perfect *ergon*" in 1:4 in particular, his emphasis on speech here and elsewhere in the letter is readily understandable in light of the intimate relationship between speech and the human *logos* posited by the Stoics. It is especially noteworthy in this connection that while "the tongue" recurs as the main subject of Jas 3:2–12, the τέλειος who is able to control "the whole body" is identified not as one who is flawless with respect to ἡ γλῶσσα, but specifically as one who doesn't "stumble" ἐν λόγῳ.[148] This is in fact the only occurrence of *logos* in James apart from 1:18 and the subsequent treatment of the implanted *logos* in 1:21 and 1:22–25. It will be recalled, moreover, that these latter two references each elaborate an element of the three-part admonition of 1:19, the remaining element of which, "slow to speak," is elaborated by a charge that the apparent religiosity of one who does not "bridle the tongue" (μὴ χαλιναγωγῶν γλῶσσαν) is "useless" (1:26). If, then, James's interest in the tongue is understood in light of the close association between human reason and speech posited by the Stoics, each of the elements of the elaboration of 1:19–27—which is itself, as we have seen, presented as an ethical inference drawn from 1:13–18 (cf. 1:18, λόγος ἀληθείας)—would thus center on the implanted *logos*.[149]

---

[147] Note esp. the fact that immediately following this exposition of the tongue, the true σόφος (cf. 3:1, διδάσκαλος) is identified as one who has *erga*.

[148] Cf. the use of πταίω to connote a transgression of the law of freedom in the statement of the general legal principle in 2:10.

[149] Note in this connection the view, espoused in different forms by E. Pfeiffer ("Der Zusammenhang des Jakobusbriefes," *TSK* 23 [1850] 163–80) and H. J. Cladder ("Die Anlage des Jakobusbriefes," *ZKT* 28 [1904] 37–57), that the three-part admo-

This would seem to provide a rather striking confirmation of this interpretation.[150]

In any event, the author considers control of the tongue to be crucial, if extraordinarily difficult.[151] The tongue itself is called an "unstable evil" (ἀκατάστατον κακόν), and said to be "full of deadly poison" (3:8). Likened to a flame which is itself lit from the very fires of "Gehenna,"[152] the tongue represents a primary conduit into the human being of the very "defilement" whose avoidance stands at the heart of "true religion" (1:26–27). It is that which "stains" (σπιλοῦσα) "the whole body" (3:6; cf. 1:27: ἄσπιλον);[153] thus control of speech is critical for bridling "the whole body" (3:2–3). Such a complete self-mastery as is enjoyed by the τέλειος who "tames" the unstable (cf. 3:8, ἀκατάστατον) tongue contrasts sharply with the ἀκαταστασία which, found wherever one finds the jealousy and social strife which the pleasures inspire, is among the hallmark features of that wisdom which is "earthly" and "demonic."[154] Such "instability," we have seen, is precisely that which characterizes the δίψυχος who, wavering in his or her faith in God's providence, is "unstable

nition of Jas 1:19 provides an organizing principle for the Letter of James as a whole. This suggestion deserves closer consideration than is normally given to it.

[150] Incidentally, one might note in this connection, in addition to the several features of Jas 3:1–12 pointed out in the preceding discussion as being especially typical of the hellenistic moralists, the very Greek distinction made in Jas 3:7–8 between "human nature" and the "natures" of various other animals. For Stoics (but, of course, among the Greeks not only the Stoics), this distinction was made on the basis of the human possession of *logos*, which, among other things, made speech possible.

[151] As is often noted, there is a certain tension between the author's notion that the religion of anyone who can't control his or her tongue is "useless" and his pessimistic view that "no one is able to tame the tongue" (Jas 3:8). Is the religion of *everyone*, therefore, "useless"? At least one of these statements (if not both) must be considered hyperbolic, and it seems to me doubtful that 3:7–8 was intended as a statement of the theoretical impossibility of controlling the tongue. Note in this connection 3:10–11, esp. 3:10b: οὐ χρή, ἀδελφοί μου, ταῦτα οὕτως γίνεσθαι; cf. Klein, *Ein vollkommenes Werk*, 79.

[152] For Johnson (*Letter of James*, 265) this reference to Gehenna conjures up the specter of the Devil; this connection is rejected by Klein, who prefers to describe the tongue, in James, as "Instrument der bösen ἐπιθυμία"; see *Ein vollkommenes Werk*, 103–106. Regardless of the relation of Gehenna to the Devil, it is clear from 4:7 that this latter figure has some connection with desire.

[153] Note also the association—however, precisely, it is to be interpreted—of the tongue with ὁ κόσμος τῆς ἀδικίας in 3:6; cf. the consistently bleak assessment of ὁ κόσμος in Jas 1:27 (associated with impurity) and 4:6 (associated with desire, enmity with God, and the devil).

[154] Jas 3:16: ὅπου γὰρ ζῆλος καὶ ἐριθεία, ἐκεῖ ἀκαταστασία; cf. 4:1–3. The contrast between τέλειος and ἀκατάστατος in James is also noted by Klein, *Ein vollkommenes Werk*, 106.

(ἀκατάστατος) in all his or her ways," and is thus comparable to a "wave of the sea being blown and tossed by the wind" (1:6–8).[155]

ἐν μηδενὶ λειπόμενοι

In contrast to the "unstable" δίψυχος who should not expect to "receive anything from the Lord" (1:7), finally, those who endure πειρασμός will be "lacking in nothing" (1:4, ἐν μηδενὶ λειπόμενοι). Once again, this statement can also be applied to the Stoic sage. The phrase is particularly reminiscent of Aristotle's discussion of the highest good, which he identifies as "happiness" (εὐδαιμονία) inasmuch as it is "final" or "perfect" (τέλεια) above all else, since "we always choose it for its own sake and never as a means to something else."[156] The "perfect" or "final" good (τὸ τέλειον ἀγαθόν), he says, "must be a thing sufficient in itself" (αὔταρκες); and being self-sufficient, means, essentially, to "be lacking nothing."[157] The Stoics, who similarly identified "being happy" as "the end (τέλος), for the sake of which everything is done, but which is not itself done for the sake of any-thing," correlated this state with virtue.[158] Thus the logic of Cicero:[159]

> ... if everything is happy which has nothing wanting (si omne beatum est, cui nihil deest) ... and if this is the peculiar mark of virtue, assuredly all virtuous men are happy ... But to me, virtuous men are supremely happy: for what is wanting (quid enim deest) to make life happy for the man who feels assured of the good that is his?

---

[155] Cf. Philo Gigant. 48–51, where it is said that one who is subjected to "the fierce mysterious storm of the soul," itself "driven" (ἀναρριπίζεται) "by life and its cares," is like one who is "in a storm or on a wave of the seething sea" (τις ἐν χειμῶνι εὐδίαν ἢ ἐν κλύδωνι κυμαινούσης θαλάττης); such a one is contrasted with Moses, whose stability (στάσις) was "stayed on the firm foundation of right rea-son." Cf. further the use of a similar image in Migr. Abr. 148, where the figure of Lot is interpreted as a type of the person whose mind has a tendency to incline variously toward what is good and what is bad: "Often both tendencies are observ-able in one and the same person: for some men are irresolute, facers both ways, inclining to either side like a boat tossed by winds from opposite quarters ... with such there is nothing praiseworthy even in their taking a turn to the better course; for it is the result not of judgment, but of drift."

[156] See N.E. 1.7.1–8, esp. 4–5. I am indebted to an anonymous reviewer of this manuscript for the Supplements series to Novum Testamentum for this reference.

[157] See N.E. 1.7.6–7, with the note b in the LCL.

[158] See Long and Sedley, The Hellenistic Philosophers, §63A (= Stobaeus 2.77.16–27).

[159] TD 5.40; note that Cicero, who expressly notes his agreement with, among others, Aristotle on this point, identifies honestum as the sole good in this context, in good Stoic fashion (5.44). Cf. Long and Sedley's comment on this passage: "the Stoics claim that a virtuous man does possess all that he needs to fulfill himself, to live well, to have his desires satisfied" (The Hellenistic Philosophers, 399).

Thus, too, Epictetus's explanation of the "freedom" (ἐλεύθερον) of Diogenes: besides the fact that he did not consider his body as his own, and that "the law, and nothing else, [was] everything to [him]," Diogenes, he said, was in need of nothing.[160]

The phrase in any case takes on a further dimension in James, which couples a general emphasis on the efficacy of prayer to the gift-giving God with a characteristic economic concern. The latter, in particular, suggests that this absence of want might not refer simply to "moral and spiritual realities"[161]—though these are no doubt most critical, as is clear from the subsequent instruction that those who "lack" (λείπεται) wisdom should request it of God.[162] In any event, given, especially, the author's insistence that all πειρασμοί originate with desire, the promise in 1:4 that those who endure πειρασμός will "lack nothing" stands in stark contrast to 4:2–6:

> ἐπιθυμεῖτε καὶ οὐκ ἔχετε . . . ζηλοῦτε καὶ οὐ δύνασθε ἐπιτυχεῖν . . . αἰτεῖτε καὶ οὐ λαμβάνετε διότι κακῶς αἰτεῖσθε, ἵνα ἐν ταῖς ἡδοναῖς ὑμῶν δαπανήσατε . . . ὁ θεὸς ὑπερηφάνοις ἀντιτάσσεται, ταπεινοῖς δὲ δίδωσιν χάριν.

Those who succumb to desire and pursue pleasure, as we have seen, are deceived regarding the source of good things. The only things achieved through succumbing to desire are sin and death; all good things come from "the God who gives to all without reserve and without reproach," but who nonetheless "resists" those who arrogantly seek fulfillment of their own desires. It is thus the one who withstands the temptation of desire who will be "lacking in nothing."

πειρασμός in James

The author of James is aware that πειρασμοί come in diverse (ποικίλοι) forms. All, however, are ultimately rooted in desire, which seduces

---

[160] Cf. Epict., *Diss.* 4.1.158, on the lips of Diogenes himself: οὐδενὸς δέομαι.

[161] Cf. Johnson, *The Letter of James*, 179: "the 'lacking' here has nothing to do with material realities (as . . . later in James 2:15) but rather moral or spiritual realities; 'lacking' means 'falling short'." Cf. Dibelius, *James*, 74 n. 26, who cites in comparison the Stoic notion of the unity of virtue.

[162] One should not overlook in this connection the similar confidence in God's providence expressed in Luke 11:9–13 (par. Matt 7:7–11) which rather clearly includes material "gifts" (cf. Luke 11:3!), though certainly not exclusively so. Cf. further in this respect Matt 6:25–34 (par. Luke 12:22–32): the "soul" is clearly primary (Matt 6:25; Luke 12:23), but gifts pertaining to bodily needs are nonetheless promised as well.

individuals into seeking to fulfill their own desires rather than simply trusting in the providence of God. πειρασμοί in general, therefore, represent "tests of faith" (1:3)—faith, above all, that God will
provide for "those who love him" (cf. 1:12; 2:5).

The immediate result of an experience of πειρασμός will be one
of two types of action: sin, if one succumbs to desire, or an *ergon*
if one successfully endures. The one who withstands such "tests,"
moreover, will be "whole," while the one who gives in to desire is
characterized as "double-souled."[163] The former will be perfect inasmuch as (s)he will be in full control of his or her "whole body,"
while the double-souled one, like a wave blown by the wind, is
"unstable in all his or her ways." And while the latter, even if (s)he
petitions "the God who gives to all without reserve and without
reproach," should not expect to receive anything (1:6–8), the former
will lack nothing. That which the one who endures πειρασμός will
ultimately "receive" (λήμψεται), in fact, is "the crown of life" (1:12),
while the one who does not so endure will find his or her end in
"death" (1:13–15).

As we have seen, James emphasizes that God, though creator of
the universe and of humanity in particular, is not responsible for
these "trials"; their root cause is rather human desire itself.[164] The
power of desire lies above all in its deceptive seduction: one is led
to believe that some good thing can be obtained by yielding to it,
though the true result will only be sin and death. God alone is the
source of good things, and he, in fact, actively "resists" those who
arrogantly pursue their own desires rather than humbly depending
upon him. In fact, far from tempting people to follow desire and
wander, deceived, down the path of sin and death, God's will is
expressed through the fact that he "gave birth to us" by means of
the *logos* of truth: the implanted *logos* that stands opposed to desire
as the way which can "save souls" from death. The question that
remains is who, precisely, this "us" is imagined to be.

---

[163] So even the one who asks God, if (s)he does not ask ἐν πίστει (1:6–8).

[164] As noted above, the question of the origin of desire, however, is not raised
by the author.

Birth by *Logos*

It is obvious by all accounts that James uses creation language in 1:18. What is disputed is whether he refers to the original creation of humanity in general, or to a new creation, experienced only by members of his own religious movement.[165] Less often realized is the fact that the term "implanted *logos*" itself has creation connotations as well: it refers to the *logos* that the deity "implanted" in human beings when creating them.

The fact that it is precisely this "birth" by *logos* which, for James, makes "us" stand apart from the rest of God's creations as "a sort of 'first fruits'"[166] militates against reading it with reference to a general creation through *logos*, whether conceived on the model of Genesis 1, the cosmic *logos* of the Stoics, or some merger of the two as in the first chapter of the Fourth Gospel.[167] Given the subsequent identification of the *logos* of truth of 1:18 as "the implanted *logos*," in fact, it can safely be assumed that the birth by *logos* mentioned in 1:18 refers particularly to God's implanting of the *logos* within "us" when he created or bore "us." But the fundamental questions remain. What particular act of creation is envisioned here? In whom, precisely, is God imagined to have implanted this *logos*?

The notion that those who join the movement experience some sort of new birth or new creation characterized some forms of early Christianity, and James's concept of a birth by *logos* has often been read in this light.[168] The concepts of re-birth found in the Fourth

---

[165] Cf. Davids, *James*, 89, commenting on 1:18: "We agree with Elliott-Binns that the author intended some reference to creation ... Yet is it not the case that redemption in the NT is often seen as a new creation, the creation terminology being used for effect?"

[166] The modification of "first fruits" with τινα signals that the author himself would not press this metaphor too far, and for this reason should caution one against reading too much into ἀπαρχήν. Cf. Philo's use of the same expression, describing Israel as "set apart out of the whole human race (τοῦ σύμπαντος ἀνθρώπων γένους) as a kind of first fruits (τις ἀπαρχή) to the Maker and Father," simply to denote Israel's special status among the rest of humanity (*Spec. Leg.* 4.180).

[167] Contrast, for example, Tsuji, *Glaube*, 69 and 108.

[168] Mayor, *Epistle of St. James*, 62–64; Dibelius, 103–107; Marty, *L'Epître de Jacques*, 43–46; Moffatt, *The General Epistles*, 21–23; Hauck, *Die Briefe des Jakobus, Petrus, Judas und Johannes*, 11; Leconte, *Les Epîtres Catholiques*, 30 note a (1st ed.) and 34 (2d ed.); Windisch, *Die katholischen Briefe*, 10; Reicke, *The Epistles of James, Peter, and Jude*, 18; Mußner, *Der Jakobusbrief*, 92–97; Fabris, *Legge*, 134–42; Davids, *Epistle of James*, 89; Popkes, *Adressaten*, 136–56; with more hesitance Ropes, *St. James*, 166. Cf. further

Gospel, 1 John, 1 Peter, Colossians and Ephesians have received special emphasis in this connection. 1 John is of particular interest here inasmuch as it associates being "born from God" (γεγεννημένος ἐκ τοῦ θεοῦ) with the reception of a "seed" (1 John 3:9, σπέρμα; cf. 1 Pet 1:23) conceived variously as *logos* or spirit, a conception which is likely to be understood in light of the Logos myth found at the beginning of the Fourth Gospel.[169] This *logos*/spirit is itself characteristically associated with "truth" (ἀλήθεια),[170] and has clear ethical implications for those in whom it "abides": "those who have been born of God do not sin, because the seed abides in them" (3:9; cf. 5:18). As in James, therefore, it is above all one's actions which ultimately reveal whether one is aligned with God or the Devil (3:10, ὁ διάβολος).[171] The concept is in several respects similar to Paul's πνεῦμα: it, too, is a divine substance, possessed only by members of a particular group, with ethical implications that can be summed up with a command to "love."[172] In both Paul and 1 John, moreover, this internalized fragment of the divine stands opposed to human desire, and functions, more generally, in the context of a supernatural and ethical dualism which pits the Devil, desire and—particularly strikingly, in 1 John—"the world" against God and his will for humanity.[173]

Such similarities between James's *logos* and the spirit of Paul or the spirit/*logos* of 1 John might be taken to suggest that the former represents a comparable divine substance possessed uniquely by Christians, only conceived along Stoic lines as a divine law "implanted"

Laws, *Epistle of James*, 75–78, 82–85; Johnson, *Letter of James*, 197–98, 202, 205. See also, however, above note 10 for those who read this with reference to the original creation of humanity.

[169] See esp. 1 John 1:1–4 and further Chapter Four, note 208. See further on being "born of God" 1 John 2:29; 3:9; 4:7; 5:1, 4, 18. Cf. in the Fourth Gospel 1:13: ἐκ θεοῦ ἐγεννήθησαν; 3:3, 7: γεννηθῆναι ἄνωθεν; 3:6, 8: γεγεννημένος ἐκ τοῦ πνεύματος; and 3:5: γεννηθῇ ἐξ ὕδατος καὶ πνεύματος.

[170] 1 John 1:6–10; 2:3–6, 20–21, 27; 4:6; 5:6; cf. 2 John 2; 3 John 3–4, 8.

[171] Cf. also 1 John 1:6–10; 2:3–6, 9–11; and *passim*.

[172] E.g., Gal 5:16–26; Rom 8:1–17. On "love" see, e.g., Gal 5:6, 13–14; Rom 13:8–10; and cf. the emphasis throughout 1 John.

[173] For the opposition of ἐπιθυμία and πνεῦμα in the thought of Paul, see again esp. Gal 5:16–26. Cf. 1 John 2:16–17, where ἐπιθυμία, moreover, is associated particularly with "the world" as opposed to God; cf. in this respect Jas 4:1–6, and further Johnson, "Friendship with the World," 170–71. For the devil see 1 John 3:8–10 (ὁ διάβολος); cf. Paul's σατανᾶς, esp. as "tempter": 1 Cor 7:5; 1 Thess 3:5; cf. 1 Thess 2:18; 1 Cor 5:5; 2 Cor 2:11; 11:14; 12:7; Rom 16:20.

by God in the context of a new creation.[174] On the other hand, the use of the term ἔμφυτος λόγος itself immediately casts doubt on this line of interpretation, for the analogous phrases in the works examined in the previous chapters—including the Christian literature—consistently denote something which is inborn in human beings in general. As was suggested earlier, the interpreter should thus be wary of assuming that the use of the concept in James is peculiar in this respect in the absence of clear evidence to the contrary. And in fact, unlike 1 Peter, 1 John and the other Christian works with which it has typically been compared in this respect, James gives no indication that it is particularly a *re*-birth or a *new* creation that is at issue.

The critical factor in determining the nature of this "birth," as was pointed out earlier in this chapter, is in any case the context in which the reference to it is made. Dibelius formulated the problem and its solution in this way:

> It is ... upon the basis of this connection [of 1:17 to 1:18] that we must examine the question of whether v 18 is intended cosmologically or soteriologically.... Now the cosmological idea does not at all suit the conclusion of v 17; for if God's good will is supposed to be depicted by a reference to the creation of human beings, then this argument has an extremely weak effect, and the fervor with which this allusion is made to something which is self-evident remains incomprehensible. The concept which is really important here is the stressing of the divine will to provide salvation, and already upon the basis of this general argument the soteriological meaning is to be preferred.[175]

The soteriological import of Jas 1:18 is in fact quite clear. As we have seen, the author stresses that the will of God, far from aiming at tempting people to pursue desire and, thus deceived, travel on the way toward death, is expressed in the fact that he has provided them with *logos*, a way characterized by "truth" which is "able to save souls." This, however, is scarcely decisive. Given James's dependence upon a philosophical understanding of law which, originally

---

[174] Cf. Klein, *Ein vollkommenes Werk*, 143f; cf. further the comparisons formulated by Fabris, *Legge*, ch. 6, esp. 191–92 (on 1 Peter), 194–203 (on the Johannine literature) and 203–211 (on Paul). As we have seen, however, Fabris denies any Stoic influence on James's understanding of *logos*.

[175] Dibelius, *James*, 103–4; cf. in this respect the apparent reasoning of Johnson, who however stresses that "no hard and fast distinction need be drawn among creation, covenant and grace, for each builds on the other, and each is an expression of the 'good and perfect gifts that come down from above'" (*Letter of James*, 205; cf. 197–98).

at least, conceived it as having been "implanted" by God in all of humanity when he created them, the assumed dichotomy between "cosmological" and "soteriological" interpretations which underlies this formulation of the problem is entirely unnecessary. Dibelius's exclusion of a reference to creation in 1:18 on the basis of its soteriological implications, in other words, is unwarranted.

What Dibelius does correctly perceive, however, is the significance of 1:17 in this connection. In this verse the author invokes God's paternity of the "lights" in the service of his larger argument that God is not responsible for the human experience of πειρασμός, sin and death. Having first drawn a distinction between God and humanity vis-à-vis the experience of πειρασμός (1:13–15), the author proceeds to draw an analogous distinction between God and the heavenly "lights": following an admonition which plays on the description of some such stars as "wanderers" (1:16, μὴ πλανᾶσθε), it is asserted that God, though the "father of lights," is not himself subject to any of the deviations which are observable among them. Here, the image of divine paternity is clearly used to denote God's (original) creation of the astral "lights," and the point is that God cannot be held responsible for their "wandering" despite the fact that he is their "father," i.e., their creator. This distinction between God's paternity of the "lights" and his responsibility for their "wandering," following upon the claim that God is not responsible when humans wander onto the path of sin and death, suggests rather strongly that a notion of God as the creator of humanity lies behind the formulation of the larger argument of 1:13–18:[176] just as God's creation of the "lights" does not entail his responsibility for the deviations in their movements, so too, one cannot infer from God's creation of humanity that he is responsible when they are tempted to wander in sin toward death. On the contrary, the "Father of Lights," when "giving birth" to humanity, endowed them with *logos*, which is characterized by "truth" and is "able to save souls."[177]

---

[176] In fact, one might find allusions to the myth of the fall of Genesis 3 in Jas 1:13–15 and to Gen 1:14–18 in Jas 1:17.

[177] Cf. also the association of God's status as "father" with the creation of human beings "in the likeness of God" (καθ᾽ ὁμοίωσιν θεοῦ) in Jas 3:9, as the author attempts to expose the depths of human hypocrisy: "with it [sc. the tongue] we bless the Lord and Father, and with it we curse the human beings who were made in the likeness of God."

In fact, while the author's use of the κτίσματα ("creatures," "creations") in 1:18 seems rather peculiar if his intention is to contrast Christians to the rest of humanity who were not so born,[178] it is readily understandable when the verse is read with reference to God's "implanting" of *logos* in humanity when he created them. The human possession of *logos*, in fact, renders humanity second only to the gods on the Stoic scale of nature.[179] Thus Cicero:

> that animal which we call man ... has been given a certain distinguished status (*praeclara quadam condicione*) by the supreme God who created him; for he is the only one among so many different kinds and varieties of living beings who has a share in reason and thought, while all the rest are deprived of it.[180]

This view of humanity's place in the universe, too, is the implicit assumption of one of Chrysippus's arguments for the existence of the gods, as reported by Cicero:

> if gods do not exist, what can there be in the universe superior to man? for he alone possesses reason, which is the most excellent thing that can exist; but for any human being in existence to think that there is nothing in the whole world superior to himself would be an insane piece of arrogance ...[181]

The Stoics, moreover, conceived of the rest of creation primarily in terms of "gifts" from the deity to humanity.[182] In the later Jewish and Christian literature, these Stoic notions are commonly combined with the Jewish concept of humanity's "dominion" over God's other creatures as found in Genesis.[183]

---

[178] Elliott-Binns considers the use of this term alone to be a "practically conclusive" indication that the author refers to creation ("James I.18: Creation or Redemption?" 155); his formulation of the problem as one of "Creation or Redemption," on the other hand, is subject to the same critique registered above in connection with the interpretation of Dibelius.

[179] See on the Stoic view of humanity's place in nature Inwood, *Ethics and Human Action*, 18–27. Note that the various astral bodies are also considered rational: see Cicero *De Nat. Deor.* 2.39–44, where it is argued, in fact, that "the motion of the heavenly bodies is voluntary" (2.44); cf. Philo, *Opif.* 73, 143–44.

[180] *De Leg.* 1.22.

[181] *De Nat. Deor.* 2.16.

[182] See, e.g., Cicero, *De Leg.* 1.25; *De Nat. Deor.* 2.37, 133, 154–62; *De Off.* 2.11; cf. Philo, *Opif.* 77; 4 Macc 5:8–9. Note further Kenter's description of this idea as "specifically Stoic" (*De Legibus*, 110).

[183] See esp. Philo *Opif.* 65ff, 77, and *passim; Abr.* 41; 45; *Jos.* 2; *Leg. All.* 1.30; 2.22; also *AC* 7.34.6; further D. Jobling, "'And Have Dominion ...': The Interpretation of Genesis 1, 28 in Philo Judaeus," *JSJ* 8 (1979) 50–82. Note in this connection

In short, while the soteriological implications of the author's reference in 1:18 to the fact that God "gave birth to us by means of a *logos* of truth" are clear, the context in which this reference is made indicates that he considers this *logos* to be the common possession of all humanity rather than the peculiar possession of Christians. While comparison with other Christian literature reveals that the author's characteristic supernatural and ethical dualism, as well as his remarkable hostility toward "the world," are quite at home within early Christian thought, there is no indication in his letter that he, like Paul and the author of 1 John, considers the *logos* which is "able to save souls" to be the unique possession of Christians. Indeed, if the interpretation of Jas 3:2 offered earlier in this chapter is correct, James's linking of the *logos* to the human capacity for speech renders such an interpretation all but impossible.

In fact, viewed within the context of the argument of 1:13–18 itself, the birth by *logos* is best understood as God's creation of humanity in general. Just as one cannot infer from God's creation of the "lights" that he is responsible when they deviate from their prescribed courses, so too, one cannot infer from God's creation of humanity that he is responsible when they "wander" from the *logos* he gave to them as their law. The subsequent identification of the λόγος ἀληθείας of 1:18 as ὁ ἔμφυτος λόγος is itself a strong indication that James's *logos*, like the ἔμφυτον σπέρμα τοῦ λόγου of Justin and the ἔμφυτος νόμος of Methodius and the *Apostolic Constitutions*, is regarded as something "implanted" by God in all of humanity when he initially created them.

Logos and Desire as "Two Ways"

The *logos* that is central to the thought of James, referred to variously as ὁ ἔμφυτος λόγος or λόγος ἀληθείας, is one imagined to have been implanted in all human beings at creation. It is intimately related, in fact, to the human capacity for speech. Its importance in James, however, lies above all in the fact that it is definitive of the

---

Jas 3:7–8, where the catalogue of the diverse types of creatures and the creation of humans (ἀνθρώπους) "in the image of God," both clearly reminiscent of Genesis (cf. esp. Gen 1:26 28; also 9:2), are understood in a very Greek manner in terms of different "natures": πᾶσα φύσις θηρίων τε καὶ πετεινῶν, ἑρπετῶν τε καὶ ἐναλίων versus ἡ φύσις ἀνθρωπίνη.

will of God for human beings. It functions, in short, as divine law, in opposition to the individual's own desire.

If in all these respects James's concept of *logos* owes much to Greek philosophical, and especially Stoic, discourse, James's treatment of it is, nonetheless, also informed significantly by Jewish and Christian tradition. The Greek opposition between *logos* and desire is here viewed in terms of the "two ways" motif of Jewish and Christian moral exhortation. Further, this opposition, as with Methodius, has been fused with the Judaeo-Christian opposition between God and the Devil, and is seen against an eschatological horizon that includes a *parousia* of Jesus and a judgment by the divine Lawgiver in accord with his law.

For James, human life—particularly, one imagines, given his thoroughly negative appraisal of "the world"—is characterized by various temptations to pursue one's own desires rather than "do" *logos*. These temptations are construed as "tests of faith"—of the faith, particularly, that God himself will provide all good gifts for those who do his will. A soteriologically effective faith, when tested, will manifest itself in *erga*, or good works; and as the implanted *logos* finds written expression in the Torah, it is through constant attention to this law that one becomes a ποιητὴς λόγου and, therefore, a ποιητὴς ἔργου.

The problem of temptation takes on a particular urgency given James's eschatological orientation. Both God's providence and the importance of endurance are emphasized in the letter's opening and closing sections. Successful endurance of temptation, for James, is nothing less than a matter of life or death. Anyone who turns the sinner who has "wandered from the truth" back from his or her erring way "will save his or her soul from death, and cover a multitude of sins" (5:19–20). This, one imagines, is precisely what the Letter of James was intended to do.

CONCLUSION

> *That James meant to speak of regeneration in I.18 and of the gospel in I.21 has no support but the expectation of what it is thought he ought to mean . . .*
>
> A. T. Cadoux, *The Thought of St. James*

The Letter of James identifies as that which is able to "save souls" an implanted *logos* that is closely associated with a perfect law of freedom. While this *logos* was interpreted in light of the Stoic theory that human reason comprises a divine, natural law by several early exegetes, the overwhelming majority of James's critical readers have rejected this line of interpretation in favor of its identification as "the Gospel." This perhaps otherwise uninteresting fact in the history of New Testament scholarship is symptomatic of the predominance of the essentialist approach in the critical study of early Christianity. The classification of James as a Christian work has generally been thought to lead naturally to the interpretation of its soteriologically central *logos* as that which is peculiarly and definitively Christian, "the Gospel"; substantive Stoic influence on the concept, therefore, is out of the question. Indeed, when the interpretation of James's *logos* along Stoic lines was re-introduced in the last century by Arnold Meyer and M.-E. Boismard, it was in both cases accompanied by a hypothesis regarding the non-Christian origin of James, or at least of the passage in question.

To be sure, the submerged logic that leads from the classification of James as Christian to the interpretation of its saving *logos* as "the Gospel" has been supported by explicit arguments against Stoic influence on James in this respect. The Stoics, it is pointed out, scarcely conceived of human reason as something that "saves souls," let alone something that can be "heard" and "done" or "received"; James's use of this language is more reminiscent of the Jewish and Christian sources. Such arguments, however, fail to reckon with the possibility that the sort of fusion of Stoic and Jewish concepts suggested by Meyer and Boismard might be operative even if James is a Christian composition. The categories "Christian" and "Stoic," or

"Judaeo-Christian" and "Greek," rather, are treated more as signifiers of static and mutually exclusive realities than as heuristic tools. In its starkest formulations, the problem has been stated as one of "Jewish" or "biblical" *versus* "hellenistic" influence on James's *logos*. At most, one finds the suggestion that a term of Stoic origin has been drained of its original meaning and filled with an essentially Christian one. Little allowance is made for the complex interweaving of traditions of diverse provenance that in fact characterizes so much of the early Christian literature.

Use of essentialist models for the classification of historical phenomena is inherently problematic, as Jonathan Z. Smith has well shown.[1] Early Christianity is not an exception. In fact, the assumption of such a model by interpreters of James has done more to obscure than to clarify its correlation of "implanted *logos*" with a law that is perfect and of freedom. The appearance of analogous terminology in Cicero's *De Legibus* and the *Apostolic Constitutions*, cited respectively by Meyer and Boismard, have been summarily—indeed, usually tacitly—dismissed as irrelevant for understanding James's *logos* when the letter is read as a Christian composition. Examination of these and other works, however, reveals that the term "implanted" (ἔμφυτος, *insita*) is regularly used in the ancient literature to describe either human reason or a natural law it comprises. This terminology has its roots in the Stoic theory that human reason, which in its perfect form as "right reason" represents natural law, develops out of "implanted preconceptions" (ἔμφυτοι προλήψεις): the innate human tendency to conceptualize moral distinctions like "good" and "bad," often described as "seeds" of knowledge or virtue. It was precisely in light of this theory that Dionysius bar Salibi described James's ἔμφυτος λόγος as "natural law," and that both he and the exegete whose interpretation of Jas 1:21 is preserved by Oecumenius and Theophylactus identified it as something inborn in all humanity, associated particularly with the ability to distinguish moral contraries.

If the discussion of *logos* in James differs in some respects from the Stoics' discussions of human reason, it is not because James alone among these ancient works has formulated the equation of "the implanted *logos*" with the perfect law entirely apart from Stoic influence. On the contrary, such divergences are found wherever the Stoic understanding of law is incorporated into worldviews alien to Stoicism.

---

[1] J. Z. Smith, "Fences and Neighbors: Some Contours of Early Judaism," 1–18.

In James, the creator of the world is the god of the Jewish scriptures, and the *logos* he has implanted in humanity finds written expression in the Torah, the "perfect law" he gave to the descendants of Abraham. Human desire, on the other hand, is associated, as by Methodius, with the mythological Tempter of Jewish and Christian tradition, ὁ διάβολος. The opposition between *logos* and desire and the problem of temptation, moreover, are seen against a looming eschatological horizon, when this god will execute a judgment in accord with his law: "the rich" will be punished for their arrogant and oppressive hedonism, while the humble poor who resist desire and love God will inherit the kingdom he has promised.

If the central feature of James's soteriology is not a "gospel" by which one can be reborn, but a *logos* implanted by God in all humanity at creation that finds written expression in the Torah, it is hardly necessary to conclude that the letter was not originally a Christian composition. Given the regular correlation of interest in Israel's twelve tribes with messianism, particularly in the literature of the early Roman period, the references to the figure of Jesus Christ are quite consistent with the letter's address "to the twelve tribes who are in the diaspora," as well as with its eschatological outlook more broadly.[2] The incorporation of the Stoic understanding of law into this worldview is itself, in fact, quite well understood in light of the ongoing early Christian debates regarding the significance of the Torah. Indeed, there is strong evidence to suggest that James's treatment of the "perfect law of freedom" was drafted particularly with an eye to Paul's formulation of the problem of the law.

It has been widely agreed throughout the history of critical scholarship that James, particularly in its discussion of faith and works in 2:14–26, interacts on some level with Paul, or at least with pauline slogans. This view, however, has not gone unchallenged. Luke Timothy Johnson, for example, has recently argued that, "[d]espite the remarkable points of resemblance" between the discussions of faith and works in Paul and James, "they appear not to be talking with each other by way of instruction or correction."[3] Johnson's conclusion that

---

[2] See on this Jackson-McCabe, "A Letter to the Twelve Tribes," 508–15. It is thus most likely that the *parousia* that will signal the time of the eschatological judgment and reversal is that of "the Lord Jesus," as in most early Christian works; see further Johnson, *The Letter of James*, 313–14.

[3] *Letter of James*, 64. For what follows, cf. my review of Johnson's commentary in *JR* 78 (1998) 102–104.

"[t]here is absolutely no reason to read this section [sc. 2:14–26] as particularly responsive to Paul"[4] is the function of two key propositions: first, that James, unlike Paul, "*never* connects *erga* to the law";[5] and second, that the "unusual concentration" of similar elements in these authors' respective treatments of faith and works is best explained by "the simple fact that both James and Paul were first generation members of a messianic movement that defined itself in terms of 'faith in Jesus'."[6] Even if one were to grant Johnson's view regarding the early date of James, there are weighty objections to both of these assertions.

Whereas the "works" which were foremost in Paul's mind in his discussions of faith and works were ἔργα νόμου, Johnson emphatically insists, as others have often claimed before him, that the author of James "*never* connects *erga* to the law."[7] It is to be noted in the first place that, even if this were true, it scarcely follows that the author of James is not interacting on some level with Paul or pauline ideas. Indeed, among the most common views of 2:14–26 is that the author either misunderstood Paul himself, or combated an "improper" development of pauline thought.[8] Whatever the case, the claim that *erga* have no connection to law in the context of James entirely overlooks 1:25, where it is said quite explicitly that it is one who gives continual attention to the "perfect law of freedom" who will become

---

[4] *Ibid.*, 249.

[5] *Ibid.*, 60, emphasis his.

[6] *Ibid.*, 250.

[7] *Ibid.*, 60 (emphasis his); note also his emphatic repetition later on the same page: "I underline the point: James' usage concerning 'works' is both unconnected to 'law' and is entirely consistent with the dominant NT usage concerning moral effort as an expression of convictions"; cf. further pp. 30, 63, 242. Cf. among many others, Ropes, *Epistle of St. James*, 204f; Dibelius, *James*, 178–80; A. Lindemann, *Paulus im ältesten Christentum: Das Bild des Apostels und die Rezeption der paulinischen Theologie in der frühchristlichen Literatur bis Marcion* (BHT 58; Tübingen: Mohr [Siebeck], 1979) 241, 247, 248f; Hartin, *James and the Q Sayings*, 238–39; G. Luedemann, *Opposition to Paul in Jewish Christianity* (Minneapolis: Fortress, 1989) 144–46. Klein, however, represents a welcome exception: ". . . zwar wird in 2,14–26 das Gesetz nicht erwähnt, aber aus dem übrigen Brief geht deutlich genug hervor, daß auch hier die Werke ἔργα νόμου sind" (*Ein vollkommenes Werk*, 200).

[8] See the works listed in the immediately preceding note, and esp. Luedemann, *Opposition to Paul*, 145 and 287 n. 21. Lindemann reports that the view that the author opposes "eine 'entartete' paulinische Tradition" is "die in der Forschung überwiegend vertretene Annahme" (*Paulus im ältesten Christentum*, 243 and n. 71). Lindemann himself, however, is rightly critical of this view, arguing not only that the author of James engages directly with Paul, but that "[d]er Vf des Jak hat Paulus durchaus verstanden" (*ibid.*, 250); cf. with this last remark, however, his comment regarding the absence of the phrase ἔργα νόμου in James on pp. 248f.

a ποιητὴς ἔργου. Johnson himself describes the connection between Jas 2:14–26 and James 1 as "obvious," at least "for the reader uncommitted to theories of literary fragmentation."[9] Regarding 1:22–25 in particular, he writes that "James had [there] insisted on being 'not only a hearer of the word' but also a doer; now, the contrast is between 'faith alone' and the doing of faith (2:18–26)."[10] Strictly speaking, of course, the author never writes of a ποιητὴς πίστεως, but only, significantly, of the ποιητὴς ἔργου (1:25), λόγου (1:22–23), or νόμου (4:11; cf. 2:12). In any case, the essential question for the author of James is whether one whose faith is tested will respond by giving in to desire, and thus sin, or will resist desire and "do" *logos*, thus effecting a (perfect) *ergon*. In short, while the author never uses the phrase ἔργα νόμου, all *erga* are nonetheless ἔργα λόγου, which is to say, deeds that result from "doing" the ἔμφυτος λόγος that is able to save souls. According to James, this *logos* finds written expression in the Torah; and thus is it said that continual attention to this "perfect law of freedom" will render one a ποιητὴς ἔργου (1:25).

It is particularly significant in this connection that James's discussion of faith and works (2:14–26) follows immediately upon its argument against partiality (2:1–13). Once again, Johnson himself emphasizes the close connection between these two sections, both with respect to their common concern for the type of behavior (particularly vis-à-vis the economically disadvantaged) that ought to accompany "faith" and their argumentative structure.[11] As Johnson sees it, in fact, the author of James "develops a single argument" in these two sections of James 2:

> From beginning to end, it concerns faith and its deeds . . . In this sense, the final part of the discussion in 2:14–26 only provides the broadest formal framework for the specifics argued in 2:1–13.[12]

---

[9] *Letter of James*, 246.

[10] *Ibid.*; cf. further his comment on 1:22, καὶ μὴ μόνον ἀκροαταὶ [λόγου]: "the use of the adverb *monon* ('alone') alerts us to the exact parallel construction concerning 'faith and deeds' in 2:24" (*ibid.*, 206).

[11] See esp. *Letter of James*, 219, 246; cf. also the recent study of D. F. Watson, "James 2," esp. p. 96: "James 2 is constituted by two related examples of this [Greco-Roman] elaboration pattern of argumentation: 2.1–13 on the specific topic of partiality and 2.14–16 on the broader, related issue of faith and works." Significant too in this connection, if less often noted, are the concerns for over-emphasis on Lev 19:18 in Jas 2:1–13 and on Deut 6:4ff in Jas 2:14–26—precisely, that is, the two passages regarded as the most important commands of the law in the synoptic gospels.

[12] *Letter of James*, 219; thus his heading for James 2 as a whole as "The Deeds of Faith."

That is to say, the author of James follows his more specific argument against "having the faith" of Jesus Christ[13] while performing acts of partiality (cf. 2:1) with a discussion of the broader problem of "having faith" while lacking *erga* (cf. 2:14). If, as Johnson rightly recognizes, 2:14–26 and 2:1–13 thus represent discussions of the same basic problem of faith and *erga* on two different levels,[14] it is quite striking that the climactic argument against showing partiality is the fact that such acts represent transgressions of the "law of freedom" by which humans will ultimately be judged (2:8–13). In light of both this connection and the fact that James says quite explicitly that it is one who looks continually into the "perfect law of freedom" who will become a ποιητὴς ἔργου, the claim of Johnson and others that the *erga* of James have nothing to do with the law is wholly untenable.

Given Johnson's sensitivity to the problems which scholarship's overriding concern for the James-Paul issue has caused for the interpretation of James,[15] it is somewhat ironic that his understanding of the relationship of law and *erga* in this work is scarcely understandable apart from his own interest in eliminating the tension that the presence of both James and the letters of Paul within the canon poses for Christian interpreters.[16] A similar concern seems to underlie his claim that the "unusual concentration" of similar language in the discussions of faith and works in James and the letters of Paul

---

[13] Precisely what the description of πίστις in 2:1 specifically as ἡ πίστις τοῦ κυρίου ἡμῶν Ἰησοῦ Χριστοῦ τῆς δόξης is intended to signify is not immediately clear. The issue rests largely with the problem of the author's understanding of the significance of Jesus Christ. What is clear is that the πίστις which is of foremost concern elsewhere in the letter is faith that God will himself be faithful to those who "do" his *logos* or law. It thus seems most likely that ἡ πίστις τοῦ κυρίου ἡμῶν Ἰησοῦ Χριστοῦ τῆς δόξης—if we are in fact dealing with an objective rather than a subjective genitive (though see W. Wachob, "The rich in faith," 146–48)—concerns above all faith that an eschatological reversal will right the wrongs which characterize the corrupt "world" at the glorious *parousia* of Jesus as lord messiah, an event understood as a fulfillment of ancient promises made by God "to those who love him" (cf. 2:5; 1:12).

[14] Showing partiality is not discussed in terms of an *ergon*. This, however, is not surprising given the author's negative focus in 2:1–13: here he argues *against* a "sin" (cf. 2:9: εἰ δὲ προσωπολημπτεῖτε, ἁμαρτίαν ἐργάζεσθε), not *for* an *ergon*. On the use of ἁμαρτία and ἔργον as oppositional categories in James, see pp. 216–21.

[15] See esp. *Letter of James*, 58–64, 111–16, 156, 245–52.

[16] This was already the case with Erasmus, as Johnson himself seems to recognize: "And on the issue of faith and works, *Erasmus harmonizes*: 'truly Paul [. . .] speaks of the observance of the law of Moses, here (James) is concerned with the offices of piety and charity'" (*Letter of James*, 141 [with emphasis added]).

is best explained not by "a hypothetical power struggle between early Christian leaders" or by "a subtle [!] literary polemic," but by the authors' similar background as "first generation members" of a movement that "defined itself in terms of the 'faith of Jesus'."[17] For while it is no doubt the case that the "necessary unity between attitude and action" emphasized in James is typical of ancient (and modern) moral exhortation generally,[18] it is equally true that the treatment of this theme specifically in terms of πίστις and ἔργα—let alone the question of whether one can be considered righteous (δικαιοῦσθαι) by πίστις χωρὶς ἔργων—is not.[19] Though Johnson characterizes the general context of James's discussion of faith and works as being "not dissimilar to the language concerning faith and deeds (erga)" in several passages from 4 Ezra and 2 Baruch,[20] these works share with James little more than the basic notion that one's actions are important vis-à-vis one's eschatological fate. Indeed, despite Johnson's characterization of the passages from these works as "concerning faith and deeds (erga)," only two of them actually pair "faith" (fides) and "deeds" (opera) (4 Ezra 9:7; 13:23) at all; only one of these even arguably envisions some significant separation of the two (4 Ezra 9:7); and in no case is the problem of the merit of "faith apart from deeds" addressed. In contrast, the author of James clearly assumes

---

[17] Letter of James, 250. Note that where James's literary relationships to other works are concerned, Johnson is quite critical of attempts to explain similarities in terms of just such a "vague 'common property of early Christianity'" (ibid., 67). Note particularly in this connection his pointed critique of Dibelius's assessment of the relationship of James to the Shepherd of Hermas: "[Dibelius's] refusal to acknowledge dependence in this case appears to rest as much on his presuppositions as on the evidence" (Letter of James, 76f).

[18] Cf. ibid., 247.

[19] Cf. esp. Jas 2:18, 20, 26 with Rom 3:28; 4:4–6. Note in this respect 1 Clem 30:3, "let us put on concord in meekness of spirit and continence, keeping ourselves far from all gossip and evil speaking, and be justified by deeds, not by words (ἔργοις δικαιούμενοι, μὴ λόγοις), with which cf. 1 Clem 32:4: "we who by his will have been called in Christ Jesus, are not made righteous (δικαιούμεθα) by ourselves, or by our wisdom or understanding or piety or the deeds (ἔργων) which we have wrought in holiness of heart, but through faith (ἀλλὰ διὰ τῆς πίστεως), by which God has justified (ἐδικαίωσεν) all men from the beginning of the world." The former statement recalls the more general discussions of "the necessary unity between attitude and action" which Johnson characterizes as "the fundamental assumption of all ancient moral discourse," albeit with the infusion of the Christian sense of δικαιοῦσθαι. The latter statement, however, which assumes a significant distinction between becoming righteous before God διὰ ἔργων, etc. and διὰ τῆς πίστεως, clearly recalls the doctrine of justification as formulated by Paul.

[20] Johnson, Letter of James, 238, citing 2 Bar. 14:12; 24:1; 51:7 and 4 Ezra 7:77; 8:32–36; 9:7; 13:23.

the existence of the position that faith apart from works is sufficient
for righteousness and eschatological salvation.[21] At least as far as can
be judged from the extant evidence, this position, which he repeatedly characterizes with the tag πίστις χωρὶς ἔργων and attacks, is
peculiarly pauline.[22]

Particularly characteristic of Paul too, moreover, is another notion
that the author presupposes and combats in the immediately previous and closely related discussion of partiality. James's argument that
showing partiality renders one a transgressor of the law regardless
of whether one "keeps the whole law" by "loving one's neighbor as
oneself," as we have seen, presupposes the use of Lev 19:18 as summary of the "whole law." The formulation of summaries of biblical
law, even vis-à-vis love of God, of one's fellow human beings, or
some combination of the two, was practiced both by Christians and
non-Christian Jews, and in a variety of ways. But it is Paul in particular who emerges from the extant ancient Jewish and Christian
literature as an advocate of the position that the author of James
seeks to defuse. While Matthew pairs Deut 6:5 and Lev 19:18 as a
summary of "the whole law" (Matt 22:34–39; cf. Mark 12:28–34;
Luke 10:25–28), Paul stands apart from the synoptics in his emphasis on Lev 19:18 alone (Gal 5:14; Rom 13:8–10).[23] Moreover, the
reductionistic tendency which most concerns the author of James,
while clearly evident neither in Matthew nor in Hillel's summary, is
among the chief services rendered by the summary use of the love
command in Paul's letters. To be sure, the author of James is aware—
and wary—of the special emphasis placed on *both* Deut 6:4ff *and* Lev
19:18 in some Christian circles.[24] However, the argument of Jas

---

[21] It is likely in connection with his attempt to discredit this position that James's
consistently positive use of the term *erga* as *good* deeds as opposed to "sin" (rather than
its usual more neutral sense of "deeds," good or bad) is to be understood. Assuming
the existence of a position which holds that *erga* are unnecessary for eschatological
salvation, James reacts by characterizing *erga* as the very mark of God's wisdom
(3:13) and of a "living," i.e., soteriologically efficacious, faith (2:14–26; cf. 1:2–4, 12).

[22] It seems most likely to me, in fact, that Paul formulated this distinction between
righteousness by faith and righteousness by works himself, to meet a specific problem
that arose in connection with his own activity: disputes regarding the extent to which
non-Jewish members of the movement were obliged to observe the Torah. An additional indication that the author of James engages particularly with pauline teaching in 2:14–26 is the importance of Gen 15:6 to his argument; see on this below.

[23] Note that Hillel's use of the golden rule as summary does not obviously refer
to Lev 19:18.

[24] See above, note 11, and further pp. 174f.

2:8–11 presupposes and combats specifically just such a sentiment as is found in Rom 13:8–10; namely, that since the various commands of the law are "summed up" (ἀνακεφαλαιόω) as "love your neighbor as yourself," "love is therefore the fulfilling (πλήρωμα) of law," so that "one who loves another has fulfilled (πεπλήρωκεν) the law."[25]

James's lavish description of the Torah as the "perfect law of freedom," too, can be understood as a response to Paul's statements regarding the soteriological impotence of the law. This is especially true of his repeated description of the Torah as a "law of freedom." As "freedom" is not mentioned elsewhere in the letter, it would seem that James's main interest in the concept is simply to make of it an attribute of the Torah. It is quite interesting, then, that Paul sharply contrasts the "freedom" of those who obtained the spirit through faith in Jesus Christ with the "slavery" that characterizes life under the Torah.[26] This contrast is expressed with particular force in Galatians, and especially in the allegory of Sarah and Hagar, where the law is in fact itself ultimately characterized as a "yoke of slavery" (4:21–5:1). Thus, too, are the "false brothers" in Jerusalem who apparently felt that Titus should be circumcised characterized as having "slipped in to spy on the freedom (τὴν ἐλευθερίαν) we have in Christ Jesus, so that they might enslave (καταδουλώσουσιν) us" (2:4).[27] Seen alongside his refutation of the notions of righteousness by faith apart from works and of fulfilling the law simply by observing the love command, James's obvious concern to associate the Torah with freedom[28]—the only explicit interest in freedom in the work—can be well understood as part of a broader attempt to counter pauline positions regarding the significance of the law.[29] Far from being a

---

[25] Cf. Ludwig, *Wort als Gesetz*, 184–87; also Popkes, *Adressaten*, 116–18, who, however, reads Jas 2:8–11 in light of a supposed polemic against later pauline "libertinists" (see below, note 29).

[26] To be sure, Paul can (at least in Romans) describe the law itself as "spiritual"—the highest compliment he could give it. It is, nonetheless, unable to effect that which Jesus Christ accomplished through his death and resurrection, namely, it could not liberate the sarkic human being from its slavery to sin; indeed, it only served to "increase the trespass." See esp. Rom 7:14–8:17, and cf. 5:20–21 and 7:13. This entire line of thinking is alien to James.

[27] See further Gal 4:1–11, noting especially Paul's characterization of the Galatians themselves as wanting to become "enslaved" (δουλεύειν) in 4:9.

[28] Note in this connection the emphatic effect created by the use of the definite article τόν before τῆς ἐλευθερίας in 1:25; noted also by Klein, *Ein vollkommenes Werk*, 138.

[29] Cf. Betz, *Galatians*, 91 n. 308; Wachob, "Rich in Faith," 284. Differently Popkes, *Adressaten*, 68–70, who suggests that "law of freedom" was a slogan developed by

"yoke of slavery," the Torah, as a written expression of ὁ ἔμφυτος λόγος, is the source of "freedom."[30]

In sum, in connection with his treatment of law, the author of James presupposes, and seeks to refute, the existence of at least two characteristically (indeed, perhaps peculiarly) pauline notions: that one can be considered righteous by faith apart from works, and that one can fulfill "the whole law" simply by loving one's neighbor as oneself. Moreover, James's obvious desire to associate the law with "freedom" is quite well understood in light of Paul's contrary equation of it with "slavery." The best explanation for these points of contact is the most straightforward: the author of James writes with an eye to undermining Paul's position on the significance of the Torah. Notably, however, James is silent on the issues that seem to have been the impetus for these pauline formulations in the first place: the importance of circumcision, diet, etc., particularly for the non-Jewish members of the movement. If, as pointed out earlier, it cannot simply be concluded from this silence that James felt that such aspects of the Torah were no longer binding at all, it seems safe to suppose that such matters were not, at least, among his primary concerns. Indeed, whatever his stance on these issues, it is quite clear from the letter as a whole, and from 2:1–13 (esp. 2:2–3) and 2:14–26 (esp. 2:15–16) in particular, that his main concerns were economic, and above all the treatment of the socially disadvantaged: the "poor" (2:1–7), the naked and hungry (2:15–16), the widow and the orphan (1:27), the hired laborer (5:4).[31] His dislike of the pauline

---

post-pauline libertinists, and is used ironically in James. Klein, who points out that there is no other evidence for such a group, finds it more likely that James's use of pauline concepts is not ironic; rather, his association of law and freedom results from the identification of the law with the *logos* by which they have become Christians and which they possess within themselves: "Dies gibt ihnen die Möglichkeit und die Freiheit, das zu tun, was dieses Wort gebietet"; see *Ein vollkommenes Werk*, 143–44. Note, though, that Klein considers this *logos* to be the functional equivalent of Paul's "spirit" (*Ein vollkommenes Werk*, 158–59); indeed, the notion of humanity's fundamental inability to live in accord with the law apart from the reception of some additional divine substance, which Klein apparently assumes to be operative in James, sounds strikingly pauline.

[30] Note that Irenaeus's interest in a "law of freedom," while undoubtedly related to his familiarity with a Greek notion of natural law, is also related to his participation in the ongoing early Christian debates regarding the significance of the Torah. Interestingly, he too is engaged particularly with the pauline view—albeit, at least in part, via Marcion.

[31] See also 1:9–11 ("rich" and "humble"); 4:13–17 (travelling merchants); 5:1–6 (condemnation of "the rich"); and further 4:1–10, which concerns acquisitiveness.

notion of πίστις χωρὶς ἔργων and his wariness regarding the placement of special emphasis upon Lev 19:18 and Deut 6:4ff, that is,
seems to be motivated less by his special interest in the particular
issues which inspired Paul's formulation of the problem of the law
than by a concern that such principles might lead to neglect, more
generally, of God's law—and particularly of those aspects of it which
concern the economically disadvantaged.[32] In this respect, perhaps,
James is not altogether different from those who leveled a more generalizing critique of Paul by caricaturing his teaching as "let us do
evil so that good may come."[33]

Whether James became familiar with these aspects of Paul's view
through oral channels alone, by direct access to some collection of
Paul's letters (including at least Romans and Galatians), or through
the writings of later advocates of the pauline position, however, is
not altogether clear. While the several points of contact might suggest his familiarity with some written work or works, it is not difficult
to imagine the individual points he counters as having been trans-
mitted as pithy slogans: righteousness is attained by πίστις χωρὶς
ἔργων; love of neighbor is the fulfillment of the law; the law is a
"yoke of slavery." A somewhat stronger indication of literary dependence, perhaps, is use of the Abraham example in the argument of
2:14–26.[34] The author is rather clearly concerned to interpret Gen
15:6, ἐπίστευσεν δὲ Ἀβραὰμ τῷ θεῷ, καὶ ἐλογίσθη αὐτῷ εἰς δικαιοσύνην,

---

Note esp., too, that while "the rich" are the arch-enemies of the letter, "the poor"
are said to have been chosen to inherit the kingdom (2:5). Significant too is his
definition of "pure religion" in terms not only of avoiding the impurity of "the
world" (with which cf. esp. 4:1–10), but care of widows and orphans (1:27).

[32] As is clear esp. from 2:1–13, proper treatment of the poor is assumed by the
author of James to be a duty required by the law. Note also in this respect his
charge that the rich withhold the wages owed to the laborers who work their fields,
with which cf. Lev 19:13, and further the Jewish literature referred to in Dibelius,
James, 238. In this respect, James is somewhat reminiscent of the story of Lazarus
and the rich man in Luke 16:19–31, which clearly presupposes an interpretation
of the law (and prophets) in which concern for the poor is both obvious and of
critical importance.

[33] Rom 3:8. The lack of evidence for the broader concerns which motivated this
caricature, however, or for the nature and aim of the particular pauline position
they mocked (though cf. Rom 5:18–6:2), prohibit drawing any firm conclusions in
this respect. Cf. however Luedemann's discussion of this passage in *Opposition to
Paul*, 109–11, noting that he also compares the caricaturization of pauline teaching in this passage with that found in Jas 2:14–26 (*ibid.*, 146).

[34] Lindemann, *Paulus im ältesten Christentum*, 245–47; Luedemann, *Opposition to Paul*,
143–46; Tsuji, *Glaube*, 189–94; contrast Penner, *Epistle of James and Eschatology*, 63–70.

in such a way that Abraham's "righteousness" cannot be said to proceed directly from his faith. To this end, he claims that this "scripture" was actually "fulfilled" when Abraham attempted to sacrifice Isaac;[35] and thus, too, was Abraham considered a "friend of God."[36] The interpretation of Gen 15:6 which he seeks to disallow, of course, is precisely that offered by Paul (Rom 4:2–3; cf. Gal 3:6–9). In fact, the question which introduces the example of Abraham in James, Ἀβραὰμ ὁ πατὴρ ἡμῶν οὐκ ἐξ ἔργων ἐδικαιώθη ... (2:21), is quite reminiscent of—and directly opposed to the thrust of—Rom 4:2, found just prior to Paul's own citation of Gen 15:6: εἰ γὰρ Ἀβραὰμ ἐξ ἔργων ἐδικαιώθη, ἔχει καύχημα, ἀλλ' οὐ πρὸς θεόν. Still, it seems at least possible that Paul's apparently peculiar use of Gen 15:6 to prove that Abraham did not become righteous ἐξ ἔργων might also have become known to the author of James apart from a direct dependence upon Romans.[37]

---

[35] Jas 2:23: καὶ ἐπληρώθη ἡ γραφὴ ἡ λέγουσα, κτλ.; note in this respect LXX Gen 22:15–18, where it is said that God will "indeed" (μήν) fulfill the promises first made to Abraham in Genesis 15 as a result of his willingness to sacrifice his son. Included among those who similarly interpret Jas 2:23 on the model of a prophetic fulfillment are Ropes, *Epistle of St. James*, 221; Lindemann, *Paulus im ältesten Christentum*, 246; Johnson, *Letter of James*, 243.

[36] It seems most likely that the καὶ which introduces the clause καὶ φίλος θεοῦ ἐκλήθη coordinates with that which begins 2:23; thus: "and the scripture was fulfilled...; and he was called a friend of God." Dibelius's argument that the statement regarding Abraham's friendship with God is "isolated and meaningless" if not read as a part of the "scripture" being cited is by no means persuasive (*James*, 164). As is clear from 4:4, being a "friend of God" is quite important to the author of James: it is, in fact, a function of resisting desire and thus, conversely, manifesting the endurance of temptation in *erga*—in this case, Abraham's *ergon* of executing God's command to sacrifice his son. Note here that Abraham's sacrifice of Isaac was often understood as one of a series of "trials" successfully completed by the patriarch, as in *Jubilees*, which in fact similarly connects Abraham's "faithfulness" in the last of his ten trials with his status as "friend of God": "he was found faithful and he was recorded as a friend of the LORD in the heavenly tablets" (*Jub.* 19:9; cf. 19:6–8; 17:15–18). If, then, one insists with Dibelius that James's clause "and he was called a friend of God" is to be read as part of the "scripture" cited in 2:23, a reference to *Jubilees* might be considered as plausible a possibility as one to Genesis. Dibelius's conclusion that Jas 2:23 "is not actually a quotation, but rather ... the sort of 'automatic' statement which is often made in devotional language" in any case seems to me to be contrary to the plain sense of the introductory formula ἡ γραφὴ ἡ λέγουσα.

[37] One cannot place too much weight on the (admittedly interesting) fact that the citation of Gen 15:6 in Jas 2:23 agrees verbatim with that of Rom 4:3, with both diverging from LXX Gen 15:6 with respect to their use of Ἀβραάμ (not Ἀβραμ) and the inclusion of the particle δέ. With respect to the former, cf. 1 Macc 2:52; with respect to the latter, cf. Philo, *Mut. Nom.* 177.

James's interaction with pauline ideas provides a secure basis for locating it within early Christianity. More specifically, the Letter of James was produced in some circle of Christians for whom the Torah remained the central expression of love of God, and thus a critical criterion for inheriting the promised kingdom that would be given to the "twelve tribes" at the *parousia* of the messiah, Jesus. Its precise date and provenance, however, remain elusive. Clearly it was not written prior to Paul's activity; and if it does assume some collection of Paul's letters, this would likely place it well after Paul's death,[38] and thus after the death of James the brother of Jesus ca. 62 CE. In fact, while the letter's emphasis on the Torah seems consistent with our evidence for Jesus's brother, its enlisting, to this end, of the Stoic view of law seems more consistent with later developments in the Christian debates about the Torah.[39] All things considered, it seems most plausible to view James as a pseudonymous work, written in the late first or early second century, perhaps in Syria or Palestine.[40] In any case, the Letter of James provides important, if all too rare evidence for a form of the Christian movement where soteriology centered not on rebirth through "the Gospel," but on observance of the Torah.

---

[38] The early history of collections of pauline letters, however, is quite obscure; see Gamble, *The New Testament Canon*, 35–41.

[39] Our knowledge of the "historical James," however, is rather limited; for a concise treatment, see R. B. Ward, "James of Jerusalem in the First Two Centuries," *ANRW* 2.26.1 (1992) 779–812.

[40] The address of the letter to the "twelve tribes" is best understood in the context of the marked increase of interest in the tribes of Israel that began around the fall of the Hasmonean kingdom and apparently waned with the failure of the Bar Kochba revolt; see Jackson-McCabe, "A Letter to the Twelve Tribes," 510–15. The earliest attestation of James in the Pseudo-Clementine *De Virginitate* and Origen's works is consistent with an eastern provenance.

BIBLIOGRAPHY

Abrahams, I. *Studies in Pharisaism and the Gospels. First and Second Series*. Edited by Harry M. Orlinsky. Prolegomenon by Morton S. Enslin. Library of Biblical Studies. New York: Ktav Publishing House, 1967.

Adamson, James B. *James: The Man and His Message*. Grand Rapids, MI: Eerdmans, 1989.

———. *The Epistle of James*. NICNT. Grand Rapids, MI: Eerdmans, 1976; reprint edition, 1984.

Agourides, S. "Apocalypse of Sedrach." *OTP* 1, 605–13.

Aland, Barbara, Kurt Aland, Gerd Mink and Klaus Wachtel. *Novum Testamentum Graecum. Editio Critica Maior, Volume IV: Catholic Letters. Installment 1: James*. 2 Parts. Edited by the Institute for New Testament Textual Research. Stuttgart: Deutsche Bibelgesellschaft, 1997.

Anderson, H. "4 Maccabees: A New Translation and Introduction." *OTP* 2, 531–64.

Baker, William R. *Personal Speech Ethics in the Epistle of James*. WUNT 2/68. Tübingen: J. C. B. Mohr (Paul Siebeck), 1995.

Balz, H., and W. Schrage. *Die "katholischen" Briefe: Die Briefe des Jakobus, Petrus, Johannes und Judas*. 11th edition. NTD 10. Göttingen: Vandenhoeck & Ruprecht, 1973.

Bauckham, Richard. *Jude, 2 Peter*. WBC 50. Waco: Word Books, 1983.

Bauer, Walter. *Orthodoxy and Heresy in Earliest Christianity*. Second German edition, with added appendices, by Georg Strecker. Translated by a team from the Philadelphia Seminar on Christian Origins. Edited by Robert A. Kraft and Gerhard Krodel. Philadelphia: Fortress Press, 1971.

Benardete, Seth. "Cicero's *De Legibus* I: Its Plan and Intention." *AJP* 108 (1987) 295–309.

Betz, Hans Dieter. *Galatians: A Commentary on Paul's Letter to the Churches in Galatia*. Hermeneia. Philadelphia: Fortress Press, 1979.

———. *Lukian von Samosata und das Neue Testament: Religionsgeschichtliche und paränetische Parallelen. Ein Beitrag zum Corpus Hellenesticum Novi Testamenti*. TU 76. Berlin: Akademie Verlag, 1961.

———. *Paul's Concept of Freedom in the Context of Hellenistic Discussions about the Possiblities of Human Freedom*. Protocol of the 26th Colloquy of the Center for Hermeneutical Studies in Hellenistic and Modern Culture. Berkeley: The Center for Hermeneutical Studies in Hellenistic and Modern Culture, 1977.

———. *The Sermon on the Mount: A Commentary on the Sermon on the Mount, including the Sermon on the Plain (Matthew 5:3–7:27 and Luke 6:20–49)*. Edited by Adela Yarbro Collins. Hermeneia. Philadelphia: Fortress Press, 1995.

Beyschlag, Willibald. *Der Brief des Jacobus*. 6th edition KEKNT. Göttingen: Vandenhoeck & Ruprecht, 1897.

Bietenhard, H. "Deuterosis." *RAC* 3 (1957) 842–49.

Black, Matthew, and Albert-Marie Denis. *Apocalypsis Henochi Graece. Fragmenta Pseudepigraphorum quae supersunt Graeca: Una cum historicum et auctorum judaeorum hellenistarum fragmentis*. PVTG 3. Leiden: E. J. Brill, 1970.

Black, Matthew. *The Book of Enoch or I Enoch: A New English Edition with Commentary and Textual Notes*. In consultation with James C. VanderKam, with an appendix on the 'Astronomical' chapters by O. Neugebauer. SVTP 7. Leiden: E. J. Brill, 1985.

Blackman, E. C. *The Epistle of James: Introduction and Commentary*. Torch Bible Commentaries. London: SCM, 1957.

Boismard, M.-E. "Une liturgie baptismale dans la Prima Petri: II—Son Influence sur l'Epître de Jacques." *RB* 64 (1957) 161–83.

Bonhöffer, Adolf. *Epictet und die Stoa: Untersuchungen zur stoischen Philosophie.* Stuttgart: Enke, 1890. Reprint edition: Stuttgard-Bad Cannstatt: Friedrich Frommann Verlag (Günther Holzboog), 1968.

———. *Epiktet und das Neue Testament.* RGVV 10. Gießen: Töpelmann, 1911.

Bousset, Wilhelm. "Eine jüdische Gebetssammlung im siebenten Buch der apostolischen Konstitutionen." *Nachrichten von der Königlichen Gesellschaft der Wissenschaften zu Göttingen: Philologisch-historisches Klasse* (1915) 438–85. Reprinted in Wilhelm Bousset, *Religionsgeschichtliche Studien: Aufsätze zur Religionsgeschichte des Hellenistischen Zeitalters,* 231–86. Edited by Anthonie F. Verheule. NovTSup 50. Leiden: E. J. Brill, 1979.

Boyle, Marjorie O'Rourke. "The Stoic Paradox of James 2.10." *NTS* 31 (1995) 611–17.

Breitenstein, Urs. *Beobachtungen zu Sprache, Stil und Gedankengut des Vierten Makkabäerbuchs.* 2d edition. Basel und Stuttgart: Schwabe & Co. Verlag, 1978.

Brink, C. O. "Οἰκείωσις and Οἰκειότης: Theophrastus and Zeno on Nature in Moral Theory." *Phronesis* 1 (1955–1956) 123–45.

Burchard, Christoph. "Nächstenliebegebot, Dekalog und Gesetz in Jak 2, 8–11." In *Die Hebräische Bibel und ihre zweifache Nachgeschichte: Festschrift für Rolf Rendtorff zum 65. Geburtstag,* edited by Erhard Blum, Christian Macholz, and Ekkehard W. Stegemann, 517–33. Neukirchen-Vluyn: Neukirchener, 1990.

Cadoux, Arthur Temple. *The Thought of St. James.* London: Clarke & Co., 1944.

Cantinat, Jean. *Les Epîtres de Saint Jacques et de Saint Jude.* SB. Paris: Gabalda, 1973.

Chaine, Joseph. *L'Epître de Saint Jacques.* 2d edition. EBib. Paris: Gabalda, 1927.

Charles, R. H. *The Greek Versions of the Testaments of the Twelve Patriarchs. Edited from Nine MSS together with the Variants of the Armenian and Slavonic Versions and Some Hebrew Fragments.* Reprint edition. Oxford: Oxford University Press; Hildesheim: Georg Olms Verlagsbuchhandlung, 1960.

Chesnut, Glenn F. "The Ruler and the Logos in Neopythagorean, Middle Platonic, and Late Stoic Political Philosophy." *ANRW* 2.16.2 (1978) 1310–32.

Cladder, H. J. "Die Anlage des Jakobusbriefes." *ZKT* 28 (1904) 37–57.

Clemen, Carl. *Primitive Christianity and its Non-Jewish Sources.* Edinburgh: T & T Clark, 1912.

Cohen, Shaye J. D. *From the Maccabees to the Mishnah.* Library of Early Christianity. Philadelphia: Westminster, 1989.

Collins, John J. *Between Athens and Jerusalem: Jewish Identity in the Hellenistic Diaspora.* New York: Crossroad, 1983.

———. "Cosmos and Salvation: Jewish Wisdom and Apocalyptic in the Hellenistic Age." *HR* 17 (1977) 121–42.

———. *The Apocalyptic Imagination: An Introduction to the Jewish Matrix of Christianity.* New York: Crossroad, 1989.

Connolly, R. Hugh. *Didascalia Apostolorum: The Syriac Version Translated and Accompanied by the Verona Fragments. With an Introduction and Notes.* Oxford: Clarendon, 1929.

Darnell, D. R. "Hellenistic Synagogal Prayers." *OTP* 2, 671–97.

Davids, Peter H. "The Epistle of James in Modern Discussion." *ANRW* 2.25.5 (1988) 3621–3645.

———. *The Epistle of James: A Commentary on the Greek Text.* NIGTC. Grand Rapids, MI: Eerdmans, 1982.

DeFilippo, Joseph G., and Philip Mitsis. "Socrates and Stoic Natural Law." In *The Socratic Movement,* edited by Paul A. Vander Waerdt, 252–71. Ithaca: Cornell University Press, 1994.

Denis, Albert-Marie. *Concordance Grecque des Pseudépigraphes d'Ancien Testament: Concordance, Corpus des textes, Indices.* Louvain-la-Neuve: Université Catholique de Louvain, Institut Orientaliste, 1997.

Deppe, Dean B. *The Sayings of Jesus in the Epistle of James.* Chelsea: MI: Bookcrafters, 1989.

deSilva, David A. *4 Maccabees.* Guides to Apocrypha and Pseudepigrapha. Sheffield: Sheffield Academic Press, 1998.

Dibelius, Martin. *James: A Commentary on the Epistle of James.* 11th edition, revised by Heinrich Greeven. Hermeneia. Translated by Michael A. Williams Philadelphia: Fortress, 1988. First German edition: *Der Brief des Jakobus.* 7th edition. KEKNT. Göttingen: Vandenhoeck & Ruprecht, 1921.

Dillon, John M. *The Middle Platonists: 80 B.C. to A.D. 220.* Ithaca: Cornell University Press, 1977.

Droge, Arthur J. *Homer or Moses? Early Christian Interpretation of the History of Culture.* HUT 26. Tübingen: J. C. B. Mohr (Paul Siebeck), 1989.

Dupont-Sommer, André. *Le Quatrième Livre des Machabées: Introduction, Traduction et Notes.* Paris: Libraire Ancienne Honoré Champion, 1939.

Edsman, Carl-Martin. "Schöpferwille und Geburt Jac I 18. Eine Studie zur altchristlichen Kosmologie." *ZNW* 38 (1939) 11–44.

———. "Schöpfung und Wiedergeburt: Nochmals Jac 1:18." *Spiritus et Veritas* (FS Karl Kundsin), 43–55. Eutin: Ozolin, 1953.

Edwards, M. J. "Justin's Logos and the Word of God." *Journal of Early Christian Studies* 3 (1995) 261–80.

Elliott-Binns, L. E. "James I.18: Creation or Redemption?" *NTS* 3 (1957) 148–61.

Engberg-Pedersen, T. *The Stoic Theory of Oikeiosis: Moral Development and Social Interaction in Early Stoic Philosophy.* Studies in Hellenistic Civilization 2. Denmark: Aarhus University Press, 1990.

Fabris, Rinaldo. *Legge della Libertà in Giacomo.* Supplementi all RivistB 8. Brescia: Paideia, 1977.

Felder, Cain Hope. "Wisdom, Law and Social Concern in the Epistle of James." Ph.D. dissertation, Columbia University, 1982.

Fiensy, D. A., and D. R. Darnell. "Hellenistic Synagogal Prayers." *OTP* 2, 671–97.

Fiensy, David A. *Prayers Alleged to be Jewish: An Examination of the Constitutiones Apostolorum.* Brown Judaic Studies 65. Chico, CA: Scholars Press, 1985.

Foerster, Werner, and Johannes Herrmann. "κλῆρος, κτλ." *TDNT* 3, 758–85.

Frankemölle, Hubert. *Der Brief des Jakobus.* 2 volumes. ÖTKNT 17. Gütersloh: Gütersloher Verlagshaus; Würzburg: Echter Verlag, 1994.

Gamble, Harry Y. *The New Testament Canon: Its Making and Meaning.* Guides to Biblical Scholarship, New Testament Series. Philadelphia; Fortress Press, 1985.

Goodenough, Erwin R. "Philo's Exposition of the Law and his De Vita Mosis." *HTR* 26 (1933) 109–25.

———. "The Political Philosophy of Hellenistic Kingship." *Yale Classical Studies* 1 (1928) 55–102.

———. *The Politics of Philo Judaeus: Practice and Theory.* New Haven: Yale University Press, 1938.

———. *By Light, Light: The Mystic Gospel of Hellenistic Judaism.* New Haven: Yale University Press, 1935.

Goranson, Stephen. "Ebionites." *ABD* 2, 260–61.

Greeven, Heinrich. "Jede Gabe ist gut, Jak. 1, 17." *TZ* 14 (1958) 1–13.

Hadas, Moses. *The Third and Fourth Books of Maccabees.* New York: Harper & Bros., 1953.

Hartin, Patrick J. "Call to Be Perfect through Suffering (James 1,2–4). The Concept of Perfection in the Epistle of James and the Sermon on the Mount." *Bib* 77 (1996) 477–92.

———. *James and the Q Sayings of Jesus.* JSNTSup 47. Sheffield: JSOT Press, 1991.

Hauck, Fr. *Die Briefe des Jakobus, Petrus, Judas und Johannes.* 6th edition. NTD 10. Göttingen: Vandenhoeck & Ruprecht, 1953.

Heidland, Hans Wolfgang. "λογίζομαι, κτλ." *TDNT* 4, 284–92.

Hengel, Martin. *Judaism and Hellenism: Studies in their Encounter in Palestine during the Early Hellenistic Period.* 2 vols. in one. Philadelphia: Fortress, 1981.

Hengel, Martin, in collaboration with Christoph Markschies. *The "Hellenization" of Judaea in the First Century after Christ.* Philadelphia: Trinity Press International, 1989.

Hollander, H. W., and M. de Jonge. *The Testaments of the Twelve Patriarchs: A Commentary*. SVTP 8. Leiden: E. J. Brill, 1985.

Holte, Ragnar. "Logos Spermatikos: Christianity and Ancient Philosophy according to St. Justin's Apologies." *ST* 12 (1958) 109–68.

Hoppe, Rudolf. *Der theologische Hintergrund des Jakobusbriefes*. 2d edition. FB 28. Würzburg: Echter Verlag, 1985.

Horsley, Richard. "The Law of Nature in Philo and Cicero." *HTR* 71 (1978) 35–59.

Horst, Pieter W. van der. "The Jewish Prayers in the Apostolic Constitutions." Presented at the 1997 annual meeting of the Society of Biblical Literature.

Hort, F. J. A. *The Epistle of St. James: The Greek Text with Introduction, Commentary as far as Chapter IV, Verse 7, and Additional Notes*. London: MacMillan and Co. Limited, 1909.

Huther, Joh. Ed. *Kritisch-exegetisches Handbuch über den Brief des Jakobus*. 3d edition. KEKNT. Göttingen: Vandenhoeck & Ruprecht, 1870.

Inwood, Brad. "Commentary on Striker." In *Proceedings of the Boston Area Colloquium in Ancient Philosophy* 2, edited by John J. Cleary, 95–101. New York: University Press of America, 1987.

———. "Comments on Professor Gorgemanns' Paper: The Two Forms of *Oikeiôsis* in Arius and the Stoa." In *On Stoic and Peripatetic Ethics: The Work of Arius Didymus*, edited by W. W. Fortenbaugh, 190–201. New Brunswick, NJ: Transaction Books, 1983.

———. *Ethics and Human Action in Early Stoicism*. Oxford: Clarendon Press, 1985.

Isaac, E. "1 (Ethiopic Apocalypse of) Enoch." *OTP* 1, 5–89.

Jackson-McCabe, Matt A. "A Letter to the Twelve Tribes in the Diaspora: Wisdom and 'Apocalyptic' Eschatology in James." *SBLSP* 35 (1996) 504–17.

———. Review of *The Letter of James: A New Translation with Introduction and Commentary*, by Luke Timothy Johnson. In *JR* 78 (1998) 102–104.

———. Review of *Wort als Gesetz*, by Martina Ludwig. In *JBL* 115 (1996) 372–75.

Jobling, David. "And Have Dominion . . .: The Interpretation of Genesis 1, 28 in Philo Judaeus." *JSJ* 8 (1979) 50–51.

Johnson, Luke Timothy. "Friendship with the World/Friendship with God: A Study of Discipleship." In *Discipleship in the New Testament*, edited with an introduction by F. F. Segovia, 166–83. Philadelphia: Fortress Press, 1985.

———. "James 3:13–4:10 and the *Topos* ΠΕΡΙ ΦΘΟΝΟΥ." *NovT* 25 (1983) 327–47.

———. "Taciturnity and True Religion: James 1:26–27." In *Greeks, Romans, and Christians: Essays in Honor of Abraham J. Malherbe*, edited by David L. Balch, Everett Ferguson, and Wayne A. Meeks, 329–39. Minneapolis: Fortress Press, 1990.

———. *The Letter of James: A New Translation with Introduction and Commentary*. AB 37a. New York, NY: Doubleday, 1995.

———. "The Mirror of Remembrance (James 1:22–25)." *CBQ* 50 (1988) 632–45.

———. "The Use of Leviticus 19 in the Letter of James." *JBL* 101 (1982) 391–401.

Jones, F. Stanely. "Freedom," *ABD* 2, 855–59.

Jonge, Marinus de. *Testamenta XII Patriarchum: Edited according to Cambridge University Library MS Ff1.24 fol. 203a–262b, with Short Notes*. PVTG. Leiden: E. J. Brill, 1964.

———. *The Testaments of the Twelve Patriarchs: A Critical Edition of the Greek Text*. PVTG 1. Leiden: E. J. Brill, 1978.

Kanel, Baruch. "Ancient Jewish Coins and Their Historical Importance." *BA* 26 (1963) 38–62.

Keck, Leander E. "The Poor Among the Saints in Jewish Christianity and Qumran." *ZNW* 57 (1966) 54–78.

———. "The Poor Among the Saints in the New Testament." *ZNW* 56 (1965) 100–129.

Kee, Howard Clark. "Testaments of the Twelve Patriarchs," *OTP* 1, 775–828.

———. "The Ethical Dimensions of the Testaments of the XII as a Clue to their Provenance." *NTS* 24 (1978) 259–70.

Kenter, L. P. M. *Tullius Cicero, De Legibus: A commentary on book I*. Translated by J. L. Leenheer-Braid. Amsterdam: Adolf M. Hakkert, 1972.

Kirk, G. S. *Heraclitus: The Cosmic Fragments Edited with an Introduction and Commentary.* Cambridge: Cambridge University Press, 1954.

Kirk, J. A. "The Meaning of Wisdom in James: Examination of a Hypothesis." *NTS* 16 (1969–1970) 24–38.

Klauck, Hans-Josef. *4 Makkabäerbuch.* JSHRZ 3.6. Gütersloh: Gerd Mohn, 1989.

Klein, Martin. *"Ein vollkommenes Werk": Vollkommenheit, Gesetz und Gericht als theologische Themen des Jakobusbriefes.* BWANT 7/19 (Der ganzen Sammlung Heft 139). Stuttgart: Verlag W. Kohlhammer, 1995.

Klijn, A. F. J. *Der lateinische Text der Apokalypse des Esra.* TU 131. Berlin: Akademie Verlag, 1983.

Kloppenborg, John S. *Q Parallels: Synopsis, Critical Notes & Concordance.* Foundations & Facets. Sonoma, CA: Polebridge, 1988.

———. "Status und Wohltätigkeit bei Paulus und Jakobus." In *Vom Jesus zum Christus: Christologische Studien. Festgabe für Paul Hoffmann zum 65. Geburtstag,* edited by Rudolf Hoppe and Ulrich Busse, 127–54. BZNW 93. Berlin and New York: Walter de Gruyter, 1998.

———. *The Formation of Q: Trajectories in Ancient Christian Wisdom Collections.* Studies in Antiquity and Christianity. Philadelphia: Fortress Press, 1987.

Koester, Helmut. "ΝΟΜΟΣ ΦΥΣΕΩΣ: The Concept of Natural Law in Greek Thought." In *Religions in Antiquity: Essays in Memory of Erwin Randall Goodenough,* edited by Jacob Neusner, 521–41. Leiden: E. J. Brill, 1970.

Kohler, Kaufmann. "The Origin and Composition of the Eighteen Benedictions with a Translation of the Corresponding Essene Prayers in the Apostolic Constitutions." *HUCA* 1 (1924) 410–25. Reprinted in *Contributions to the Scientific Study of Jewish Liturgy,* edited by Jakob J. Petuchowsky, 52–90. New York: Ktav Publishing House, Inc., 1970.

———. "Ueber die Urspünge und Grundformen der synagogalen Liturgie. Eine Studie." *MGWJ* 37 (1893) 441–51, 489–97.

Kühl, Ernst. *Die Stellung des Jakobusbriefes zum alttestamentlichen Gesetz und zur paulinischen Rechtfertigungslehre.* Königsberg i. Pr: Verlag von Wilh. Koch, 1905.

Lauer, S. "Eusebes Logismos in IV Macc." *JJS* 6 (1955) 170–71.

Laws, Sophie. *A Commentary on the Epistle of James.* Black's. London: Black, 1980.

———. "Does Scripture Speak in Vain? A Reconsideration of James IV.5." *NTS* 20 (1973–74) 210–15.

Leconte, R. *Les Epîtres Catholiques de Saint Jacques, Saint Jude et Saint Pierre.* Paris: Les Editions du Cerf, 1953; 2d edition, 1961.

Lindemann, Andreas. *Paulus im ältesten Christentum: Das Bild des Apostels und die Rezeption der paulinischen Theologie in der frühchristlichen Literatur bis Marcion.* BHT 58. Tübingen: J. C. B. Mohr (Paul Siebeck), 1979.

Lisçu, Marin O. *Etude sur la Langue de la Philosophie Morale chez Cicéron.* Paris: Société d'Edition «Les Belles Lettres», 1930.

Lohse, Eduard. "πρόσωπον, κτλ." *TDNT* 6, 769–81.

Long, A. A. "Heraclitus and Stoicism." *Philosophia* 5/6 (1975–76) 133–56.

———. "The Logical Basis of Stoic Ethics." *Proceedings of the Aristotelian Society* 71 (1970–1971) 85–104.

Long, A. A., and D. N. Sedley. *The Hellenistic Philosophers.* 2 volumes. Cambridge: Cambridge University Press, 1987.

Ludwig, Martina. *Wort als Gesetz: Eine Untersuchung zum Verständnis von "Wort" und "Gesetz" in israelitisch-frühjüdischen und neutestamentlichen Schriften. Gleichzeitig ein Beitrag zur Theologie des Jakobusbriefes.* Europäische Hochschulschriften 23/502. Frankfurt am Main: Peter Lang, 1994.

Luedemann, Gerd. *Opposition to Paul in Jewish Christianity.* Minneapolis: Fortress Press, 1989.

Manns, F. "Une tradition liturgique juive sous-jacente a Jacques 1,21b," *RevScRel* 62 (1988) 85–89.

Martens, John W. "Philo and the 'Higher' Law." *SBLSP* 30 (1991) 309–22.

Martin, Ralph P. *James*. WBC 48. Waco, TX: Word, 1988.

Marty, Jacques. *L'Epître de Jacques. Etude critique*. Paris: Librairie Félix Alcan, 1935.

Mayer, Günter. *Index Philoneus*. Berlin and New York: Walter de Gruyter, 1974.

Mayor, Joseph B. *The Epistle of St. James: The Greek Text with Introduction, Notes, Comments and Further Studies in the Epistle of St. James*. 3d edition. London: MacMillan, 1913. Reprint edition: Classical Commentary Library. Grand Rapids, MI: Zondervan, 1954.

McKnight, Scot. "James 2:18a: The Unidentifiable Interlocutor." *WTJ* 52 (1990) 355–64.

Meinertz, Max, and Wilhelm Vrede. *Die katholischen Briefe*. 4th edition. Die heilige Schrift des Neuen Testaments 9. Bonn: Peter Hanstein, 1932.

Meshorer, Ya'akov. *Ancient Jewish Coinage. Volume II: Herod the Great through Bar Cochba*. Dix Hills, NY: Amphora Books, 1982.

Meyer, Arnold. *Das Rätsel des Jacobusbriefes*. BZNW 10. Gießen: Töpelmann, 1930.

Mitchell, Margaret M. "Rhetorical Shorthand in Pauline Argumentation: The Functions of 'the Gospel' in the Corinthian Correspondence." In *Gospel in Paul: Studies in Corinthians, Galatians and Romans for Richard N. Longenecker*, edited by L. Ann Jervis and Peter Richardson, 63–88. JSNTSup 108. Sheffield: Sheffield Academic Press, 1994.

Mitsis, Philip. "Natural Law and Natural Right in Post-Aristotelian Philosophy. The Stoics and their Critics." *ANRW* 2.36.7 (1994) 4812–50.

Moffatt, James. *The General Epistles: James, Peter and Judas*. MNTC. London: Hodder and Stoughton, 1928.

Mußner, Franz. *Der Jakobusbrief*. 3d edition. HTKNT 13/1. Freiburg: Herder, 1975.

Neitzel, Heinz. "Eine alte crux interpretum im Jakobusbrief 2,18." *ZNW* 73 (1982) 286–93.

Nickelsburg, George W. E. *Jewish Literature Between the Bible and the Mishnah: A Historical and Literary Introduction*. Philadelphia: Fortress, 1981.

———. "Riches, the Rich and God's Judgment in 1 Enoch 92–105 and the Gospel According to Luke." *NTS* 25 (1979) 324–44.

Pembroke, S. G. "Oikeiôsis." In *Problems in Stoicism*, edited by A. A. Long, 114–49. London: The Athlone Press, 1971.

Penner, Todd. *The Epistle of James and Eschatology: Re-reading an Ancient Christian Letter*. JSNTSup 121. Sheffield: Sheffield Academic Press, 1996.

Perdue, Leo G. *Wisdom and Creation: The Theology of Wisdom Literature*. Nashville: Abingdon, 1994.

Perkins, Pheme. *First and Second Peter, James and Jude*. IBC. Louisville: John Knox, 1995.

Pfeiffer, Ernst. "Der Zusammenhang des Jakobusbriefes." *TSK* 23 (1850) 163–80.

Philippson, R. "Das erste Naturgemässe." *Philologus* 87 (1931–32) 445–66.

Plessis, Paul Johannes du. *ΤΕΛΕΙΟΣ: The Idea of Perfection in the New Testament*. Kampen: Kok, 1959.

Pohlenz, Max. *Freedom in Greek Life and Thought: The History of an Ideal*. Dordrecht-Holland: D. Reidel; New York: The Humanities Press, 1966.

———. *Grundfragen der stoischen Philosophie*. Abhandlungen der Gesellschaft der Wissenschaften zu Göttingen 3/26. Göttingen: Vandenhoeck & Ruprecht, 1940. Reprinted in *Stoicism*, edited by Leonardo Tarán. Greek and Roman Philosophy 38. New York and London: Garland, 1987.

Popkes, Wiard. *Adressaten, Situation und Form des Jakobusbriefes*. SBS 125/126. Stuttgart: Verlag Katholisches Bibelwerk, 1986.

Redditt, Paul L. "The Concept of *Nomos* in Fourth Maccabees." *CBQ* 45 (1983) 249–70.

Reesor, Margaret E. *The Political Theory of the Old and Middle Stoa*. New York: J. J. Augustin, 1951.

Reicke, Bo. *The Epistles of James, Peter, and Jude: Introduction, Translation and Notes*. AB 37. Garden City, NY: Doubleday, 1964.

Rendall, Gerald H. *The Epistle of James and Judaic Christianity.* Cambridge: At the University Press, 1927.

Renehan, Robert. "The Greek Philosophic Background of Fourth Maccabees." *Rheinisches Museum für Philologie* 115 (1972) 223–38.

Rist, John M. *Stoic Philosophy.* Cambridge: Cambridge University Press, 1969; reprint edition, 1990.

Ropes, James Hardy. *A Critical and Exegetical Commentary on the Epistle of St. James.* ICC. Edinburgh: T & T Clark, 1916; reprint edition, 1991.

Sandbach, F. H. "Ennoia and Prolêpsis in the Stoic Theory of Knowledge." *Classical Quarterly* 24 (1930) 44–51. Reprinted with supplementary notes in *Problems in Stoicism*, edited by A. A. Long, 22–37. London: The Athlone Press, 1971.

Sanders, E. P. "Jewish Association with Gentiles and Galatians 2:11–14." In *The Conversation Continues: Studies in Paul and John in Honor of J. Louis Martyn*, edited by Robert T. Fortna and Beverly R. Gaventa, 170–88. Nashville: Abingdon, 1990.

———. *Judaism: Practice and Belief 63 BCE–66 CE.* London: SCM; Philadelphia: Trinity Press International, 1992.

———. *Paul and Palestinian Judaism: A Comparison of Patterns of Religion.* Philadelphia: Fortress Press, 1977.

———. "The Covenant as a Soteriological Category and the Nature of Salvation in Palestinian and Hellenistic Judaism." In *Jews, Greeks and Christians: Religious Cultures in Late Antiquity. Essays in Honor of William David Davies*, edited by Robert Hamerton-Kelly and Robin Scroggs, 11–44. Studies in Judaism in Late Antiquity. Leiden: E. J. Brill, 1976.

Schlier, Heinrich. "ἐλεύθερος, κτλ." *TDNT* 2, 487–96.

Schnabel, Eckhard J. *Law and Wisdom from Ben Sira to Paul: A Tradition Historical Inquiry into the Relation of Law, Wisdom and Ethics.* WUNT 2/16. Tübingen: J. C. B. Mohr (Paul Siebeck), 1985.

Schnackenburg, Rudolph. *The Johannine Epistles: Introduction and Commentary.* Translated by Reginald and Ilse Fuller. New York: Crossroad, 1992.

———. *Ephesians: A Commentary.* Translated by Helen Helen Heron. Edinburgh: T & T Clark, 1991.

Schneider, Joh. *Die Brief des Jakobus, Petrus, Judas und Johannes: Die katholischen Briefe.* 9th edition. NTD 10. Göttingen: Vandenhoeck & Ruprecht, 1961.

Schoedel, William Richard. "The Appeal to Nature in Graeco-Roman and Early Christian Thought." Ph.D. dissertation, The University of Chicago, 1963.

Schofield, Malcolm. *The Stoic Idea of the City.* Cambridge: Cambridge University Press, 1991.

Schökel, Luis Alonso. "James 5,2 [sic] and 4,6." *Bib* 54 (1973) 73–76.

Sedlacek, I. *Dionysius bar Salibi in Apocalypsim, Actus et Epistulas Catholicas.* CSCO, Scriptores Syri 2.101. Rome: de Luigi, 1901.

Segal, Alan F. *Rebecca's Children: Judaism and Christianity in the Roman World.* Cambridge, MA: Harvard University Press, 1986.

Seitz, Oscar J. F. "Afterthoughts on the Term 'Dipsychos." *NTS* 4 (1957–1958) 327–34.

———. "Antecedents and Signification of the Term ΔΙΨΥΧΟΣ." *JBL* 66 (1947) 211–19.

———. "James and the Law." In *Studia Evangelia II*, edited by Frank L. Cross, 472–86. TU 87. Berlin: Akademie Verlag, 1964.

———. "Relationship of the Shepherd of Hermas to the Epistle of James," *JBL* 63 (1944) 131–40.

Sidebottom, E. M. *James, Jude and 2 Peter.* Century Bible, New Edition. Greenwood, SC: The Attic Press, Inc., 1967.

Simon, Louis. *Une ethique de la Sagesse: Commentaire de l'Epître de Jacques.* Geneva: Labor et Fides, 1961.

Smith, Jonathan Z. *Imagining Religion: From Babylon to Jonestown.* Chicago and London. University of Chicago Press, 1982.

Smith, Morton. *Clement of Alexandria and a Secret Gospel of Mark*. Cambridge, MA: Harvard University Press, 1973.

Smyth, Herbert Weir. *Greek Grammar*. Revised by Gordon M. Messing. Cambridge: Harvard University Press, 1956.

Spitta, Friedrich. *Der Brief des Jakobus*. Göttingen: Vandenhoeck & Ruprecht, 1896.

Sterling, Gregory E. *Historiography And Self-Definition: Josephos, Luke-Acts and Apologetic Historiography*. NovTSup 64. Leiden, New York and Köln: E. J. Brill, 1992.

Stone, Michael E. *Fourth Ezra: A Commentary on the Book of Fourth Ezra*. Hermeneia. Minneapolis: Fortress Press, 1990.

Strack, H. L., and Günter Stemberger. *Introduction to the Talmud and Midrash*. Translated and edited by Markus Bockmuehl. Second printing, with emendations and updates. Minneapolis: Fortress Press, 1996.

Striker, Gisela. "Following Nature: A Study in Stoic Ethics." *Oxford Studies in Ancient Philosophy* 9 (1991) 1–73.

———. "Origins of the Concept of Natural Law." In *Proceedings of the Boston Area Colloquium in Ancient Philosophy* 2, edited by John J. Cleary, 79–94. New York: University Press of America, 1987.

Tcherikover, Victor. *Hellenistic Civilization and the Jews*. Reprinted with a preface by John J. Collins. Peabody, MA: Hendrickson, 1999.

Todd, Robert B. "The Stoic Common Notions: A Re-examination and Reinterpretation." *Symbolae Osloenses* 48 (1973) 47–75.

Townshend, R. B. "The Fourth book of Maccabees." *APOT* 2, 653–85.

Tsuji, Manabu. *Glaube zwischen Vollkommenheit und Verweltlichung: Eine Untersuchung zur literarischen Gestalt und zur inhaltlichen Kohärenz des Jakobusbriefes*. WUNT 2/93. Tübingen: J. C. B. Mohr (Paul Siebeck), 1997.

Vander Waerdt, Paul A. "Philosophical Influence on Roman Jurisprudence? The Case of Stoicism and Natural Law." *ANRW* 2.36.7 (1994) 4851–4900.

———. "The Stoic Theory of Natural Law." Ph.D. dissertation, Princeton University, 1989.

———. "Zeno's *Republic* and the Origins of Natural Law." In *The Socratic Movement*, edited by Paul A. Vander Waerdt, 272–308. Ithaca: Cornell University Press, 1994.

Vouga, François. *L'Epître de Saint Jacques*. CNT, d.s.13a. Geneva: Labor et Fides, 1984.

Wachob, Wesley Hiram. "'The Rich in Faith' and 'the Poor in Spirit': The Socio-Rhetorical Function of a Saying of Jesus in the Epistle of James." Ph. D. dissertation, Emory University, 1993.

Wahl, O. *Apocalypsis Esdrae. Apocalypsis Sedrach. Visio Beati Esdrae*. PVTG 4. Leiden: E. J. Brill, 1977.

Ward, Roy Bowen, Jr. "The Communal Concern of the Epistle of James." Ph.D. dissertation, Harvard University, 1966.

Ward, Roy Bowen. "James of Jerusalem in the First Two Centuries." *ANRW* 2.26.1 (1992) 779–812.

———. "Partiality in the Assembly: James 2:2–4." *HTR* 62 (1969) 87–97.

Watson, Duane F. "James 2 in Light of Greco-Roman Schemes of Argumentation." *NTS* 39 (1993) 94–121.

———. "The Rhetoric of James 3:1–12 and a Classical Pattern of Argumentation." *NovT* 35 (1993) 58.

Watson, Gerard. "The Natural Law and Stoicism." In *Problems in Stoicism*, edited by A. A. Long, 216–38. London: The Athlone Press, 1971.

Weiss, Bernhard. *Die katholischen Briefe. Textkritische Untersuchungen und Textherstellung*. Leipzig: J. C. Hinrichs'sche Buchhandlung, 1892.

Williams, Frank, ed. *The Panarion of Epiphanius of Salamis. Books II and III (Sects 47–80, De Fide)*. NHMS 36. Leiden: E. J. Brill, 1994.

Windisch, Hans. *Die katholischen Briefe.* 3d edition. HNT 15. Tübingen: J. C. B. Mohr (Paul Siebeck), 1951.

Winston, David. *Logos and Mystical Theology in Philo of Alexandria.* Cincinnati: Hebrew Union College Press, 1985.

Wolmarans, J. L. P. "The Tongue Guiding the Body: The Anthropological Presuppositions of James 3:1–12." *Neotestamentica* 26 (1992) 523–30.

Wolverton, W. I. "The Double-Minded Man in the Light of Essene Psychology." *ATR* 38 (1956) 166–75.

INDEX OF ANCIENT LITERATURE

A. Jewish Bible/Old Testament
B. New Testament
C. Apocrypha, Pseudepigrapha, and Dead Sea Scrolls
D. Philo
E. Rabbinic Literature
F. Apostolic Fathers
G. Other Early Christian Literature
H. Graeco-Roman Literature

A. JEWISH BIBLE/OLD TESTAMENT

B. New Testament

C. Apocrypha, Pseudepigrapha, and Dead Sea Scrolls

D. Philo

E. Rabbinic Literature

H. Graeco-Roman Literature

INDEX OF MODERN AUTHORS

SUPPLEMENTS TO NOVUM TESTAMENTUM

ISSN 0167-9732

2. Strobel, A. *Untersuchungen zum eschatologischen Verzögerungsproblem auf Grund der spätjüdische-urchristlichen Geschichte von Habakuk 2,2 ff.* 1961. ISBN 90 04 01582 5

16. Pfitzner, V.C. *Paul and the Agon Motif.* 1967. ISBN 90 04 01596 5

27. Mussies, G. *The Morphology of Koine Greek As Used in the Apocalypse of St. John.* A Study in Bilingualism. 1971. ISBN 90 04 02656 8

28. Aune, D.E. *The Cultic Setting of Realized Eschatology in Early Christianity.* 1972. ISBN 90 04 03341 6

29. Unnik, W.C. van. *Sparsa Collecta.* The Collected Essays of W.C. van Unnik Part 1. Evangelia, Paulina, Acta. 1973. ISBN 90 04 03660 1

31. Unnik, W.C. van. *Sparsa Collecta.* The Collected Essays of W.C. van Unnik Part 3. Patristica, Gnostica, Liturgica. 1983. ISBN 90 04 06262 9

34. Hagner, D.A. *The Use of the Old and New Testaments in Clement of Rome.* 1973. ISBN 90 04 03636 9

37. Reiling, J. *Hermas and Christian Prophecy.* A Study of The Eleventh Mandate. 1973. ISBN 90 04 03771 3

43. Clavier, H. *Les variétés de la pensée biblique et le problème de son unité.* Esquisse d'une théologie de la Bible sur les textes originaux et dans leur contexte historique. 1976. ISBN 90 04 04465 5

47. Baarda, T., A.F.J. Klijn & W.C. van Unnik (eds.) *Miscellanea Neotestamentica.* I. Studia ad Novum Testamentum Praesertim Pertinentia a Sociis Sodalicii Batavi c.n. Studiosorum Novi Testamenti Conventus Anno MCMLXXVI Quintum Lustrum Feliciter Complentis Suscepta. 1978. ISBN 90 04 05685 8

48. Baarda, T., A.F.J. Klijn & W.C. van Unnik (eds.) *Miscellanea Neotestamentica.* II. 1978. ISBN 90 04 05686 6

50. Bousset, D.W. *Religionsgeschichtliche Studien.* Aufsätze zur Religionsgeschichte des hellenistischen Zeitalters. Hrsg. von A.F. Verheule. 1979. ISBN 90 04 05845 1

52. Garland, D.E. *The Intention of Matthew 23.* 1979. ISBN 90 04 05912 1

53. Moxnes, H. *Theology in Conflict.* Studies in Paul's Understanding of God in Romans. 1980. ISBN 90 04 06140 1

56. Skarsaune, O. *The Proof From Prophecy.* A Study in Justin Martyr's Proof-Text Tradition: Text-type, Provenance, Theological Profile. 1987. ISBN 90 04 07468 6

59. Wilkins, M.J. *The Concept of Disciple in Matthew's Gospel, as Reflected in the Use of the Term 'Mathetes'.* 1988. ISBN 90 04 08689 7

64. Sterling, G.E. *Historiography and Self-Definition.* Josephos, Luke-Acts and Apologetic Historiography. 1992. ISBN 90 04 09501 2

65. Botha, J.E. *Jesus and the Samaritan Woman.* A Speech Act Reading of John 4:1-42. 1991. ISBN 90 04 09505 5

66. Kuck, D.W. *Judgment and Community Conflict.* Paul's Use of Apologetic Judgment Language in 1 Corinthians 3:5-4:5. 1992. ISBN 90 04 09510 1

67. Schneider, G. *Jesusüberlieferung und Christologie.* Neutestamentliche Aufsätze 1970-1990. 1992. ISBN 90 04 09555 1

68. Seifrid, M.A. *Justification by Faith.* The Origin and Development of a Central Pauline Theme. 1992. ISBN 90 04 09521 7

69. Newman, C.C. *Paul's Glory-Christology*. Tradition and Rhetoric. 1992.
    ISBN 90 04 09463 6
70. Ireland, D.J. *Stewardship and the Kingdom of God*. An Historical, Exegetical, and Contextual Study of the Parable of the Unjust Steward in Luke 16: 1-13. 1992.
    ISBN 90 04 09600 0
71. Elliott, J.K. *The Language and Style of the Gospel of Mark*. An Edition of C.H. Turner's "Notes on Marcan Usage" together with other comparable studies. 1993.
    ISBN 90 04 09767 8
72. Chilton, B. *A Feast of Meanings*. Eucharistic Theologies from Jesus through Johannine Circles. 1994. ISBN 90 04 09949 2
73. Guthrie, G.H. *The Structure of Hebrews*. A Text-Linguistic Analysis. 1994.
    ISBN 90 04 09866 6
74. Bormann, L., K. Del Tredici & A. Standhartinger (eds.) *Religious Propaganda and Missionary Competition in the New Testament World*. Essays Honoring Dieter Georgi.1994. ISBN 90 04 10049 0
75. Piper, R.A. (ed.) *The Gospel Behind the Gospels*. Current Studies on Q. 1995.
    ISBN 90 04 09737 6
76. Pedersen, S. (ed.) *New Directions in Biblical Theology*. Papers of the Aarhus Conference, 16-19 September 1992. 1994. ISBN 90 04 10120 9
77. Jefford, C.N. (ed.) *The* Didache *in Context*. Essays on Its Text, History and Transmission. 1995. ISBN 90 04 10045 8
78. Bormann, L. *Philippi – Stadt und Christengemeinde zur Zeit des Paulus*. 1995.
    ISBN 90 04 10232 9
79. Peterlin, D. *Paul's Letter to the Philippians in the Light of Disunity in the Church*. 1995.
    ISBN 90 04 10305 8
80. Jones, I.H. *The Matthean Parables*. A Literary and Historical Commentary. 1995.
    ISBN 90 04 10181 0
81. Glad, C.E. *Paul and Philodemus*. Adaptability in Epicurean and Early Christian Psychagogy. 1995 ISBN 90 04 10067 9
82. Fitzgerald, J.T. (ed.) *Friendship, Flattery, and Frankness of Speech*. Studies on Friendship in the New Testament World. 1996. ISBN 90 04 10454 2
83. Tilborg, S. van. *Reading John in Ephesus*. 1996. 90 04 10530 1
84. Holleman, J. *Resurrection and Parousia*. A Traditio-Historical Study of Paul's Eschatology in 1 Corinthians 15. 1996. ISBN 90 04 10597 2
85. Moritz, T. *A Profound Mystery*. The Use of the Old Testament in Ephesians. 1996.
    ISBN 90 04 10556 5
86. Borgen, P. *Philo of Alexandria - An Exegete for His Time*. 1997. ISBN 90 04 10388 0
87. Zwiep, A.W. *The Ascension of the Messiah in Lukan Christology*. 1997.
    ISBN 90 04 10897 1
88. Wilson, W.T. *The Hope of Glory*. Education and Exhortation in the Epistle to the Colossians. 1997. ISBN 90 04 10937 4
89. Peterson, W.L., J.S. Vos & H.J. de Jonge (eds.). *Sayings of Jesus: Canonical and Non-Canonical*. Essays in Honour of Tjitze Baarda. 1997. ISBN 90 04 10380 5
90. Malherbe, A.J., F.W. Norris & J.W. Thompson (eds.). *The Early Church in Its Context*. Essays in Honor of Everett Ferguson. 1998. ISBN 90 04 10832 7
91. Kirk, A. *The Composition of the Sayings Source*. Genre, Synchrony, and Wisdom Redaction in Q. 1998. ISBN 90 04 11085 2
92. Vorster, W.S. *Speaking of Jesus*. Essays on Biblical Language, Gospel Narrative and the Historical Jesus. Edited by J. E. Botha. 1999. ISBN 90 04 10779 7
93. Bauckham, R. *The Fate of Dead*. Studies on the Jewish and Christian Apocalypses. 1998. ISBN 90 04 11203 0

94. Standhartinger, A. *Studien zur Entstehungsgeschichte und Intention des Kolosserbriefs.* ISBN 90 04 11286 3 *(In preparation)*

95. Oegema, G.S. *Für Israel und die Völker.* Studien zum alttestamentlich-jüdischen Hintergrund der paulinischen Theologie. 1999. ISBN 90 04 11297 9

96. Albl, M.C. *"And Scripture Cannot Be Broken".* The Form and Function of the Early Christian *Testimonia* Collections. 1999. ISBN 90 04 11417 3

97. Ellis, E.E. *Christ and the Future in New Testament History.* 1999. ISBN 90 04 11533 1

98. Chilton, B. & C.A. Evans, (eds.) *James the Just and Christian Origins.* 1999. ISBN 90 04 11550 1

99. Horrell, D.G. & C.M. Tuckett (eds.) *Christology, Controversy and Community.* New Testament Essays in Honour of David R. Catchpole. 2000. ISBN 90 04 11679 6

100. Jackson-McCabe, M.A. *Logos and Law in the Letter of James.* The Law of Nature, the Law of Moses and the Law of Freedom. 2001. ISBN 90 04 11994 9